DEFENDING GOVERNMENT: WHY BIG GOVERNMENT WORKS

Max Neiman

University of California, Riverside

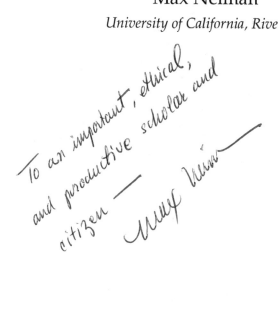

To an important, ethical, and productive scholar and citizen —

PRENTICE HALL, UPPER SADDLE RIVER, NEW JERSEY 07458

Library of Congress Cataloging-in-Publication Data

NEIMAN, MAX.
  Defending government: why big government works/Max Neiman.
    p. cm.
  Includes bibliographical references and index.
  ISBN 0-13-373044-1
    1. United States—Politics and government—20th century.   2. Administrative
  agencies—United States—Evaluation.   3. Government productivity—United States.
  4. Quality of life—Political aspects—United States.   5. Democracy—United States.   I. Title.

  JK421.N4 2000
  320.51'3—dc21   99-054022

Editorial director: Charlyce Jones Owen
Editor in chief: Nancy Roberts
Senior acquisitions editor: Beth Gillett Mejia
Editorial assistant: Brian Prybella
Marketing manager: Christopher DeJohn
Editorial/production supervision: Kari Callaghan Mazzola
Electronic page makeup: Kari Callaghan Mazzola and John P. Mazzola
Interior design and electronic art creation: John P. Mazzola
Cover director: Jayne Conte
Cover design: Joseph Sengotta
Cover photo: Hisham F. Ibrahim/PhotoDisc, Inc.
Buyer: Ben Smith

This book was set in 10/12 Palatino by Big Sky Composition
and was printed and bound by Courier Companies, Inc.
The cover was printed by Phoenix Color Corp.

© 2000 by Prentice-Hall, Inc.
Upper Saddle River, New Jersey 07458

Printed in the United States of America
10 9 8 7 6 5 4 3 2 1

ISBN 0-13-373044-1

PRENTICE-HALL INTERNATIONAL (UK) LIMITED, *London*
PRENTICE-HALL OF AUSTRALIA PTY. LIMITED, *Sydney*
PRENTICE-HALL CANADA INC., *Toronto*
PRENTICE-HALL HISPANOAMERICANA, S.A., *Mexico*
PRENTICE-HALL OF INDIA PRIVATE LIMITED, *New Delhi*
PRENTICE-HALL OF JAPAN, INC., *Tokyo*
PEARSON EDUCATION ASIA PTE. LTD., *Singapore*
EDITORA PRENTICE-HALL DO BRASIL, LTDA., *Rio de Janeiro*

CONTENTS

PREFACE   ix

CHAPTER 1   AN INTRODUCTION TO THE ISSUES   1

Approaches to the Explanation of Government Growth   7
Organization of the Book   9

CHAPTER 2   HOW BIG HAS GOVERNMENT GOTTEN
            IN THE UNITED STATES?   13

The Need for Context   13
Growth in Levels, Proportions, and Burdens: The Fiscal
    Dimension   16
The Growth of Government Regulation   35

CHAPTER 3   MACRO-DETERMINISTIC EXPLANATIONS
            OF GOVERNMENT GROWTH   43

Changes in Social and Demographic Characteristics
    of the Population and in the Scale and Growth
    of Government   44
Some Frequently Used Macro-Deterministic Approaches   47
Marxist Explanations of Government Growth   62

CHAPTER 4   PUBLIC CHOICE EXPLANATIONS OF GOVERNMENT SIZE
            AND GROWTH   68

The Political Economy Origin of Public Choice   68
A Marriage of Convenience: Government as a Tool
  to Increase Market Efficiency   70
Market Failure: When Government Should and Does Grow,
  According to Public Choice Theorists   71
Can Remedying Market Failure Lead to Government
  Failure?   78

CHAPTER 5   FOR WHOM THE EVIDENCE MATTERS:
            CONCLUSIONS REGARDING THE CAUSES
            OF GOVERNMENT GROWTH   87

Wagner's Hypothesis   88
Peacock and Wiseman: The Displacement Effect   90
Democratization and Institutional Change   95
Public Choice Explanations   96
Explanations of Government Growth: Some Conclusions   113

CHAPTER 6   BLAMING GOVERNMENT: THE CASE OF ECONOMIC
            PERFORMANCE   115

Government Size, Growth, and Economic Performance   116
Conclusions   129

CHAPTER 7   DOES AN ACTIVE GOVERNMENT NECESSARILY MEAN
            OPPRESSIVE GOVERNMENT?   132

Labor and Consumers   141
White Collar Crime   144
Expensive Lessons, Expensive Reruns   148
The Discounted Marketplace   150

CHAPTER 8   HITLER DIDN'T COME TO POWER VIA THE HEALTH
             DEPARTMENT   157

The Big Brother Road to Dictatorship   157
The Antigovernment Spin   161
Consider This Perverse Argument   169
Meaning and Interpretation   177

CHAPTER 9   BEING DISMAL IN POLICY ANALYSIS OR LEARNING
             TO LOVE POLICYMAKING   182

The Flight from Politics   182
Fretting about Democracy and Redistributive Demands   183
Public Choice and Metropolitan Organization   186
Rational Models as Blueprints and the Lack of Resource
    Fluidity   194
A Realistic Role for Policy Analysis   201
Limited Government as a Common Property Resource   202
Being Rational Is a Difficult and Sometimes Undesirable
    Thing to Try   205

CHAPTER 10   THE FREEDOM TO CHOOSE DEMOCRATIC POLITICS   208

Summary   211
Issues Regarding Future Public Sector Involvement   214
Some Remedies for Some Problems   218

REFERENCES   222

INDEX   249

PREFACE

It is important that readers know my orientation to the subjects of *Defending Government: Why Big Government Works*. I am not an apologist for the failures of previous policy. I am not indifferent to the worries of people regarding crime and public safety, nor do I dismiss their chagrin regarding wasteful and ineffectual public policies. I worry that an alienated, angry white working class increasingly believes that social justice means only remedying the injustices to women, gays, and people of color. I also worry about people who feel angry or foolish for struggling to make ends meet while thinking that there are mythical legions of loafing welfare cheats who live in luxury at the expense of the working stiff. I am sympathetic to the need to encourage and to respect work and investment. I am scornful of the tendency to replace results with motives as the test of successful public policy. On the other hand, I also celebrate the efforts of the public to use the powers of democratic governing to improve the lives of people.

Although liberals have contributed to the current rancor in the public discourse over domestic and social policy, they have not, in recent decades, influenced policy to the same extent as have those in the conservative mold. With few exceptions, liberal militants are today relatively invisible and mute; certainly they are disorganized and less successful in reaching a large, receptive audience. The liberal legacy has been defeated by the ironic, if not tragic, view that "the poor are seen as a 'special interest' while the wealthy are not" (Dionne, 1991: 144). Although criticism of government and politics from the left has been forceful, it is less salient in the current public discourse. Today, the chief barrier to a newer, principled pragmatism of the moderate center is the dominance of neoconservative

American political dialogue. My attention is therefore focused on the conservative attack on the public sector, especially its explanation for and evaluation of the size and growth of the public sector in the United States.

My parents and those of my wife are World War II concentration camp survivors. During World War II, much of my family disappeared in the execution pits in what is today the Ukraine and in the smoke that wafted out of the crematoria of Auschwitz and other Nazi hells-on-earth. As a child, in 1956, I remember being mesmerized by the magazine, newspaper, and television coverage of the Hungarian Revolution and the brutal response it evoked from the "people's" Soviet military. In other words, I am very aware of how the power of the state can be abusive. I do not ignore the anxieties that individuals might have regarding irresponsible and oppressive governments. I mention these things because this is a book that ultimately defends the use of the tools of governing in *democratically* organized societies, so that people can make their lives more rewarding, more productive, and more just. In today's America, notwithstanding the modest successes of a politically wounded, lame-duck Democratic president, the use of government has been blamed in recent decades for economic malaise and has even been posed as a serious threat to personal liberty. The conservative spirit, with its celebration of the private market and its fear, if not loathing, of government policies and public officials, dominates the prevailing political mood. As part of this conservative festival there has been a growing effort to make it more difficult for the public to use governing power to meet public ends. Cutting taxes, constraining revenues, weakening previous legislation, and debunking public agencies (particularly those with social- and health-related functions or those required to finance public activities) are the focus of the conservative agenda that prevails in the United States. I believe that the current dominance of conservative forces might seriously undermine the well-being of many disadvantaged Americans, threaten the health of many others, and make it more difficult to achieve broader national objectives in the fields of economic security, public health, efficiency, and environmental objectives. We will talk about all of that later.

I have, in short, an agenda. Most people, including scholars, who write books do. I believe that I am systematic and try to be rigorous in what I do here, but I am clearly guided by values and my own personal history. I remember quite clearly that when I arrived in the United States as a refugee with my mother in late January of 1952, I enrolled almost immediately in a Philadelphia public school. Among my clearer recollections are those of teachers taking a keen interest in me, teaching me English, and otherwise easing my sink-or-swim entry into a new nation. The attention and dedication of these teachers and the pleasure they seemed to have in my progress as a new American will remain lovingly stored in my memory. Perhaps it is this personal connection with publicly supported institutions that has made me fairly sanguine about the importance of vigorous and effective public institutions.

I also recall my years of coming home from school and waiting for my mother to arrive home from work. On the one hand, I enjoyed the freedom I had in the hours between arriving home and my mother's arrival. Playing on the streets and having countless adventures in my Strawberry Mansion, north Philadelphia neighborhood was loads of fun. Yet I also remember my mother coming home from her millinery job fairly late. She worked long hours, often six days a week. I was disappointed when we could not attend certain events because she was tired or obligated to work. My mother explained to me that she was afraid she would lose her job if she were unwilling to work when she was asked to do so. When she became ill or sometimes suffered some work-related injury to her back or hands, she still went to work for fear of losing her job. I know that my first sense of what it means to be an employer or business owner was influenced by my view, perhaps distorted by time, of how my mother was treated by her corporate-factory bosses. Public school teachers, public parks and public recreation, public swimming pools, public camps during the summers, and the mounted police in the parks were very visible sources of pleasure and security for me. The most difficult thing facing my family was the need to work and the fear of losing one's job.

Yet, my parents, when they were reunited in 1961 (don't ask, that's another story), were also small business owners. Indeed, from the time of his liberation at Dachau in 1945, my father was always an entrepreneur. He was incapable of "working for someone else." It was as if his body would rebel, at the physical and psychological levels, if he were an employee. His one sojourn of working for others nearly destroyed his spirit. In any case, my father has always been incredibly grateful for the opportunity he had in the United States to run his own business (he ran a couple of bakeries). While the streets were not paved with gold, my parents were able to earn a decent living and accumulate their own retirement, mostly through their incredible investment of labor. I appreciate tremendously the willingness of people to take legitimate risks in establishing and developing their businesses, and I also understand that for most of us there is much hard work involved in what we are able to achieve. When demands are placed on our labor, say in the form of taxes, or when some of us are obliged to give to others, the result can be resentment. If the recipients of public help are seen as undeserving, and if some people are made to feel foolish for working hard while others receive benefits, that is a very painful perception. So, while I feel blessed for having been helped by publicly supported institutions and policies, I am also very aware of the sensibilities of those who work and invest in the unique insecurities of the private sector.

So this is a book by a person who believes strongly in the benefits of well-designed, democratically inspired public policies. I believe in a vigorous public sector. Moreover, I do not believe that a productive, competitive, or innovative private sector is necessarily undermined by a vigorous, even large, public sector. Many of these issues are embraced by the continuing controversy over the implications of the size of government, which is the major focus of this book. This controversy is very complex, of course, and includes issues having to do with the following questions:

- What do we mean by a large public sector?
- How large is our public sector, in absolute or relative terms, when compared to previous times or other nations?
- What is the relationship between the size of the public sector and other things about which we are concerned, such as economic performance and personal liberty?
- Insofar as government size is a "problem," what are the suitable remedies for the problem?
- What is the role of democratic politics as a means of disciplining the growth and operation of government? Can we trust "politics" to manage these issues?

I am very grateful to a number of individuals who have provided ongoing and long-term moral and material support as I have worked on this book: Nicholas Lovrich, Michael Desch, Francis Carney, Jon Sonstelie, and Stephen Stambough. As my boss and dean of the College of Humanities, Arts, and Social Sciences at the University of California, Riverside, Carlos Vélez-Ibáñez was critical in both material and spiritual ways. I consider him a model scholar, with a passion for social justice and for doing rigorous scholarship. I extend a heartfelt thanks to Mark Lichbach, a prolific and inspiring scholar who took over as chair of my Political Science Department and thereby improved the quality of my scholarly environment in a very big way. I am grateful to the following reviewers who read and commented on the manuscript: Peter Steinberger, *Reed College*; Mark Baldassare, *University of California, Irvine*; Jeffrey R. Henig, *George Washington University*; and Larry Elowitz, *Georgia College and State University*. I am grateful as well to those social scientists, conservative and liberal and in-between, whose main focus is making life better for as many people as possible. The ends of social science are the people and their interests, rather than the means by which we study them, and I am inspired by the continuing presence and work of colleagues who share that view.

Expressions of gratitude for the support of my family can never convey how important they are to everything I have done here and elsewhere. Unfortunately, since she died I can no longer work with the nourishment of my mother's great soups and her boundless hope that life is worth living, even in the most constrained circumstances. My father, Benjamin Neiman, provided an occasional safe haven, and I don't think he realizes how important that has sometimes been to me. Joshua and David, my sons, have needled me, lifted my spirits, and made me feel much more capable and important than I can ever be. I am the lucky beneficiary of their wit, joy, and intelligence. Then there is Sarah Deborah, my best, most enduring, and patient friend and wife. Yes, of course, this book would not have been possible without the path she cleared for me and the burdens she took on to make my life and schedule as uncluttered and simple for me as possible. Like so many other spouses, Sarah tolerated the usual array of bad and inconsiderate behaviors that authors seem to justify as part of their poetic license. And so I am grateful for the chance to let her know that without her this work and anything else I have done or will do is, for me, meaningless.

Max Neiman

CHAPTER 1

AN INTRODUCTION
TO THE ISSUES

In January 1996, in his State of the Union Address, President Clinton stated the following:

> We know big government does not have all the answers. We know there's not a program for every problem. We know, and we have worked to give the American people a smaller, less bureaucratic government in Washington. And we have to give the American people one that lives within its means. The era of big government is over.

What did President Clinton mean? Did he mean that a monster called the Big Bad Government had been slain, and citizens could now rest easy and not worry about being terrorized by the agents of government? Or did he mean that there was a time when Americans profitably used government to achieve public ends, but that this time had passed? Most of the public discussion about the president's declaration concerning "big government" focused on whether he really meant it, or whether he was merely co-opting a theme from his antigovernment opponents and cashing in on the nation's prevailing mood of skepticism regarding just about anything we try to do through government, a tactic over which his critics claim the president has assumed unmatched mastery. The president, it seems, was sincere in expressing a kind of surrender and was waving a white flag to those who resist any major new initiatives from government. After experiencing the political debacle of his medical care and health industry initiatives in the first two years of his first term, the president was voicing his own commitment to policy gradualism and his decision to employ and harness private sector energy as a means of achieving policy.

This book will focus on a variety of issues and questions associated with what President Clinton and others have referred to as "Big Government." This book, then, is necessarily about government size—for example, what is meant by Big Government? How do we define it? How do we measure it? How do we explain it? Why do we worry about it? If Big Government is bad, how can it be controlled without undermining the capacity of citizens to achieve worthwhile ends?

Much of the discussion here hinges on an implicit distinction between government and governing. The term *government* refers to the array of people and policies that happen to prevail or to characterize a society at some time. The following are all attributes that characterize a government: who is in control of the legislature, what particular system of taxation is used, what the level of taxes is, how the tobacco industry is being treated, what methods are used to regulate the telephone industry, how elections are organized, and what the terms of citizenship are. The term *governing* refers to the process by which individuals make choices about the things they wish to affect. Governing does not imply a particular set of policies, and the results of governing might be deplorable, wasteful, dangerous, effective, or commendable. In a well-ordered democracy, the public is entitled to and provided with meaningful opportunities to use the tools of governing to achieve humane, prudent, effective, and equitable objectives. Some of the tools of governing are taxing, spending, regulating, designing incentives, imposing fines and sanctions, and issuing honors and awards.

Over the past twenty-five years or more the attack on government has involved not only a sophisticated critique of government programs, but also a focused effort to make it more difficult for the less privileged of society to have access to governing authority. If the assault on public programs and the capacity to produce them is permanently and broadly successful, then making life fairer and better for the least advantaged and less politically connected members of society will be more difficult.

There are many reasons that this assault on governing has achieved many successes, if not total victory. Very important in this antigovernment campaign has been the work of conservative thinkers, corporate sponsors, conservative foundations and think tanks, and opportunistic pundits and talk-show hosts. Of course, the assault on public institutions and on the very idea of using government tools like taxes, redistributive programs, and regulation, is not monopolized by conservatives. Indeed, thinkers and activists on the left have also been intrepid, sometimes savagely so, in their criticism of policies, politicians, and political institutions. However, in the United States the most recent, effective, and widely accepted attacks on those who wish to use the tools of government for a variety of purposes have emerged from the right. It is not necessary to prove, nor do I believe, that there is a vast, concerted, right-wing conspiracy to "get" nonconservative politicians or a plot to undermine public confidence in its ability to achieve useful ends through governing. The effort to impugn government workers and elected officials or to denigrate and ridicule public institutions is obvious and up front. It is not subtle or conspiratorial at all. President Clinton's attempt to hide his private sexual misconduct from Americans and the efforts of Republicans to press the impeachment process have independently contributed to further dismay with government and politics. Although the assault from the right is not coordinated as some grand conspiracy, it does proceed with self-consciousness and common purpose. Conferences, meetings, common publications, foundations, and the acceptance of a language of disdain for government—all function to reinforce fears of and loathing for politics and government. It really is irrelevant for our purposes if the assault on governing is a conspiracy. The view here is that if it is a conspiracy, it is one of history's least well-guarded ones. In any case, public criticism of government, governing, politicians, and government employees is perfectly legitimate, if often exaggerated and incorrect. It seems, in some sense, grandly patronizing to mention that it is appropriate and exalted for people to engage in public discourse, even when it does not support one's views. It does no good to demonize one's opponents in the competition over ideas, just because one is losing the argument.

It is true, though, that the critics of governing and government generally have been getting the better of it. While they are not demons, they often seem to get away with avoiding some key issues, such as their implicit fear of democracy. Even though President Clinton revealed a proposed balanced budget in early 1998 for the first time in thirty years, and even though public support for selected programs remains high, there is a kind of prevailing sense that "The Era of Big Government Is Over." Grand and dramatic efforts to achieve public objectives are very problematic in the current political climate, except in the most unusual of circumstances. Similar constraints have operated to strap the policy options of local and state governments. Public support for programs is, at best, limited to military spending, education, penal institutions, and income security for the elderly. We have also recently had inflicted on us a tawdry, national pillorying of President Clinton. In a sense, this sorry spectacle of what began as an investigation of President Clinton as part of the Whitewater Affair has mutated into the most absurd expression of life imitating popular art. This victory of the hot-button, talk-show motif in our public discourse and in the current political flagellation of President Clinton makes the point.

Americans have always been generally suspicious and skeptical about government and governing. I am not going to retrace this old story in its entirety. My concern is about several things. First, in recent decades the expression of antigovernment sentiment has escalated to very high levels, notwithstanding any current outbreak of "good feelings" associated with economic prosperity. Second, the language of antigovernment sentiment and the accompanying political success of antigovernment politicians have produced an interpretation of government growth and a view of government size that serves the political ends of the prosperous and powerful, at the expense of those who are not. Third, important changes in the world economy and continuing issues at home (job safety, environmental and consumer protection, income, security, tax reform, and the like) will be shaped by the rhetorical and political constraints posed by antigovernment sentiment.

In recent decades, Americans' distrust of government has achieved a kind of fervor and pervasiveness not seen since the conflict between Federalists and Anti-Federalists during debates over the ratifying of our constitution. There are reasons for this. There is, of course, the general antigovernment thrust that pervades American history and politics. Then, particularly since the mid-1960s, there has been a sense of unremitting failure and embarrassment around a number of issues and problems. These include the perceived failure to achieve the social welfare objectives of Kennedy's New Frontier or of Lyndon Johnson's Great Society, despite considerable expenditure of public resources; the appearance of ineptitude and deception that prevailed during the conduct of the Vietnam War; the corruption and abuse of power revealed during the Nixon administration and the Watergate scandal; the inability of government to manage a generally sputtering, if not stagnating, economy during the 1970s and much of the 1980s and early 1990s; the intensification of partisan confrontations in Congress and between Congress and the president; and the most recent spectacle of the Clinton presidency which has, for one reason or another, been associated with a never-ending stream of charges—ranging from alleged wrong-doing in land investments while the president was still governor of Arkansas, his campaign finance practices, and accusations about foreign influences in American elections, to the sordid charges regarding sexual misconduct and perjury that metastasized into an impeachment trial in the U.S. Senate. Although there is a modest resurgence of good feeling due to the impressive economic gains of the mid-to-late 1990s, the erosion of trust and the decline of civic nobility and a more elevated public discourse will require much more than improved paychecks to heal. The fact is that most Americans still find that politics is not an elevating activity.

The Ronald Reagan presidency (1980–88) produced an enduring legacy and successfully altered budget priorities. Now and for years to come the domestic agenda will orbit around issues such as budget balancing, budget cuts, and tax cuts. Despite the occasional failure to achieve some antigovernment or conservative objective, such as the mixed success of the Contract with America, there is a kind of continuing drumbeat in the popularity of antigovernment activity and the sneering use of "politics" and "bureaucrat" as epithets of loathing and disgust. Government budgets do, to be sure, continue to grow, but they do so at a notably slower rate. Policy innovations that seek to deal with an array of social problems are rare, especially if they require money or tax increases. At the federal level, a variety of actions make government budgets, even with their modest growth, less responsive to the concerns of the less affluent. Now there is tightened eligibility for food stamps, lowered assistance to students, strict limits on length of eligibility for welfare, and increased minimum payments required among the elderly for Medicare. Programs designed to help the poor with energy costs and housing have been severely curtailed, along with a host of government policies and expenditures in older, developed localities with disproportionate numbers of minorities, the poor, and a host of other attributes associated with difficult social challenges. Even the presence of a budget surplus in fiscal 1999 does not open the door to major new initiatives, demonstrating the enduring quality of commitment to budget balancing and tax expenditures. It is true that crime control, education, military investments, and income security for the elderly occupy a privileged policy position and there is some willingness to spend in these arenas. But these policy areas are exceptions, perhaps to be joined with spending for streets, highways, and bridges. Commitments to a revived social agenda—for the working or abject poor, for struggling working-class citizens, or even the insecure middle classes—are likely to be in the cold for a while longer, if they are invited back in at all. Virtually all of the efforts of liberals are necessarily devoted to seeing if any of the current and expected budget surpluses will be available for something other than military spending, Social Security, or tax cuts.

In short, even if the Reagan-Bush presidencies symbolized the high-water mark of the antigovernment tide, there have been a number of durable changes in the political landscape of the United States. There have been important shifts in the spending priorities at the national level and among states and localities, including drastic reductions of intergovernmental revenues and grants, extensions of deregulation to a greater variety of activities, curtailment of federal mandates imposed on states and localities, and efforts by the national administration to shift current federal programs to state and local governments. There have also been efforts to impose fundamental, more stringent limitations on the ability of government to raise revenues, especially, and most successfully, at the state and local level. There have been some major reductions in government service levels and personnel. There have been both statutory and constitutional efforts to curtail federal government growth, for example in the Gramm-Rudman legislation governing congressional budget management and in the persistent and continually appealing idea of a balanced budget requirement to be incorporated in the federal constitution.

Whether we recall the horrors of Hitler's Nazi Germany or Stalin's Soviet Union or the more prosaic waste and inefficiency that sometimes infects public policy in democratic regimes, it is clear that there is plenty of room to worry about the government arena. Notwithstanding the legitimate anxiety about the proper exercise of governing power, much of the debate regarding the growth, scale, and application of government is wrong-headed, appealing to popular prejudices about elected officials and public employees. The resulting climate of cynicism and antigovernment mood enables strategic efforts of particular groups, interests, and organizations to undermine the public's control over private sector excesses and misconduct. It is the primary purpose of this book to analyze a number of issues associated with discussions about the size of government. In the course of doing this, a number of important conceptions or assumptions are critically addressed, including the following:

1. The belief in the superiority of market exchange and market outcomes over those produced through processes of governing and politics (e.g., elections, bargaining, negotiation, and democratically imposed compulsion)

2. The belief that the distinction between coercion and voluntarism is clear and that coercion is a feature of big, powerful, and dangerous government; put differently, the belief that compliance based on non-coercive methods is "better" or less dangerous than compliance induced through coercion

3. The belief in a kind of bureaucratic determinism, in which the self-interests of government employees are used to explain changes in government scale and growth

4. The belief in the idea that market failure is episodic and that private sector dynamics or civil society operate in generally felicitous fashion (consequently, public or government intervention is justified largely as a "touching-up" or "fine-tuning")

5. The claim that the size of government in the United States, reflected in the scope of government activities and the magnitude of government budgets, is the cause of the nation's poor economic performance in recent decades, in comparison to earlier periods of rapid improvement in economic and social well-being (further, the implication is that fiscal discipline and slow government growth have stimulated the economic gains of the mid-1990s)

There is a need to examine carefully the assumptions, the logic, and the empirical basis of current diagnoses and prescriptions regarding the government size problem. Clearly, not everyone who resists and laments and fears government growth and size lacks public spirit. The concern here is with those who exploit the antigovernment tradition and sentiment, who use the current failures and frustrations of policy as a lever by which to redirect our governing institutions away from addressing social justice and away from managing many other problems, ranging from economic insecurity to environmental protection. There is a real danger that the quick and warm embrace of antigovernment ideology only serves to disarm the many who have greatly benefited and the many more who are yet to benefit from a vigorous, democratically responsive government.

Advanced, industrial societies have achieved a variety of important social justice objectives and produced many cultural and scientific achievements.

These accomplishments were made possible, in some important ways, by the capacity of democratically organized publics to use governing institutions to focus and direct the resources, good will, and intelligence of a society's members. In the United States a variety of public policy achievements have contributed to a more pleasing life, including the following: more civilized relationships among races, ethnic groups, and religions; a greater regard and care for the many of us who are vulnerable to the unpredictable winds of commerce and trade; a disciplining of abusive private power; and the mobilization of resources in science and culture. The capacity of our governing institutions to use the tools of taxation, spending, and regulation—that is, *governing*—is critical in achieving these ends.

Assumptions used by any analyst might produce interesting, even comforting, visions of the world, but they might be illusory at best and dangerous if taken too seriously. For example, many of the things that government does are not especially effective; indeed they are often downright stupid. Yet, the "cause" of the policy and perhaps its persistence, despite its apparent lack of wisdom, might have more to do with the tendency of the policy's beneficiaries (who might be a relatively small number of individuals) to press for the policy's adoption and continued support. It is not especially effective to lament the policy as an expression of special interest greed, when interest group egotism is the rule of democratic political life rather than the exception, unless one has good reason to believe otherwise. Similarly, many economists employ the concept of market failure and related concepts to specify the conditions under which government does and ought to intervene into previously private matters. The idea is that market failure and attendant concepts will help to discipline and rationalize the management of government growth. However, what if market failure, rather than being episodic, as many economists seem to assume, turns out to be pervasive? Does that imply that public intervention must also be pervasive?

In short, in reviewing the material on why government grows, the major points to be made are as follows: (1) The literature pinpoints a variety of compelling forces that produce new government involvement; and (2) the choice of explanations for government growth often flow from prior value commitments. The conclusions about government size and growth are, therefore, instrumental, in the sense that such explanations are often as important for supporting prior values as they are for their conformity with reality.

Approaches to the Explanation of Government Growth

This book is mainly about controversies over government size, and as one surveys the explanations and the relatively few empirical studies on the causes of government growth, one is impressed by the very long list of factors that are alleged to affect government scale. These factors range across several levels of analysis (individual, group, national, and international), as well as varying on the basis of which particular aspect of government growth one is talking about. For example, an increased level of government regulation of the environment might be explained in terms of changes in the individual preferences of a society's members, as when public opinion polls indicate greater preferences for protecting the environment. Or greater government involvement in environmental protection might be explained in terms of the greater affluence of the society and the commensurate increase in the demand for high quality amenities. Or environmental protection might be seen as the expression of bureaucratic budget building among those officials who see, in environmental protection, opportunities for enhancing their agency's budgets or their individual status and income. In any case, a given increment of government growth in a given policy area might be explained in terms of a host of different factors. One might find relevant such matters as social and economic diversity, responsiveness of officials, group pressures, fluctuations in the business cycle, stage of economic development, elite attitudes and interests, citizen support, oscillations in income levels and income distribution, utility maximizing behavior by citizens and officials, or war and disaster. Surely the task of making sense of the scholarship in this area can be fairly challenging.

Although there are many ways in which the literature explaining government growth can be divided, for our purposes three categories are used: (1) macro-deterministic; (2) public choice; and (3) group conflict and competition. However, it is important to emphasize that these categories are not intended to encompass isolated clusters of variables, unrelated to each other. Variables in the macro-deterministic category (e.g., the onset of a severe economic downturn) might produce changes in the scale of government, but such changes might be filtered through aspects of group conflict and group competition. For example, the choice of managing an economic downturn by enacting major tax benefits for business investment or, alternatively, by stimulating employment and consumer demand, is partly a function of how sensitive a particular regime is to the groups that are adversely affected by the economic downturn and by the groups' relative capacity to influence public policy.

Another example of cross-category connections is the often-hypothesized interplay between the level of fiscal decentralization within a nation, the utility-maximizing behavior of individuals, and the size of the public sector. For example, according to Brennan and Buchanan (1980), the more decentralized the source of government revenue, that is, the greater the number of different jurisdictions that raise taxes and spend for public services, the greater the opportunity for people to pursue fiscal gains by moving from one jurisdiction to another. In a highly decentralized government system, households and businesses, it is argued, will be able to determine whether they can benefit from relocating from one jurisdiction to another. Insofar as households and businesses desire to minimize paying taxes or wish to evade paying for services they do not use, they might find locational choice to be a useful strategy for improving their "stock of utility" (Tiebout, 1956). In the face of such utility-maximizing individuals, governments are obliged to compete for businesses and households by keeping service costs and tax burdens lower. As Oates has observed (1985: 748), "Such competition among governments in a federal system that places heavy reliance on 'local' fiscal decisions will greatly limit the capacity of Leviathan to channel resources into the public sector." In short, decentralization of taxing and spending authority will, assuming utility-maximizing behavior on the part of officials and citizenry, operate as a functional equivalent of a formal fiscal constraint.

The thing to keep in mind is the importance of multicausality in surveying the causes of government growth. As in many other topics in the social sciences, there is a tendency in the study of government growth to rely excessively on single-factor explanations. But Rose states the following:

> The size of government is the sum of all the programmes for which government is responsible. Yet it is growth in particular programmes that results in the aggregate phenomenon commonly known as 'big government.' It follows from this that the causes of government growth must be sought in the determinants of particular programmes as well as in pervasive attributes of government. Given a multiplicity of programme and resource measures, it is entirely reasonable for each of a number of theories of the growth of government to be correct in part, and no one theory to be true for all programmes and all resources. (1985: 22)

In short, while the categorizing of variables can provide an important organizational function, it is also true that these variables often operate in complex ways across and within categories. Consequently, as varieties of "causes" and explanations for government growth are reviewed in subsequent pages, some of the intricacy among the variables or phenomena within categories is likely to be neglected.

ORGANIZATION OF THE BOOK

The focus is primarily on the United States, although there is significant discussion of its peer communities in Japan and in other advanced, democratic, and postindustrial societies. There is a lively debate on whether market-oriented as compared to government-directed policies should prevail among less developed nations. However, the questions and issues at the core of this book are most usefully examined in the context of those countries that are categorized as economically advanced and democratic. Issues regarding the contrasts and differences in government scale are sensible only in societies in which there is accorded to the private sector a considerable, if not prevailing, autonomy. Consequently, the discussion here is not concerned, for the most part, with those nations that are or were recently largely state-planned. The extremely important and complex matter of comparing market against state-planned systems is not engaged here.

Chapter 2 examines the various dimensions of government growth, with particular attention to the problem of selecting measurements of government scale and the preoccupation with fiscal indicators of government size and growth. There is a brief discussion regarding nonfiscal aspects of government size, including government regulation. Data are also examined to assess the issue of how "burdensome" government has allegedly become in late-twentieth-century America.

Chapters 3 and 4 deal with theories of why government grows. Chapter 3 is an explication of macro-deterministic approaches to government growth, including discussion of traditional approaches to government growth.

Chapter 4 explicates the public choice approach to changes in government scale and growth. In approaching public or rational choice models, the focus is on connecting this approach to the venerable social contract tradition of American political thought (Lovrich and Neiman, 1984). It is argued that public choice models seek to provide not only explanations of the causes of government growth, but also a set of methods and concepts to delimit the appropriate circumstances for government intervention.

Chapter 5 reviews studies of government growth and how they square with extant theory. The empirical evidence generally indicates a need for a multidimensional approach to explaining government growth, that is, the data indicate that the question of why government grows cannot be understood in terms of a single process, much less a small set of variables or a lone factor, such as class conflict or income levels. After all, government growth occurs at different levels, involving different components of government activity, driven by different demand-generating entities operating at both the individual and organizational level.

Chapter 6 concentrates on the contention that government size and growth has impeded economic progress. Specifically, the claim is often made that the modern welfare state in market societies has imposed such a heavy burden upon the productive elements of society that too little untaxed capital or too little individual motivation exist to supply the investment and purchasing needs of a growing economy. What is the available evidence regarding the association between the scale and growth of government and economic performance? The evidence is perplexing and often contradictory, and it challenges us to be more sophisticated about the nexus between government activity and the performance of the economy. Moreover, clarifying this issue is important, since much of the public's low regard for government is related to its view of government as a cause of economic malaise.

Is an active government, one that does a wide range of different things, necessarily an oppressive government? That is the central question of Chapter 7, which examines the tradition of suspicion regarding the consequences of government growth for personal liberty. In a society such as ours, which views governing institutions as subsequent to the existence of a fundamentally felicitous private order, there is also a tendency to see the role of government as a mere lubricant for civil society. In short, a prevailing belief has existed in both popular and many intellectual forums that with increases in the scale and scope of government there are coincident, if not commensurate, losses in personal freedom. Equally important is the idea, held by individuals, that as government does more, its capacity also grows to employ the tools of governing for the purposes of abusing members of society.

While not down-playing the potential for the abuse of power that growth in government or government size entail, evidence is plentiful that private sector power can also be a source of abuse and a threat to personal liberty. Powerful concentrations of abusive, private power is a problem that might only be remedied through the countervailing strength of public authority. For example, what of the role of government in resisting discrimination and unfairness based on race, religion, national origin, or any other characteristic that has no rational or reasonable basis? Or what of economic blacklisting by private firms and individuals on political grounds? As we come to understand that certain behaviors are based on prejudice and fear, might it not be necessary for the public to discipline itself through the extension of government prohibitions of objectionable conduct? For example, if modern technology and modern therapeutic methods make it possible to gainfully employ greater proportions of handicapped individuals, is it a restriction of freedom to prohibit employers from denying employment, on a general basis, to handicapped people?

Chapter 8 extends the previous chapter as a conceptual discussion of what is meant by such terms as government growth and government size. Specifically, the chapter addresses the tendency to lump together the range of activities that government can do as if each one is of equal relevance to such issues as liberty or efficiency. But this obviously is a problem, since some things that government does involve more resources or greater intrusions and impositions on citizens than others. After all, Hitler did not come to power or exercise rule by consolidating the various social and welfare agencies of the former Weimar Republic. Can one casually assume that government initiatives in environmental or workplace safety are incremental steps to an authoritarian society? Are government proscriptions on discrimination and bigotry to be equated with regulation of political activity? More specifically, do government prohibitions against the segregation of schools or public accommodations imply a loss of freedom and liberty in the same way as, say, government prohibitions of certain political activity (e.g., criticizing government officials in the press)? In addressing these conceptual issues, the chapter also deals with the problem of cross-national comparisons of government growth and the role of language and meaning in judging whether an array of government actions constitute a threat to liberty.

The difficulties of evaluating government performance are the focus of Chapter 9. Particular attention is devoted to the debate over whether the delivery of government services of public policy should rely more heavily on "noncoercive," more market-like mechanisms. It is this issue that underlies much of the controversy over the privatization of public services and the lack of regard of many citizens as they assess the efficiency of government services. Although there is considerable opportunity for achieving benefits by introducing market incentives in the production and delivery of public services, there are also a number of risks. Moreover, regarding the general matter of judging governmental performance, this chapter highlights the need to incorporate an understanding of the multiplicity of objectives contained in a given public service. Finally, the chapter addresses a number of ironies and paradoxes associated with the reliance on incentives-based, market-like mechanisms in producing and delivering public services. For example, it can be argued that government reliance on market-like methods, preferred by conservatives who worry about the excessiveness of government, will result in greater involvement by government in private society, which is presumably abhorred by proponents of government reliance on incentives (Neiman, 1980). This chapter also addresses the ascendancy of economics-based models as the dominant mode of analysis regarding government policies and services. A major theme is that the use of such models is dominated by the quest for principles to limit the scale and scope of government. That is, the effort of this mode of analysis is to contribute to the venerable tradition of finding nonsubjective, "nonpolitical" bases for defining the circumstances under which the government should intervene in previously private matters and the methods that should be employed in circumstances when government must, unfortunately, be expanded. In assessing the role of economics-based approaches to describing and evaluating government policy formation, the chapter reviews a variety of concepts that economics have provided and that are often applied, including the notions of market failure, externalities, public goods, and common property resources, to name a few. Additionally, a number of applications of these concepts to institutional design and to the delivery of services are reviewed.

Chapter 10 concludes with an assessment of how the issue of government size has been deployed politically and with what effect. Since the view of this book is that much good has been done and remains to be done through public policy, the final chapter seeks to defend the idea of democratic governing. After summarizing previous material, the chapter addresses some continuing problems that can usefully be managed by public intervention, both in domestic matters and on a regional and international level. For example, what are the implications of globalization for the role of political intervention in the market for goods, services, finance, and labor? Finally, the chapter broaches a number of issues that have to do with institutional changes to affect how individuals are linked to politics.

CHAPTER 2

HOW BIG HAS GOVERNMENT GOTTEN IN THE UNITED STATES?

Government budgets provide wonderful material for political rhetoric and political jokesters. Stories about which celestial body can be reached by the pile of one-dollar bills comprising government spending or entertaining references to how many times the earth can be circled by these same dollar bills are conventional elements on the fiscal politics comedy circuit. Few subjects lend themselves more to purple prose than the subject of government spending and taxing.

THE NEED FOR CONTEXT

This chapter will not end the jokes regarding government growth. The key thing is that the size of government is viewed by most people to be bigger and more burdensome, and it is government taxing and spending that for most people symbolize this sense of imposition. Unfortunately, discussing government spending and taxing is hampered not only by the comedy it produces, but also by a tradition of public discourse that is dominated by inappropriate comparisons to family and business budgets. In these contrasts between public sector and family and business budgets there is a sense in which families and businesses are somehow constrained by market forces in ways that governments are not. Families are seen as more disciplined, frugal, and likely to invest in things that are tailored to what they want. Of course, there is much truth to this view. By contrast, government budgets are viewed as profligate, bloated, rapacious, and foolish, often supporting services and producing goods that few people want or enjoy. In actuality, though, the rate of borrowing among families or business has generally grown more rapidly in recent years than has government debt, except during times of war. In celebrating the private over the public, we charitably overlook how individuals, families, and businesses can make a host of self-destructive, ineffective, unproductive and short-sighted investments without necessarily going out of business, and we exaggerate the extent of government fiscal and budgetary misfires. We exaggerate equally the extent to which government mismanagement occurs with impunity. It is also conventional to dismiss the critical importance of the multitude of public sector investments in infrastructure, law and civic administration, social and human investments, and long-term personal security. Indeed, among antigovernment critics, the language of taxing and spending is mobilized entirely in service of an effort to undermine support for public programs, and in recent years this antigovernment sloganeering has dominated any discussion about government spending and taxing.

Clearly the public believes that its governing institutions are too expensive and too intrusive. However, it is difficult to pinpoint the specific things that people are referring to as they express opinions about how their government is bigger or more burdensome. Although studies of government growth and most claims concerning the burden of government focus on fiscal measures (taxing and spending), such measures constitute a very limited, albeit very important, aspect of government growth. There are, after all, other important things that public agencies do that do not involve money. The development of rules and regulations governing personal and economic conduct (e.g., civil liberties, business regulation, and environmental protection) requires money for their administration. Money is not necessarily the most important aspect of these policies. Rather, it is the impact such policies have on personal liberty and security or on economic behavior and growth. Many of us see in government spending and taxing some obvious indicator of the burden of government, but it is not at all clear how specific increases in taxes and spending produce some proportional increase in "the burden" or scope of government. For example, if we increase the income security of some individuals, we can certainly say that there is a kind of increase in government involvement. Yet, if the increase is only proportional to the cost of living, we can hardly think of this *quantitative* increase in an existing program as some significant breakthrough in the public sector. On the other hand, in a society in which public programs to help individuals supplement their incomes do not exist, and after a period of debate and political conflict, such programs are established, we have a *qualitative* change, representing a real change in the substance of the public sector. Or, once having such a program, we might move from a policy designed to keep pace with inflation to one by which we seek, through redistributive payments and higher taxes on the rich, to increase the relative share of income held by less affluent retirees. This is certainly a more important increase in the public sector than a mere proportional increase in income supplements paid by the public. In short, quantitative changes in current government programs are different from qualitative additions to the public sector. Of course, quantitative increases might feel like qualitative changes, if they begin to impart a sense of burden and to produce taxpayer resistance, as when taxpayers begin to resent the cost of government programs. In other words, judgments made concerning the size and scope of government have an important *subjective* component. Programs with high levels of legitimacy and support *feel* less oppressive, and government might not be perceived to be as "large" to the individuals who feel that way. No matter how objectively small the budget of a regime might be, if people feel programs are unfair, ineffective, and inefficient, the size of the public sector will be, to them, a burden indeed.

Consequently, the discussion in this chapter takes a cautious position regarding increased government spending and taxes. Notwithstanding the very limited nature of fiscal measures of growth and size, the focus is on describing the fiscal aspects of government growth. The discussion will, of course, deal with the absolute size of government growth, but there is also an effort to compare government fiscal growth to previous historical periods, as well as to overall price increases and economic growth. For now the focus is mainly on the most conventional manner in which government growth is defined—increased government taxing and spending. The discussion also includes a brief overview of government regulation. Whether the growth of government spending, taxing, and regulating is "good" or "bad," whether such growth contributes to economic growth or stagnation, or whether it financially distresses the citizenry are aspects of an intriguing and complex puzzle. That puzzle is addressed in subsequent chapters.

In order to assess some of the claims that are often made regarding the effects of government size and growth, it is necessary to place the growth of government in historical perspective. For many people it is entertaining to describe the growth of government in absolute terms, because the numbers involved are so gigantic. However, it is also necessary to compare the growth of government relative to the growth of the economy in general and to the income of the people who pay the revenue for government outlays. It is obvious, for example, that comparing the absolute size of government budgets with those at the turn of the century fails to account for price differences across time (i.e., the impact of inflation). If today's budgets were expressed in 1900 dollars, the numbers involved would be considerably smaller, an obvious point that needs to be constantly remembered.

Among those who chafe under what they perceive to be the oppressiveness of government it is common to point out that today's taxpayer in the United States pays considerably more in taxes than his or her 1900 counterpart. But what is the suggestion? Is it that the turn-of-the-century taxpayer was better off? Or that the contemporary citizen is saddled with more burdensome government obligations than were the residents of the United States in 1900? We seem often to suggest that the answers to these questions are an obvious "yes." But a major objective here is to underscore how problematic it is to arrive casually at such conclusions. If one examines a copy of a 1900 *New York Times*, one would discover that it was not only government that was relatively inexpensive in absolute terms. A modern, comfortable apartment in downtown New York City could be rented for forty dollars a month, an imported, fashionable wool coat could be purchased for a mere twelve dollars, or an evening at one of the best restaurants could be had for a few dollars. Since comparable items and services are today many times more expensive, should we conclude, then, that today's consumers are not as well-off as those of yesteryear? Of course, 50 percent of the urban workers in the United States of 1910 earned less than $900 (King, 1915). Certainly government was less expensive in early twentieth century America. But residents of the United States earned much less, and they did not receive much in the way of publicly supported higher education, secondary education, income security, or protection from the exploitation of private firms.

GROWTH IN LEVELS, PROPORTIONS, AND BURDENS: THE FISCAL DIMENSION

Taxing and spending by government have produced major political controversies no matter what interval of American history is explored. Violent insurgencies associated with the efforts of the states and the federal government to tax existed at the earliest points in the founding of the Republic [Brennan and Buchanan, 1977; Musgrave, 1981; Bruchey, 1988). Academic and political objections to government growth can be illustrated at practically any point in U.S. history. In 1909, Professor Henry Jones Ford (no relation to the automobile baron) delivered and published a series of lectures entitled *The Cost of Our National Government: A Study in Political Pathology*. In the text, Professor Ford quoted the then chairman of the Senate Finance Committee, Nelson Aldrich, who was lamenting the growth of government expenditures and deficits:

> In no period except in time of war have the expenditures of our National Government increased so rapidly, both in the aggregate and per capita, as these expenditures have increased during the past eight years. This fact may well cause our people not only to pause and consider the cause of this very large increase in the annual expenditures of the Government, but also to consider the necessity of checking this growing tendency toward excess. (Ford, 1974: 3)

Perhaps of greatest alarm to the period's contemporaries, however, was the 1909 federal budget deficit of $90 million, representing a 13 percent shortfall of revenues over outlays. At the time, it was perhaps the largest federal budget deficit since the Civil War. Moreover, Professor Ford's and Senator

Aldrich's apprehensions were expressed at a time when the *total* federal budget was just under $700 million dollars and total federal government spending represented approximately 2 percent of GNP.

In comparison to the absolute magnitude of outlays, expenditures, and debt of today's government budgets, the anxiety expressed by observers of early-twentieth-century America might seem misplaced or quaint. Seen historically, however, one might understand the concern. Beginning with the end of the Civil War, the federal budget experienced a quarter of a century of uninterrupted surpluses and relative stability in both spending and taxing. For example, in 1866, one year after the Civil War, federal expenditures were at just over $500 million and the budget was in surplus. By 1870, federal expenditures slid to $309 million and the federal budget had a $102 million surplus. In fact, in 1890, twenty years later, federal expenditures were only at $318 million, with an $82 million surplus. Between 1866 and 1893, then, federal expenditures declined thirteen times over the previous year and the average percentage of the surplus of revenues over expenditures was approximately 20 percent. Between 1880–90, budget surpluses were especially high, with the ratio of receipts to outlays averaging 37.4 percent above 1.00 (a ratio of 1.00 indicates a balanced budget, a ratio below 1.00 indicates a deficit). No wonder, then, as deficits and spending increased after 1893, due to a number of sharp reversals in economic conditions, that Professor Ford and other contemporaries became alarmed. Equally fretful expressions about expenditures and taxes and deficits appear at various points during the twentieth century. Each of these fiscal anxiety attacks appears with its own set of circumstances. In short, to understand reactions to the level of government spending and taxing during given periods, one must place the fiscal growth of government into historical perspective.

GROWTH IN THE ABSOLUTE SIZE OF FISCAL DIMENSIONS

The absolute size of the numbers associated with the growth of government since the founding of the Republic is daunting. Examining the enumeration of federal government outlays and receipts reported in Table 2.1 (on page 18) reveals how far we have come, from a $5 million federal expenditure in 1792, with a $1 million deficit, to a 1987 expenditure that exceeded $1 trillion for the first time, with a budget deficit of approximately $155 billion. By 1997, federal government expenditures reached $1.7 trillion. As the decades have advanced, then, when measured in absolute, current dollars, government taxing and spending levels have also swelled, at times in very dramatic fashion. Additionally, Figures 2.1–2.4 pinpoint the periods of surge and decline in outlays (expenditures) and receipts (all sources of revenue, including taxes, tariffs, and fees). These figures also suggest some of the differences that exist in different fiscal epochs. For example, during the first fifty years of the nineteenth century (Figure 2.1, on page 19), spending levels trailed revenues

**TABLE 2.1   SUMMARY OF FEDERAL RECEIPTS, OUTLAYS,
AND SURPLUS/DEFICITS, 1792–1994**

YEAR	*RECEIPTS (MILLIONS)*	*OUTLAYS (MILLIONS)*	*SURPLUS OR DEFICITS (MILLIONS)*	*RATIO OF RECEIPTS TO OUTLAYS*
1792	4	5	–1	0.80
1800	12	11	1	1.09
1810	9	8	1	1.12
1820	18	18	0	1.00
1830	25	15	10	1.67
1840	19	24	–5	0.79
1850	44	40	4	1.10
1860	56	63	–7	0.89
1861	42	67	–25	0.63
1862	52	475	–423	0.11
1863	113	715	–602	0.16
1864	265	865	–600	0.31
1865	334	1298	–964	0.26
1866	558	521	37	1.07
1870	411	309	102	1.33
1880	334	268	66	1.25
1890	403	318	85	1.27
1900	567	521	46	1.09
1910	675	693	–18	0.97
1917	1100	1956	–853	0.56
1918	3645	12677	–9032	0.29
1919	5130	19492	–14362	0.26
1920	6649	6358	291	1.05
1930	4058	3320	738	1.22
1940	6548	9468	–2920	0.69
1941	8712	13653	–4941	0.64
1942	14634	35137	–20503	0.42
1943	24001	78555	–54554	0.30
1944	43747	91304	–47557	0.48
1945	45159	92712	–47553	0.49
1946	39296	55232	–15936	0.71
1947	38514	34496	4018	1.12
1950	39443	42562	–3119	0.93
1960	92492	92191	301	1.00
1970	192807	195649	–2842	0.98
1980	517112	590920	–73808	0.88
1990	1031321	1252705	–221384	0.82
1997	1505425	1631016	–125591	0.92

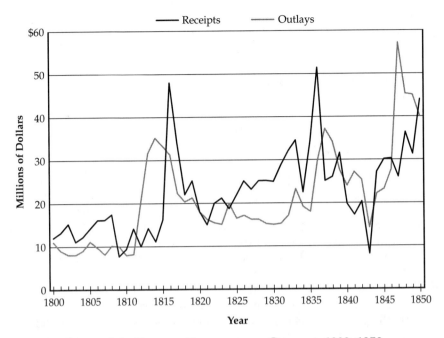

FIGURE 2.1   FEDERAL RECEIPTS AND OUTLAYS, 1800–1850

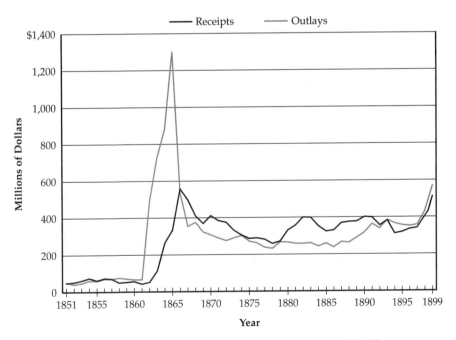

FIGURE 2.2   FEDERAL RECEIPTS AND OUTLAYS, 1851–99

fairly consistently. The exceptions were the War of 1812 (1812–15), the economic downturn in the late 1830s to early 1840s, and the Mexican-American War period (1847–49). The latter half of the nineteenth century is dominated by the impact of the Civil War (Figure 2.2, on page 19).

Expenditures surged between 1861–65, but then remained constant and well below receipts until the late years of the century, when the appearance of modern economic downturns and the Spanish-American War affected fiscal behavior. The first half of the twentieth century is dominated by the impact of war on spending, but we also see the effect of severe economic downturns (Figure 2.3).

There is a spike in expenditures during World War I. We also see the decline in both spending and receipts that occurred in the aftermath of the 1929 collapse of the American economy. Moreover, the Roosevelt New Deal policies are reflected in the post-1932 increase in expenditures, which regularly exceed receipts. Indeed, expenditures exceeded receipts from 1931–47, the longest such period in U.S. history till that time. Of course, the run-up in World War II expenditures comprised the largest percentage increase in expenditures and revenues since the Civil War. The fiscal surges and declines in the first half of the twentieth century were, in historical terms, much greater than anything that has been experienced in the post-World War II period (Figure 2.4). The most notable feature of the latter half of the twentieth century is

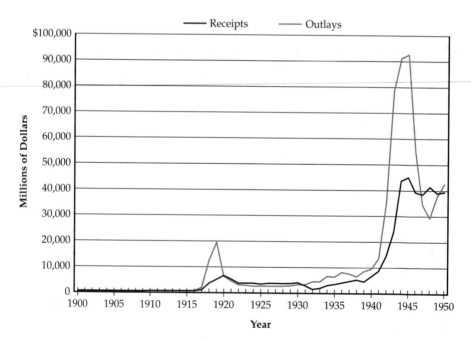

FIGURE 2.3   FEDERAL RECEIPTS AND OUTLAYS, 1900–1950

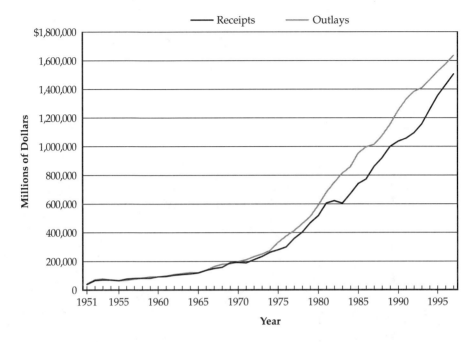

FIGURE 2.4 FEDERAL RECEIPTS AND OUTLAYS, 1951–97

the sustained increases in both spending and receipts, along with a period of notable but not historically large deficits, especially in the years following the election of Ronald Reagan. Indeed, while the Reagan administration took office on an antispending and antideficit train, driven by a powerful antigovernment locomotive, spending and deficits in particular increased dramatically during the Reagan years. Although the post-World War II period is marked largely by unremitting growth in government spending, the period is also fairly stable, being smoother and less erratic in terms of dramatic declines and increases in revenues and expenditures.

RELATIVE FISCAL GROWTH

As the previous section has shown, examining government fiscal data in current and absolute dollar terms provides some astonishing figures. However, a proper assessment of government's fiscal growth requires us to evaluate such data in terms of its relationship to the total economy. The standard method has been to express government fiscal data as a percentage of the Gross National Product. The data in Table 2.2 (on pages 22–23) suggest several conclusions regarding the relative growth of government spending in the United States during the twentieth century. First, until World War II, state and local government spending represented a greater proportion of GNP

TABLE 2.2 GOVERNMENT SPENDING, INCOME, AND CORPORATE TAXES AS PERCENT OF GNP

YEAR	FEDERAL OUTLAYS (BILLIONS)	STATE-LOCAL OUTLAYS (BILLIONS)	PERCENT GNP FEDERAL OUTLAYS	PERCENT GNP STATE-LOCAL OUTLAYS	PERCENT GNP TOTAL GOV'T OUTLAYS	TOTAL PER CAPITA GOV'T OUTLAYS	INDIVIDUAL INCOME TAXES AS PERCENT OF TOTAL FED. REVENUE	CORPORATE TAXES AS PERCENT OF TOTAL FED. REVENUE
1902	0.6	1.1	2.2	5.1	7.3	21.0		
1913	1.0	2.3	1.8	5.8	7.5	31.0		
1922	3.8	5.7	4.4	7.7	12.0	86.0		
1927	3.5	7.8	4.2	8.2	12.4	104.0		
1932	4.3	8.4	8.0	14.5	22.5	84.0		
1934	5.9	7.8	10.2	12.0	22.0	98.0	14.2	12.3
1936	9.2	8.5	10.2	10.3	20.5	113.0	17.2	18.3
1938	8.4	10.0	8.0	11.8	19.8	141.0	19.0	19.1
1940	10.1	11.2	9.5	11.3	20.8	142.0	13.6	17.9
1942	35.5	10.9	22.2	6.9	29.1	208.0	22.3	18.2
1944	100.5	10.5	43.4	5.0	48.4	476.0	45.0	33.9
1946	66.5	14.1	26.5	6.8	33.3	441.0	41.0	30.2
1948	35.6	21.3	11.6	8.3	19.9	469.0	46.5	23.3
1950	44.8	27.9	14.9	9.8	25.7	456.0	40.0	26.5
1952	48.9	30.9	19.6	8.9	28.5	693.0	42.2	32.1
1954	76.8	36.6	19.4	10.0	29.4	760.0	42.4	30.3
1956	74.7	43.2	16.8	10.3	27.1	624.0	43.2	28.0
1958	86.1	53.7	18.4	12.0	30.4	780.0	43.6	25.2
1960	97.3	61.0	18.3	12.1	30.4	893.0	44.0	23.2

Table 2.2, continued

Year	Federal Outlays (Billions)	State-Local Outlays (Billions)	Percent GNP Federal Outlays	Percent GNP State-Local Outlays	Percent GNP Total Gov't Outlays	Total Per Capita Gov't Outlays	Individual Income Taxes as Percent of Total Fed. Revenue	Corporate Taxes as Percent of Total Fed. Revenue
1962	113.4	70.1	19.1	12.5	31.6	946.0	45.7	20.6
1964	125.9	80.6	18.7	12.7	31.4	961.0	43.2	20.9
1966	143.0	94.9	17.9	12.7	30.6	1219.0	42.4	23.0
1968	184.5	116.2	20.6	13.4	34.0	1415.0	44.9	18.7
1970	208.2	148.1	20.0	15.2	35.2	1750.0	46.9	17.0
1972	242.2	188.8	19.0	15.6	34.6	1984.0	45.7	15.5
1974	297.2	226.0	18.3	15.3	33.6	2492.0	45.2	14.7
1976	391.1	363.8	20.8	20.4	41.2	2930.0	44.2	13.9
1978	479.3	414.9	20.4	18.4	38.8	3682.0	45.3	15.0
1980	617.2	518.6	21.6	19.0	40.6	4491.0	47.2	12.5
1982	796.5	621.7	23.6	19.6	43.2	5445.0	48.2	8.0
1984	928.2	710.7	22.6	18.8	41.4	5954.0	44.8	8.5
1986	1096.4	718.3	23.7	17.0	40.7	6765.0	45.4	8.2
1988	1214.8	981.3	22.2	20.1	42.3	7716.0	44.1	10.4
1990	1393.1	1153.5	21.8	18.5	40.3	8792.0	45.6	10.4

Sources: United States Department of Commerce, Bureau of the Census. Historical Statistics of the United States, Colonial Times to 1970, Bicentennial Edition, part 1. Washington, D.C.: U.S. Government Printing Office, 1975: 224, 1104–5; United States Bureau of the Census, Statistical Abstract of the United States, 1987.

than did federal spending. Second, reexamining Table 2.1 and inspecting Table 2.2 indicate that the growth of government spending, in absolute terms and in terms of percentages of the national economy, occurs at particular times, with the sharpest climbs occurring during the War of 1812, the Civil War, World War I, and World War II. Total peacetime government spending as a percentage of GNP reached a peak in 1982 (at 43.2 percent), which is approximately 10 percent greater than the immediate postwar figure of 33.3 percent in 1946. In fact, in recent years there has been a decline and then steadying of the percentage representing government taxing or spending as a proportion of GNP (Wildavsky, 1998). Although government spending as a percentage of GNP crept up steadily until 1980, as a percentage of GNP this growth was modest and, as is suggested in Table 2.2, in recent years has hardly changed at all. The data indicate that for approximately twenty years total government spending did not advance substantially as a percentage of GNP (See Figure 2.5).

Figure 2.6 also reports the proportion of total federal revenue derived from income taxes. Clearly, individuals are presently contributing to federal revenue more from their income than was the case before World War II. Prior to World War II, individual and corporate income taxes were roughly similar as proportions of total federal revenue. Both corporate and individual

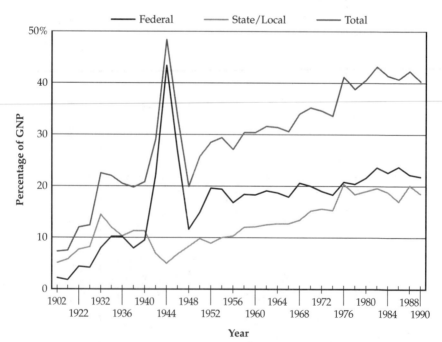

FIGURE 2.5   PERCENT OF GNP REPRESENTED BY FEDERAL, STATE/LOCAL, AND TOTAL GOVERNMENT SPENDING, 1902–90

FIGURE 2.6   PROPORTION OF FEDERAL BUDGET DERIVED
FROM INDIVIDUAL AND CORPORATE INCOME TAXES, 1932–92

income taxes, as a proportion of federal revenue, rose dramatically during World War II, although individual income taxes grew somewhat more than corporate taxes. Even after World War II, levels of support from individual income taxes declined only slightly from 45 percent in 1944 to 41 percent in 1946, after which they rose again. However, since World War II, individual income taxes as a proportion of federal revenue peaked at 48.2 percent and have most often represented around 45 percent of all government revenue. Individual income taxes as a source of federal revenue have, since the mid-1960s, hovered around the 45 percent level, sometimes rising a little higher and sometimes falling a little lower.

The distribution of the percentage of total federal revenue derived from corporate taxes has been quite different. Until the end of World War II, this proportion rose steadily, reaching a maximum in 1944, at 33.9 percent of total federal revenues. Since then, the contribution of corporate taxes to total federal revenue has declined steadily, reaching a low in the 1982–88 period. Indeed it would not be unreasonable, in light of the pattern in Figure 2.6, to suggest that as a proportion of total federal revenues, corporate income taxes have plummeted. Prior to World War II, individual and corporate taxes seemed to grow together. In 1940, individual income taxes actually contributed somewhat less to total federal revenue than did corporate taxes. It seems a

little ironic that the period prior to the Great Depression seems to be associated with a kind of business-dominated epoch, while the post-Great Depression period presumably marked the onset of the welfare state in the United
States, with a coincident decline in corporate power. Given the general feeling that taxes have become more burdensome and "progressive" over the
years, it is curious to observe how individual income taxes have been established as the paramount source of government revenue, while corporate income taxes as a proportion of total federal government revenue have declined
steadily for most of the period after World War II.

In the sense of income devoted to taxes, government's burden at the
federal and no doubt at the local/state levels has increased. The term *burden*
is, however, complex. After all, the actual burden of government for any individual citizen is the difference between what that person would voluntarily pay for and what that person actually pays, as well as the sense of
"burden" actually perceived by individuals. Surely, if all government services disappeared, an individual might still wish to arrange, if possible, for
personal security, education, street maintenance, garbage collection, or enforcement of contracts (presumably through private "enforcers"). The idea
that all government revenues would, if eliminated, wind up as "disposable"
income in the pockets of frustrated taxpayers is often suggested by the very
nature of how we talk about taxes in public forums. We all know, of course,
that people would surely have to use these resources to purchase goods and
services that are currently provided through the public sector. Transportation and streets, education, public safety, contract enforcement, and national defense would have to be paid for privately, assuming funds could be
raised for these services privately or voluntarily. Evaluating the size and burden of a government is, therefore, a more complex matter than we might ordinarily think.

GOVERNMENT DEFICITS

The size and burden of government is today often expressed in terms of the
large deficits that have been generated to sustain government spending.
Moreover, the deficit is agonized over as a major cause of a lagging economic performance. If one were to judge the origins of the "deficit problem"
and had only the discussions of the past fifty years to study, one would
conclude that the issue only emerged since the end of World War II. However, growth in government deficits is not unprecedented in the United
States, notwithstanding the current celebration over the balanced budget
(Savage, 1988). Data indicate that although government deficits have recently reached high levels in absolute terms and even in relative terms,
government deficits are certainly not new in U.S. history. Figure 2.7 reports
the pattern resulting from plotting the ratio of federal government receipts

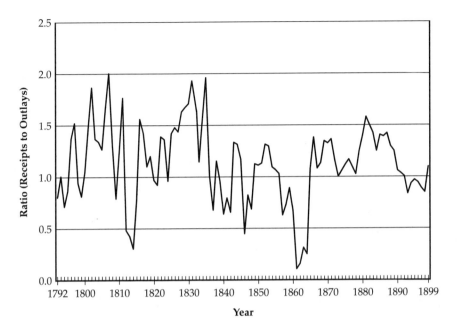

FIGURE 2.7   RATIO OF RECEIPTS TO OUTLAYS, NINETEENTH CENTURY

to outlays between 1792–1899 and 1900–1997 respectively. A value of 1.00 indicates a balanced budget, a value greater than 1.00 indicates a surplus, while a ratio of less than 1.00 indicates a deficit.

The pattern suggests that U.S. budgetary history is pockmarked by substantial episodes of deficit spending. Indeed, the Civil War period produced perhaps more red ink, relatively speaking, than any period other than World War II (Keller, 1977: 20–22). Indeed, in 1862 federal revenues comprised only 11 percent of expenditures. In 1919, at the height of World War I mobilization, federal revenues only covered 26 percent of expenditures. Recall that while hostilities ended in 1918, the peace was not formalized until 1919, and the United States signed a separate peace treaty with Germany in 1921. During World War II, in 1943, revenues accounted for only 30 percent of expenditures. Even though the nineteenth century was fiscally conservative, with great commitment among government officials to avoiding and retiring government debt, the data indicate that a number of periods of sustained deficit spending can also be found prior to the twentieth century (see Figure 2.7). These include the periods associated with the War of 1812 (1812–15), the Mexican-American War (1846–48), the Civil War (1861–65), and the depression generated by the Panic of 1893 (1894–1900).

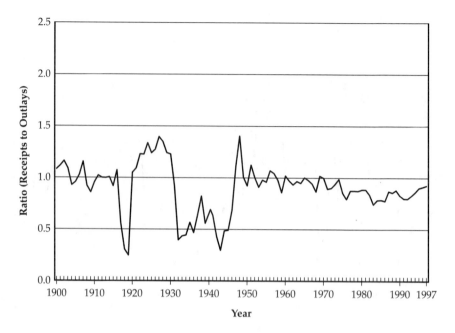

FIGURE 2.8   RATIO OF RECEIPTS TO OUTLAYS, TWENTIETH CENTURY

Figure 2.8 highlights intervals in the twentieth century with sustained deficits that have been associated with *economic* downturns (1903–10; 1932–40). However, as was the case in the nineteenth century, wars in the twentieth century produced the steepest onsets of deficit spending, especially in the cases of World War I (1917–19) and World War II (1941–45). In comparison, the Korean War (1950–53) and the Vietnam War build-up (1965–68) produced fairly minor, if noticeable, deficit increases. However, even though it is likely that government deficits grew substantially as a consequence of war mobilization, the post-World War II period has been marked almost entirely by deficits, some small and others quite large, regardless of whether war or other military action existed. Indeed, a comparison of Figures 2.7 and 2.8 indicates that the nineteenth century was marked by substantial periods of budget surplus, sprinkled with occasional, even dramatic, bouts of deficits. After the onset of World War II, the twentieth century trend was nearly uninterrupted deficit spending at the federal level, with the ratio inclining to larger deficits after 1965. Indeed, much has been made of this pattern. Politicians, citizens, and scholars have lamented the fact that since 1945 the budget has balanced only nine times (including the most recent balanced-budget victory in fiscal 1997–98), and, since 1960 and prior to fiscal 1998, the budget has balanced only once—in 1969.

It is possible, however, to exaggerate the importance of this pattern. Between 1945 and 1970, the federal budget was balanced or within five percent of being balanced seventeen out of twenty-six times. Although the recent growth in deficits was striking, the data indicate that federal budget deficits being produced, as a percentage of GNP, were not unprecedented, viewed in historical terms. In fact, until 1976, federal deficits had been declining as a percentage of GNP, as had been the total debt owed. Nevertheless, the data do indicate that a chronic deficit problem emerged in recent years, with its burden increasing somewhat after 1976 and accelerating in the early 1980s after the Reagan administration spearheaded major tax cuts and reforms that made the tax yield less robust. Whether this trend is a long-term one or merely one interlude of deficit growth among previous periods of deficits is an unsettled question, especially in light of the recent fiscal success in producing budget surpluses and balancing the federal budget.

Figure 2.9 highlights some concerns about budget deficits. The data indicate the step-like increases in the role of federal budget deficits in the 1970s. On the one hand, the data indicate that budget deficits between 1960–96 as a percentage of GNP remained between 1.32 and about 3.20 percent. These were

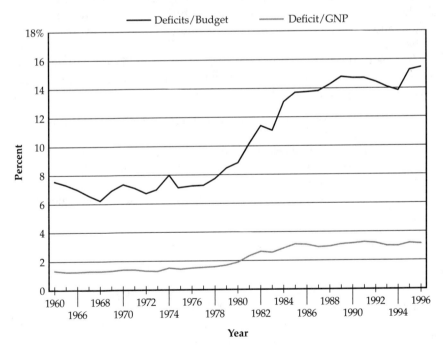

FIGURE 2.9   BUDGET DEFICIT AS PERCENT
OF TOTAL FEDERAL BUDGET AND GNP

not dramatic swings. As a percent of GNP, the annual budget deficit varied between fairly inconsequential to noticeable, but not harrowing. On the other hand, the change in the budget deficit as a percentage of the total federal budget nearly doubled between the mid-1970s and mid-1990s. Moreover, growth in payments for interest on the national debt were dramatic. Indeed, as a percentage of federal budget outlays, it was among the most rapidly increasing items, rising from about 6 percent of federal outlays in 1968 to nearly 15 percent by 1989.

Clearly the budget deficit, while not reaching the dizzying levels of wartime deficits, has in recent years come to produce much anxiety among elected officials, scholars, and citizens. Nevertheless, the federal budget grew only from 2.0 percent of the GNP in 1980 to 3.2 percent of GNP by 1990, and even this latter percentage is considerably lower than in other periods of American history. Although the absolute numbers are impressive, even frightening to those concerned about deficits, between 1984 and 1990 the growth of interest paid on the national debt, as a percentage of GNP, grew by only 0.2 percent. These data seem to suggest that deficits and the interest paid to service them are perhaps more important as they function to limit the choices of policymakers. When seen in terms of their size relative to the overall economy, their magnitude is somewhat less imposing. It might be that the salience of "the politics of deficits" has more to do with the symbolism of budgetary politics and less with the actual impact of budget deficits on the performance of the national economy.

Some of these issues can be further clarified in Figure 2.10, which depicts the changes in federal government expenditures in five general categories, as percentages of the federal budget:

1. *National Defense,* which involves all direct expenditures on the military branches
2. *Human Resources* (Social Security, income security, Medicare, health, education, training, employment, and other social services)
3. *Physical Resources* (energy, natural resources and environment, commerce and housing credit, transportation, community and regional development)
4. *Interest* (payments on the national debt)
5. *Other* (international affairs and assistance, science, space, technology, agriculture, administration of justice, general government)

The declining role of defense expenditures in the federal budget, particularly after the Korean War (post-1954), are clearly illustrated in these figures. Only during the height of the Vietnam War and a relatively minor reversal during the 1980s did military spending not decline. The pattern seems very similar for defense spending as a percentage of GNP. Human resource spending seemed to be a reversal of the defense pattern, rising steeply as a percentage of the federal budget and of GNP until the late 1970s. Finally, the rising

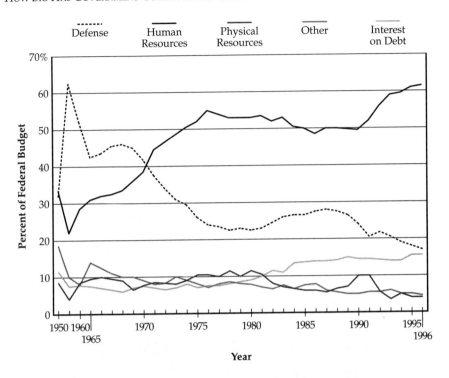

FIGURE 2.10   PERCENT OF FEDERAL BUDGET IN SELECTED ITEMS, 1950–96

national debt is reflected in the rise of payments for interest on the national debt, particularly since the post-1980 period. Indeed, interest payments and defense spending as a percentage of the federal budget are on converging paths, with interest payments appearing to pass defense spending levels, as the latter falls in the budget and as a proportion of the GNP.

THE COMPARATIVE SIZE OF U.S. SPENDING AND TAXING

Although government spending and taxing activity has grown substantially since the founding of the Republic, another way in which to get a sense of how large government has become is to compare the size of the public sector in the United States with other, comparable nations. Table 2.3 and Figure 2.11 (both on page 32) illustrate the size of government spending in the United States in comparison to selected countries, in constant 1985 prices. These data, compiled by the Organisation for Economic Cooperation and Development, indicate that when compared to most of the advanced, Western European nations, the United States appears to have among the smallest public sectors. It is notable, too, that total government expenditures as a proportion of Gross Domestic Product seems to be stabilizing or declining among nearly all of the

TABLE 2.3   TOTAL GOVERNMENT EXPENDITURES AS PERCENT OF GDP, 1960–92

COUNTRY	1960	1970	1980	1990	1992	MEAN FOR COUNTRY
Sweden	22.2	24.6	27.7	27.0	28.5	26.0
Denmark	18.7	21.7	26.7	24.1	23.8	23.0
Unit. Kingdom	22.6	20.9	22.0	19.3	20.4	21.0
Canada	19.9	22.8	20.8	20.1	20.8	20.9
United States	20.7	21.4	17.9	17.8	17.9	19.1
France	21.0	18.3	18.5	18.5	19.0	19.1
Greece	17.9	15.8	18.3	20.8	20.6	18.7
Germany	18.7	18.6	20.0	18.2	17.7	18.6
Austria	21.6	18.5	18.5	17.0	17.2	18.6
Ireland	16.8	17.4	20.2	14.3	13.7	16.5
Switzerland	10.6	11.8	12.7	14.0	14.3	12.7

Source: OECD National Accounts Main Aggregates, vol. 1, 1960–92

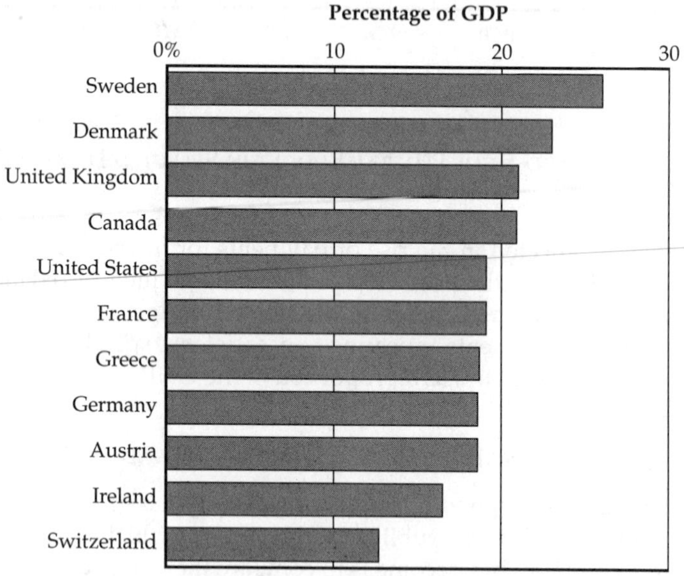

FIGURE 2.11   TOTAL GOVERNMENT EXPENDITURES
AS PERCENT OF GDP, MEAN FOR 1960–92

nations listed in the table. Finally, Table 2.4 (on page 33) and Figure 2.12 (on page 34) report the proportion of taxes as a percent of GDP among twenty-four nations, as of 1988. Only Turkey, with a percentage of taxes relative to GDP at 22.9 percent, is lower than the United States.

TABLE 2.4   ALL TAXES AS A PERCENTAGE OF GDP
AMONG OECD MEMBERS, 1965–95

COUNTRY	1965	1970	1975	1980	1985	1990	1995	MEAN FOR NATION 1965–95
Sweden	35.0	39.8	43.4	48.8	50.0	55.6	51.3	46.3
Denmark	29.9	40.4	41.4	45.5	49.0	48.7	49.7	43.5
Netherlands	32.8	37.1	43.0	45.2	44.1	44.6	46.5	41.9
Belgium	31.2	35.7	41.8	44.4	47.3	44.4	44.5	41.3
France	34.5	35.1	36.9	41.7	44.5	43.7	44.0	40.1
Norway	29.6	34.9	39.9	42.7	43.3	41.8	46.5	39.8
Austria	34.7	35.7	38.6	40.3	42.4	41.0	42.2	39.3
Luxembourg	27.7	28.0	38.8	42.0	46.7	43.4	44.0	38.7
Finland	30.3	32.5	37.7	36.9	40.8	45.4	41.4	37.9
Germany	31.6	32.9	36.0	38.2	38.1	36.7	39.2	36.1
Unit. Kingdom	30.4	36.9	35.5	35.3	37.9	36.4	38.2	35.8
Ireland	25.9	31.0	31.3	33.8	36.4	34.8	41.5	33.5
New Zealand	24.7	27.4	31.1	33.0	33.6	38.1	41.3	32.7
Canada	25.9	31.3	32.4	31.6	33.1	36.5	33.9	32.1
Italy	25.5	26.1	26.2	30.4	34.5	39.2	37.2	31.3
Greece	22.0	25.3	25.5	29.4	34.5	36.5	35.3	29.8
Iceland	26.2	27.0	29.6	29.2	28.4	31.4	31.2	29.0
Switzerland	20.7	23.8	29.6	30.8	32.0	31.5	33.8	28.9
Australia	23.2	24.2	27.6	28.4	30.0	30.8	28.5	27.5
United States	24.3	27.4	26.7	26.9	26.0	26.7	27.9	26.6
Portugal	16.2	20.3	21.7	25.2	27.8	31.0	34.0	25.2
Japan	18.3	19.7	20.9	25.4	27.6	31.3	30.9	24.9
Spain	14.7	16.9	19.5	24.1	28.8	34.4	33.8	24.6
Turkey	10.6	12.5	16.0	17.9	15.4	20.0	22.5	16.4
Annual Mean	26.1	29.2	32.1	34.5	36.3	37.7	38.3	

Source: "Revenue Statistics of OECD Member Countries," Annual Reports, Organization for Economic Co-operation and Development, Paris, France.

It is possible that the public sector in the United States is, according to one or another standard, too large or burdensome. However, when compared to other nations in terms of expenditures or revenue, relative to the size of the total economy, the public sector in the United States does not appear impressively large.

Notwithstanding complaints and criticism concerning the growth, burden, or impact of the public sector in the United States, the fact that the public sector in the United States appears relatively small when compared across nations has a number of important implications. Assuming that a larger or growing public sector should diminish economic performance, then the

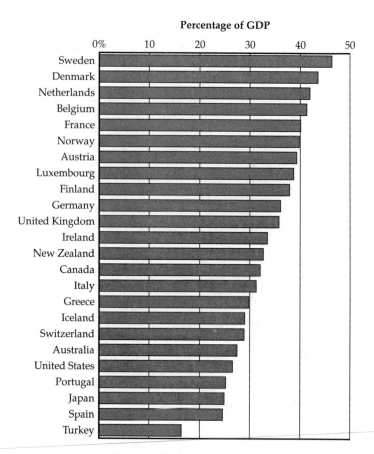

**FIGURE 2.12   ALL TAXES AS PERCENT OF GDP
AMONG OEC COUNTRIES, MEAN FOR 1965–95**

United States, all other things being equal, should be consistently performing better than most other nations, since its public sector is smaller and has grown at a slower rate than its peer nations. Although the U.S. economy has performed enviably in recent years, over the long run the data indicate no clear relationship between conventional measures of public sector size and economic performance. Indeed, even in the United States, the most recent period of economic growth has been accompanied by a slight growth in the size of the public sector and the levels of taxes. President Clinton's political opponents hyperbolically refer to these tax increases as "the largest tax increase in American history." Of course, the economic expansion during the post-1982 Ronald Reagan administration was also precipitated by a very unconservative, very Keynesian spurt of cosmically large budget deficits. As will be shown in later chapters, some nations with very large and rapidly growing public sectors also had lively, growing economies, while others with smaller, slower growing public sectors did relatively poorly. Reviewing the post-World War II period as a whole, among the major capitalist advanced nations the general issue of whether a correlation between public sector size and economic performance exists is problematic.

The Growth of Government Regulation

Regarding the nonfiscal dimensions of government growth, perhaps the most important is the greater involvement by government in what is called regulation. The meaning of the term *regulation* is a matter of some considerable discussion. However, for our purposes, the discussion adopts Alan Stone's definition (1982: 7); that is, regulations involve "a state-imposed limitation on the discretion that may be exercised by individuals or organizations, which is supported by the threat of sanction." The topic of regulation is extraordinarily rich in studies and controversy and it is difficult to resist the temptation to become preoccupied with it. Nevertheless, it is important to note at least briefly why regulation has become an important public policy issue:

1. The concern that greater regulation reduces personal liberty and contributes to excessively powerful government
2. The concern that regulation tends not to work in the manner in which it is intended
3. The concern that regulation militates against economic efficiency, resulting in a number of related bad consequences (e.g., reduced competitiveness, lowered productivity, misallocations of resources, and loss of investment in research and development)

Later chapters address a number of these issues in greater detail, while the remainder of this chapter concentrates on depicting the main dimensions and periods of regulatory growth. The concern is not to replicate the historical details of regulation, but to outline the pattern of regulatory growth. A number of excellent historical summaries can be found in other recent texts (Gerston, Fraleigh, and Schwab, 1988: 39; Bernstein, 1955; *Congressional Quarterly*, 1982: 7–20; Bucholz, 1989: 176–84; Hoberg, 1986; Kemp, 1987; Lilly and Miller, 1977; Wilson, 1980).

It is conventional to point out that, prior to the Civil War, government in the United States regulated society very little. This is not to say, however, that Americans had no regulatory experience before that. It was more likely that the lower levels of regulation reflected the smaller scale of colonial and pre-Civil War society, rather than an absence of government authority to regulate. During the colonial period and among the states in the postrevolutionary period, regulation existed across a rather broad range of social and economic activity (Bourgin, 1989; Farnam, 1938). For rather obvious reasons, the kind of regulation associated with the emergence of the modern business corporation and its exercise of economic power, the formation of urban ag-glomerations, and the intensification of social and class conflict was not pre-sent until these conditions intensified in the latter half of the nineteenth century. Although large-scale federal regulation is relatively recent, it would be an error to believe that the United States had no regulatory experience until the closing decades of the nineteenth century.

Much of the federal regulation that developed was modeled after the already existing state regulatory institutions that had developed throughout the nineteenth century (Bernstein, 1955). Clearly, however, the *federal* role in regulation was minor until the Civil War, when government expanded its powers and role in managing the war effort. Although there existed, prior to the Civil War, a number of federal agencies that sought to promote econom-ic development (e.g., Patent and Trademarks), it was not until the Civil War and its aftermath that major federal involvement began to regulate industry in order to alter the commercial/economic behavior of individuals and firms through sanctions.

In discussing the regulations that emerged during these times, it is use-ful to use the now conventional distinction between economic and social reg-ulation (Fritschler and Ross, 1980: 41–42; Bucholz, 1989: 173–76). Economic regulation refers to government efforts to manage competitiveness, improve the performance of specific industries, and smooth labor-management rela-tions. As Fritschler and Ross claim (1980: 41), economic regulation seeks "to protect and enhance competitive forces in the economy, not to supplant them." In addition, economic regulation focuses on improving the performance and promoting the prosperity of business generally or by focusing on particular businesses or industry (e.g., utilities, airlines, or commodity and stock ex-change), while maintaining public confidence in legitimacy of profits. Eco-nomic regulation, then, seeks to promote business and to avoid the excesses of "ruinous competition."

Social regulation, often referred to as "the new regulation," tends to cut across sectors of the society, rather than focus on particular industries. Social regulation is defined by Fritschler and Ross as follows:

> ... [Social regulation is] defining what goods should or should not be pro-duced. They provide product specifications and procedures in industrial processes designed for industrial safety. These regulations define modes of environmentally acceptable production, types of employees who should be hired, acceptable working conditions, pay conditions, retirement sys-tems, and similar issues. (1980: 42)

Or, as another observer has said, social regulation "... is not economic policy but social policy. It is an effort to advance a conception of the public in-terest apart from, and often opposed to, the outcomes of the marketplace and, indeed, the entire idea of a market economy." (Weaver, 1978: 45). Social regulations apply not only to the private sector but to the nonprofit and public sector as well. State and local agencies and churches, as well as the federal government, must today comply with a host of workplace safety, equal opportunity, and environmental regulations. Indeed, as Neiman and Lovell (1981; 1982) have shown, local governments are among the most severely affected by the imposition of regulations by federal and state governments.

SUMMARIZING PERIODS OF REGULATORY GROWTH

It is possible to identify a number of periods of regulatory growth, each of which contains both economic and social regulation. Each of these periods, however, tends to be dominated by particular events and circumstances giving rise to new regulatory laws and new regulating agencies. The first period extends from the Civil War years to the New Deal (1861–1932). During this time the national government established a federal role in regulating markets and industries, often at the behest of industry because of the pressure of such groups as farmers and bank depositors. The watershed events in the development of federal regulation were the establishment of the Interstate Commerce Commission in 1887 and the enactment of the Sherman Antitrust Act of 1890. The Interstate Commerce Commission preempted state regulation of railroads and, later, other forms of transportation, while the Sherman Act involved the federal government in the regulation of business conduct, with the intent of managing methods of competition.

Subsequent regulation involved efforts to oversee banking, culminating with the establishment of the Federal Reserve System in 1913. Throughout the early years of the twentieth century, regulatory enactments extended the federal government's role in such areas as unfair and uncompetitive trade practices, import trade, commodities trade, and hydroelectric projects within federal jurisdiction. The period included what is often considered the first instance of federal social regulation, which involved the creation in 1906 of the Food and Drug Administration. The period also witnessed the emergence of regulations designed to rationalize and promote new industries, including the radio and airline businesses.

This period was dominated by a number of themes associated with late-nineteenth and early-twentieth-century reform. On the one hand, government was employed to prevent abuses of market power by large and powerful corporations. Simultaneously, government power was deployed in order to rationalize the development of new industries and to minimize public distrust of business profits. The period was marked not so much by the pace of new regulation, unprecedented as it was, but by the assertion of a new, potentially powerful regulatory role by the federal regime.

The second period, running from the New Deal to World War II (1932–40) was dominated by the travail and disruption associated with the

Great Depression. The underlying impetus for regulation was the effort to develop new regulatory authority in order to reestablish confidence in a number of major business institutions, as well as to promote harmony among major social classes in the face of increasing class friction. Also, regulations designed to promote a number of rapidly expanding new communication and transportation technologies, as well as to manage the competition among them, were also developed. These included radio and television broadcasting, interstate transmission of electricity, trucking, and airlines. The period also witnessed the next major piece of social regulation in the formation of the National Labor Relations Board in 1935. Clearly, however, new regulations designed to revive public confidence in saving and lending institutions and other major economic actors were the ones that marked the character of the period. This was a confidence-building era, involving additional, incidental regulatory inroads into newly developing communications and transport businesses.

In the 1960s there began a whirlwind of regulatory enactments, accelerating well into the 1970s. The period was marked especially by the domination of social regulation across the fields of consumer protection, workplace safety, product liability, equal opportunity, environmental protection, and historical preservation. A number of the most important and controversial regulatory agencies were created at this time, including the Equal Employment Opportunity Commission (1963); the Occupational and Health Administration (1970); the Environmental Protection Agency (1970); the Consumer Product Safety Commission (1972); the National Transportation Safety Board (1975); the Nuclear Regulatory Commission (1975); and the Federal Energy Regulatory Commission (1977). During the 1970s regulatory agencies and commissions were granted ever-more-powerful methods of affecting industry and individuals, as well as state and local government compliance with federal rules and regulations.

It is generally understood that, although there exists today a considerable regulatory apparatus, the growth in regulation was in large part associated with specific periods, especially the economic collapse of the 1930s and the social activism of the 1960s and 1970s. As Gatti says:

> ... the bulk of the growth in the number of agencies is attributable to three decades: that of the Great Depression—the 1930s, and the decades of increased social activism—the 1960s and 1970s. Of the more than 200 years covered, those 30 years account for 70 percent of all agency growth. (1981:3)

Not only did the vast amount of agency growth occur in a very short time, but, perhaps not surprisingly, the great proportion of the legislation enabling the growth happened concurrently. These points, highlighted in Table 2.5 and Figure 2.13 (on page 39) and Table 2.6 and Figure 2.14 (on page 40), demonstrate that there was a rapid growth in expenditures and personnel

TABLE 2.5   COSTS OF FEDERAL REGULATORY
AGENCIES, 1970–87 (MILLIONS OF DOLLARS)

YEAR	SOCIAL REGULATION	ECONOMIC REGULATION
1970	1273	1587
1975	3306	3860
1980	5717	6763
1985	7022	8505
1987, est.	7691	9387
% Change		
1970–80	349	326
1980–87	35	39

Source: Bucholz, 1989: 191.

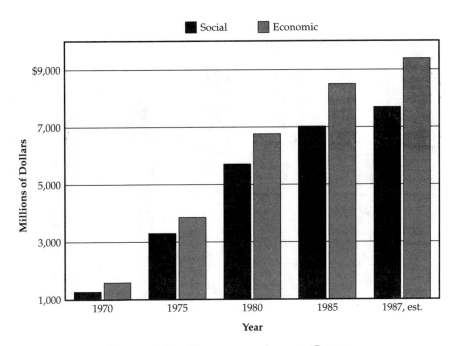

FIGURE 2.13   REGULATORY AGENCY COSTS

during the 1970s. Moreover, the growth was concentrated in the social regulation agencies, with the agencies dealing with economic regulation hardly growing at all. Indeed, if there had not been a resurgence of regulatory growth in finance and banking due to the savings and loan crisis stemming from deregulation, economic regulation figures would have been even smaller

40

CHAPTER 2

TABLE 2.6   NUMBER OF FEDERAL REGULATORY
PERSONNEL 1970–87 (PERMANENT, FULL-TIME POSITIONS)

YEAR	SOCIAL REGULATION	ECONOMIC REGULATION
1970	65481	20679
1975	95075	25314
1980	103038	27863
1985	87047	24897
1987, est.	86908	26453
% Change		
1970–80	59	35
1980–87	−16	−5

Source: Bucholz, 1989: 192.

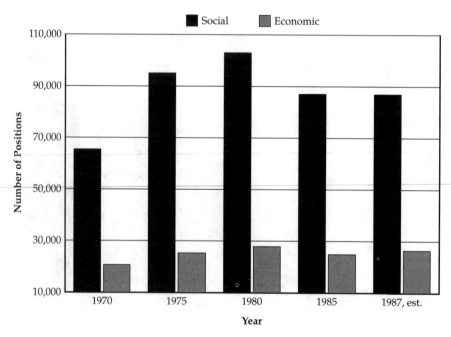

FIGURE 2.14   NUMBER OF PERMANENT
FULL-TIME REGULATORY AGENCY POSITIONS

than those for social regulation. In short, the growth of post-World War II regulation has historically been explosive and confined to rather specific times. In the decades of the 1960s and 1970s, moreover, the growth was primarily in the areas of social regulation.

With the exception of the savings and loan industry, during the 1980s the regulatory impetus as a whole was severely curtailed. Deregulation in transportation, both in the trucking and airlines industries, and in communications and finance was accomplished in the 1970s and early 1980s. Although there have been moments that produced a new infusion of government regulation, as in the area of finance and banking after the savings and loans crisis of the late 1980s, or in the tobacco industry, or as a result of the managed care crisis in the health care industry, the main theme today is a presumption of resistance to government regulation. Deregulation of transportation, communications, and financial services has produced more competition and lower prices for customers. Although regulations to protect the environment and a variety of consumer safeguards are supported by the public, advocates of such regulation spend most of their time maintaining the safeguards that exist, rather than devoting much attention to extending public regulation. There are exceptions, as in the recent battles over extending government regulation of the cigarette industry or the debates over "the patient's bill of rights." However, the times now seem to favor a presumption against regulation as a matter of principle. Gerston, Fraleigh, and Schwab refer to the current period as the "third wave" in the regulation story, as many conservative thinkers and politicians successfully focus energetic criticism on regulation (1988: 34). "Regulatory unreasonableness" has become the preeminent concern (Bardach and Kagan, 1981). The reasons for this are not hard to understand. By the onset of the 1980s, the nation had endured an unprecedented run-up in inflation rates. The nation also began to comprehend the dimensions of the decline in the U.S. position regarding economic performance in world markets, productivity, and standard of living. In the late 1970s, the time of the ascendancy of the Reagan administration and the activities of articulate critics of public regulation, the public discourse emphasized the role of regulation in hampering economic performance and contributing to a host of other economic maladies.

Just as it is clear that government has grown with respect to taxes and spending, so it is with nonfiscal aspects of government growth, especially in the area of government regulation. In recent decades it is clear that a variety of laws have produced real costs for the private sector as businesses seek to comply with regulations regarding workplace safety, equity in hiring and firing, environmental protection, energy conservation, historic preservation, consumer safety, and many other objects of government regulation. In any case, it is unlikely that we can establish a precise fix on the "net" burden of regulation in U.S. society. There are enough unwise and bizarre regulations to warrant a certain skepticism regarding the workability of regulations in some fields. There is, of course, little justification for regulations that clearly and invariably generate greater costs than benefits. But determining the aggregate burden of regulation relative to the overall economy is a very problematic task. The puzzles and problems associated with assessing regulation and its burdens are discussed more fully in later chapters.

Regulations that are burdensome for some people often *reduce* burdens for others. For example, regulations that deal with equal opportunity in employment, schooling, and public accommodations have made life more complicated for businesses, local governments, and the managers or owners of such facilities as restaurants, "private" clubs, housing, and stores. However, racial, religious, and ethnic minorities have acquired more freedom as a result. Undoubtedly, requirements to allow women to join all-male clubs prevent some men from excluding women, and, in that sense, some men will see government involvement in this field as imposing a kind of burden or limit on their freedom. Similarly, environmental protection regulations or limits on the use of such amenities as wilderness areas impose limits and burdens on some segments of society. But, in principle, those whose health or choices are limited by the decline of environmental quality or whose activities are threatened by the loss of some resource will perhaps find their freedoms enhanced. Regulatory burdens have increased, although by how much is uncertain. What the increase in regulation means in terms of the overall level of well-being or freedom experienced by members of society is an even murkier issue to sort out. We have, moreover, not even discussed public regulation at the state and local levels, where important matters regarding land use development, building inspection, occupational licensing, health and public safety regulations, and a host of other areas are involved. These also have their agencies and personnel. These also involve benefits, as well as costs. How one feels about the array of government regulations at the federal, state, and local level has to do with how much relative weight one places on perceived regulatory benefits and costs.

CHAPTER 3

~❦~

MACRO-DETERMINISTIC EXPLANATIONS OF GOVERNMENT GROWTH

When the labor movement secured the right to organize and bargain collectively, that right profoundly affected the choice of labor's strategies and management's approach to labor. Transformations of technology in communication and transportation changed in momentous ways the decisions of individual builders, businesses, and households about where to develop, invest, and reside. The capacity of businesses to separate phases of their operation, or of households to separate home from workplace, dramatically altered the relative attractiveness of various locational options available to individuals. In short, change at the societal (macro) level often alters the likelihood that certain behaviors will be adopted by individuals. These macro or societal level variables can include many characteristics: social, technological, or even geographical. They are assumed to affect how social actors (e.g., individuals, households, businesses, local governments, organized interests) behave and the kinds of choices that social actors are likely to find more or less attractive or feasible.

Macro changes, in turn, create special challenges and demands for government. Land use disputes and problems, for example, generated by competition over the use of land, result from the decisions of individual businesses, governments, and households—decisions that are made possible or incited by previous macro-level developments (e.g., national government policy and changes in technology). Consider, for example, the relationship between mass ownership of the automobile and an array of costly federal and state subsidies for home ownership on the urban fringe. Clearly, the impact of car use and suburban development has had much to do with current demands for greater public controls over land use. Or what of the increasing power of genetic engineering and the host of complex ethical and legal issues these pose for the public and government? In other words, there are a variety of factors that operate at the level of society, and they form the context or the environment of a society's members, creating new options, new forms of disputes, and new forums to consider the boundaries between the public and private sectors.

Although many approaches to social explanation account for the behavior of subsocietal actors (e.g., businesses, subnational governments, organized interests, and households) with reference to macro-level factors, the tendency is to assume that macro factors must in some way affect individual behavior. How these macro factors actually operate to generate particular individual-level behaviors tend not to be observed *directly*. It is in this sense that these approaches tend to be *macro-deterministic*. There is plausibility in the way these approaches explain the growth of government. On the other hand, there is a kind of phantom quality to these explanations too, because there is precious little, if any, discussion of people actually behaving or exerting political influence. Social phenomena like population growth or income levels are connected to things like the need for more government without much assessment of how these social forces are linked to the efforts of individuals. Many of the grand theories of social systems do this, whether one is talking about the linkages between functions and structures (Turner and Maryanksi, 1979; Holmwood, 1996; Meehan, 1967), social and ecological environments and the emergence of political system stress (Easton,1965a; 1965b), or the connection between class conflict and political structure (Barrow, 1993; Dahrendorf, 1959; Harvey, 1982; Parenti, 1995). Among the various factors that come into play in macro-deterministic studies are the following:

1. Changes in the social and demographic characteristics of the population
2. Altered states of technology and changes in the economic base
3. Institutional features and rights of the society's members
4. Differences in the functions and operations of public organizations as compared to private ones
5. Transformations in general beliefs and values

CHANGES IN SOCIAL AND DEMOGRAPHIC CHARACTERISTICS OF THE POPULATION AND IN THE SCALE AND GROWTH OF GOVERNMENT

The study of social change has a long tradition of focusing on the impact of population characteristics on government policy. Generally, such population characteristics are quite numerous and include such things as the absolute size, the density, and the social heterogeneity of the population. The classic article by Lewis Wirth, "Urbanism as a Way of Life" (1938), is an excellent example of a macro-deterministic explanation of government growth, hypothesizing demographic characteristics as causes of greater government scale. In the article, Wirth, relying on a variety of grand social theorists such as Durkheim and Weber, indicates how a series of phenomena are triggered by increasing population size, density, and heterogeneity. Increasing magnitudes of these variables result in such things as greater alienation, deviant and criminal conduct, and tension and competition among hostile but previously isolated groups. The result is greater government involvement in ameliorating social tensions, as well as more government entanglement in previously private matters, such as the education and the socialization of individuals into dominant societal norms.

Other population characteristics that are often viewed as important stimulants of government size and growth are personal income, age, and ethnic background. With respect to income levels, the connections made to the growth of government are usually direct; that is, greater income provides more resources for government policies or reduces citizen resistance to taxes. Indeed, some have suggested that as general income rises, there is both a greater preference for government services and a heightened concern for government policies to maintain and secure these income gains (Aharoni, 1981). A number of theories of government growth make the connection between greater levels of affluence and advancements in economic growth and the higher demand for and capacity to support government services.

Finally, some population characteristics become important determinants of government scale and growth because previous government actions make public policy sensitive to changes in these population variables. A regime might provide for various services with explicit eligibility requirements, which by themselves entitle individuals to government services and benefits; then the rate of increase or decline among those eligible for the program will be a critical determinant of government size, especially measured as expenditure. Naturally, when population changes occur in unpredictable fashion, there might be unanticipated increases of government expenditure or greater pressure to extract the needed resources, should they not currently be there. When the number of college-age students rises so quickly that eligible students are routinely kept out of college, the demand for higher education facilities increases. Or, when strong institutional commitments exist to supplement the incomes of retired citizens, the rapid and large increases in the proportions of such individuals will clearly drive up, in dramatic fashion, the costs of government programs.

ECONOMIC BASE, TECHNOLOGY, AND GOVERNMENT SIZE AND GROWTH

At least since the onset of the Industrial Revolution, it has been standard to attribute a relationship among economic structure, technological change, and the resulting effect on the scope of government activity. It would, of course, take us far afield to review the many different treatments of this relationship. The classical liberal (today called a conservative) and Marxist traditions have their roots in the great transformation from agrarian to industrial systems. While classical liberalism arose during the infancy of the industrial age, Marxist analysis of the economy/government nexus developed with the ascendancy of the factory system and the intensification of urbanization, along with periodic visitations of sharp, disruptive oscillations in the business cycle.

Regardless of the ideological perspective guiding analysis, advancements in knowledge and technology have altered economic relationships and created a host of challenges to societies, as well as new capabilities. Despite their occurrence in differing national environments, these challenges and capabilities have expressed themselves in dramatically altered systems of state-society relations and have been associated with greater levels of government activity.

INSTITUTIONS, RIGHTS OF CITIZENSHIP, AND CHANGE IN GOVERNMENT SCALE AND GROWTH

Changes in the rules governing policy formation, the selection of and access to officials, and the exercise of political rights can affect the scope of government and the rate at which government grows. Such changes are produced through their impact on group competition and group conflict. The focus here is not on the groups, their actions, maneuvers, successes, or failures. However, in considering the importance of formal government institutions as macrodeterministic variables, it is important to focus on the effects of the institutions and rights of citizenship in general terms. As avenues of political access, rights of participation, or various aspects of the law are altered, so it is that the influence of various groups and interests might also be changed.

In addition to aspects of citizenship, participation, and grants of government authority, many institutional characteristics are used to account for certain features of government growth. For example, a number of theorists link such things as election systems, party government, and, as mentioned earlier, the degree of government centralization to the rates of government growth (Amacher, Tollison, and Willett, 1975; Dye, 1976; Gould, 1983; Key, 1964; Zysman, 1983).

POLITICAL CULTURE AND THE SCOPE AND GROWTH OF GOVERNMENT

Although the role of norms, ideas, and values in explaining political matters is somewhat controversial, there is a respected tradition that claims political culture has an important influence on public policy. It is suggested that political culture can shape the public's view concerning the policies government should pursue. At least since the classic work of de Tocqueville (1966) and the influential work of Louis Hartz (1955), there have been a number of treatments regarding the manner in which certain attitudes and expectations among individuals affect the demand and support for government services.

Insofar as one hypothesizes a political system with responsive officials and opportunities for participation among the public, it is reasonable to expect a linkage between changing values and public expectations and the scope and growth of government. It is true, however, that precise, quantitative descriptions of such linkages between attitude change and policy change are quite difficult to provide.

Usually, such cultural changes result from dramatic changes in social, demographic, and technological events. For example, the following all result in a variety of changes in outlook: the emergence of the large corporation in the middle to late nineteenth century; recurrent and severe downturns in the economy; dramatic events like birth defects due to insufficiently tested drugs; widespread ecological damage due to oil spills or air pollution; and sympathy-inducing portrayals of the plight of farm workers, minorities, handicapped people, abused children, or exploited women. Such changes can often lead to public support for increased government involvement in previously private matters (Brooks, 1974; Doyle, 1995; Campbell, 1995; Easton, 1965a and 1965b; Levi, 1988; Maier, 1987; Schott, 1984).

Public attitudes and values regarding the scope and substance of public policy tend to persist at stable levels until some disturbance or other factor changes perceptions, expectations, attitudes and, ultimately, political demands. These emerging expectations constrain government from returning to previous, lower levels of government activity. Severe economic downturns and major natural disasters can traumatize an entire generation of citizens, who strongly support new programs that purport to prevent repetition or at least mitigate the effects of various social and economic maladies. We are, of course, familiar with the usual interpretation of the New Deal as a response to the Great Depression, when a host of new programs governing agricultural production, social insurance, bank regulation, labor-management relations, government and the arts, and macro-economic policymaking were developed. And for decades, the public supported refinements and additions to these New Deal programs, as well as extensions to previously uncovered groups. This extension of government activism continued, to an important degree, because of the pain and deprivation that was seared into the social memories of tens of millions of Americans during the Great Depression (Conklin, 1967; Leuchtenburg, 1963; Skocpol, 1980).

SOME FREQUENTLY USED MACRO-DETERMINISTIC APPROACHES

WAGNER'S LAW

Over one hundred years ago, Adolph Wagner, a German political economist, formulated his explanation of the relationship between government growth and the advancing development of the economy. There was an irony in this, for until Wagner popularized the claim of a connection between economic progress and public sector growth, there had been for several hundred years an opposite perspective. As Tarschys (1975: 9) claimed, "In the age of Enlightenment it was a common view that the scope of government actions would diminish through the moral and economic evolution of mankind." Indeed, the classical liberal tradition (conservative) saw government as largely superfluous, with the exception of a number of night-watchman functions. The Marxist tradition posited the disappearance of government as a consequence of a successful socialist evolution in which class conflict disappeared. In this sense, there was a historical irony since Marxists and classical liberals saw government, under ideal conditions, as a fairly unimportant institution.

It is far from the focus of this discussion to pursue the fascinating question of why, on the one hand, some thinkers view social progress as inevitably requiring a withering or minimizing of the state. On the other hand, others cannot comprehend substantial social progress without the active participation of a large state apparatus. In our own history, we find this clash of views in the confrontation between the statism of Alexander Hamilton and the minimalism of Thomas Jefferson (Hartz, 1955). Notwithstanding the preference for a small over a large government, during the past several hundred years there has been a dramatic transformation of government and far greater involvement by the state in managing the economy, extracting revenues, and otherwise regulating the conduct of its citizens in subtle and overt ways.

The work of Adolph Wagner, until recently, generated most of the empirical work exploring the connection between social change and its effects on the growth and scale of the public sector (Herber, 1975). Wagner hypothesized that for a variety of reasons, economic progress—in the form of higher personal income, more productive manufacture, more complex forms of business organization, and transformations in the work force—would both support and necessitate greater government involvement. This greater involvement would be manifested in both greater tax burdens for individuals and higher expenditure levels by government, as well as more government involvement in previously private matters. Wagner's formulation is often called "The Law of Increasing State Activity." The hypothesized positive relationship between economic progress and government growth was for Wagner both empirically obvious and ideologically desirable.

It would be naive to ignore the manner in which Wagner's formulation was shaped by German history (Borchardt, 1991; Lee, 1991). Until the middle of the nineteenth century, Germany was divided into hundreds of separate, sovereign jurisdictions. Moreover, what was to become modern Germany was largely agrarian well into the nineteenth century. With the emergence of modern German nationalism, and propelled by the Bismarckian vision of a Germany that rivaled the military and industrial power of Britain, there occurred in Germany one of the great economic takeoffs of history. There were rapid increases in German personal income, along with dramatic increases in the level and value of manufacture and industry. German international involvement became more notable, including the acquisition of and intense competition for colonies. By 1900, German industrial production surpassed Great Britain's, its population had vastly increased, and its military power was viewed as unexcelled.

During this approximately fifty-year period, friction among social classes intensified. German labor movements emerged, coalescing around mass-based, militantly socialist parties. In the famous program formulated by Bismarck to deflect social unrest, Germany also developed a substantial commitment to finance social insurance of various sorts. It is generally believed that these programs were designed to attenuate labor's ardor for radical political movements and to increase popular support for the German state and its nationalist and imperial objectives (Ashley, 1912; Hennock, 1987). It is not surprising, then, that Wagner saw in the German example a general model for explaining the growth of the public sector, expressed in terms of its larger budgets and its greater involvement in previously private matters.

Most of the research that has examined Wagner's formulation fails to focus on the mechanisms that he claimed accounted for the increasing scale and growth of government. In that sense, his approach manifested that typical quality of macro-deterministic approaches—a lack of discussion of individual behavior and a reliance on linking aggregate social forces with one another. It is worth examining these in some detail.

Wagner believed that economic progress would intensify military competition and enhance the quality and sophistication of weapons. Consequently, he believed that one major cause of government growth would be military spending. Moreover, the greater revenues required to finance escalating military spending would create new forms of taxation that would produce greater amounts of revenue for other purposes as well. Equally important, the requirements and consequences of industrialization in the nineteenth and early twentieth centuries produced pressures for greater government involvement in previously private matters. For example, the growth of large urban settlements was a universal accompaniment of industrialization. One immediate result was the concentration of large numbers of laborers in relatively compact, usually inhospitable environments. The result was higher levels of social friction. The ominous shadow of the city mob was always present for the more affluent urban resident. Additionally, regional antagonisms within the nation intensified as agrarian workers, displaced from diverse places, with passionate memories of religious and ethnic conflict, congregated and competed in the closeness of harsh city neighborhoods. The rise of professional police departments and rules governing street conduct (e.g., problems regarding criminal conduct, prostitution, and drunk and disorderly conduct, and the emergence of large numbers of homeless, unemployed, and abandoned children) were inevitable results of rapid industrial urbanization, whether in Britain, the United States, or Germany.

Of course, the extremely rapid concentrations of population in the growing cities engendered more than social problems. The spread of fire and disease, and the collapse of infrastructure (bridges, streets, and water lines) due to the volume and frequency of use led to such modern government services and professions as public health, public housing, and urban planning. And as both the social and physical challenges to government increased, there emerged public institutions and facilities in which to train and house the growing government bureaucracy. Finally, as industrialization and manufacture proceeded, there developed new forms of economic exchange and conduct, which ultimately required greater government oversight. New forms of money and credit and new economic actors, especially the modern corporation, would invariably bring the government and society together in new and complex ways.

The government and society nexus was both promotional and regulatory. On the one hand, government was involved in smoothing the social, technical, and physical frictions that impeded the advance of private accumulation of wealth. So, for example, government involvement in transportation (roads, canals, and railroads) and government-sponsored research were part of the new and greater promotional role for government. The government's role in facilitating business activity also expressed itself through such ameliorative actions as governmentally supported social insurance programs and such policies of social control as regulating or suppressing labor solidarity. Not to be forgotten was the further claim by Wagner that as economic progress proceeded, incomes of the society's citizens also increased. Consequently, there was a greater ability for the state to provide and the citizenry to support higher levels of culture and education. Moreover, experience indicated that the private sector would invariably under-supply a variety of goods with collective consumption characteristics—often termed public goods. Public goods are goods and services that provide little incentive for producers to supply them, since the consumers cannot be charged or nonpayers excluded from consuming the goods (Hardin, 1982; Samuelson, 1955). Higher incomes tend to increase the public demand for such goods, including public education, parks and recreation, and the protection of certain environmental amenities. Consequently, higher incomes combined with the collective nature of certain services result in higher levels of government support. According to interpreters of Wagner (Herber, 1975: 372–73), in the preindustrial, agricultural era the public sector grew slowly, and during the industrial period the public sector rose more rapidly than the private. With regard to the future, Wagner did suggest that there must be some limit to public sector growth. He did not envision the public sector devouring the entire social product, thereby implying that in some unspecified future period the rate of government growth would slow substantially relative to the public sector.

During the preindustrial period, goods and services were overwhelmingly provided by the private sector. Consequently, as incomes rose in this period, it was the private sector that grew more rapidly, relative to public sector expansion. With industrialization, however, the demand and need for a greater variety of goods and services with collective and social goods properties increased rapidly (e.g., transportation, regulation, national defense, cultural amenities, and public education). Historically it has been government that has more often provided goods with high, fixed initial costs of production and collective or public goods characteristics (Hardin, 1982). In this stage, consequently, the value of government goods and services, according to Wagner, grows more rapidly than the value of private sector exchange. According to Herber (1975: 373), as society evolves into a postindustrial stage, the public will begin to resist further public sector burdens and the efficiency gains of further public sector production will decline. Hence, in the postindustrial era, public sector growth should decline, relative to private sector expansion.

PEACOCK AND WISEMAN'S DISPLACEMENT EFFECT HYPOTHESIS

While Wagner is the most noted nineteenth-century scholar of government growth, many claim that Alan Peacock and Jack Wiseman are the most notable twentieth-century investigators of the subject. Encompassing the period of 1890 to 1955, they charted the growth of government spending in the United Kingdom. Their influential book, *The Growth of Public Expenditure in the United Kingdom* (1961), was inspired by a number of shortcomings in the work of Wagner, particularly his assumption of a smoothly and exponentially growing public sector. Rather than seeing the public sector expand in automatic fashion, Peacock and Wiseman found periods of stability, with new inroads by government requiring an antecedent, catalytic event. In presenting their findings, Peacock and Wiseman also provided a number of useful, if simple, concepts, including *tax tolerance, public sector plateaus, displacement, inspection,* and *concentration effects.*

According to Peacock and Wiseman, during a given period of time the public sector comprises a fairly constant level of public spending, relative to the overall economy. That is, government spending is a stable proportion of overall economic activity. During relatively tranquil times, the public tends to have fixed ideas or preferences regarding the appropriate mix, level, and burden of government services. More importantly, during such periods the public tends to resist new taxes and greater tax burdens; that is, the public operates at a fixed level of *tax tolerance.* During these stable periods, then, the proportion of the economy represented by government spending constitutes a *plateau.* This plateau is maintained over time by the public's *resistance to new taxes.*

However, societies inevitably face major crises or conditions that *displace* the existing levels of tax tolerance and create new expectations of government and greater demands for public services. In the past, wars have been the most frequent and greatest source of such displacement.

Since the late nineteenth century, major downturns in the economy have also been important, although much less so than war, in escalating public sector growth. This has resulted in part from the effort of government to stimulate economic activity during recessions and downturns through a variety of programs, as well as from such "automatic stabilizers" as unemployment and welfare expenditures, which tend to increase during poor economic times. Peacock and Wiseman not only provide a refinement to Wagner's explanation of government growth, but also highlight how modern, advanced societies experience major government growth in the face of deteriorating economic conditions. Recall that Wagner saw *economic progress* as the driving force of government growth. Due to perturbations of the modern business cycle, culminating in the traumatic, worldwide economic calamity of the 1930s, government spending to maintain economic growth and to underwrite social insurance has also been a major source of public sector growth. Major sources of growth in government spending, especially since World War II, tend to increase, at least in part, as institutionalized, counter-cyclical policy instruments designed to reduce and reverse economic distress.

Although Peacock and Wiseman do not specifically apply their analysis to less cataclysmic sources of government growth, their concepts can explain a number of other important factors that might displace a given plateau of government activity. While wars and depressions have been major sources of upheaval and have stimulated new tax tolerance levels, thereby enabling government spending to grow to a higher plateau, other factors like natural disasters or very rapidly increasing incomes can also result in greater public tolerance of government growth.

As the pace and scale of government spending increases, a new resistance to tax increases begins to form, posing a new barrier to government growth; the result is a new plateau and a new period of relative stability in the government's share of societal resources. While there might be some retreat from the summit of the new plateau, there is no return to earlier and lower plateaus. There are many reasons for this, although Peacock and Wiseman do not explore them in detail. The reasons include the public's expectation of new services, vested interests (in both public and private sectors) that form around the new public sector mix, and the range of wants and needs, as well as unanticipated obligations, that result from new public sector involvement. Indeed, the recognition of a host of new obligations and problems that are now viewed as government responsibilities is referred to by Peacock and Wiseman as the inspection effect.

As higher plateaus of government spending are reached, as the proportion of total societal resources represented by government increases, Peacock and Wiseman claim there is also a tendency for the expenditures of national, central authorities to grow at faster rates than that of local or regional entities. Some of this results from a greater desire or demand for uniformity in service levels, which tend to homogenize at higher rather than lower levels. For example, when greater pressures existed in the United States to reduce disparities in social welfare expenditures across the respective states, the result was to raise the spending among the lower spending states, rather than reduce the levels among the higher spending locales. In some cases it might also be that economies of scale push service responsibilities to "higher" government levels. The superior revenue-raising tools of central authorities might also shift responsibilities from localities and regions as the burden of the required revenue increases. Finally, equity considerations might argue for greater uniformity of treatment among jurisdictions, when interdependencies make it clear that certain problems cannot be reasonably viewed as local responsibilities. Air pollution, illegal immigration, unemployment, public schooling for children, and natural disasters are judged to have national implications and are no longer problems seen as the sole responsibility of local communities. If the national authorities are to locate major national facilities in a particular location, such as a military base or missile range, it has appeared reasonable that the national government should contribute to the funding of local services. Others in the United States have pointed out that policing the nation's boundaries and regulating immigration into the United States is a national responsibility. Insofar as there is a major local burden in educational, health, housing, and welfare services resulting from massive influxes of illegal immigrants, some have argued that the federal government should contribute to the funding of the relevant services or stem the tide of these individuals.

Peacock and Wiseman do not say much about the *limits* on growth in public spending. It is reasonable to suggest that with each breakthrough to new levels, the subsequent differences between plateau summits will decline. In this sense, government initially grows in large "steps." As the public sector tackles large, new issues (e.g., social insurance, public education, modern military investments, transportation), there eventually are fewer new areas into which government intervention can occur. It is helpful to refer to a distinction made by Lawrence Brown (1983: 7–11) between *breakthrough* and *rationalizing* politics. Breakthrough politics involves the movement of government into new areas of public sector activity, while rationalizing politics primarily focuses on issues of managing the delivery of already existing policies. The processes involved in establishing Social Security or the federal government's first major inroad into supporting health care—Medicare—are examples of breakthrough politics, where great new assertions of public authority and prodigious commitments of public resources were involved. Current debates regarding greater control over existing entitlement programs illustrate the more narrowly focused issues surrounding rationalizing politics. Initial breakthroughs tend to involve large areas of social life and unprecedented commitments of resources, but with time, as the agenda of government already contains a broad array of government programs, more attention is devoted to rationalizing the existing policy commitments. New, large public commitments then become less frequent as politics tends to be dominated more by issues of administering and making more efficient the current array of services, rather than by moving into new areas. This is not to say that breakthroughs will not occur in a nation with a "large" public sector. Rather, the assertion is that the relative emphasis on rationalizing policies tends to increase over time as the public sector increases.

The timing of policy breakthroughs, their magnitude, and the rate at which rationalizing politics intensifies while breakthrough issues wane depend in very important ways on the many complex factors that characterize different nation-states. For example, in the United States, public sector breakthroughs tend to occur later and are less frequent. The point at which public resistance emerges to the overall size and burden of the public sector is likely to erupt earlier in the United States than among nations with long histories of substantial state-society interactions. Our antigovernment tradition and the institutional framework in which policy must be introduced, ratified, and implemented tend to foster such a pattern. In other nations, with traditions of strong government authority and more centralized policy institutions, breakthroughs occur perhaps earlier and more expansively. In any case, *ceteris paribus*, the public sector tends to grow, first, in larger steps (the domination of breakthrough politics). Later, the breakthrough steps decline in size, as rationalizing politics become more salient.

INSTITUTIONS, MAJORITARIAN DEMOCRACY, AND THE SIZE OF THE PUBLIC SECTOR

The idea of democratic government assumes that there is an important connection between what citizens prefer and what their government officials do. Sometimes there is disagreement as to what topics should be of concern to the electorate or how extensive the public's control over policy should be. Often there is controversy over how binding the voters' views should be on officials. Notwithstanding these differences, there is a general belief that in a democracy public opinion should have a significant bearing on the agenda and policy content of government.

The paramount method by which citizens and government actions are linked in modern democracies is through the electoral process. Hence, policies and laws that constrict the rights of political participation or limit the subjects over which the electorate exercises control will necessarily constrain the range of politically relevant demands and preferences. Insofar as the electorate is restricted to rather small segments of the total society, one can reasonably expect that officials will have a more confined view of their respective constituencies. They will, thus, perceive a narrower range of topics and issues as relevant for the political agenda. If members of particular races, gender, religions, national origins, or socioeconomic classes are excluded by statute and official policy from electoral participation, then the interests, needs, and desires of these individuals will necessarily have less political weight.

Although many citizens of the United States were permitted under the law to participate in elections when the Constitution was adopted, the fact is that the right to vote was substantially restricted to white, male property owners. Indeed, blacks were not considered full persons at all, and only for purposes of determining representation in the Congress were blacks considered three-fifths of a person. Among the newer states, those entering the Union after 1790, very few property qualifications existed, largely because of difficulty in accurate and rapid recording of property ownership. By 1850 property qualifications were mostly eliminated, especially in the newer states and territories. (Williamson, 1960). By the mid-nineteenth century, anxiety and hostility regarding immigrants, particularly Irish-Catholics, resulted in a number of states promulgating literacy tests designed to curtail the political strength of immigrants (Connecticut in 1855 and Massachusetts in 1857). Nevertheless, it is generally believed that by 1860 almost universal white, male suffrage was achieved (Williamson, 1960; Flanigan and Zingale, 1987). Blacks were accorded the formal right to vote as a consequence of the Fourteenth and Fifteenth Amendments, although after 1877, with the withdrawal of federal troops from the South, numerous formal and informal barriers to Black political participation in the South were created. These barriers included poll taxes and literacy tests, reinforced by various forms of psychological and violent intimidation.

Although the poll tax was eliminated by constitutional amendment, substantially universal, effective Black political participation did not become a routine feature of the American political system until the middle 1960s, with the enactment of Civil Rights Acts in 1964 and 1968, and with the vigorous enforcement of these acts by national authorities (Franklin, 1978). Two other major additions to the national electorate occurred: first, in 1920, when women were granted voting rights via adoption of the Nineteenth Amendment to the Constitution; second, in 1971, when the right to vote was extended to those eighteen years of age or older, also by constitutional amendment. It is true that registration and residency requirements and other methods of disqualifying electors might affect the size of the electorate today. Still, the guarantees against racial and ethnic discrimination regarding voting eligibility, the elimination of sex discrimination in voting rights, and the provision of voting rights for those eighteen years old or older represent the major extensions of the American electorate.

As the number of individuals participating in the electoral process increases, so the components of different interests swirling in the brew that comprises the politically relevant public will also increase. Assuming responsive legislators, the larger and more heterogeneous the electorate becomes, the greater the range of demands, the higher the number of laws enacted, and the greater the scope and rate of government growth. In other words, as the right to vote and participate in formal avenues of political participation is extended to incorporate greater segments of society, the scope of demands on government increases, and, assuming responsive officials, the range of government activity increases as well. The democratization of political participation is a force for government growth.

There has always been, among the more advantaged members of societies, the fear that increasing the range of participants in the political arena, especially participants from the less affluent classes, will produce policies that provide benefits for the poor at the expense of the nonpoor. In other words, it has been expected not only that a growing electorate will produce more government, but also that these new increments of government will involve redistributive, if not confiscatory, government policies. Indeed, a number of the early restrictions on electoral participation in the United States, especially those based on property ownership and poll taxes, were directed at those potential voters who would have a self-interest in voting for programs that would benefit them but that would be paid for by others. It is exactly such reasoning that underlies in large part the idea of the median voter model of government growth to be discussed in the next chapter. For example, note the following comments of two major contemporary researchers and theorists of government growth:

> In most Western countries, property or status requirements for voting have been abolished during the last hundred years. Extension of the franchise is always in the interest of voters with incomes below the median because the spread of the franchise increases the number and proportion of voters who favor redistribution. As the franchise spreads downward through the income distribution, the proportion of votes going to candidates who promise redistribution increases. Progressive taxes increase the gain to the majority by taking a larger fraction of income from voters with incomes above the median to pay for programs like health care, which is available to everyone, or housing allowances, which go mainly to voters with incomes below the median. (Meltzer and Richard, 1978: 117)

Or as Tarschys (1975: 15) claims, democracy and universal suffrage underlie the "demand side" explanations of government growth; in his words, "... given a multi-party system and universal suffrage, it is ultimately the citizens and consumers of public goods who decide on the scope and substance of government action." This view of the link between democratization and public sector size is labeled by Hewitt (1977) as the "simple democratic hypothesis," in which "the existence of democratic institutions—especially the enfranchisement of all citizens—virtually guarantees relatively egalitarian policies" (Moon and Dixon, 1985: 669).

Although many scholars of government growth understand that extension of voting rights might have engendered more government, some applaud the presumed relationship while others, especially those adopting economic theories of government growth, tend to be somewhat critical of universal suffrage. That is, a number of scholars see in the restrictions on the right to vote, particularly property qualifications, a felicitous bulwark against government growth. Rarely are such defenders of restricting the political rights of the propertyless and the poor as candid as Gottfried Dietze, a venerable libertarian political philosopher, who claimed the following:

> Even if one agrees with the generally accepted opinion that there ought to be no property qualifications, one can hardly deny that their abolition watered down the rationality of the electorate. As a rule, property owners are more reasonable than those who have no property, for it generally takes more brains to acquire and keep property than not to acquire or lose it. Even if one agrees with the generally accepted opinion that suffrage should not be restricted on account of race, color, or previous condition of servitude, one can hardly deny that the Fifteenth Amendment extended the right to vote to a relatively uneducated part of the population whose rationality was likely to be affected by their want of education. The same applies to the bulk of immigrants. (1968: 264–65)

Most critics of unqualified voting rights tend not to put as many cards on the table as Dietze does, and he should at least be commended for his candor in claiming that majoritarian democracy is inconsistent with his conception of freedom. After blaming the expansion of civil rights under the Warren Court for urban unrest, he concludes:

> The greater the number of those having the right to vote, the greater the probability that this right, supposed to influence the making of laws, will entice people to take the law into their own hands and in turn to break it. The power to vote thus tends to corrupt into the assumption that it justifies the right to act illegally. Furthermore, the greater the number of persons with the right to vote, the more the government is representative of the whole people and the more the ruling majority will feel entitled to carry out its mandate at the expense of the minority. (1985: 266)

In all fairness to those who are concerned about a tyrannical majority unjustly expropriating material benefits from a wealthier minority, such a concern does not necessarily have to express itself as a preference for restricted voting rights. Indeed, American political doctrine, generally acknowledged to be most clearly expressed in *The Federalist Papers*, has always been infused with a fear of property rights and wealth being confiscated by inflamed and unrestrained majorities. It is a testimony to the genius of our most influential political thinkers, Madison in particular, that their solution was not to advocate extensive restrictions on the rights of individuals to participate in politics but, rather, to advocate enlargement of territory, in order to encompass "a greater variety of parties and interests." As Plattner claims, the purpose of the large, heterogeneous republic is as follows:

> ... to make the various distributions of property more politically salient than its "unequal" distribution. If both the poor and the rich earn their livelihood in a great variety of ways, there will be divergent and competing interests within each group, as well as certain common interests cutting across economic strata. (1982: 15)

Moreover, in a large regime, large election districts are possible, with the result that men of wealth are most likely to stand for and win electoral office. "In sum, the large republic is meant to be structured so as to minimize the likelihood that a poor majority will coalesce and violate the property rights of the more prosperous" (Plattner, 1982: 15). Notwithstanding the braking effect that a large, heterogeneous nation has on the ability of one interest to dominate others, history suggests that extension of the franchise increases the range of demands, which results in more government, produced by responsive legislators. To the extent that this extension of the franchise involves less affluent citizens, the theory suggests, for good or ill, that there will be general growth in the scale of government and greater emphasis on redistributive policies. Of course, other factors might work to constrain such government growth and blunt the impulse to redistribute wealth, such as the cost of campaigns or other forms of political competition, the required size of a winning coalition in the electorate, or the number of opportunities provided minorities to contest policy in other policymaking venues.

Another important institution affecting the pattern of government growth is the court system. Particularly important is the relatively unique power of courts in the United States to review legislation and to strike down legislation or administrative actions that are judged to be unconstitutional or in violation of statute. And throughout U.S. history, the courts have made decisions that have affected the role of the government in managing the economy and in securing the economic and civil liberties of citizens (Braeman, 1988; Pacelle, 1987). The size of government budgets, the burden and incidence of taxes, and the scope of government authority is from time to time directed and shaped by court decisions. Whereas in the United States, particularly in the latter half of the nineteenth century and the early decades of the twentieth century, the courts functioned to limit government growth, John Burton (1985) points out that Parliament had at one time operated as the principal "constitutional" constraint on government growth in Britain. Burton, writing as a critic of "the modern Leviathan" (1985: 15), points out that until the nineteenth century, Parliament operated mostly to resist government growth by restraining the impositions of the executive branch of the state. It was the independent federal judiciary that resisted government growth in the United States in the years of rapid economic change in the late nineteenth and early twentieth centuries.

In the United States there emerged after the Civil War a movement by legal scholars and jurists, first gradually and then with greater acceleration, to limit the capacity of government to regulate property rights and a variety of business practices. Although there had always been instances of government regulation of business activities, there had also been a tradition of viewing property rights as having a special status (Williamson, 1960; Hartz, 1955; Machan, 1995). Nevertheless, localities and states regulated businesses, granted monopolies, publicly financed private enterprises, and did a variety of things to protect public safety and morals under the police power.

During the nineteenth century, state courts occasionally nullified local government and state legislative activity believed to be inimical to property rights, with particular attention to what is referred to as "vested rights." For example, in 1856 the Court of Appeals of New York struck down a state-wide prohibition on the sale of liquor (*Wynehamer v. People*, 13 N.Y. 378 [1856]). The grounds for the court's action rested on the idea that those individuals who in good conscience purchased liquor for sale and invested in distribution facilities prior to the law were being unjustly deprived of property. As the Civil War approached, the federal courts began to reinforce a constitutional foundation to limit property rights restrictions, with particular attention to the Fifth Amendment. It is worth examining the content of the Amendment fully:

> No person shall be held to answer for a capital, or otherwise infamous crime, unless on a presentment or indictment of a Grand Jury, except in cases arising in the land or naval forces, or in the Militia, when in actual service in time of War or public danger; nor shall any person be subject for the same offence to be twice put in jeopardy of life or limb; nor shall be compelled in any criminal case to be a witness against himself, nor be deprived of life, liberty, or property without due process of law; nor shall private property be taken for public use, without just compensation.

It is generally believed that this provision of the Constitution was intended to ensure fairness and justice in *criminal* trials. Very early, however, the courts generally applied the due process provisions not only to ensure proper legal procedure, but also to protect individuals from the substance of regulations on the use of property imposed by local or state governments, even when such regulations were enacted in procedurally correct fashion.

By the middle of the nineteenth century, substantive due process as a bulwark to protect property reached a watershed when the U.S. Supreme Court nullified the exclusion of slavery from U.S. territories under the Missouri Compromise. The U.S. Supreme Court, resting its case on the Fifth Amendment, stated it was an unjust limit on the rights of property to prohibit individuals from transporting slaves into the territories, since slaves were property (*Scott v. Sandford*, 19 How. 393, 450 [1857]). Presumably, since it would have been unjust to prohibit the bringing in of wagons, tables, and other property, the Court could not accept what to them was an unjust prohibition against the movement of slaves, who were regarded as merely as another article of property.

By the middle of the nineteenth century, with the emergence of major changes in the structure and technology of economic activity (e.g., the rise of the modern corporate form, the increased importance of railroads and utilities, and the appearance of a variety of economic practices that included price fixing and other attempts to control market forces) several states began to trade off economic freedom against the need to regulate economic activity for the public benefit or on behalf of groups seeking protection against the exigencies of an increasingly volatile, national economy.

The Fourteenth Amendment of the U.S. Constitution was ratified in 1868 and was clearly designed to secure a number of objectives involved in the recently concluded Civil War, expressed in Section 1 of the Amendment:

> All persons born or naturalized in the United States, and subject to the jurisdiction thereof, are citizens of the United States and of the State wherein they reside. No State shall make or enforce any law which shall abridge the privileges or immunities of citizens of the United States, nor shall any State deprive any person of life, liberty, or property, without due process of law, nor deny to any person within its jurisdiction the equal protection of the laws.

It is also important to mention that Section 5 of the Fourteenth Amendment gave Congress the power to enforce the amendment, "by appropriate legislation." The amendment dealt with a number of matters, but the paramount concern was to secure the equality of civil rights for blacks emancipated during the Civil War and through the ratification of the Thirteenth Amendment.

In 1869, Louisiana granted a twenty-five-year livestock and slaughterhouse monopoly to a private corporation in an area comprising New Orleans and several adjacent parishes. As a consequence, a group of butchers excluded by the monopoly sued on the grounds that the monopoly violated the Thirteenth and Fourteenth Amendments. An important claim made by the butchers was that their trade constituted property and that a regulation that prevented them from practicing their trade, in effect, deprived them of property without due process or just compensation (*Slaughterhouse Cases*, 16 Wall. 36 [1873]). By a 5–4 majority, the U.S. Supreme Court rejected the claims of the lawyers representing the nonmonopoly butchers. The Court suggested that the petitioners were seeking to have the federal government enable businesses to develop unimpeded by state regulation. The mechanism sought to accomplish this was to grant to the corporation, a legal artifact of state policy, something that could hardly be claimed to have existed in a prior state of nature. That is, the corporation was for legal purposes a "person" with all of the privileges and immunities granted to other persons, including the shelter of the equal protection and due process provisions of the Constitution.

Although the legal critics of the *Slaughterhouse* monopoly were very influential, the ramifications of upholding their argument compelled a bare majority of the Court to uphold state legislation. They recoiled from the prospect of becoming the "perpetual censor upon all State legislation." In 1876, the U.S. Supreme Court, in the face of an intense assault from the legal community that was spearheaded by the house lawyers of the railroads, some of whom had sat as state supreme court justices, rejected again an effort to incorporate into federal legal doctrine an omnibus shield against procedurally correct regulations (*Munn v. Illinois*, 94 U.S. 113 [1876]). The Court asserted again that the states were permitted under their grant of the police power to regulate the prices and charges of businesses "affected with a public interest."

In any case, the pressure to incorporate *laissez faire* economics into the Constitution did not abate (Twiss, 1942). And after some changes in Court membership, in a series of cases between 1897 and 1915, the federal government asserted a close oversight on government regulation of economic activity, especially that of the states (*Allgeyer v. Louisiana*, 165 U.S. 578 [1897]; *Lochner v. New York*, 198 U.S. 45 [1905]; *Adair v. United States*, 208 U.S. 161 [1908]; *Coppage v. Kansas*, 236 U.S. 1 [1915]). In 1905, the U.S. Supreme Court invalidated a New York state law regulating maximum daily and weekly working hours (*Lochner v. New York*), and in 1926 the Court struck down the efforts of Congress to enact minimum wages in the District of Columbia (*Adkins v. Children's Hospital*). In both cases, the Court's decisions were based on an interpretation of the due process clause of the Fifth Amendment of the U.S. Constitution. The Court majority believed that state and federal efforts to regulate the conditions of employment interfered with the right of contract.

This interpretation of the due process provisions reached a climax in the late 1930s when, in a series of cases between 1935 and 1936, the Court declared unconstitutional most of the New Deal's policies designed to manage the Great Depression. Through its narrow interpretation of interstate commerce and unprecedented and expansive view of freedom of contract, the Court operated as a bulwark against much, although not all, proposed legislation at the state and federal level to regulate business. It was not until the breakthrough decisions of 1937, representing a kind of anticlimactic denouement, that judicial barriers to major new forms of government activity were overcome. Now the facilitating role played by the courts in allowing and encouraging government involvement in a variety of social and economic areas has become the source of substantial contemporary dispute. Many conservatives argue that activist jurists have supplanted legislatures through an expansive interpretation of the Constitution's general welfare and interstate commerce clauses.

MARXIST EXPLANATIONS OF GOVERNMENT GROWTH

Those referred to today as liberals sometimes wistfully harken back to such periods as the New Deal and other intervals of major growth in government activity. They perceive such times, perhaps through a romanticized hindsight, as epochs during which the people were served by a responsive government, propelled by bursts of popular political strength to fashion new institutions and champion new rights, thereby increasing the economic security of people and restoring stable, economic growth. Those referred to today as conservatives tend to see government growth as the result of government having been, from their viewpoint, too sensitive to societal pressures to undermine, distort, and otherwise mismanage the natural workings of the market system. Their contention is that the correct response to economic distress is to allow market forces to sort themselves out; government intervention will only result ultimately in more severe economic distress and produce losses in the freedoms of citizens. Consequently, conservatives tend to be skeptical and anxious about such periods of government growth as the Progressive Era, the New Deal, or the post-World War II efforts to manage macro-economic policy and to reduce socioeconomic inequality.

Marxists reject both liberal and conservative views of the growth of government, especially as regards government responses to economic distress. In a kind of irony, however, Marxists share with conservatives a skepticism about government growth in capitalist societies, albeit for profoundly different reasons. Conservatives tend to worry about the effectiveness of government interventions in private society and the effects of such action on personal liberty. Marxists, on the contrary, tend to believe that most important government interventions in market societies are primarily designed not for the popular majority or the downtrodden but, rather, to perpetuate patterns of power and inequality. Although Marxists are far from being in agreement about explanations for the causes of government growth, particularly during such dramatic periods as World War I or during severe economic downturns like the Panic of 1893 or the decade of the Great Depression, they do share important outlooks and conclusions. As Skocpol and Feingold state:

> As for Marxism, its various adherents would all tend to agree on one conclusion: Capitalists as a class should benefit most from politics in capitalist society. Some Marxists would attribute this to capitalists' direct control over the state or political resources; other neo-Marxists would say, instead, that the state can be expected to intervene 'relatively autonomously' for the objective interests of the capitalist system (and class), regardless of whether or not capitalists control political decision making. Either way, however, political outcomes (short of revolution) should work disproportionately to the benefit of capitalists. (1982: 259)

Similarly, Greenberg (1985) asserts, "... the transformation of government in the United States since 1789 may be explained primarily as a product of political leaders' need to respond to the various problems thrown up by a dynamic and ever-changing capitalist economy—and particularly to its periodic crises." In short, Marxists are in agreement that the changes in the scale and scope of government in market societies are generally in the direction of preserving the well-being of the capitalist social order and the status, power, and privilege of the capitalist class.

Although it is easy to locate simplistic formulations by some Marxists, in which governing bodies and officials are seen as nothing more than direct appendages of a monolithic, smoothly functioning ruling class, it would be unfair to characterize most contemporary Marxist analysis in that way. In fact, Skocpol (1980: 158, 160–99) identifies three types of Marxist theory regarding the growth of the state: (1) instrumentalist; (2) political functionalist; and (3) class struggle. Instrumentalist approaches are characterized by an emphasis on the direct control by a monolithic capitalist class. Those emphasizing the instrumentalist approach argue that capitalists have crucial advantages either when they take on official positions or in their private capacities. Many important government officials, it is contended, tend to have capitalist backgrounds or aspire to careers in the private sector, and even professional government workers are inculcated with strong commitments to the legitimacy and inevitability of market system values. Furthermore, it is argued that the accumulation of a host of other advantages directly controlled by the capitalist class provides a set of winning resources in its competition with other social classes; higher status, solidarity, and money give capitalists a winning edge over their working-class competitors. Instrumentalists claim that while capitalists do not always appear to win or operate in concert, when it counts, during times of crisis, they will function as a distinct, mobilized class. As Skocpol (1980: 161) states, increasing government intervention during periods like the Progressive Era and the New Deal involve "the deliberate extension of state action by a class-conscious vanguard." And a vanguard of the proletariat, Marxists would say, it is not.

Political functionalist Marxists developed partly out of concern for the manner in which instrumentalist viewpoints apparently oversimplified the complexities of class competition. Instrumentalist viewpoints have been criticized for ignoring the fact that capitalists do not act in concert, are not monolithic, and sometimes are obliged to make significant concessions to noncapitalist classes. Moreover, the instrumentalist view of the government as a mere reflection of capitalist will and whim ignores the evidence of state autonomy. According to functional Marxists, the regime often operates in a manner that is contrary not only to the expressed demands of the general public or working classes, but also to the expressed interests of the capitalist class. Functionalist Marxists see the state as sometimes rising above the pettier, self-interested demands of capitalists and noncapitalists. The state, in functionalist formulations, is compelled instead to adopt policies that presumably further the workings of capitalism, occasionally requiring policy to be in conflict with the demands of extant groups, capitalist or otherwise. In characterizing the functionalist view of government interventions like the New Deal, Skocpol (1980: 171) states, "... New Deal economic policies were not simply a response to the demands of capitalists; rather they addressed the interests of competing groups both within the ranks of the capitalist class and between capitalists and noncapitalists." Indeed, a host of reforms during the Progressive Era and during the New Deal were adopted by the state over substantial opposition by important capitalist interests. Whereas instrumentalists tend to claim that state intervention in private society is primarily a consequence of the agitation by a monolithic, mobilized capitalist class, functionalists see the state as adopting policies that are contrary to the demands of many capitalist groups. Instrumentalists and functionalists do agree, however, that public policy in market societies will operate in the long-term interest of capitalists.

What Skocpol (1980) refers to as the class struggle perspective is perhaps more aptly characterized as a *state management* perspective. In a sense, this perspective is an elaboration on the functionalist perspective. It attempts to identify the processes and mechanisms whereby the state in a market society will operate, sometimes in considerable conflict with capitalists, to facilitate the workings of capitalism. Very important to this perspective is the idea that there is a division of labor between the managers of capital and the managers of the state, the latter including elected officials as well as the bureaucracy. In market systems, capitalists are assumed to be incapable of acting on behalf of the long-term interests of capital. The class struggle or state manager view, then, concentrates on how one explains (1) the manner in which state managers often adopt policies opposed by important components of the capitalist class; and (2) why it is that such policies in the long run are constrained to be in the general interest of capitalism. The explanation goes something like this: In market systems, particularly those with widespread political participation and in a more fitful way in less democratic market systems, officials are held responsible for the performance of the economy and for managing other social ills (e.g., crime and environmental quality). State managers are motivated to maintain their positions, which requires them to avoid serious socioeconomic distress, since society's members will tend to blame them by replacing them with other state managers. Moreover, the salaries and budgets of state managers and the agencies they run depend on a growing market economy, just as does the profit and well-being of other institutions in a market society. Most often, intervention in the private sector by state managers is resisted, especially among the capitalist class. Skocpol describes it as follows:

> ... [C]apitalists are almost by definition too short-sighted initially to accept, let alone to promote, major reforms or extensions of state power. Such changes come primarily in opposition to capitalist preferences. And they

mostly come when, and because, state managers are strongly prodded to institute reforms by the working class.... [According to class struggle theorists], the biggest spurts forward in state activity come during major crises such as wars or depression. During wars capitalists can not easily undercut state managers, and during depressions the decline of business confidence is not such a potent threat. Moreover, especially during economic crises, class struggle and pressures from below are likely to intensify. Thus state managers may find it expedient to grant concessions to the working class. Yet they will do so only in forms that simultaneously increase the power of the state itself. What is more, over the longer run, especially as economic recovery resumes or a wartime emergency ends, the state managers will do the best they can to shape (or restructure) the concessions won by the working class in order to make them function smoothly in support of capital accumulation and existing class relations. Thus it can come to pass that reforms and extensions of state power originally won through "pressure from below" can end up being "functional for" capitalism.... (1980: 183–84)

The major differences among the three approaches are (1) the degree to which they concentrate on mediating factors that operate between class conflict and government growth, (2) the degree to which capitalists operate directly and decisively to control policy, and (3) the degree to which government institutions and officials are accorded any independence as a source of policy and action.

With the exception of a strictly instrumentalist application of Marxism, government is not viewed as a mere extension of the will of the dominant economic class or as some conspiratorial outcome of the machinations among a putative ruling class. Rather, government responds to "the tensions and contradictions that threaten the system's stability (Greenberg, 1985: 42)." The degree of payoff to noncapitalist classes, how well new government actions perform, either as mechanisms for capitalist accumulation or as "bribes" for working class acquiescence, and whether genuine social progress can occur within the capitalist setting are matters of some considerable dispute among Marxists (Barrow, 1993; Block, 1977; Nordlinger, 1981; Skocpol, 1980; Skocpol and Feingold, 1982). Moreover, it would be inaccurate to suggest that Marxists view social dynamics as the simple interplay between two cohesive and opposing classes. Marxists understand, moreover, that intraclass composition can vary dramatically and that there can be substantial oscillation in levels of conflict within and across class categories.

During the latter half of the nineteenth century, there emerged in the United States a number of major social challenges, rivaling the unrest that existed in the years after the Revolutionary War. There appeared the great waves of growing agrarian and industrial unrest, the initial government efforts to regulate the economy, the emergence of the modern business cycle, the need for mass war mobilization, and the task of managing deep, chronic economic depression, especially during the Panic of 1893 and the onset of worldwide depression in 1929. In explaining the growing government role in dealing with these problems, Marxists saw government's increased role in managing business activity and economic performance as primarily a function of maintaining the capitalist order in the face of changing and threatening conditions. Although the precise conditions and the relative power and privilege of the dominant classes vis-à-vis the mass of society might vary, "Marxian social theory understands the capitalist state as an institution that attempts to maintain the system of unequal distribution of power and benefits, and thereby advances the general interests of the owners of the means of production" (Greenberg, 1985: 42).

Consequently, the following all operated to create discontent among the populace generally and among certain traditional sources of social reform: the social unrest of the late nineteenth century; the increased severity of social distress wrought by the gyrations of the business cycle; the vulnerability of agriculture to the fluctuations of national and world commodity prices as well as its discontent at the high, often "fixed" prices of transport and credit; the very hard conditions imposed on industrial workers and urban residents; the excesses in production practices among certain businesses; and the inability of corporations to manage privately the coordination of prices, profits, and product quality.

It is often suggested that these sources of reform were successful as a political movement in promulgating and enacting a number of important policies, including such things as the Sherman Anti-Trust Act, the Meat Inspection Act, the Pure Food and Drug Act, and the Federal Reserve Act. These policies, which were all enacted by 1914, are often regarded as major achievements of the Progressive Movement. Marxists, while occasionally conceding that the Progressive Movement was in some sense important in creating the impetus for a growing state apparatus, still view these "achievements" of the reformers as manifestations of capitalist hegemony. As Greenberg says:

> The Age of Reform was primarily an effort by leading members of the business community to bring order, stability, and predictability to the competitive chaos of the emerging industrial order, to incorporate labor into the business system through conservative unionism, and to prevent social revolution through the distribution of minimal relief benefits of the poor. (1985: 75)

Similarly, the New Deal, which involves another ratcheting-up of the role of government in the society, is understood by Marxists as primarily directed to the preservation of capitalist dynamics. So the establishment of the Federal Deposit Insurance Corporation was enacted to manage the banking crisis and enhance trust in the financial community; the Agricultural Adjustment Act was provided to stabilize and ensure the well-being of the major agricultural producers by creating scarcity and raising prices; industrial unrest was addressed by the National Industrial Recovery Act and the consequent National Recovery Administration; and the enactment of the Social Security Act and the Wagner Labor Relations Act were designed to reduce the drift by many of the working class toward anticapitalist action and to ameliorate labor-management strife. Again, in words similar to those characterizing the "achievements" of the Progressives, Greenberg states:

> ... [T]he New Deal is best understood as a series of attempts to save a faltering and depressed capitalist system by further regulating and rationalizing the economy, by bringing important elements of the labor movement into established political life, and by staving off social disruption and revolution through expansion of the welfare role of government ... the New Deal represents, paradoxically, a conservative expansion of government activities. While it is traditional to define any expansion of government activities as "liberal," I would argue that since this expansion was directed toward preserving and cementing the position of capital and maintaining the social class system, it must, in the end, be judged "conservative." (1985: 93)

Contemporary Marxists understand the many anomalies that traditional Marxism finds difficult to explain—such as the tendency of capitalists to operate in ways that conflict with one another or that are actually detrimental to capitalist interests, and the tendency of workers to resist attacking capitalist institutions. Contemporary Marxist work sometimes departs from traditional concerns, especially in its focus on explaining the decline of communist states or in its effort to understand macro-economic policymaking in competitive democracies (Wallerstein, 1984).

CHAPTER 4

PUBLIC CHOICE EXPLANATIONS
OF GOVERNMENT SIZE AND GROWTH

Previous chapters have reviewed some of the traditional ways in which scholars have explained the growth of government in western societies. Since the end of World War II, the classic interest in how government comes to intervene in previously private matters has been increasingly marked by a fascination with applying the concepts and tools of economic analysis to political life (Baumol, 1965; Buchanan and Tullock, 1962; Buchanan, 1968; Coleman and Fararo, 1992; Frey, 1978; Friedman, 1996; Green and Shapiro, 1994; Higgs, 1971; Johnson, 1991; Lybeck, 1986; McLean, 1982, 1987; Meltzer and Richard, 1981; Monroe, 1991; Niskanen, 1971; Olson, 1968; Riker, 1962; Tullock, 1976).

THE POLITICAL ECONOMY ORIGIN OF PUBLIC CHOICE

"Public choice" approaches to politics (often termed rational choice, social choice, collective choice, or economic choice) are a facet of what has been called political economy. Public choice approaches have come to be among the most important ways in which scholars tackle the explanation and evaluation of government intervention in society, especially as regards economic matters.

As McLean defines it, public choice approaches infer various conclusions regarding the behavior of individuals as if they were

> ... rationally pursuing their goals in a highly simplified model world. It [the public choice approach] then gradually makes its model world more

complicated in order to make it resemble the real world more closely. Finally, it compares its findings with what actually happens in the real world, in the hope that the model-building process will throw some light on why and how real people do the things they do. (1982: 20)

The "model world" of public choice is based on abstract principles defining a free, competitive market. As Buchanan has said (1967: 3), "Individuals, separately and in groups, make decisions concerning the use of economic resources. They do so in at least two capacities: first, as purchasers (sellers) of goods and services in organized markets, and, second, as "purchasers" ("sellers") of goods and services through organized political processes." In public choice theory, then, rational, self-interested economic roles prevail in *both* private markets and government sectors.

A discussion about private or political markets, moreover, is not just a discussion about conventional economic activity (e.g., producing, selling, and purchasing cars, apples, televisions, or computer games). For public choice theorists nearly every kind of interaction can be understood in economic terms. When a person commits or refrains from perpetrating a crime, it is a matter of weighing the risks and penalties associated with being convicted of the crime against the potential gains (Brigham and Brown, 1980). When a person beautifies his home so that it is more pleasing and attractive than surrounding properties, he is providing a "public good" for his neighbors, whose levels of satisfaction are improved as a consequence. In other words, nearly any kind of interaction among people can be interpreted, explained, and judged as a kind of exchange, a weighing of benefits and costs.

Of course, costs and benefits are not only material but also involve psychic costs and benefits. For example, a program redistributing income involves the concrete dollars and cents that are moved from one person to another. Those whose incomes are taxed to support such a program might experience a sense of imposition, not simply because they are contributing to someone else's income, but also because they might feel that the public is doing something objectionable. It is possible, no matter how meritorious a welfare program appears to be to its proponents, that others might believe the program is unfair, wasteful, or even immoral according to some set of values or opinions. When some citizens resist public support of abortions for poor women or birth control programs, they are expressing more than their ire at the financial cost of such actions. If a taxpayer believes that most welfare recipients are able-bodied and lazy, no matter how inaccurate the view, that person's opposition expresses resentment at more than the dollar value of the welfare payments. Citizens who decry violence and espouse pacifist views react to more than the revenues expended in the support of military expenditures. These kinds of feelings, then, constitute examples of psychic costs. If, on the other hand, people experience "good feelings" because the government is trying to eliminate poverty, reduce teen pregnancies, or reduce the spread of AIDs among intravenous drug users, then these programs are providing a psychic benefit. In short, the calculation of costs and benefits is greatly complicated when psychic dimensions are involved in peoples' assessments of their net benefits and costs. Most often, even a specific public policy poses for the individual complex mixtures of costs and benefits, both material and psychic. Commuters might feel that they need more roads to facilitate their travel, but they might simultaneously lament the scarring of the landscape and the loss of environmental amenities required in the construction of new freeways.

A MARRIAGE OF CONVENIENCE: GOVERNMENT AS A TOOL TO INCREASE MARKET EFFICIENCY

There is an intriguing ambivalence in the way public choice theory explains how government comes to intervene in previously private matters. On the one hand, government involvement is viewed as necessary to *improve* overall economic efficiency. In this remedial capacity, government is viewed as a prescription for market failure, applied by rational citizen-consumers. Recent public choice appraisals of growth in government, however, claim that government meddling in previously private affairs detracts from efficiency. In its *initial* expressions, the expansion in government tended to be viewed by public choice theorists as a remedy for market failure. In recent years, however, many public choice analysts have concentrated on the deleterious effects of government involvement in society generally and in the economy in particular. In this sense, government activity and growth are seen through public choice lenses as *government failure*. On the one hand, public choice theorists, particularly prior to the mid-1960s, tended to focus on remedying market failure through some form of government or collective action. On the other hand, more contemporary public choice theorists tend to concentrate on the defects of government activity, that is, government failure. Although, in actuality, managing the problems of market and government failure poses intertwined puzzles for citizens, officials, and scholars, there is a tendency to discuss market and government failures as separate processes (Wolf, 1988). The important point to be made is that government growth has been explained both in terms of society's members acting rationally and self-interestedly to deal with market shortcomings *and* in terms of the tendency of governments to produce excessive public sectors. Attention is directed first toward those explanations that see government growth as the consequence of rational societal actors (citizens, businesses, and officials) managing the shortcomings of private markets.

MARKET FAILURE: WHEN GOVERNMENT SHOULD
AND DOES GROW, ACCORDING TO PUBLIC CHOICE THEORISTS

Among public choice theorists there is the belief that private sector exchanges and transactions are, in the main, efficient (Apgar and Brown, 1987). Public choice theorists claim that in private, free markets the stock of productive capital and wealth is efficiently utilized and that the level of satisfaction among individuals is, therefore, maximized. A private economy is generally considered preferable because private markets provide goods and services by (1) using methods that have the lowest production costs, (2) producing the quantity and mix of goods most valued by society's members, and (3) distributing the goods and services to those individuals who value them the most, thereby maximizing societal satisfaction (utility).

The market system relies, moreover, on persons expressing freely and individually their own choices as to what to produce and consume (the principle of *consumer sovereignty*). In the theoretically postulated world of an idealized, private market the only factor constraining and shaping the expression of consumer preferences is *willingness to pay*, which, in turn, is a function of the interplay among personal tastes, preferences, and personal income. Personal income is a constraint: People obviously want to consume or experience all the things they like, but since incomes are limited, they need to pick and choose. Of course, there is less picking and more consuming for those who have more, rather than less, personal wealth. If we also hoist atop our idealized, private market the assumption that there are no objections regarding the *initial* distribution of income or the *initial* pattern of tastes and preferences, many public choice theorists will conclude that the distribution of goods and services is optimal, from an efficiency view. Finally, because exchanges and distributions of goods, services, satisfactions, and dissatisfactions are engendered through apparently voluntary behavior, private markets are also viewed as maximizing personal liberty and the "freedom to choose" in society.

There is, however, a very important qualification that complicates the private market model. The difficulty is the phenomenon of *market failure*. Indeed, market failure is a critical concept in the public choice approach to government growth; it is the paramount phenomenon used to *justify* increasing government growth among public choice theorists. Public choice theorists realize that certain circumstances require government involvement. However, most public choice theorists want public involvement to occur in a manner that replicates the workings of the market as much as possible. It is for this reason that market failure and its complementary concepts (e.g., public goods and externalities) are critical—*they provide a justification for government growth and size that rests on narrow technical and efficiency grounds.* Put differently, the concept of market failure, as it is used among public choice theorists, is important because it specifies situations where distribution, production, and consumer efficiency are *not* maximized by private, market exchanges.

In order to discuss the conditions under which public choice theorists believe there is market failure and, hence, some possible justification for government intervention, it is necessary to enumerate the conditions (assumptions) that define market efficiency. To the extent these assumptions are not manifested in real world situations, then actual market outcomes might not be efficient. These assumptions are as follows:

1. Information regarding goods and services used in production and consumed by individuals is widely shared by society's members.
2. The number of producers and consumers is sufficiently large to prevent any individual producer or consumer from exercising identifiable control over prices or supply.
3. Transactions for various goods and services affect only those who produce and consume them.
4. Exchange of goods and services, that is the actual transaction of a good or service, involves no costs other than a decision to offer a good or service at a certain price or a decision to consume at a certain price; in short, bargaining among market members involves no time or other resource costs.
5. People who do not pay for a given good or service are prevented from receiving any utility from the production or consumption of that good or service; as one person uses a good or service, nonpayers are prevented from using that good or service.

When these assumptions are violated by real-world conditions, market efficiency is threatened. For example, if a firm has some information regarding a product that it produces and the information is not shared among other producers in the same field, it is possible that a decline in competition might result, producing a number of inefficiencies. Perhaps a firm has exclusive knowledge of government tests indicating that some product it produces is hazardous and that the government is about to ban its production. The firm having the exclusive information would then be in a comparatively favorable economic position vis-à-vis its competitors. The result would be to undermine competitiveness in that field.

In any case, since there are a number of circumstances that detract from the degree to which the free market assumptions apply in the real world, public choice theorists employ a number of market failure categories to assess the nature of societal responses to market failure. It is worth reviewing what these categories of market failure are and how they pose problems for market efficiency and, assuming a society of rationally acting citizens, produce pressures for government involvement in previously private matters.

MONOPOLY

Monopoly refers to situations in which there is only a single producer. The many sources of monopoly will not be investigated here; the important thing to know is that when a firm is a monopoly it can, because of its individual action, manage the prices of its goods and services by manipulating output. Consequently, monopoly firms might produce *less* of a good or service, *at a higher price*, than a competitive market would produce. Consumers that purchase monopoly-supplied goods and services will presumably be doing so at higher than competitive prices; other consumers will not be able to afford or will eschew the good or service at the monopoly price. Not only will consumer welfare be adversely affected, but societal resources will tend to be misallocated and reduce productive efficiency in other businesses. In short, the result is that net social welfare is not maximized.

EXTERNALITIES

Recall that a major assumption of market efficiency is that the exchange of goods and services affects only those who produce and consume them. In actuality, this assumption is often violated. In modern, urban societies the presence of externalities is ubiquitous, rather than exceptional. It is also important to understand that externalities can confer benefits (*positive externalities*) as well as costs (*negative externalities*). Positive externalities result when individuals benefit from the effects of transactions to which they are not a party. When a city provides a lovely, well-policed, well-maintained park, the homes adjacent to the park increase in value, even though the costs of the park might be borne by the city residents as a whole. When a homeowner invests heavily in the beauty of his residence, then the neighbors benefit aesthetically and economically, too.

Negative externalities result when costs are imposed on parties not involved in a transaction, as when a factory uses a waterway as a repository of its waste and thereby imposes a variety of costs on others downstream, including the loss of recreational potential and possible health hazards. Externalities produce market failure because of the misallocation of resources they engender. In the case of positive externalities, certain goods and services might be *under-supplied*, since the producer of positive externalities is not compensated for providing them. Homeowners might be reluctant to increase investments in their residences if they believe there is no way to recover the cost of providing the increased value provided to neighbors who do much less to maintain their home. Home maintenance investment might be under-supplied. Businesses might under-supply training if there is no guarantee that the workers they train will stay with their firms. Positive externalities, in short, pose the problem of under-supply in goods or services whose greater supply would increase social welfare.

The reverse applies in negative externalities. A firm that uses the atmosphere or waterways as a convenient place to dump the waste by-product of its production passes along a production cost to individuals who are perhaps not consumers of the good or service produced. Moreover, the product consumers reap benefits because the price of the good or service is lower than it would be if it were produced without using the air or waterways as waste receptacles or if the firm had to pay in order to use the air and waterways for this purpose. Since the consumers of such goods and services pay a *lower* price than they might if they were "charged" with the true cost of delivering such goods and services, their demand for these goods and services is also *higher*. In such situations, there is an *over-supply* of a good or service and a misallocation of resources. Positive externalities pose the problem of under-supply and negative externalities create prospects of over-supply.

PUBLIC GOODS

Some have referred to public goods as "an extreme type of positive externality" (Apgar and Brown, 1987: 227). The critical features of a public good are (1) nonexcludability and (2) nonrivalry in consumption. Recall that an efficient market requires that individuals not paying for a good or service are excluded from its benefits. However, there are some goods and services that are available even to those who do not pay. National defense, public health programs, or efforts to improve the seismic safety of buildings represent programs that, if produced, cannot exclude those who do not pay for their provision. Public goods also manifest the quality of nonrivalry. When national defense is provided to a jurisdiction, then the sense of security one person gains does not reduce the level of defense available to anyone else. If a public immunization program is provided, the lower risk of contracting an illness is the same for all those vulnerable to the illness. In this sense, national defense and immunization benefits pose no rivalry in consumption.

Of course, goods and services can have more or less of the qualities of nonexcludability and nonrivalry. For example, some public goods could be delivered in a manner to exclude nonpayers, as in the extensive use of toll roads and barriers in financing streets and sidewalks. Some goods involve nonrivalry only to a point, as when a public beach eventually has enough people on it so that the presence of an additional person reduces the pleasure for other users. In any case, the effects of public goods on market efficiency are quite substantial. Obviously, there is little incentive for individuals to produce public goods for beneficiaries who cannot be excluded from use when they do not pay. Nonexcludable consumers of public goods, since their pleasure or use is not affected by the use of others, will have very little incentive to pay for these public goods and services. This is often referred to as the *free-rider* problem. Public goods, then, are likely to be under-supplied by purely private markets, since their producers have no capacity to exclude free riders or recover the costs of production from them.

EQUAL DISTRIBUTION, IMPERFECT INFORMATION

It is assumed in market models of efficiency that there is a cost-free and equal distribution of knowledge *and* ignorance among producers and consumers. This is obviously rare. Businesses often withhold information or benefit from inside information, and consumers are often unaware of prices or quality differences among goods and services. In the case of certain ingredients in standard, everyday consumption items (e.g., food and medicine) the consumer often finds it costly to assess benefits versus risks in consumption.

When information or ignorance is unequally distributed, resource misallocation can result, since factors of production are not necessarily used where they produce the most satisfaction. For example, consumers will often find the cost of determining the quality of and prices for goods and services quite high, and hence they cannot make the most optimal decision when purchasing a good or service. When purchasing a house or car or selecting a health care provider, the consumer is faced with a considerable information problem regarding the apparent or less obvious shortcomings of the house, car, or health service. If the house seller or auto dealer knows more about the particular product (e.g., where the leak in the roof is or what the flaws in the car are), then clearly the assumption about free and equally flowing information is inaccurate. Surely, most individuals will find it a complex, time-consuming, and expensive matter to compare different health maintenance organizations or health insurance plans. It is highly questionable whether individuals in the workforce are aware of which jobs bring the highest return to them or which jobs pose unique hazards. Nor are consumers using new drugs likely to have knowledge about the full range of their side-effects. Discontinuities and inequalities in the availability of knowledge between and among producers and consumers or employers and employees can lead to a variety of inefficiencies regarding the allocation of resources.

Another important area in which information problems can produce market failure is that of considering the costs and benefits of the future (Ahrens, 1983; Norgaard, 1992; Sikora and Barry, 1978). Individuals often are not cognizant of the hazards of having insufficient income at retirement. It is, after all, hard for people to visualize their retirement needs when they are in the midst of their working years. Consequently, there is a good chance that, on the average, people will under-invest in their future—that is, they will not, on their own, save enough during their working years for their income. Given the uncertainties of the future, it is very hard for individuals to assess what the appropriate level of saving should be. After all, inflation might be higher or lower than what is anticipated. People are likely to maximize near-term satisfaction by under-investing in the future. They are far more likely to invest in making the here and now as pleasant as possible. That will often come at the expense of future well-being. That is why, in the absence of strong incentives by government or some other entity, many citizens will be completely unprepared to deal with their retirement years. Of course, the nature of public policies concerning income security is controversial, although a sound public choice justification for some government involvement is obviously possible.

TRANSACTION COSTS

If a person has to negotiate privately with possible competitors to ensure that some new product will not be duplicated, then the cost of innovation and invention will be substantially higher. Under such circumstances, the rate of innovation, since its cost will be higher, will decline. The economy will have fewer new, higher quality products. When the costs of coordinating the benefits and costs of a transaction are greater than the net benefits of the transaction itself, it is possible that certain exchanges and interactions will not occur, although they could improve social welfare. This is the classic justification for the government's role in enforcing patent rights.

Another example involves the difficulty a household might have in getting neighbors to agree to limits on the kind of activities they will conduct in the neighborhood. Defining the extent of a neighborhood, getting all the parties to agree to limitations on the use of one's property, forming an enforceable contract, and executing the contract might make *private* coordination of local land use very expensive. In these circumstances, no individual property owner actually will initiate or pay for such agreements and, hence, the neighborhood would not achieve the quality of life they might otherwise enjoy. Some argue that such situations justify government involvement in land use regulation, such as zoning ordinances.

In all these cases of market failure, private outcomes lead to diseconomies, sometimes involving an under-supply or over-supply of goods and services and, hence, a misallocation of resources and a less than optimal level of net social well-being. In some of these settings, public choice theorists contend that government intervention will improve efficiency, although the nature of such intervention is itself usually a matter of some debate. Indeed, Friedman (1962) argues that it is often more efficient to tolerate market failures in order to avoid public intervention in private matters. Notwithstanding the hard-line on government intervention held by libertarians, for most public choice theorists it is the effort to manage market failure that produces government growth.

It should be pointed out, however, that for public choice theorists market failure does not automatically explain or justify government growth. Public choice theorists claim that in the face of market failure it is still critical to determine first what is the most optimal form of government intervention. Should the government provide free information; should it tax; should it regulate; or should it provide incentives? And, once an optimal method of intervention is identified, are the costs of the government intervention less than the cost of market failure? After all, it is possible that living with a market failure is economically more efficient than trying to remedy it. For example, there is currently a great dispute over the sale and use of some drugs. Most argue that drug use occurs because of considerable lack of information, sometimes because the user is too young to process the information, sometimes because addiction makes consumer decisions irrational, and sometimes because of the external health effects of widespread, illegal drug use. However, the highly coercive, regulatory approach, the criminalizing of drug use, is viewed by many as producing more inefficiencies than the direct costs resulting from the use of the drugs. Some analysts argue, therefore, that decriminalizing drug use is superior to trying to stop drug use, even though everyone believes even a private, freely arrived at choice to use certain drugs is probably not a good thing for society.

In education, the idea that the purely private sector will under-supply primary education is accepted. The traditional response has been compulsory, universal education for youngsters. However, while it might be claimed that public intervention is needed to increase the supply of public education, it is still unclear what form that intervention should take. Disagreement over this issue is reflected in disputes over the use of school vouchers as a substitute for the current neighborhood school system in order to enable parents to send their children to schools of their choice within the school district.

Put differently, public choice theorists might acknowledge the presence of market failure, but they can also point out that a public remedy for the failure must be avoided unless it can lead to greater benefits. Even if a government remedy is justified, the public choice theorist will contend that the government's actions should attempt to replicate the workings of a market as closely as is possible.

In any case, public choice theories can be used to explain government growth in market societies. After all, the attempt to regulate railroad and utility monopolies, government consumer protection, and environmental regulation programs can be interpreted as efforts to deal with various aspects of market failure. Even when it can be shown that the private market produces efficiently and maximizes consumer satisfaction according to prevailing efficiency criteria, it is possible to justify government modification of the resulting distribution of goods, services, resources, and income on the grounds of *equity* and *merit wants* (Apgar and Brown, 1987: 302).

For example, the provision of shelter or nutritional assistance might be demanded of government when certain norms are violated. These would perhaps be the result of a concern for equity, that is, a sense of fairness and conscience. Additionally, merit wants have to do with the goods or services that are viewed as necessary, even if consumers act as if they are unwilling to demand them through the market. Museums, historic preservation, mass transportation, conservation of resources, or compulsory retirement savings are examples of such things. As Musgrave (1959) pointed out, the claims that government should become involved in providing merit goods is contrary to the belief in consumer sovereignty. Although there is a prevailing belief that most of what is produced, distributed, and consumed should be determined by private markets, merit wants and equity considerations suggest many instances in which market results are considered unacceptable. Often the result is some demand for government provision of such merit goods.

CAN REMEDYING MARKET FAILURE LEAD TO GOVERNMENT FAILURE?

Interestingly, then, the initial offerings of public choice theory were directed at showing how government direction—whether obtrusive or subtle—must correct for market failure. It was such correcting that presumably accounted for the growth of government in market societies. And, of course, there are many examples that would accord with a public choice explanation of government growth (North, 1981). This initial thrust among public choice theorists was fostered by some of the earlier analysts, such as Pigou (1946) and Musgrave (1959). In more recent years, however, public choice analysis has come to be dominated by the work of such individuals as Buchanan, Tullock, Stigler, and Niskanen, who view the growth of government as a source of economic inefficiency. They see government in democratic, market societies as a potential Leviathan, feeding insatiably on private resources, endangering personal liberties, and undermining economic efficiency (Mitchell and Simmons, 1994; Machan, 1995; Ball, 1984; Bennett and Johnson, 1980; Borcherding, 1977; Burton, 1985; Freeman, 1975; Hughes, 1977; Galloway, 1976). According to this view, a number of mechanisms and actors are causing excessive government, including simple majority rule, budget maximizing behavior of bureaucrats, public employee voting, underestimating by voters of the costs of public services because of "fiscal illusion," and relying on deficit finance among governments. Let us examine more carefully a number of these mechanisms and the behaviors that presumably engender more government than the public would really want, which presumably, then, detracts from economic efficiency.

MEDIAN-VOTER REDISTRIBUTION

Downs argued some time ago that under a number of circumstances the preferences of the median voter will tend to prevail. For this to occur in a democracy, with voting and majority rule as key public policy choice mechanisms, the conditions under which median voter domination (equilibrium) exists are as follows:

1. Voters have single-peaked preferences on given issues of concern. Each voter has a point where utility declines or remains constant as one moves from it.
2. Voters decide issues without considering other issues; that is, individual decisions are independent of one another.
3. Voters always decide issues by comparing one with another; that is, choices are between an alternative and the current choice.
4. Voters always vote for their preferred alternative at the time.
5. Decisions are by majority rule. (Larkey, Stolp, and Winer, 1981: 180–81)

It can be shown that under these conditions, the median voter's preferred choices will prevail. Of course, when the previous assumptions are violated, the predicted outcome is no longer tenable. Nevertheless, the median voter model, along with its assumptions, is often used to account for growth in government as follows. As indicated, much of the public choice literature emphasizes the importance of competition for votes. Officials seeking votes offer services to garner public support. Voters judge officials on the basis of the package of services and/or benefits they provide. As Meltzer and Richard (1978: 116) say: "Each member of the electorate compares the benefits he expects to receive from expanded government programs to the costs he expects to pay. Voters choose candidates who promise to act in their interest and re-elect those who do." One of the factors affecting the manner in which voters decide to choose or reject certain packages of candidates and policies is the gap between the income of the median voter and the income of the average earner. Considering only self-interest, the voter with an income below the average can gain if incomes above the average are taxed, and the revenues redistributed as benefits to him and others like him.

Public choice theorists claim, therefore, that in a democracy, growth in government results from the differences between the distribution of income among voters and the distribution of income in society. As voting rights are extended to include voters whose incomes are below the median family income, the demand for services that redistribute income will increase. How much redistribution occurs will, of course, depend on the propensity of these citizens to exercise their right to vote.

What prevents a self-interested majority, however, from confiscating the wealth of individuals in the higher classes of income? At some point the incentive to work and earn among individuals who are more affluent is reduced at greater rates than the return from higher taxes on such individuals. It becomes "less rational" for lower income voters to continue to tax higher income citizens, since there would be greater losses in revenue than gains in benefits. Similarly, lower income voters might find that the increases to be received are not worth the costs of organizing or otherwise investing in whatever political action is required to achieve further tax benefit gains. Meltzer and Richard describe it as follows:

> Progressive taxes increase the gain to the majority by taking a larger fraction of income from voters with incomes above the median to pay for programs like health care, which is available to everyone, or housing allowances, which go mainly to voters with incomes below the median. But if high taxes reduce incentives greatly, income is lowered, the size of net benefits from redistribution declines, and there is an increase in the number of voters favoring lower tax rates and smaller government. (1978: 117)

The democratic competition among officials for votes and the rational, self-interested conduct of citizens produce a powerful incentive to increase the demand for and supply of government services. The result is that democracy in the context of rational behavior leads to a larger government. Whether this is a good or bad thing is a very tough puzzle to solve. Meltzer and Richard express the difficulty in the following statement (1978: 118): "Although large government poses a threat to many of our freedoms, government grows in every society where the majority remains free to express its will." Are Meltzer and Richard suggesting that, in order to restrain government, the free expression of the majority's will must also be restrained?

BUREAUCRATIC DETERMINISM

Government agencies have always been the object of suspicion and sometimes of fear. Citizens routinely believe that government agencies are always seeking new things to do, new restrictions to fasten on the backs of citizens, and new reasons to extract more tax revenue. Although it is relatively well known that public service and politicians are generally regarded with a mixture of disdain and derision, public choice theorists suggest that bureaucracies be depicted mostly in terms that are more neutral, if not positive. As Tullock says:

> Most of the existing literature on the machinery of government assumes that, when an activity is delegated to a bureaucrat, he will either carry out the rules and regulations or will make decisions in the public interest

regardless of whether it benefits him or not. We do not make this assumption about businessmen. We do not make it about consumers in the market. I see no reason why we should make it about bureaucrats. (1976: 26)

Niskanen, in his *Bureaucracy and Representative Government* (1971) presented the most widely cited formal model of "bureau behavior." His major claim is that it is in the self-interest of government bureaus and agencies of government to maximize budgets. As echoed in the words of Gordon Tullock:

> As a general rule, a bureaucrat will find that his possibilities for promotion increase, his power, influence, and public respect improve, and even the physical conditions of his office improve, if the bureaucracy in which he works expands. This proposition is fairly general. Almost any bureaucrat gains at least something if the *whole* bureaucracy expands. He gains more, however, if *his* Ministry expands, and more yet if the *sub*-division in which he is employed expands. (1976: 29)

It is important to understand that in the supply of collective goods, it is very difficult to maximize per unit prices to maximize budgets. A major portion of what governments provide are collective goods, and even where feasible many governments operate without user charges. When these charges are implemented, they are usually pegged at some fixed price, regardless of demand, or only at cost recovery levels. Governments find it very difficult to utilize demand-driven prices. Consequently, the usual manner of maximizing government agency budgets is to have the entire budget authorized in advance at the highest level by public authority.

Not only do bureaus presumably seek larger budgets through the budgetary process, according to public choice theorists, they are also the beneficiaries of the political activity of their personnel. Many employees of government agencies, it is charged, will vote for legislators and policies that will enhance their respective agencies' budgets. And, in some circumstances, they will be able to advertise publicly, lobby, and otherwise struggle on behalf of themselves in the budgetary process.

Generally, public choice theorists see bureaucracies as relatively autonomous and free of legislative oversight, able to outflank elected officials and hide critical information from them. It is argued, furthermore, that legislative oversight is undermined when legislators seek access to committees that oversee policies that the legislators are interested in advocating. They devote their energies, consequently, to advocating larger budgets for their constituencies and supporters.

However, legislative-bureau relations might *lower* spending beyond expectations. For example, if a bureau produces more than one good and the legislature has a strong preference for the lower cost one, then legislators might reduce spending for the more expensive one to provide more units of the preferred and less expensive good. In other words, the results of the agency budget-maximization model depends considerably on the precise mix of control over the budget process among legislatures, bureaus, and executives. Finally, it is not at all clear that maximizing the size of the bureaucracy always means maximizing spending, especially among agencies dispensing transfer payments. As Larkey, Stolp and Winer (1981: 190) point out, "Items that may appeal to the individual voter, such as straight transfer payments, have little appeal to the bureaucrat." Why? Because these payments might have no bearing on increasing salaries or power; in fact, they might only increase the workload. Although other instances in which bureaucratic politics might not necessarily produce higher spending or more government will be reviewed, it is fair to describe most public choice theorists as proponents of the view that bureaucracy is itself a major force for more government.

FISCAL ILLUSION ANALYSIS

The fiscal illusion analysis suggests that taxpayers are willing to tolerate higher than "optimum" levels of government because they underestimate the cost of services or are not fully conscious of the burden of taxation. The cause of the misperceptions among voters is the manner by which taxes are levied. Taxes raised in the course of many small purchases (e.g., sales taxes), subtracted weekly from payrolls, or disguised in the costs of goods and services, make it difficult for voters to sense fully the burden and cost of government activity. Related to the directness and size of individual tax payments are such matters as whether the budget process requires balanced budgets, which would require either service cuts or higher taxes to support newer services. When decisions to spend are made independently of how these expenditures are to be financed, we are also more likely to spend. In a related way, when the public imposes costs on private actors through regulations, the costs of complying with these regulations are hard to discern. Such costs might be considerable and come to be reflected as costs in privately exchanged goods and services. The costs of medicine, fossil fuels, or office space can reflect the cost of ensuring safe pharmaceuticals, environmental quality, or worker safety. But since these costs are, in a sense, hidden in the retail price of these goods and services, it is harder to assess the trade-off between the benefits of regulatory policies.

In all of these cases, then, a kind of "illusion" exists, the result of which is to have citizens and decision makers lose sight of the actual burden or cost of public services or regulation. The result is an over-supply of public services or excessive regulation, since their costs are underestimated and the public's demand, thereby, inefficiently inflated.

ECONOMIC CHOICE MODELS OF INTEREST GROUP BEHAVIOR

Popularized by the work of Olson (1965), a number of efforts have highlighted the role of groups in demanding and getting publicly produced private benefits. Rational economic behavior inclines individuals to benefit from the goods and services produced by others, especially when people cannot be excluded from benefiting from publicly produced goods and services. Consequently, most individuals will not organize to prevent others from extracting government benefits. Many government programs, then, are governmentally produced benefits for smaller groups of citizens. Among such benefits are those going to particular industries, professions, or even government agencies when government employees seek the expansion or creation of programs primarily to enhance their own prestige and status.

The costs of benefits produced by the public are often diffused widely, so that any individual would gain very little by the termination of any particular special interest program. On the other hand, special interest members who receive the benefits have much greater motivation to resist efforts to end such benefits. The bias of government, then, is to over-supply government programs, since they are produced one at a time. Even though collectively all members of society might very well prefer government to produce fewer benefits for various groups, individuals are motivated to protect their own benefits and not to invest equal time in resisting the benefits provided to others. The benefit of stopping others from receiving benefits is often, especially for large groups, considerably less than the gain of seeking one's own benefits. As Lieberson stated in describing the persistence of "The Military-Industrial Complex":

> If each group attempts to generate the greatest *net* gain for itself, then a given policy need not be the product of simply the majority of interest, nor need it mean that a small set of interests is dominant. Rather, the policy may mean that the losses to a majority of interests are small, whereas the gains to some sectors are substantial. (1971: 582)

Groups seek benefits for themselves, with far less incentive to obstruct the attainment of benefits for other groups. The policymaking system is, therefore, according to the public choice view of interest groups, biased in favor of expanding government through the provision of quasi-private benefits for a variety of special interests.

THE ANOMALOUS CASE OF A DECLINING PUBLIC SECTOR PREDICTION

In 1960, Anthony Downs wrote an article entitled "Why the Government Budget Is Too Small in a Democracy." The claims made in the article are important, since unlike most other public choice theorists, Downs contends that the size of government, rather than being too large, tends to be too small in a democracy. The argument is as follows. Governments set expenditures and revenue levels to enhance the hold they have on elected office. Hence, the budget results from an interplay of how expenditures and revenues function to maximize electoral support. In the words of Downs (1960: 542), "The governing party looks at every possible expenditure and tries to decide whether making it would gain more votes than financing it would lose." Voters, equally rational and self-interested, will support those politicians and vote for those individuals and parties that *maximize* benefits. It is assumed, of course, that voters know the issues, differentiate between parties and their respective programs, weigh the costs of the benefits associated with particular parties, and can calculate a cost/benefit ratio regarding an array of government services.

Of course, all of this is complicated because benefits and costs can include symbolic and psychic dimensions. In actuality, politicians might not support policies that would increase majority voter support because the policies are so contrary to deeply felt beliefs of some subset of voters. Such highly motivated voters might prevent enactment of policies that provide substantial benefits to a larger set of voters who respond less intensely toward the same benefits. Additionally, citizens might not punish officials for enacting policies that are harmful in the long run but whose effects are, in the short-term, salubrious and, hence, make voters "feel good." Tax cuts that provide higher levels of current disposable income at the expense of producing growing, long-term budget deficits are a good example of such policies. Of course, this kind of an analysis makes a number of assumptions regarding the capacity of government to know the effects of its decisions.

Using standard assumptions, Downs posits the following thesis (Downs, 1960: 544): rational ignorance among the citizenry leads governments to omit certain specific types of expenditures that would be there if citizens were not ignorant. Downs terms the condition as one of "rational political ignorance." The condition arises because parties must know what voters want if they are to form policies that maximize voter support. For voters to maximize benefits, they must know what the parties offer. Of course, information for officials, parties, and voters is costly, both in terms of time and resources. Since the respective impact of individuals' votes are very tiny, individuals have little incentive to invest in information. Rational behavior generally leads to pervasive political ignorance.

Downs identifies three types of political ignorance (Downs, 1960: 544–45)—"zero ignorance" (perfect knowledge of all actual or potential budget items and their associated costs and benefits); "partial ignorance" (knowledge of all actual or potential items, but not all costs and benefits); and "preponderant ignorance" (ignorance of most or all actual items in budget as well as their associated costs and benefits, with possible exception of only those items of most immediate interest or concern). For Downs then a "correct" budget is one that emerges from the democratic process if both citizens and officials had perfect information (zero ignorance) regarding budget items and their associated benefits and costs.

Budgets are too small or large, depending on the mix of ignorance regarding benefits and costs. If perception of costs is high while benefits are low, then budgets might be smaller since the electorate reacts more strongly to costs. If benefits are perceived more strongly than costs, then the public sector budget might be too large. In the public sector, the costs of benefits are usually separated. Taxes are paid at times that are different from when benefits are received. In the private sector, payment usually occurs at the time of sale. For many public services, a *quid pro quo* basis for paying is not feasible (they are public goods) and in other cases there is a desire to provide redistribution of income for the less well-off. Payment for public services is generally enforced coercively, rather than through the apparent voluntarism of the private sector. We invariably pay for some things that we do not want. In short, "no one ever attains marginal equilibrium in his dealing with the government" (Downs, 1960: 548). Put differently, only a few individuals are likely to have the cost of government equal exactly the benefits they receive. More often, individuals bear greater public service burdens in comparison to the sum of satisfaction received from government goods and services.

Downs then makes the most important statement in his argument: Everyone is paying for some public goods and services he does not want. "Therefore, every citizen believes that the actual government budget is too large in relation to the benefits he himself is deriving from it." (Downs, 1960: 550). The budget is too large in the sense that these "excess" government expenditures supported by individuals could be invested in consuming private benefits or other public benefits of greater utility.

Governments in democracies tend to provide benefits that voters are aware of and willing to support by voting for the party that produces the benefits. Governments will not provide benefits that might provide utility if the recipients are unaware of them or do not support public officials for producing them. The remoteness of public transactions makes it difficult for many voters to assess the benefits of government expenditures (remoteness in terms of time, space, or comprehensibility; Downs, 1960: 551). Examples of government actions with such remote benefits include foreign aid, environmental protection, resource conservation, social security, and education. Governments in democracies can be expected, then, to spend less on producing remote, less visible benefits. The uncertain nature of government benefits also reduces the tendency of voters to perceive benefits and reward suppliers. Consequently, individuals are more aware of the government's policies affecting their role as income-earners rather than as consumers of government benefits.

Because Downs believes that taxes will inevitably be more apparent than benefits, budgets are expected to be smaller. That is because taxes are perceived in an immediate sense whereas future benefits are not. The result is, according to Downs, that *the forces for increasing government spending are not as great as those restraining government spending*. In contrast to most other public choice theorists, then, Downs suggests that democratic politics will produce a *smaller* public sector than might otherwise be the case.

CHAPTER 5

FOR WHOM THE EVIDENCE MATTERS: CONCLUSIONS REGARDING THE CAUSES OF GOVERNMENT GROWTH

People have always been ready to produce theories and explanations of government size and growth. They have been even more prepared to *judge* the consequences of government size and growth. There has been far less interest in the task of empirical examination and suitable data gathering in order to determine which explanations and theories and evaluations are more or less consistent with the evidence. In this chapter the major work that has been done to test theories and explanations of government growth and size is appraised. The purpose of such an evaluation is not to referee among the various accounts of how government has grown. A review of competing theories and explanations about social phenomena is not like a zero-sum game, where support for one explanation necessarily detracts from another.

What makes things so difficult, however, is that while some factors are important in explaining certain aspects of government scale and growth, they are less important or even irrelevant for other features. For example, the amount of growth in government expenditure for a particular program in a given year might be the consequence of the growth in revenues and the condition of the economy at the time. In this case, economic factors and the process of "incremental" decision making might best account for the growth in that program in that year. On the other hand, the factors that account for why the laws authorizing the program were enacted or subsequently eliminated might be altogether different. Wagner's Hypothesis posits a positive relationship between advancing economic development and the size of government. This linkage might be more suitable among developing countries, those transforming from agrarian to nonagrarian societies. In economically advanced societies the connection is more complicated, and it is clear that in many cases it is economic *decline* that stimulates the growth of government as governments introduce programs to supplement incomes or remedy economic malaise.

Even when focusing on the United States exclusively during the post-World War II period, differences in the causes of change in government size are apparent. In the words of one analyst, "Our analysis would imply that the mechanisms shaping the rates of expansion of the tax state in advanced industrial democracies vary over time" (Schmidt, 1983: 281). During the 1950s, a period of very rapid growth in the size of the U.S. government sector, the advance of government was fueled by the growing increments of government revenue made possible by the tax systems and tax tolerances of World War II and the Korean War. On the other hand, the expansion of government programs in the 1960s and 1970s was nurtured by robust economic growth. In contrast, after the mid-1970s government growth slowed considerably, and the management of economic decline became a dominant theme.

The growth in government size must be seen as the result of an amalgam of causes. The effort here is devoted to synthesizing the existing research, rather than merely dismissing some factors as "less important" than others. In the words of a prominent student of government size:

> ... [W]e should not expect any one cause to determine the growth of all the major programmes of government. We should ask: Under what circumstances and to what extent do a variety of political, economic and social structure influences affect the programmes that do most to determine the size of government in the aggregate? (Rose, 1985: 25)

Or, as Berry and Lowery (1987: 97) state in their account of government size, "Given the vast scope of the phenomenon being explained, the size of government in the postwar era, it is naive to expect any one of these single-factor explanations to work."

WAGNER'S HYPOTHESIS

As explained earlier, Wagner has claimed that the social pressures and infrastructure requirements that result from economic progress engender a variety of government advancements into previously private matters. One can find extensive treatments of Wagner's hypothesis regarding increasing government activity. Obviously the secular growth of modern government activity in the past four centuries has been concurrent, more or less, with great economic advances among the world's nations. Of course, the pace of government growth regarding social welfare expenditures and the regulation of economic activities has been largely a development of the past 150 years. It is clear that modern governments have become more involved in previously private matters not only as a function of economic progress but also as a consequence of economic decline. As Cameron found in his 1978 comparative study of modern government growth, increases in public sector involvement were not related to economic growth, but, instead, to downturns and recessions. Indeed, some of the most important government initiatives and programs in the United States occurred during the Great Depression (1932–40) and some of the deeper recessions in the post-World War II period as counter-cyclical efforts. Additionally, among the less developed countries (LDCs), the evidence regarding the relationship between government sector size and economic growth is rather muddied in the twentieth century. There are a number of LDCs that have experienced rapidly growing economies (e.g., Singapore, Thailand, and Indonesia), but whose public sectors, relative to those of less rapidly growing LDCs (e.g., Egypt, Algeria, and Zaire) are smaller. It also seems that places like Indonesia, Thailand, Malaysia, and Taiwan are today experiencing considerable growth in government involvement in the economy because of the severe economic downturns in those nations brought about by the financial crisis of 1998. In any case, Wagner's formulation is expressed at such a general level that one can find substantial evidence for his ideas, as well as a number of exceptions.

Furthermore, Wagner's hypothesis is too deterministic, without explicating the kind of mechanisms, processes, and behaviors that produce more government in the context of economic growth. Flora and Alber (1981) do attempt to provide just such a set of explanations. They describe how economic progress was historically associated with industrialization and urbanization, which, in turn, produced working class mobilization, the development of worker-based political parties, parliamentary democracy, widespread suffrage, and, consequently, greater government involvement in social welfare (accident, unemployment, retirement, and health insurance), as well as greater international, hence, military competition. The combination of democratic participation and the advance of capitalism contributes to the growth of government (Flora and Heidenheimer, 1981: 22). It might be necessary to tailor theories of why government grows to the stage of economic development that is being discussed. Does the relevance of Wagner vary between advanced societies and LDCs? While for many LDCs there might very well be a positive relationship between government growth and economic progress, in advanced societies the relationship can be both positive and negative. In advanced nations, when there have been very rapid and large increases in personal income, citizens have often been tolerant of increases in expenditures for public services. However, the interplay between economic growth and growth in the public sector is inverse when economic downturns also increase government size in the form of counter-cyclical spending and the provision of income security benefits and other social services.

Gould (1983) also points out that among advanced, democratic societies revenue constraints, taxpayer resistance, the desire to substitute private for public consumption, and ideology might function to weaken the relationship between economic advance and government growth. As the data have indicated, in the latter half of the nineteenth century, when the U.S. economy grew very rapidly and was transformed from agriculture to industry, government sector growth was, contrary to what Wagner's Hypothesis would have predicted, flat. The promotional role of the U.S. government in terms of such activities as land grants and open immigration, support of research and development in mechanics and agriculture, and the federal government's modulation of the demand for greater social regulation, was substantial. The fiscal growth of government during that period, however, was very slow. This languid pace of growth in budgetary terms was, in substantial part, due to a strong political and ideological antagonism to government intrusions into private sector matters. This aversion was militantly expressed in a generalized, if not uniform, federal court resistance to government efforts to control or regulate business behavior or economic conditions (Twiss, 1942).

PEACOCK AND WISEMAN: THE DISPLACEMENT EFFECT

Recall that the work of Peacock and Wiseman was partly a response to the Wagner Hypothesis. In addressing some of the shortcomings of Wagner, Peacock and Wiseman were particularly concerned about the fact that in western democracies there does develop, from time to time, a resistance to the growth of government on economic and ideological grounds. Resurgent conservative ideology and popular resistance to higher taxes and "more" government have served as constraints on government in the United States and even among nations with traditions of expansive governments (Dogan, 1995; Eulau and Beck, 1985; Maier, 1987; Manza, Hout, and Brooks, 1995). In light of the oscillation between periods of growth in government and resistance to its expansion, Peacock and Wiseman conceptualized the step-like pattern for government growth described previously.

Of course, public sector rates of growth have rarely been completely flat, especially during the twentieth century. It is more plausible to think of growth in government in terms of periods of relative stability, interrupted by periods of rapid growth, followed by periods during which government growth again slows down. An examination of the pattern of public sector growth in the United States before the 1960s reveals that prior to the Great Depression there were long periods of relative stability regarding the scope and burden of government. Although it is rare that government size remains on some clearly identifiable plateau, when measured by any of the usual indicators of government size (e.g., spending/taxing relative to GNP or personal income), there are periods when such growth is relatively slow. There are other times when the pace of growth accelerates rapidly before once again slowing. War, economic decline, and occasional instances of unusual prosperity in the face of highly particularized political factors can account for the step-like increases in government growth.

In the U.S. experience it was clearly the impact of war that propelled increases in the scale of government. After the late eighteenth century, the preparation for and conduct of war tended to accelerate the growth of government. This propensity accelerated with the advent of total war, involving the mobilization of mass armies and national resources, as well as capital. In contrast, prior to the modern era, war often tended to accompany the disintegration of regimes and societies. Prior to the War of 1812, between 1792–1811, federal government spending ranged between $5 million and $11 million. Moreover, most of the period was marked by large budget surpluses. Receipts were sometimes twice the level of outlays. For example, in 1807 federal government receipts were $16 million, while outlays were $8 million. With the onset of war, outlays skyrocketed in 1812 to $20 million, an increase of 150 percent over the previous year, peaking at $35 million during 1812. Although there were concurrent increases in the revenue-extracting efforts of the federal government, these efforts did not match expenditures, as reflected in the very large budget deficits incurred during the War of 1812. During 1814, receipts were only about 31 percent of the outlays. With the end of the war, outlays and revenue seeking by the government declined dramatically. However, taxes and spending did not decline to the pre-war days.

There are similar patterns for other periods of war as well. For example, in the years preceding the Civil War, federal government receipts and outlays in 1850 and 1860 were $56 million and $63 million respectively. The zenith of federal government receipts was $558 million in 1866, while expenditures peaked during the final war year (1865) at $1.3 billion. Outlays and receipts by the federal government declined consistently thereafter until the late 1870s, although they never declined to the prewar levels. By 1870, federal government receipts were 633 percent above the 1860 level, while expenditures were 390 percent above the 1860 level. The much higher revenue figure and huge surpluses reflected, of course, the commitment to retiring Civil War debt.

Clearly, in all the wars in which the United States was involved, including the very short Spanish-American War in 1898, one can discern spurts of expenditures, followed by less dramatic increases in revenue. There can be little doubt that wars precipitate substantial accelerations in government taxing and spending to new levels. As Arthur Stein remarks in his documentation of the domestic consequences of war-making on the United States, "... war makes the state" (1980: 4). Although social welfare involvements and business regulation account for significant increases in the cost and burden of government, these have been much less important catalysts than have been military commitments. Insofar as restraining the size and growth of government is an important objective, then avoiding the need for military expenditures seems to be the most effective strategy.

War and military tension create a number of opportunities for government to increase, as a result of the public's support of war aims or its greater willingness to support higher taxes and government intrusion. In his marvelous exploration of the latter half of the nineteenth-century civic affairs in the United States, Keller remarked on the impact of the Civil War on the growth of government:

> The war created new possibilities of power for civilian as well as military authority. Men in public office, traditionally hamstrung by localism, individualism, and hostility to the state, now found it possible to assert themselves as never before. (1977: 17)

As recounted by Keller (1977), the Civil War not only involved more and new forms of government revenue extraction and spending, but also involved government intrusions in the form of newspaper censorship, military draft, suspension of habeas corpus, and a very large increase in the federal civil service (200,000 personnel in 1865, compared to 40,000 in 1861).

Historically, the cost of military preparedness and the conduct of war have most forcefully and extensively driven the growth of government. Since the 1930s, however, economic decline and business regulation have also played a role in fostering government growth. Consider the response of receipts and outlays in the severe economic downturn of the early 1890s with the Great Depression. In the decades preceding industrial take-off and prior to the Great Depression, economic downturns tended to produce declines in both revenue and spending, although revenues tended to decline more rapidly than spending, hence producing deficits. The economic malaise of the 1890s illustrates the situation. In 1890, federal revenues stood at $403 million, with expenditures at $318 million. Generally declining revenues sank to $306 million by 1894, while expenditures grew to $368 million, resulting in the first deficit in nearly thirty years. Even while in deficit, however, the economic malaise of the 1890s resulted in declining revenues and expenditures. Economic slowdowns prior to the Great Depression seemed to operate as a drag on government growth. The data support the Wagner hypothesis that economic progress is associated with economic growth. Other studies of the business cycle also support the idea that economic decline prior to the Great Depression slowed, even reversed, the tendency for the public sector to grow (Hansen, 1964).

With the Great Depression, however, the pattern changed dramatically. Federal government receipts plummeted between 1929 and 1932. On the other hand, federal outlays grew rapidly after 1932, as a host of government programs were initiated as part of the effort to manage economic decline, social distress, and political unrest (Barber, 1985; Conklin, 1967; Keller, 1963; Leuchtenburg, 1963; Olson, 1988; Fraser and Gerstle, 1989). In the post-Great Depression era, economic decline posed the kind of disturbance to the system that engendered new opportunities for government intervention. Of course, government involvement in the United States to deal with economic decline was not as extensive and fundamental as it was in a number of other nations where, for cultural, political, and institutional reasons, the government's role in dealing with economic distress was more fundamental and developed much earlier. For example, the differences in general social welfare and income security policy among the United States and a number of Western European nations are well-documented (Flora and Heidenheimer, 1981; George and Wilding, 1976; Rothstein, 1998). Even focusing on problems less dramatic than national health insurance or public financing of maternal leave reveals the same pattern of belated and anemic public involvement in the United States. As Hooks revealed in his 1984 comparative study of factory-closing policies in the United States, France, and Sweden, the government response in the United States was the slowest in coming and the least concerned with equity and social welfare questions, and it imposed the fewest requirements on businesses closing their facilities in communities.

Economic distress and military threats, then, have come to operate as displacement factors, supplanting existing notions of what is acceptable in the way of government involvement and government burdens. New taxes are accepted, and more intrusive actions by government agencies are tolerated, if not celebrated (assuming they are directed at enemies of the nation or the perpetrators of economic decline). From time to time, however, great upsurges in economic well-being and unique political factors might also produce new public commitments, which in the long run will produce relatively greater levels of government. For example, the administrations of Presidents Kennedy and Johnson involved expensive new ventures in social welfare in the areas of education, hunger, housing, urban redevelopment, social and medical insurance, research and development in science, and income inequality. These programs packaged in the labels of Kennedy's New Frontier and Johnson's Great Society were enacted during the years when unemployment was lowest and real, disposable income grew most rapidly. In fact, real disposable income grew more during 1965–69, when most of the major social welfare programs were enacted, than in any other previous five-year period after World War II (Hibbs, 1987: 91). Additionally, in 1964 President Johnson was running for presidential election, with the nation's sympathy bestowed on him in the aftermath of the assassination of President Kennedy the year before. Moreover, President Johnson's opponent, Arizona's Senator Barry Goldwater, was an ineffective candidate whose very conservative message and call for greater military expenditures and anticommunist militancy seemed out of touch with this period of liberal dominance. The result was a landslide victory for President Johnson and the election of a host of very liberal Democratic congressmen who provided critical support for the passage of the Great Society agenda. The combination of general prosperity and unusual political circumstances served to provide the basis for new government initiatives that would prove to be among the nation's costliest domestic policy burdens (e.g., the currently skyrocketing costs of federally subsidized health care and social security).

Evidence for the inspection effect discussed by Peacock and Wiseman is plentiful. Certainly as regards the growth effects of war, demobilization tends to reduce government size from the peak levels during the war, although the subsequent point at which government stabilizes will be substantially higher than before the war. However, the inspection effect is most clearly observable during the late New Deal period (1937–38) and the conservative, antigovernment resurgence in the United States. A similar pattern occurred throughout the major advanced democracies starting in the late 1960s, accelerating in the 1970s, and culminating in the ascendance of conservative governments. In the United States, this was associated with the election of Ronald Reagan, although his predecessor, Jimmy Carter, also campaigned on a strong antigovernment, efficiency-in-government theme in the presidential election of 1976.

Since the Nixon administration (1968–74), the rate of government growth has decelerated dramatically, once inflation, population growth, and demographic changes have been taken into account. On a variety of fronts, it has become increasingly difficult to sustain real increases in government spending at all levels of government. A pervasive resistance to higher taxes, spending, and deficits have overlaid all domestic politics, making it extraordinarily difficult to initiate major new programs and involvements by government, especially those government programs that are associated with the traditional social welfare agenda (Hoover and Plant, 1989). Slade Kendrick, an observer and scholar of government growth during a period of rapid government spending increases in the immediate post-Korean War environment, anticipated this mass resistance to further impositions from government:

> The question therefore arises whether, under the new conditions, past experience will be repeated. The increase in civil expenditures generally, unlike the increase in military outlays, is not under the compulsion of necessity. Nor does such an increase have the inevitability of the larger interest payments that follow an increase in the national debt or of the greater outlay for discharged veterans as their numbers mount. There is choice, and accordingly the pressure for additional civil functions is less. Moreover, resistance to larger expenditures increases: Taxes already high will become higher, or if the financing is by borrowing, the consequences of adding to an already great debt will give pause. These factors are likely to

moderate or to check previous tendencies toward a relatively greater
growth in civil than in military outlays. (1955: 54)

It is hard not to admire this instance of a fairly accurate prediction of what tran-
spired in the post-World War II decades. It remains to be seen if the budget surpluses at the federal and state levels of 1998 will fuel sustained federal
increases. The Clinton-Gingrich-Lott budget of 1998 seems more like an one-
time infusion of preelection opportunism than some blue-print for a new period of government growth. Whether or not the prosperity of the late 1990s
continues and budget surpluses are sustained will have a lot to do with continued support for more public spending.

Insofar as Peacock and Wiseman and those using related approaches
(Hibbs, 1987) focus on the topography of government growth, their accounts
and explanations have substantial support in research. Moreover, the emphasis on the premier role of military preparedness and the conduct of war in
driving the scale and growth of government seems generally supported by the
data. Undoubtedly it is the military threat and wars that have the greatest capacity to displace public resistance to new taxes and government involvement in previously private matters. Scholars also acknowledge, however, the
relatively less important but still significant role of economic distress in driving government into new areas. And, finally, there is the occasional convergence of public generosity, made possible by a combination of affluence and
receptive political institutions (e.g., the 1964–67 Great Society initiatives).

DEMOCRATIZATION AND INSTITUTIONAL CHANGE

It is very difficult to define precisely a statistical relationship between growth
in the public sector and increased democratization of society. However, as
discussed in previous chapters, there has always been and there continues to
be concern that making officials more responsive will produce more government activity than is, according to certain standards, desirable. The fear of democratization has been present from the start. Contemporary conservative
critics of government size and policy contend that it is the empowering of
groups and the "activism" of such institutions as the courts that have made
government grow more rapidly.

The role of democratization in expanding the size of government is taken
pretty much as a given. In his fascinating account of the impact of the demand
for security, Aharoni declares:

> ... [A]s political power has spread from a few aristocrats and property
> holders, with the advent of universal suffrage, to take in—at least poten-
> tially, the entire adult population, the relative power of propertyless work-
> ers, women, and minority groups, has increased, and they have learned

that they can achieve more for themselves using the political clout available to them than they would if they relied solely on the market. The result has been growing demands on government, no longer simply to protect the poor and the unfortunate or to supply free education or subsidized transportation; but for a complete array of insurance services to all citizens against almost every hazard. (1981: 3)

But is this really the case? It is difficult to deny that the public sector in the United States is probably larger and has grown more rapidly because governing institutions and the governing process have been substantially democratized. The case is an easy one to make. Surely if only white, male, Christian, and European-stock members of society counted as citizens, the public sector would be smaller than it is today. But there are still difficulties for those who might otherwise assume a kind of uniform equity in public benefits. Aharoni (1981), like so many others, seems to imply that democratization has resulted in uniformly greater protection claims for all citizens against nearly every form of unpleasantness and hazard. Undoubtedly government is more responsive to the modestly endowed segments of the population as a consequence of democratization, and, therefore, there is a larger public sector than would otherwise be the case. Yet examination of those social programs for which the government exerts the greatest effort indicates that it is not the lower classes who have benefited the most. Rather it is the middle classes that have gained the most in the social welfare field (Page, 1983). As none other than Tullock, a leading conservative thinker, has said:

> The income transfer system in the United States is very largely a transfer from one group of middle class citizens to another. We do help the poor to some extent, and we do to some extent take money away from the wealthy, but both of these are minor phenomenon compared to the transfers within the middle class. (1983: 26)

Examining the flow of benefits in terms of which segments of society receive what, one readily sees that redistribution from the wealthy to the poor simply does not occur or, if it does, only at very modest levels.

PUBLIC CHOICE EXPLANATIONS

MARKET FAILURE

From a public choice perspective, government intervention in previously private matters results from the failure of the market to optimize allocations and distributions of goods and services. As previously discussed, the types of market failure are legion. Although there is considerable disagreement concerning what the appropriate collective response to market failure should be, to the extent that public choice theorists acknowledge a need for government intervention, it is under the conditions associated with market failure.

Clearly the advance of industrialization and its attendant social processes—for example, urbanization, frictions among social classes, and environmental stress—generate many instances of market failure in the public choice sense of the term. Particularly in the U.S. experience the market failure view of government growth has empirical appeal. Initially in the United States, so much was left in the hands of private parties: Street maintenance, water supply, policing, highway construction, and welfare were, in fact, largely private matters. Notwithstanding the tendency to ignore the fact that governments *did* do a variety of things, even during the colonial era, the role of the regime, whether at the local, state, or federal levels, was minimal at the start of the nation (Bourgin, 1989; Hughes, 1977). In this sense, then, the history of the United States can be charted in terms of its movement from a system of governing in which the powers and responsibilities of the regime were very limited to one in which government has grown to quite significant proportions in terms of the resources it requires and the range of things that it does.

Moreover, many of the activities of U.S. government did appear to come about in response to such market failures as free-rider problems and externalities. The pattern became rather clear in the emergence of a host of standard government activities, including fire protection, street maintenance, building regulation, land use regulation, public health regulation, and primary and secondary education. The processes of industrialization, with the increases in population size, density, and heterogeneity (Wirth, 1938), all increased the probability of market failures occurring. With the massive increases in population density came homes and other structures closely packed in space. Built in a relatively unregulated environment, such structures were designed to minimize costs to owners, with respect to materials and resources. Structures built at the least cost and at the highest density led to a number of problems, all of which could be assessed as major externalities and market failures. Consequently, building structures were more likely to erupt in flames, and since the density of housing was very high, these fires tended to spread very rapidly. Additionally, tenement housing for less affluent urban residents was unsanitary and poorly ventilated. Consequently, respiratory and other communicable diseases spread more rapidly in these circumstances. Government's role in providing fire protection, regulating land and buildings, and monitoring, policing, and promoting public health were all outgrowths of the externality effects of the industrial city.

There is a kind of superficial fit between the pattern of government growth in such areas as public health and safety, education, public works and sanitation, and land/building regulation and the market failure analysis. Thinking of the growth of government in terms of the mechanisms of public choice, however, is somewhat strained. The notion of market failure and government intervention suggests a kind of rational decision-making structure that monitors the relevant jurisdiction for market failure events. Of course, such market failures are assessed for their magnitude, the costs of managing them properly, presumably calculated relative to their cost. When intervention by government is seen to produce some gain, then, *voila*, there is a new increment of government!

Things are not usually that neat, however. In the United States, for example, many years of stupendous losses due to urban conflagrations preceded the development of the professional, government-employed fire department. Staggering losses of life due to the ravages of fires, floods, and such diseases as typhoid fever, pneumonia, tuberculosis, and flu, made worse by the unsanitary and densely packed city populations, persisted for decades before the emergence of effective public health departments. Tragedies like the Triangle Shirtwaist fire in New York City (Llewellyn, 1987) galvanized reform and contributed to the institutionalization of the urban planning profession, as well as to the enactment of building codes. The combined effect of pervasive externalities produced new government involvement, *but not as an expression of a rational model calculus*. Rather, the externalities produced intervention only when these were sufficiently dramatic and persistent to propel individuals and groups into the political process. Indeed, the nature of negative externalities, by virtue of the harm and costs they impose, provides the basis for legitimating the demands for some remedy. *Their mere existence, however, is no explanation for something being done about them.* Whether, in fact, remedies are forthcoming through government policies is a matter of politics, demand-making, responsiveness, and a host of other characteristics that affect the nature of policymaking.

The question here is whether the idea of market failure provides an adequate empirical account of why government has grown. The conclusion is that market failure as an empirically grounded idea makes some sense, particularly for the United States. Notwithstanding the desire for public choice theorists to see public policy decisions guided by the idea of market failure, efforts to manage externalities quite often fail or do not receive notice from authorities, despite their technical or rational appeal. When government does intervene to remedy an instance of market failure, then, it must be seen as a possible consequence of political processes, triggered by the externalities.

Similar issues apply in other instances of market failure. Problems of monopoly existed for decades and produced a variety of economic and political problems before they were addressed by government. The fact of monopolies in railroads, steel, sugar, and in other areas of the U.S. economy was not the propellant that drove government into the arena of monopoly regulation. Monopolistic abuses existed for years before legal doctrine and political force transformed citizen disquiet with monopolies into public policy. Government responses regarding consumer protection, particularly in the nature of information required for health, safety, and welfare were not forthcoming, despite the long-standing evidence of hazards in the food and drug industries.

MEDIAN VOTER MODEL

Recall that the median voter model of government growth posits that, given a certain distribution of income (where the median income is substantially below the mean income) and the existence of vote-seeking officials, the public sector will grow. The further implication is that the growth is a reflection of cultivating support among the less affluent by sprinkling them with public programs that supplement their incomes. This is a view rooted in the reaction to the nineteenth-century rise of socialist movements and leftist political parties. It was believed that democratization would permit the formation of worker-based political parties, which would then enact radical changes and introduce greater equality and social justice (Przeworski, 1991). As Meltzer and Richard explain it (1978), those voters whose incomes are below the *median* income level will, if rational and self-interested, seek to increase income by taxing income above the average (mean) level and redistributing the resulting revenues to voters below the median income level. The consequence is, then, according to Meltzer and Richard:

> Large government thus results from the difference between the distribution of votes and the distribution of income. Government grows when the franchise is extended to include more voters below the median income or when the growth of income provides revenues for increased redistribution. It is not necessary that everyone vote or that each voter fully perceive the effect of his vote on society. A voter need only choose the candidate who promises net benefits; majority rule does the rest. (1978: 116)

As will be shown, there is much skepticism about the median voter model. Scholars have indicated (Esping-Anderson, 1985) that under certain circumstances, government officials, elected and otherwise, do have an interest in and sympathy for the needs of the less well-off and they are often motivated to act on that impulse.

Although working-class political parties and large, powerful labor unions have advanced the redistributive causes of those below the median income level, it has been observed by a plethora of scholars that the conditions for successful political competition by the poor are especially infelicitous in the United States (Esping-Anderson, 1985; Frey, 1971; Olson, 1983; Tullock, 1976; Weatherford, 1983). The median voter model seems to have more relevance in other national contexts, even though a mini-industry has emerged to describe and offer explanations for the decline of class voting throughout the advanced industrial world (Dalton, 1988; Dogan, 1995; Manza, Hout, and Brooks, 1995). Notwithstanding the decline in class voting in the post-1970 period, there are reasons why other nations had strong working class movements reflected in political parties that moved working class and lower income agendas. Among these are the following: earlier experiences with government involvement in the economy; war and competition between antagonistic economic classes; more disciplined, worker-based political parties; higher levels of voting rates among those below the median family income level; and ideologies that are more supportive of the goals of social welfare. (Flora and Heidenheimer, 1981; Lybeck, 1986; Maier, 1987; Wilensky, 1981). Generally, then, empirical work has supported the hypothesis that the greater participation of the less affluent results in a growing public sector (Lindbeck, 1985). However, the degree to which the less affluent actually make such demands, and whether the growing public sector stems from responding to redistributive demands, varies among nations.

Perhaps the greatest exception to the median voter process can be found in the United States. Meltzer and Richard (1983) have tested their theory on U.S. data and claim to have found empirical evidence for the median voter model. Specifically, they have found that the ratio of mean to median income is positively related to growth in government expenditures for a variety of social welfare programs. That is, the higher the mean income is relative to the median income, the greater the growth in social welfare programs. As Tullock (1983), a *conservative* thinker, pointed out in his critique of the Meltzer and Richard work, the relationship between income distribution and changes in the public sector cannot be causally connected, since income distribution in the United States has remained relatively stable for a very long time. If one examines the post-World War II period, there is no evidence that there were major income distribution shifts during the time when real value-government transfer payments grew the most—that is, the time between 1945 and 1968. If welfare payments, then, reflect rationally motivated politicians seeking support through the provision of benefits to those below the median family income level, then one would expect such benefits to reduce the degree of income inequality. That issue will be discussed shortly.

There has been a fair amount of empirical work that bears on the impact of the process outlined by the median voter model. The results are rather mixed. For U.S. data, the empirical support for the median voter hypothesis is quite weak. Higgs (1987) specifically addresses the median voter model's adequacy in his history of public sector growth in the U.S. context. He refers to the median voter model as "The Political Redistribution Hypothesis" (1987: 12). Higgs concludes:

> The explanation fits the historical facts poorly. Extensions of the franchise apparently have had no independent effect on the growth of government, and the most dramatic extensions of governmental power have occurred in periods of stagnant or falling real civilian income, during the world

wars and the trough of the Great Depression. Furthermore, to assume that government always transfers income to lower-income recipients flies in the face of facts too numerous and familiar to require recitation. (1987: 12)

And in one of the most exhaustive reviews of the literature associated with the median voter model, Romer and Rosenthal declare:

The various studies we have reviewed have not provided strong, broadly based support for the median voter hypothesis. We found methodological problems that made tests of the hypothesis inherently difficult; and we found that the median voter models were inadequately tested against competing models. (1979: 162)

Although there are many among public choice theorists who rely on the median voter model to account for certain aspects of government growth, it is also the case that the model has a number of very stringent conditions for it to apply (Larkey, Stolp, and Winer, 1981: 181). There are three major reasons why, in actuality, there is such mixed support for the median voter model:

1. First, the conditions associated with maximizing the political influence of those below the median family income do not occur often in reality.
2. Second, the motivation and resources of those who resist the redistributive efforts of the less affluent are greatly underestimated by median voter theorists.
3. Third, the growth of the public sector has been associated with the success of the more affluent in eliciting programs to help them and secure their incomes.

The problem is especially severe in the United States, where working and lower class voting and political participation rates have plummeted more drastically than elsewhere (Burnham, 1987). Even when the ratio of mean to median income is related to government size, it is not clear whether the growth in government involves programs that do in fact redistribute income to the less affluent, at the expense of those whose incomes are above the mean. Simply because the ratio of mean to median income is positively related to the size of the public sector does not mean that the public sector has been growing due to the swelling of redistributive program budgets.

As the data have indicated, those who are of more modest income generally participate less in politics and have fewer resources to invest in demand-making and influence-generating activities. What causes the disparity among income groups is a matter of considerable dispute (Manza, Hout, and Brooks, 1995). Biased voting registration laws, declining personal efficacy among the less affluent, or declining party competition have been posited as explanations for the differences in voting rates among income and class groups (Burnham, 1987; Highton, 1997; Piven and Cloward, 1988).

Additionally, the median voter model suggests that voters are uniformly aware of the implications for their respective incomes of the views taken by individuals running for public office or the implications of the various proposals before important law-making institutions such as legislatures and courts. Again, the data tend to undermine the assumption that voters generally have knowledge regarding these matters. For much of the past thirty years, U.S. working-class citizens and less affluent citizens have sometimes supported political candidates and political parties that have *eroded* redistributive programs and cut services to the less affluent. Some observers and scholars, especially those on the left, claim that economic insecurity among working class and moderate income Americans in recent decades has resulted in scapegoating and denuding of programs designed for the very poor. Rather than turning attention to the more affluent or reacting to policies that have favored the affluent, much of the white, working class has either withdrawn from politics or voted more conservatively, evidently more concerned about issues such as prayer in schools, flag-burning, affirmative action, immigration levels, and gay rights than about pressing for a redistributive policy agenda (Piven and Cloward, 1988).

Perhaps the major flaw of the median voter model is its assumption that the mere existence of large numbers of qualified voters with incomes below the median family income level will translate into demands for redistributive policy on their behalf. If such a group, even a sizeable one, is characterized by lack of cohesion, insufficient levels of information regarding its group interests, and low rates of political participation, or preoccupation with supporting officials who will chase down illegal immigrants and propose constitutional amendments against flag-burning, then its needs might be given short shrift in the policy agenda.

The usual explanation for why the less affluent participate less frequently than do the more affluent has to do with the presumably greater resources and skills found among the latter. However, there are other social psychological reasons to explain why less affluent citizens might be less likely to seek redistributive benefits and why the more affluent would be more successful in resisting such policies. The median voter model assumes that the perceived value of a unit of redistribution is at least equal to the cost of redistribution. That is, a less affluent person is *ceteris paribus* just as motivated to seek a unit of redistribution as a more affluent person is to *resisting* such an act. But there are a number of reasons to believe that people are more likely to resist the loss of some currently held value than others are to seek some future, currently nonexistent benefit. Of course, one might assume that the marginal utility lost from each redistributed dollar is much lower than the gain to the recipient of such a dollar. However, such actions cannot be evaluated in isolation. Even though a rich person might not value the last $1,000 earned, he might react strongly to its being "taken away" from him through some redistributive act. The redistributive policy might represent a much greater loss than that represented by the market value of the money or even than the satisfaction gained by the recipients of the money. If the propensity to resist redistribution is greater than the propensity to seek redistribution, then one would not expect gaps between median and mean income levels necessarily to produce demands for redistributive policies. Organizing, lobbying, or otherwise investing in political activity that elicits redistributive policies requires longer-term commitments. All other things being equal, then, more affluent residents, who presumably are more sensitive to the benefits of long-term investments, are more likely to anticipate the burdens of redistribution as well as to be more inclined to resist such policies (Barry, 1970; Downs, 1960; Wilson, 1980). If it is assumed that (1) those from whom resources are taken are more likely to resist than the recipients are likely to demand, that (2) those who are more affluent have longer-term perspectives than the less affluent, that (3) the expression of demands and lobbying for redistributive policies is a long-term process, and that (4) the affluent are likely to pay for redistributive policies demanded by the poor, then it is plausible to infer that redistributive policies are likely to be successfully resisted by more affluent individuals who bear the cost of such policies.

There are lots of reasons to believe that affluent citizens will be more successful in eliciting policies that redistribute income from the less affluent to themselves. While the question of the net redistributive impact of public policy among various social groups is a complex, controversial matter, there are many scholars who believe that most distributive policies involve gains for the income groups above the median family income, often at the expense of those below (Best and Connolly, 1982; Downs, 1960; Edsall, 1984). Although it is possible to identify a number of important government programs that make critical resources and services available to some of the poor (e.g., food stamps and housing assistance), there are sound reasons to contend that government benefits for the more affluent (certainly above the median family income) are much more valuable. The total worth of mortgage interest deductions, social security payments, government procurement (especially defense and highway construction), government sponsored research and development, publicly subsidized reliance on auto-based commuting, land use policies that oversupply residential land use for single-family detached housing, or government support of higher education far exceed the dollar values of programs for citizens below the median family income.

A simple examination of the data for tax expenditures underscores these points. A tax expenditure refers to the "outlays" of public funds through reductions in the tax liabilities enacted in the tax laws. When tax expenditures benefit particular groups, the cost of these benefits must be provided either through higher taxes on others or through larger deficits when governments believe, for one reason or another, that they cannot confront their citizens with higher taxes or reduced services to finance the revenue cuts. Tax expenditures, then, represent publicly provided benefits to particular categories of taxpayers, implemented through various forms of exclusions, deductions, favored treatment, deferrals of tax liability, and deductions. Table 5.1 reports the estimated dollars associated per tax return for several categories of deductions. The 1992 data are the average values per return filed, and the pattern presented in these tables have not changed. Together, the three deductions for real estate, state-local income taxes and personal property taxes, and mortgage interest accounted for nearly $80 billion in 1992 revenue foregone by the public through benefits in the Internal Revenue Code. The mortgage interest deduction alone accounted for approximately $41 billion, an amount far greater than any direct expenditure for housing assistance to the poor.

The pattern depicted in Tables 5.1 and 5.2 is generalizable to almost all benefits provided as tax expenditures—the higher the income the greater the benefit provided, at least in absolute dollar terms. In the case of the real estate tax deduction, for example, those in the income level category of $200,000 or more receive, on average, $1,990 per return filed—nearly seventeen times the amount of those in the less-than-$10,000 category and over fifteen times that of the average tax return in the $10–20,000 category. For the mortgage interest deduction, those individuals in the $200,000 or greater range received, on average, a tax benefit of $5,425, which is nearly thirty-one times greater than the average tax benefit for those in the less-than-$10,000 category and sixteen times that of the individuals in the $20–30,000 category. It also appears that the most lucrative benefit for the wealthiest tax filers is the deduction for state and local income taxes and for personal property taxes.

Even so, it is possible that the wealthiest taxpayers might only be getting a higher share of tax benefits as a reflection of their proportionately higher

TABLE 5.1   MEAN TAX EXPENDITURE
FOR VARYING INCOME CATEGORIES, 1992 (DOLLARS)

INCOME CATEGORY	REAL ESTATE TAX DEDUCTION	STATE/LOCAL/ PERSONAL PROPERTY TAXES	MORTGAGE INTEREST DEDUCTION
Less than $10,000	$125	$25	$176
$10,000–19,999	131	70	339
$20,000–29,999	142	123	435
$30,000–39,999	207	247	755
$40,000–49,999	229	558	821
$50,000–74,999	368	579	1338
$75,000–99,999	588	1059	2120
$100,000–199,999	878	1950	3461
$200,000 or greater	1990	9081	5425
Average Tax Return	**455**	**968**	**1574**

Source: U.S. Congress, Joint Committee on Taxation. *Estimates of Federal Expenditures for Fiscal Years, 1993–97.*

TABLE 5.2   SHARES OF TAX EXPENDITURES BY INCOME CATEGORY,
RELATIVE TO SHARE OF TAX LIABILITY

INCOME CATEGORY	PERCENT OF TOTAL INCOME TAX LIABILITY	PERCENT OF REAL ESTATE TAX DEDUCTION	PERCENT OF STATE/LOCAL/ PERSONAL PROPERTY TAX	PERCENT OF MORTGAGE INTEREST DEDUCTION
Less than $10,000	0.0[1]	0.0	0.0	0.0
$10,000–19,999	1.7	0.6 (–1.1)[2]	0.1 (–1.6)	0.6 (–1.1)
$20,000–29,999	6.1	2.3 (–3.8)	1.0 (–5.1)	2.2 (–3.9)
$30,000–39,999	8.7	6.0 (–2.7)	3.4 (–5.3)	6.2 (–2.5)
$40,000–49,999	9.4	7.0 (–2.4)	7.3 (–2.1)	7.5 (–1.9)
$50,000–74,999	10.8	27.1 (6.3)	19.6 (–1.2)	28.1 (7.3)
$75,000–99,999	12.4	19.5 (7.1)	15.8 (3.4)	19.7 (7.3)
$100,000–199,999	15.2	21.5 (6.3)	21.3 (6.1)	24.1 (8.9)
$200,000 or greater	26.0	16.0 (–10.0)	33.1 (7.1)	11.7 (–14.3)
Total in Millions	**$475,577**	**$12,227**	**$26,062**	**$40,767**

[1]Each cell is the percentage of the total. Tax returns with income of less than $10,000 did not have a tax liability.
[2]Figures in parentheses are the difference between that income category's tax liability and its share of the total tax expenditure in that category.
Source: U.S. Congress, Joint Committee on Taxation. *Estimates of Federal Expenditures for Fiscal Years, 1993–97.*

contribution to tax revenues. Table 5.2 explores this issue by comparing the share of the total tax benefit for each of the three tax expenditures discussed previously, relative to the share of total tax liability of the income category.

For example, the total amount of 1992 dollars paid in income taxes was approximately $476 billion. The second column lists the proportion for each income category of the total income tax paid. Those filing returns of $200,000 or more, for example, paid about 26 percent of the total. Those in the less-than-$10,000 paid nothing, and those in the $10–20,000 range paid about 1.7 percent of the total. Those in the $40–50,000 range paid about 9.4 percent of the total. If the tax benefit system were neutral, then each group would receive about the same share of a tax benefit as its share of the tax liability. If, as is the case, individuals in the $40–50,000 range paid 9.4 percent of the total income tax, then they would receive, in a neutral scheme, 9.4 percent of the benefits. But a review of the data indicates that is not the case. Far from being neutral with respect to these important tax benefits, the pattern suggests generally that individuals earning more than $50,000 received a disproportionately greater amount of the benefits. There is a notable exception, in that the *highest* income groups did not receive a greater share of the tax benefits for real estate deductions or deductions for mortgage interest; indeed, their share of these benefits was considerably less than their actual contribution to the total tax collections. The exception for the wealthiest income tax returns was the greater share that the $200,000 income category had of the state/local income tax and personal property tax deduction. Not a surprising result, since the rates for such taxes, while not exceptionally high by historical standards, tend to fall most heavily on the wealthiest individuals. The filers in the $50–199,999 categories tend to receive greater shares of tax benefits. Individuals in the lower income categories receive far fewer of the tax expenditure benefits.

The amounts of money involved are quite significant. For example in the mortgage interest deduction column, families in the $100,000–199,000 range paid 15.2 percent of the total tax liability. Applying this percentage to the value of the mortgage interest deduction would produce a tax benefit to this category of individuals of nearly $6.2 billion. This group, however, received 24.1 percent of the mortgage interest deduction benefit, with a value in 1992 of $9.8 billion, nearly $4 billion more than if the tax benefit were proportional to the tax liability.

Most income maintenance or social welfare programs (educational, job, retraining, income) for the less affluent population rely on *direct* payments, administered by government agencies. After all, the poor have little, if any, deduction on their income taxes, assuming they have any tax liability at all. Benefits administered as direct payments through government agencies are generally directed to families and individuals with lower incomes, with affluent individuals often denied any benefit altogether. Tax benefits seem, on the other hand, to stand everything on its head, so that the benefits quite often tend to increase as income increases. Clearly, the entire tax expenditure system operates to blunt, perhaps even reverse, whatever modicum of progressivity there is in the tax code or in the implementation of social welfare programs.

MEDIAN VOTER MODEL AND INCOME DISTRIBUTION

If the median voter model accurately accounts for government growth, then more income redistribution would result—that is, with greater democratization and political participation, there would be a lessening of income inequality. Regarding the United States, however, the data do not suggest such a pattern. In a wide variety of different kinds of works and studies, the overall conclusion is that income distribution in the United States has changed very little. The conclusion is less controversial when regarding income before taxes and in-kind government transfers (e.g., food stamps or housing vouchers) (Verba and Orren, 1985: 11). In fact, according to Williamson and Lindert (1980), the greatest accentuation of income inequality in the United States occurred during the early decades of the nineteenth century and the end of the Civil War. This was occurring at the same time as the participation of those below the median level was increasing more rapidly than at any time in U.S. history. Income distribution patterns seem virtually unrelated to the democratization of society or the increased participation among the poor. Recent episodes of redistributive politics made some very modest increases in the share of income among the less affluent, although the trend was very brief. As the data indicate, the redistributive impulse has probably been stabilized or even reversed slightly by the policies of recent years (Osberg, 1984). In fact, Pechman and Mazur (1985: 36) claim that before tax and transfer income has become "more unequal over the past three decades. Thus the share of society's product accruing to the top 15 percent of families has increased steadily over this period." While transfer payments between World War II and 1980 increased dramatically, their effect has been at best to moderate the tendency to greater income inequality. But even the redistributive consequences of transfer payments have been reversed by a number of cutbacks since the election of Ronald Reagan in 1980. As one observer of national politics stated as he watched the surging conservative tide in the early 1980s:

> The cuts, eventually enacted into law, eliminated the entire public service jobs program, removed 400,000 persons from the food stamp program, eliminated the Social Security minimum benefit, and reduced or eliminated welfare and Medicaid benefits for the working poor. Residents of public housing would be required to pay 30 percent of their income toward rent instead of 25 percent. A formula allowing welfare recipients with part-time jobs to retain a portion of their benefits as their income increased, providing an incentive to work, was eliminated. The cuts, in effect, chipped away at the margin of the most marginal incomes. (Edsall, 1984: 17)

These cuts were followed later in the summer of 1981 with the Economic Recovery Act of 1981, which substantially reduced the tax burdens of the most affluent segments of the population. Considering the subtle benefits received by the more affluent through the tax code, lavishly generous treatment of the capital gains on homes, public support of higher education, and the like, it is safe to conclude that the main effect of transfer payments, such as they are, is to prevent economic inequality from becoming far more severe. More recent data indicate that inequalities of income and wealth worsened well into the 1990s (Braun, 1991; Maxwell, 1990; Peterson, 1994; Ryu, 1998; Weinberg, 1996). With respect to wealth, the bottom 90 percent of the population owned 51 percent of private wealth in 1976; by 1995 it dropped to 29 percent. During this interval, the top 1 percent increased its share of private wealth from 19 to 40 percent. Between 1979 and 1993, the bottom fifth of the families in the United States experienced a 17 percent decline in real income, while the top fifth celebrated an 18 percent increase. The bottom 60 percent of families also lost real income during this time (Wolff, 1996). If public sector growth were reflecting the dynamics of the median voter model, then there should have been some significant leveling of income. That has not happened, not by a long shot.

IDEOLOGY AND THE CONSTRAINT ON MEDIAN VOTER REDISTRIBUTION

Another important reason for not finding the degree of increased government involvement in welfare and redistribution that can be reasonably expected in the United States is the constraining influence of the dominant ideology. Regarding questions of government's role in alleviating poverty and minimizing inequality, the United States has always operated in a climate that emphasizes individualism, personal responsibility, and the right of those blessed with advantages to savor and use them (Kluegel and Smith, 1986). This is in marked contrast to such places as Sweden, Norway, or the Netherlands, where citizens prefer to minimize inequality and expect the state to intervene quite substantially in satisfying the preference for equality (Szirmai, 1988).

Although Americans today accept a much greater social welfare role for government than Americans did in the periods prior to the Great Depression, in relative terms Americans still place great emphasis on characteristics of individuals in explaining the causes of poverty and prefer quite limited roles for government intervention. In their extensive study of a national sample of U.S. residents over the age of 18, Kluegel and Smith (1986: 104–13) found the following:

1. Fifty-three percent disagreed that "More equality of income would allow my family to live better."
2. Fifty-one percent agreed that "Incomes should *not* be more equal since the rich invest in the economy creating jobs and benefits for everyone."
3. Fifty-three percent agreed that "If incomes were more equal, life would be boring because people would all live in the same way."
4. Seventy-three percent agreed that incomes *cannot* be made more equal since it's human nature to always want more than others have.
5. Sixty-four percent agreed that "Incomes *should* not be made more equal since it's human nature to always want more than others have."
6. Sixty-eight percent agreed that "Making incomes more equal means socialism, and that deprives people of individual freedoms."

Even during periods of marked economic distress, the tendency for the less affluent *not* to place demands on the affluent is quite marked. In the midst of the Great Depression it was very difficult for the Congress to raise taxes at all, and it was especially difficult to raise taxes against the incomes of the most affluent. Leff (1984: 15) observed in his study of fiscal policymaking in the Great Depression era that "… the quest for business confidence tended to paralyze the tax system or force it into regressive channels." The economic malaise, stagflation, economic decline, or however one wants to characterize the economic conditions of the previous two decades, has not produced increased demands for social welfare and calls for more equal distributions of income. Rather, particularly in the United States, for good or ill there has been a diminishing of the power of organized labor, a proliferation of wage and benefit concessions among workers, a decline in support for the parties of the left, a dismantling of or severe cutbacks in social welfare programs, an increase in tax benefits for the affluent, putatively investing classes, and a stiffening resistance to new government programs. Even while there is a moderation of the antigovernment sentiments that have dominated American politics for over a decade, political opportunities to affect income distributions have not been used very often, or, when used, the effort has failed.

CONCLUSIONS REGARDING MEDIAN VOTER MODEL

When reality is not consistent with the assumptions of the median voter model, then a number of consequences predicted by the model are simply not likely to occur. Perhaps most important are those factors that facilitate or impede the political participation of those below the median family income. The greater their level of political involvement in the context of democratic institutions, then the more likely the government is to grow in the arena of social welfare and redistributive policies (Mueller and Murrell, 1985; Barry, 1970; Peltzman, 1980). Median voter model proponents are sensitive to these issues, in all fairness, although they might not always appreciate the extent to which the median voter model assumptions fail to jibe with reality.

Also important is the tendency for median voter model proponents to dismiss the importance of ideology in constraining demand making by the less affluent. Especially for the United States, data indicate that even those below the median family income tend to accept the relatively high degree of inequality in income. Moreover, there is a general repugnance with the idea of radical equalitarianism, along with substantial public grants of legitimacy to the system of unequal rewards (Kluegel and Smith, 1986; Ladd and Bowman, 1998). Indeed, a system of unequal rewards is seen as an important component in the proper working of the system. Consequently, it is not merely those at the top who naturally defend the status quo, but many of the less blessed of the society often support the basic workings of distribution as well.

In market systems, even median voter model adherents note that the less well-off will only impose taxes on the wealthy to the point at which the gains are greater than the cost. If the redistributive burden increases too much, then the share going to the less well-off might decline. In other words, the less well-off might only be getting a greater share of a shrinking pie. If the pie begins to shrink too much, then increasing the share might only result in a spiral of even more declining benefits. Consequently there is, in a sense, an optimal point of redistribution, beyond which those below the median family income would not find it in their interest to go. Even in western industrial nations like Sweden, Norway, or the Netherlands, the top quintiles of the population still have disproportionate amounts of income. The

Netherlands, for example, is seen as having an equitably distributed personal income structure. But even there, in the late 1960s and early 1970s, the top 20 percent of households represented 36.3 percent of income and the lowest 20 percent had only 9.1 percent. For that period, the comparable U.S. figures were 42.1 percent and 4.9 percent respectively (Osberg, 1984: 27). Regardless of how well-mobilized the working class or the poor, no matter how long it has been since the welfare state was initiated, no matter how extensively social welfare programs have been supported, it is doubtful that one can find any advanced, western democracy where the top income groups still do not account for substantially disproportionate amounts of wealth. Whether that is good or bad, whether this should be celebrated or mourned, is not easy to decide.

BUREAUCRATIC DETERMINISM MODEL

The claim that public employees and government agencies become an important source of government growth has also been a matter of some empirical study. The short version is that most empirical work provides little support for the claim that the public sector, through its public employees (bureaucrats), becomes an independent force for more government. Recall Niskanen's central claim (1971: 30): "Although the nominal relation of a bureau and its sponsor is that of a bilateral monopoly, the relative incentives and available information, under most conditions, give the bureau the overwhelmingly dominant monopoly power." This power is then presumably used for the aggrandizement of agency size and budgets.

With very few exceptions (Ferris and West, 1996; Huang and McDonnell, 1997), this scenario tends not to be supported by the evidence. Murrell (1985) finds that public employment, rather than being a cause of government size, is a reflection of left-wing voting and greater political participation among the poor, especially during periods of unemployment, which tends to be associated with increases in government employment. In their extensive analysis of the causes of government growth, Berry and Lowery (1984) conclude that the bureaucratic determinism model of government growth is unsupported. Rather, they claim that some amount of public sector growth relative to the private sector is due to the relatively higher labor intensiveness and lag in productivity growth among public employees, not to any imperial impulse of public sector employees.

Weingast (1984) claims that Congress does control agencies by affecting turnover in the membership of agency management. Deregulation by Congress of a number of agencies, as well as congressional curtailment of agency activism, such as that of the FTC in the 70s, were accomplished by the Congress. Weingast's extensive analysis of congressional control of federal agencies incites him to conclude that a belief in agency dominance "seems clearly inconsistent with the evidence" (1984: 183–84).

Breton and Wintrobe (1975) list a number of conceptual drawbacks to the main thesis of bureaucratic determinism. These include the following:

- Opposition parties in democracies would take advantage of the appearance of "excessive government" if incumbents merely allowed bureaucrats to have all they wanted.
- Managers of agencies are not always interested in increasing the size of their agency.
- Incumbent politicians have the power and incentive to control agencies.
- Individual well-being or income of a particular employee, including managers, of an agency are not necessarily related to the agency's size or overall budget.

Additionally, Courant, Gramlich, and Rubinfeld (1979) observe that there is considerable mobility among private sector actors, who retain the right to leave the jurisdiction. This option will restrain high and rising taxes required to finance growing agencies or higher pubic employee salaries, since it is in the interest of public employees to retain their revenue base. Such behavior is especially noticeable in state and local government contexts, where the exit and relocation options are more feasible. Indeed, there is a growing body of literature that theorizes about the impact of globalization and mobility of capital in limiting the growth, even requiring the diminishing, of public sectors (Sassen, 1996). Private sector voters do respond to public sector costs and have incentives to force down the level of public employment. And, in perhaps the most extensive conceptual critique of the bureaucratic determinism approach, Dunleavy (1985: 300) claims that adherents of the bureaucratic determinism approach fail in these respects:

- They posit overly general, poorly defined definitions of bureaucrats' range of values.
- They assume that bureaucracies are idealized, hierarchical line agencies in which the monolithic values of agency management can be imposed on agency personnel.
- They assume that systems of agencies have agencies whose behavior is independent of one another; that is they ignore inter-agency rivalry.

The implications of these observations for the bureaucratic determinism approach are rather devastating. For example, in most agencies no one public employee has complete control. Increases in the budget have the characteristics "of a collective rather than an individual good" (Dunleavy, 1985: 301). If no one agency person can control the agency, there is no necessary control over whether a budget increase can be rendered into an increase in the individual utility of agency personnel. A budget increase might merely increase the workload but not the salary of agency managers or line personnel.

Whether a budget maximizing approach dominates agency personnel (hence creating pressure to increase the size of government) is a function of a number of things. These include the degree of agency hierarchy, the distribution of bureaucrats in terms of rank, the relative influence of different ranks of bureaucrats, the costs of advocating budget increases, and the degree to which individuals are motivated by nonpecuniary aspects of public employment (e.g., status, job security, or performance of certain activities such as soldiering, policing, or dealing with certain public [i.e., collective] problems). In any case, Dunleavy lists a number of plausible situations in which agency budgets are not likely to be increased, where agency personnel might not find it individually rational to seek budget increases, or where budget increases do not imply any benefits to agency personnel. Finally, Dunleavy concludes his analysis by claiming that if bureaus are narrow-budget maximizers then the pattern of government growth should be dominated by the growth of large-line bureaucracies. He finds that this is not the case (Dunleavy, 1985: 301–28).

Of course, government agencies do not come and go the way private firms do. The popular view is that public agencies never disappear, that they persist beyond the time when their usefulness or worth has dissipated. Perhaps it is more difficult to cancel public programs and agencies. Certainly they do not merely disappear the way a private firm that is losing money does. But when agencies seem to persist past their useful time, it is not usually because of "agency domination" or the unique power of the bureaucratic classes to resist the desire for efficient government management. There are other social actors, both private and public, that participate in the prolongation of life among "useless" agencies. Included in those things leading to agency persistence is only one factor that might be viewed as reflecting agency domination (Kaufman, 1976: 3–11):

1. Statute provides longevity or difficulty in elimination or oversight.
2. Congressional committees and staff develop protective relationships with agencies.
3. Agencies benefit from the inertia of budgetary incrementalism, where policymakers find it is rational to accept agency budgets and deal only with increments.
4. Agency personnel are motivated by idealism to defend an agency and even to expand it.
5. Supporters of an agency and its clients seek to protect and enhance the agency.

Nevertheless, in perhaps the most extensive analysis of why government organizations "die," Kaufman (1976) does find that there are a significant number of agencies that disappear, even though more persist than disappear. But in this case, the exception disproves the rule, since the bureaucratic determinism model provides no explanation for the cessation of a public agency or program. Kaufman lists a number of hazards to the life of public agencies, including the following:

- Inflexibility and inability to respond to changing conditions
- Competition among other agencies
- Outlived usefulness after accomplishing mission
- Public disaffection or public hostility due to agency mistakes or scandals
- Enemies of agency work to undermine it
- Hostility of administrations with different priorities or values
- Reorganization by heads of departments

The evidence regarding the bureaucratic determinism model provides little support for the claim that in advanced, western democracies public employees or their managers cause substantial growth in government. Public employees are motivated by more diverse sources of happiness than is often understood: Public agencies are not as autonomous as believed; competition among agencies is more intense than is realized; and the utility-enhancing properties of higher budgets are exaggerated and often simply wrong. Bureaucracies can create pressures and demands for more government, of course, but the conditions under which that happens are far more limited than proponents of bureaucratic determinism suggest.

Even though empirical support for the bureaucratic determinism model might be lacking, it has at least one very important value: to point out that public agencies very often act like any other economic actor—that is, public agencies and their respective personnel can best be understood as utility maximizers whose interests and that of the individual taxpayer might diverge, even conflict. The primary error of public choice uses of the bureaucratic determinism model is to suggest that budget and personnel maximization are the *only* sources of agency satisfaction. The evidence suggests, however, that the matter is more complex. There are even situations in which public agency personnel might receive satisfaction in the decline of government and growth.

Explanations of Government Growth: Some Conclusions

Large scale societies, organized in complex systems of social, economic, cultural, and physical terms are likely to have correspondingly large governments. As suggested in Wagner's Hypothesis, the displacement of simpler forms of social organization (agrarian) by more intricate arrays of economic, demographic, social, and cultural overlays produces the need for greater government involvement. The evidence for this is quite clear, and regardless of whether there is debate over the legitimacy of some increment of government activity—some program, expenditure, law, or sanction—for most analysts the greater size, interdependence, and impacts of economic progress engenders greater government involvement. As economic progress and populations are more vulnerable to the side-effects of production, distribution, and consumption, so too has government played an increasing role in managing the flows of these "externalities" or "spillovers." Democratization, too, has played a role. As the number of actors and interests increased in the political process, and as officials have become more responsive to the demands placed on them, so has the range of policy demands increased as well. This has inevitably increased the role of government in dealing with previously private matters.

The role of government in the economy has been an explicit item on the policy agenda since the founding of the Republic, when the Federalists and their opponents contended over government's role in promoting economic growth. However, the electorate has always tended to reward and punish its officials on the basis of judgments about the performance of the economy, even when the capacity of officials to make major impacts on the economy is limited. But as a number of scholars have pointed out (Lewis-Beck, 1988; Higgs, 1987; Hibbs, 1987; Tufte, 1978; Alt and Chrystal, 1983), officials act on the assumption that their political well-being is decisively shaped by the performance of the economy. Democratization has, therefore, contributed to the melange of forces that have combined to propel government into a greater role in the economy and society as a whole. How much any one of the factors discussed and studied has contributed to some given level of public sector size is an almost insurmountable estimation problem.

However, in choosing from among the many contributors to government growth, *war-making or preparing for war stand out as the premier causes of government growth*. Ordinarily, public resistance to greater taxes or intrusive government occurs and constrains government growth. The threat of war displaces these ordinary barriers to government growth. One important way for individuals interested in limiting government growth to achieve their objectives, then, is to avoid the conditions that give rise to real or imagined military threats.

CHAPTER 6

BLAMING GOVERNMENT: THE CASE OF ECONOMIC PERFORMANCE

By the late 1960s there had developed in the United States a strong critique of government efforts to deal with the problems of social injustice and inequality. The contention was that government efforts to remedy poverty, redistribute income, regulate business, and generally smooth out the business cycle were at best fruitless and wasteful. At worst, it was claimed, government activity had imposed so heavy a burden on the productive elements of society that too little untaxed private capital remained to supply the investment and purchasing needs of the economy (King, 1987).

Beginning in the late 1960s, the United States and many of its competitors in the industrial world experienced various symptoms of economic malaise. Inflation and unemployment in tandem (so-called stagflation), sometimes at double-digit levels, as well as very slow increases in economic growth, seemed to afflict the entire economically advanced world. A number of nations experienced actual declines in the aggregate standard of living. In the United States, moreover, a pervasive sense arose that the nation was slipping as a world economic leader. As the nation's productivity lagged, manufacturing activity seemed to disappear and economic downturns seemed to be deeper and more persistent. The result was a rise in conservative political strength, including not only the rise of Ronald Reagan and Margaret Thatcher in the United States and Britain respectively, but also the resurgence of more conservative political parties in such democratic socialist bastions as Norway and Sweden, where conservative governments came to power, in some cases, for the first time in decades (Esping-Anderson, 1985: 97–99; Dalton, 1988).

The emergence of conservative political strength in all of these places was strongly associated with (1) dissatisfaction regarding the decline in income and economic growth, and (2) the increasingly popular view that the rapid public sector growth in the post-World War II period, especially with respect to social spending, was the cause of these economic reversals (King, 1987). Since the electorate in the advanced economies often associated declining economic fortune with the apparently large and rapid increases in public sector burdens, it was not surprising that voters were often convinced that the premier remedy for economic difficulties was to constrain, if not shrink, the public sector. Growth in government, measured in terms of both the level and increase in government spending and taxing, was seen as the cause of such things as high inflation, high unemployment, meager levels of capital formation, slow or declining rates of economic growth, and lowered productivity. But what is the evidence regarding the association between indicators of government size and economic growth?

GOVERNMENT SIZE, GROWTH, AND ECONOMIC PERFORMANCE

Much of what occurs among individual nations in the advanced industrial world happens in tandem. In other words, changes in unemployment, inflation, and economic growth tend to happen together. For example, as inflation raged in the 1970s in the United States, so it did elsewhere. As unemployment in the United States began to soar in the early 1980s, so it did everywhere in the advanced economic world (Bean, Layard, and Nickell, 1986; Eulau and Lewis-Beck, 1985; Norpoth, Beck, and Lafay, 1991). Perhaps more so in the United States and Great Britain, but in lesser degrees almost everywhere in the advanced capitalist world, voters seemed to blame these economic difficulties on the growth and size of their respective nations' public sectors.

With respect to some of the specific indicators of economic performance, there is no evidence that nations with large or more rapidly growing public sectors experience less robust economic performance. In fact, the United States, when compared to such nations as West Germany, France, the Scandinavian countries, Austria, Belgium, or the Netherlands, has among the smallest public sectors. Table 6.1 reports total government spending in the United States and other nations (including transfer payments as well as final consumption expenditures).

The data indicate not only that the United States has among the smaller public sectors, when measured as total spending relative to total GDP, but also that its public sector has grown slowly when compared to other nations. In 1970, total government spending was 30 percent of GDP, and in 1998 total government spending was estimated to be 31.6 percent. Compared to other nations, then, the United States has a relatively small public sector, when measured in this way. Insofar as government size and growth

Table 6.1   Total General Government Outlays as a Percent of GDP

Country	1970	1975	1980	1985	1990	1995	*(Est.)* 1998
Sweden	42.8	48.4	60.1	63.1	59.1	65.6	59.6
France	38.3	43.4	46.1	52.2	49.8	54.3	53.9
Denmark	30.0	na	na	na	54.5	56.3	52.5
Finland	38.5	37.6	38.1	43.8	45.4	57.9	51.7
Belgium	41.5	50.8	57.0	61.0	53.6	53.8	51.6
Switzerland	36.7	na	na	38.5	40.6	46.5	50.3
Austria	37.6	44.3	47.1	50.3	48.6	52.5	49.9
Italy	19.0	41.5	42.1	51.2	53.6	52.7	49.5
Netherlands	34.9	50.2	55.8	57.1	54.1	51.3	47.5
Germany	38.3	48.4	47.9	47.0	45.1	49.5	47.4
Portugal	19.8	28.5	23.6	40.9	41.9	46.0	45.7
Norway	34.9	39.8	43.9	41.5	49.7	47.6	44.7
Canada	34.1	39.2	39.6	46.0	46.7	46.5	41.6
Greece	na	27.9	30.4	42.9	48.2	47.4	41.3
Spain	42.8	24.3	32.2	41.2	42.0	44.8	41.3
United Kingdom	30.0	44.4	43.0	44.0	39.9	43.0	39.2
Japan	19.0	26.8	32.0	31.6	31.3	35.2	35.6
Australia	na	31.4	31.4	36.5	34.8	36.2	34.6
Ireland	na	na	48.2	51.0	39.0	38.0	34.5
United States	30.0	32.8	31.4	32.9	32.8	32.9	31.6
Turkey	na	na	na	28.7	27.9	26.5	23.6
South Korea	na	na	19.3	17.6	18.0	20.5	21.2
Mexico	na	na	na	21.5	17.2	17.7	14.8

Source: *Economic Outlook*, no. 63, June 1998, OECD, Analytical Data Bank, 1998; the data in the table are based on final consumption expenditures.

are obstacles to economic progress, the United States should presumably have an advantage on that score. All other things being equal, if having a larger public sector is a drag on the performance of the economy, then the United States should be advantaged, since its public sector is so small in comparison. Only Turkey, South Korea, and Mexico, among the nations described in Table 6.1, are estimated to have a smaller proportion of the GDP represented by total government spending.

In the following pages, a number of standard aspects of economic performance are examined to determine whether there is evidence for the presumed inverse relationship: that as the size of the public sector *increases*, the performance of the economy *declines*. The level of total government spending as a share of GDP among economically advanced countries is used as a measure of government size. All of the findings discussed are not altered by using other measures of public sector size (e.g., size of the public employee workforce, level of tax burdens, amount of transfer payments, or final government consumption expenditures).

CAPITAL FORMATION

Capital formation growth rates are important because they presumably reveal something about how competitive and efficient an economy is likely to be. Greater capacities to generate GDP per hour of labor are connected to higher rates of capital formation. If the data supported a clear or simple relationship between the size of the public sector and growth in capital formation in the manner suggested by critics of government size, then we would expect growth rates in capital formation to be slowest among the nations with higher public sectors. In fact, as Cameron indicated (1982), after 1975 the countries with the highest public sectors seemed to suffer steeper declines in net capital formation rates than the nations with smaller public sectors, *although declines were occurring among all the countries.* As the data in Table 6.2 indicate, however, nations with large public sectors are represented at both the higher and lower ends of the capital formation spectrum. During the 1960–95 period, Norway, Finland, and Austria had capital formation rates higher than a number of nations with smaller public sectors. The United States, moreover, is near the bottom in terms of 1960–95 capital formation rates. The data indicate that the United States was trailing the nations with the *highest* public sectors for much of the time. The United States appeared to lag considerably for the entire 1960–95 period. For the data reported here, the rate of capital formation for the United States seemed highest during the 1974–79 period, and even then the United States was tied for the lowest rate among the nations described in these data. It is not possible to explore the role of capital formation growth in the performance of the economy here, but it is true that public sector size has been called an impediment to growth in the rate of capital formation. The data seem to indicate that differences in rates of capital formation growth are not very strongly related to public sector size. It is also striking to find that no matter what the relationship between the public sector and the rate of capital formation, the United States often trailed considerably behind nations with larger and smaller public sectors. It is probably unwarranted, then, to suggest that the problems of capital formation in the United States can be explained simply by the size of the government sector or the level of taxation, both of which are, in the United States, relatively small in comparison to many U.S. competitors and peers.

NATIONAL WEALTH AND INCOME

The conventional indicator of economic progress for cross-national comparisons is Gross Domestic Product. Table 6.3 (on page 120) reports the mean growth in GDP over the 1960–95 period with the nations arrayed on the

TABLE 6.2 AVERAGE ANNUAL GROSS FIXED CAPITAL FORMATION
AS A PERCENTAGE OF GDP AMONG OECD NATIONS

COUNTRY	1960–73	1974–79	1980–89	1990–95	1960–95
Japan	32.6	31.8	29.1	30.0	31.0
Norway	27.8	32.7	27.0	20.7	27.2
Greece	27.6	28.1	24.1	21.3	25.7
Switzerland	28.1	22.8	24.6	23.4	25.5
Finland	26.4	27.3	25.0	18.7	24.9
Australia	25.5	23.7	24.3	20.9	24.1
Austria	24.8	24.5	22.2	23.5	23.8
Spain	24.1	24.5	21.1	21.7	22.9
Italy	24.6	24.1	21.4	18.3	22.6
Netherlands	25.6	21.5	20.1	19.8	22.4
Germany	24.6	20.5	20.2	22.2	22.3
France	23.8	23.6	20.6	19.5	22.2
Canada	22.4	23.5	21.5	19.1	21.8
Sweden	23.3	20.5	19.4	16.7	20.7
Denmark	23.8	22.1	17.9	15.8	20.6
Ireland	20.0	25.1	21.1	15.6	20.4
Belgium	21.6	21.8	17.1	18.5	19.9
United States	18.4	19.4	18.9	16.3	18.3
United Kingdom	18.3	19.4	17.5	16.2	17.9

Source: Historical Statistics, OECD Economic Indicators, page 73.

basis of their average rate of GDP growth between 1960–95. The median
GDP average growth rate is 3.3 percent, and there is a fairly diverse mix of
nations above and below the median when considering public sector size
as a percentage of GDP. On the one hand, when considering nations with
public sectors that are greater than 50 percent GDP, only Italy has average
GDP growth greater than the median level of 3.3 percent. Of the seven other
nations with public sectors above 50 percent of GDP (when measured in
terms of total government outlays as a percent of GDP), none of them experienced during the 1960–95 period GDP growth above 3.3 percent (the
median GDP growth rate). In this sense there is some very modest support
for the idea that economic growth is related to public sector size, with large
public sectors producing slower GDP growth rates. Among the nations in
Table 6.3, those with public sector sizes above the median have an average
GDP growth rate of 3.1 percent for the 1960–95 period, while for those with
public sectors below the median (smaller public sectors) the average GDP
growth rate is 3.9 percent. On the other hand, among nations experiencing
below the median rates of GDP growth, there are also a number of nations
whose public sectors are well below the median. In any case, the average

TABLE 6.3   PUBLIC SECTOR SIZE AND GROWTH
IN THE GDP FROM 1960–95

COUNTRY	AVERAGE ANNUAL GDP GROWTH, 1960–95	PUBLIC SECTOR SIZE AS PERCENTAGE OF GDP, 1995
Japan	5.5	35.2
Ireland	4.4	38.0
Greece	4.2	47.4
Spain	4.1	44.8
Norway	3.8	47.6
Canada	3.8	46.5
Australia	3.8	36.2
Italy	3.4	52.7
France	3.3	54.3
Austria	3.3	52.5
Netherlands	3.2	51.3
Finland	3.1	57.9
Belgium	3.0	53.8
Germany	2.9	49.5
United States	2.9	32.9
Denmark	2.8	56.3
Sweden	2.5	65.6
Switzerland	2.3	46.5
United Kingdom	2.3	43.0

Source: Historical Statistics: OECD Main Economic Indicators, pages 50 and 70.

GDP growth rates of the nations above the median in public sector size and those below the median in government size are not very different. However, there are also nations with fairly small public sectors, such as Switzerland and the United States, with slower rates of GDP growth. These are not large differences, to be sure. A closer look at the 1960–95 period reveals that there are points at which nations with larger public sectors grow more rapidly than nations with smaller public sectors. An examination of U.S. GDP growth rates during the past five years shows that the United States has done exceptionally well as a nation with a relatively small public sector. Different intervals over the past forty years show no consistent relationship between the GDP growth rates and public sector sizes among a variety of advanced nations.

With respect to income and earnings, as mentioned, residents of all the advanced nations sometimes experienced slow growth and income declines. With respect to manufacturing wages, the United States lagged considerably behind a number of countries with larger and smaller public sectors. Table 6.4 illustrates the relatively poor performance of the United

TABLE 6.4   ANNUAL RATE OF GROWTH,
REAL MANUFACTURING WAGES AMONG OECD COUNTRIES

COUNTRY	1960–73	1973–79	1979–89	1989–95	1960–95
Italy	10.8	22.1	11.8	5.4	12.0
Ireland	10.9	20.0	10.0	4.5	11.0
Finland	10.4	14.2	9.5	5.1	9.8
France	9.3	14.9	8.2	3.2	8.8
Norway	8.8	12.6	9.3	3.9	8.7
Japan	13.5	11.8	4.1	2.5	8.5
Belgium	9.5	12.5	4.9	3.1	7.5
Germany	8.9	7.2	4.3	4.9	6.6
Canada	6.1	11.6	6.3	3.0	6.5
United States	4.7	8.6	4.6	2.8	5.0
Switzerland	6.2	4.9	4.1	3.5	4.9

Source: OECD Historical Statistics, Main Economic Indicators, pp. 100–101.

States regarding *growth* in the hourly earnings of workers in manufacturing when compared to most of the countries included in these data. Table 6.4 illustrates that the United States trailed in the growth of hourly manufacturing wages for much of the post-1960 period. It might be that the U.S. economy was growing more in other sectors, hence the focus on manufacturing wages might underestimate wage growth in the economy as a whole. Table 6.5 illustrates that the United States has generated fairly modest increases in GDP per person employed, which might also account for some of the lagging salary growth in manufacturing services. It is possible, too, that lagging salaries and incomes can shed light on the increased levels of resistance to public sector growth. The data described in Table 6.4 reveals how, since the mid-1970s, there has been virtually no real growth in median family income in the United States, with the late 1970s and early 1980s experiencing the most severe post-World War II decline in family income. Although

TABLE 6.5   PERCENT CHANGE IN REAL GDP PER PERSON EMPLOYED

COUNTRY	1870–1950	1950–60	1960–73	1973–79	1979–89
France	1.9	4.4	5.5	2.3	2.0
Germany	1.5	6.9	5.4	2.7	1.5
Japan	1.6	5.7	9.3	2.8	2.6
Netherlands	1.4	3.4	5.4	2.1	2.2
United Kingdom	1.4	2.2	3.9	1.3	1.9
United States	2.3	2.3	2.6	0.2	0.7

Source: OECD Main Economic Indicators, 1997; Maddison, 1984: 61 (for 1870–1973).

the family income level in 1986 had recovered to $29,458, that figure was still below the 1978 median family income level of $29,629. While there have been periods of gradually rising family incomes in the past twenty years, they have been accompanied by the income declines of the early 1990s. Family incomes in the United States have not grown at anything like the rates between the end of World War II and the mid-1970s.

UNEMPLOYMENT AND INFLATION

Another standard performance indicator is the level of employment. Figure 6.1 describes the relationship between the size of the public sector and the mean annual levels of unemployment between 1960 and 1995. The nations in Figure 6.1 are arrayed by the size of the public sector along with their mean 1960–95 unemployment rates. Although Keynesians would obviously disagree, conservative critics of government performance in recent years have

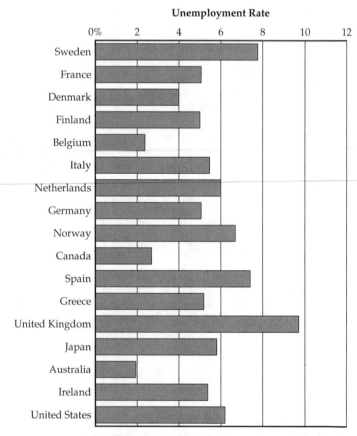

FIGURE 6.1   AVERAGE ANNUAL UNEMPLOYMENT RATE,
1960–95, ARRAYED BY SIZE OF PUBLIC SECTOR

argued that higher public sector levels should, over the long haul, produce greater unemployment because of slower economic expansion. The countries are arrayed from highest public sector to lowest, and if this relationship were to hold, then the heights of the bars in Figure 6.1 would decline as the size of the public sector declines. That seems not to happen, however. If there is a discernible trend it is a slight tendency for average unemployment levels between 1960–95 to rise as the size of the public sector declines. Still, there are some nations with larger public sectors but higher than average unemployment rates (Sweden), and nations with small public sectors and high unemployment, such as Spain, the United Kingdom, and the United States. There are, it seems, nation states with lower and higher unemployment rates on either end of the public sector size continuum.

Regarding inflation, Figure 6.2 suggests that, among the nations examined, those with larger public sectors are not likely to have distinctively higher inflation rates. The nation with the highest 1960–95 inflation rate is

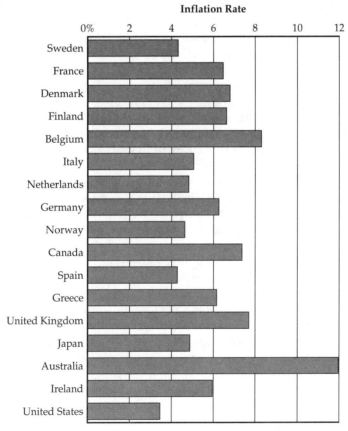

FIGURE 6.2   AVERAGE ANNUAL INFLATION RATE,
1960–95, NATIONS ARRAYED BY SIZE OF PUBLIC SECTOR

Australia, which also has among the smallest public sectors, at least as measured in terms of government spending relative to GDP (Cameron, 1988). The data indicate that there is very little relationship between the size of the public sector and any systematic cross-national patterns regarding either unemployment or inflation for most of the post-World War II period.

When government size is measured in terms of deficits, that is, government spending in excess of revenues, the findings are equally inconclusive. In the first place, most of the studies find no relationship between economic performance indicators and government deficits. As Nell (1988: 60) concludes, "... the two most common claims—that deficits cause inflation, and that they cause high interest rates—are clearly false, as a matter of fact." In the United States, during a time (1981–88) when federal budget deficits were roaring ahead at unprecedented peacetime levels, interest rates and inflation declined instead. Despite the persistence and growth of government deficits in the previous ten years, there seems to be no evidence of a deleterious effect of budget deficits on either inflation or employment levels (U.S. Congress, 1987). It is possible, of course, that depending on the time and the place and the level of government budget deficits, inflation, interest rates, and employment levels will be related. However, the data indicate that if a relationship exists, it is likely to be fairly complex and not a simple linear relationship, where each increment of deficits produces a measurable effect on interest rates, employment levels, and prices.

In Cameron's analysis of taxes, expenditures, and deficits across the advanced capitalist nations, he finds that "budget deficits account for a very insignificant portion of the upward drift in prices" (1985: 266). Indeed, he finds that each 1 percent of GDP attributable to government deficits accounted for less than two tenths of a percent change in prices. Although it is possible to find nations that experienced inflation surges along with growth in government budget deficits, it is also possible to find countries with large increases in deficits relative to GDP that had far-below-average inflation rates for given periods (e.g., Japan, the United States, and Switzerland). How governments finance deficits can have an important impact on inflation, but that is a different matter altogether. The conservative argument against deficits rests in large part on the claim that government budget deficits generally produce higher interest rates, which, in turn, produces less borrowing, less business expansion, less consumer debt, and a slowing, even declining, economy. The final consequence should, therefore, also include higher unemployment. But, since the data seem to find only an occasional relationship between government size, either in terms of spending or deficit levels and inflation rates, then the link between spending and deficits, inflation, interest rates, economic slowdown, and unemployment cannot be said to exist on some general basis. It is difficult to imagine that in any given country an uninterrupted, inexorably *growing* rate of inflation would not at some point produce dire economic consequences. However, the relationships clearly are not stable or simple and the range within which interest rates and inflation can rise without producing ill effects is variable and not easily predictable. It is not at all clear that dropping spending and deficit levels will necessarily reduce interest rates. The worldwide demand for capital and the fluidity of capital and money across national boundaries means that the worldwide demand for, say, dollars, also affects interest rates. That is why interest rates in the United States might remain high, relative to inflation, despite declining spending or lower deficits, if German money instruments offer high relative interest rates. Although the 1998 Asian economic crisis and the economic stagnation among key Latin American nations and a number of the nations of the former Soviet Union, not the least of which is Russia, have perhaps dampened world demands for capital, in the longer term, capital intensive economies are emerging throughout the world, particularly in the Pacific Rim (South Korea, Philippines, Singapore, Indonesia) and Latin America (especially Brazil, Chile, Argentina, and perhaps Mexico). It is not unthinkable that even Russia might turn things around, and other previously communist regimes will also enter world capital markets, driving higher the demand and, hence, the cost of capital. There is so much now affecting the demand for U.S. dollars and capital that it is reasonable to claim that the role of a given percentage increase in spending, public sector size, or budget deficits will explain less and less in the oscillation of interest rates in the nation. Put differently, it is possible for domestically generated pressures for inflation (e.g., government budget deficits or oscillation in agricultural harvests) to be negated by countervailing forces from outside the national boundaries. In the late 1970s, U.S. national deficits, which appeared relatively high, had much less to do with the period's growing inflation rates than did the impact of worldwide commodity prices, particularly those associated with imported petroleum. In the late 1990s, despite a plummeting unemployment rate and rapidly growing economy, the United States experienced little pressure on wages or commodities because of the Asian, Brazilian, and Russian fiscal crises as well as the worldwide drop in commodity prices, especially petroleum.

GOVERNMENT SIZE AND PRODUCTIVITY

Even though the United States has been experiencing very high productivity increases in the closing years of the twentieth century, for most of the 1965–95 period the concern was stagnant, even declining U.S. productivity, usually measured in terms of the amount of GDP produced per man hour of work. As in so many other economic performance indicators, the matter of measuring productivity is complex and often controversial. But the GDP/Man-Hour indicator is among the most widely used measures, and it is used here. As Table 6.5 (on page 121) indicates, the United States, along with other advanced economies, experienced a drop in the growth of productivity after the 1970s. The much slower rate of productivity growth at that time is often blamed primarily on the size and growth of government. As Maddison (1984: 73) explains, the argument for the deleterious impact of government size on productivity growth goes as follows:

1. High taxes reduce the incentive to work and save.
2. High levels of transfer payments lower the incentive to work at all or to work at the highest level.
3. High taxes increase investment and time in tax avoidance, leading to bartering and other features of underground economic activity.
4. Government provision of public services distorts efficient allocation of resources through overproduction of such services.
5. Government regulation of economic activity increases cost of production and distribution, adding to resource misallocation.

As Table 6.5 indicates, the United States is not alone in experiencing slower rates of growth in productivity, although it has lagged behind a number of countries for much of the post-World War II period. Even so, the most severe declines in this measure of productivity have been in Germany and Japan, although the United States has been notable in its slower productivity growth as well. Table 6.5 also reveals that while the United States has lagged in productivity growth rates for much of the post-World War II period, it is highly touted Japan that experienced the most severe drop in productivity growth rates in the post-1973 period. Moreover, Japan has a public sector that is relatively small in comparison to other advanced industrial economies. Throughout the 1990s Japan slipped increasingly into worsening economic performance. Several of the countries in Table 6.5 have better productivity gains in the post-World War II period, even while they have larger government spending and taxing levels than that of the United States (e.g., Netherlands). Like the other measures of economic performance, most studies of government size and productivity conclude that little loss in productivity can be attributed to the level of government spending. But the most extensive analyses of the interplay between public sector size and productivity changes conclude that there is no systematic relationship or, if one is discernible, it is relatively unimportant in comparison to the many other factors that affect productivity change (Maddison, 1984; Denison, 1983).

In the United States it has become popular to point to regulation of the economy and business as the cause of the economic difficulties of the 1970s and 1980s (Weidenbaum, 1977). On the one hand, it is difficult to assess the benefits relative to costs when it comes to regulation, and most assessments of regulation focus almost exclusively on the cost-generating aspects of regulatory policy. On the other hand, while there is disagreement regarding the overall effect of government regulation on productivity, there is agreement that the impact of these policies has declined since the sixties and seventies. Evidently, as the initial compliance costs have been incorporated, the longer-term costs of regulation have declined. In addition, it might be that the impact of government regulations derives more from the manner of implementation. Maddison, in his review of the evidence regarding the impact of government policy, claims that non-U.S. styles of regulation tend to be less detailed and less adversarial in nature, thereby reducing the costs of compliance and standards setting. The United States, he claims, has a tradition of adopting "an abrasive adversary posture in administering new rules, involving more litigation and less regard to business costs than in Europe" (Maddison, 1984: 76–77). So it might be that government regulation in the United States engenders greater costs and possibly hampers productivity as a consequence of the regulatory "style" and not because of the inherently adverse nature of regulation (Vogel, 1986).

Since capital formation is a critical component in generating productivity gains, the lack of capital formation in the United States is an important variable in this problem area. However, most studies attribute the low level of capital formation, at least to an important degree, to the low level of savings in the United States. Table 6.6 (on page 128) reports the level of national saving relative to GDP among advanced economies. The data indicate clearly the relatively low level of saving occurring in the United States. Although data indicate that the United States produces a low savings rate, compared to other nations, there seems to be a trend for all nations to be declining in their savings rates. After 1970, most of the advanced economies experienced declines in capital formation, savings, and investment. The experience of the United States, along with a number of other nations, disproves the idea that it is larger public sectors that contribute to lower productivity by diminishing savings and investment. Several of the nations with larger public sectors have also had substantial savings. Those nations rely heavily on consumption taxes (thereby discouraging spending), and, along with other policies, might in fact be encouraging saving. Norway, Austria, Netherlands, and France are among the higher savers and yet have large public sectors. On the other hand, the United States, Ireland, and the United Kingdom have relatively small public sectors and the lowest savings rates. Many analysts suggest that if the United States is to ensure consistently higher rates of capital formation, it has to adopt a number of government policies to help bring about the private sector changes in investment and efficiency that are deemed requisite to productivity improvements, including better education, incentives for personal saving,

TABLE 6.6   GROSS NATIONAL SAVINGS
AS A PERCENT OF GROSS DOMESTIC PRODUCT

COUNTRY	1960	1965	1970	1975	1980	1985	1990	1995	1960–73	1974–79	1980–89	1990–95	1960–95
Japan	34.7	33.4	39.9	32.5	31.3	31.5	33.5	30.8	35.7	32.8	31.7	32.8	33.6
Switzerland	31.1	31.8	34.2	29.0	27.1	29.8	33.1	28.4	31.6	29.3	30.1	29.3	30.4
Norway	26.2	27.7	28.6	27.5	30.3	30.4	25.2	27.0	32.0	28.6	28.6	25.4	29.4
Austria	27.7	27.1	30.1	26.1	25.6	23.0	26.1	22.5	28.5	26.4	23.7	23.7	26.0
Netherlands	30.4	27.4	26.9	24.0	21.0	24.5	26.2	24.6	27.6	23.5	23.1	24.5	25.1
Italy	23.9	22.8	24.1	19.8	24.8	21.8	20.0	20.5	27.6	25.5	21.8	18.7	24.1
Finland	29.2	26.9	30.7	29.0	26.6	22.9	22.9	19.7	26.0	25.2	23.7	16.6	23.7
France	25.8	26.6	27.2	23.9	23.1	18.8	21.5	19.7	26.6	24.9	20.4	19.9	23.5
Germany	29.9	28.4	29.9	23.4	22.5	23.1	27.8	21.3	25.3	21.2	21.2	21.8	22.9
Australia	24.7	24.4	25.7	24.3	22.2	19.3	17.1	17.3	24.8	22.7	20.3	16.9	21.9
Belgium	19.3	23.5	27.1	23.2	19.3	17.4	23.3	22.6	23.4	21.4	16.4	21.4	20.8
Canada	19.6	23.3	21.7	21.0	22.9	19.8	17.1	17.1	21.7	22.6	20.1	15.0	20.3
New Zealand	20.3	23.3	23.8	19.7	17.9	18.5	16.8	18.4	21.9	20.7	18.5	16.6	19.8
Sweden	24.3	25.9	24.5	22.8	18.4	18.1	18.6	16.6	23.8	19.9	17.3	14.8	19.8
Denmark	22.1	22.4	22.4	18.7	14.8	15.5	18.6	17.6	23.3	19.1	14.8	17.3	19.3
United States	19.6	21.3	18.3	17.2	19.3	17.2	15.7	15.8	19.9	19.5	17.5	14.9	18.3
Ireland	13.5	17.3	18.2	16.6	11.1	10.7	16.3	19.5	17.9	19.1	15.5	19.2	17.7
United Kingdom	18.1	20.2	21.9	17.1	19.1	18.6	15.5	13.9	18.9	16.8	16.6	13.4	17.0

Source: Historical Statistics, OECD Main Economic Indicators, 1997.

government inducements for research and development, more effective negotiation for favorable international trade terms, differential tax treatment for investment activity, and disincentives to spend for personal consumption. There is at least as much evidence that much of the poor economic performance in the U.S. economy stems from the lack of effective government involvement, rather than too much involvement (Reich, 1983). Some of these new programs might involve more expenditures (e.g., education and research and development), while others might involve negligible or modest resources (e.g., improved, more efficient implementation of government regulations; more effective bargaining with trading partners; or higher taxation on consumption).

CONCLUSIONS

Although there are possible reasons for criticizing the nature, substance, and scale of government growth in the United States, there is an irony in the emphasis that such criticism places on economic performance. Although much of the current criticism of government links public sector growth to the sometimes anemic economic performance of the U.S. economy, the data reviewed in this chapter suggest that the criticism is largely misplaced and often wrong. In fact, the entire advanced economic world has experienced important economic shocks and has experienced, at best, very modest economic improvements in the past twenty-five years.

Considering all the advanced economies, there seems to be virtually no single aspect of economic performance that is correlated in any direct, simple, or consistent way with standard measures of government size and growth, whether government revenues, expenditures, or deficits are considered. What is the nature and role of this criticism of government in the United States if the facts are that government growth has so little to do with explaining economic malaise? The criticism obscures the fact that the United States remains in fundamental ways the largest, most powerful single economy in the world. When in the post-World War II period its economy lagged, it reflected in an important way the catching-up of the rest of the world after the United States rose above the dust, smoke, destruction, and waste of World War II as the planet's economic behemoth. Despite its real suffering during the wars of the twentieth century, the United States was spared the enormously destructive costs of World Wars I and II, which laid waste to property, resources, and physical plants, not to mention dissipating vast segments of whole generations of human capital among the trading competitors of the United States. Economic decline in the United States might only have involved an accommodation to the rest of the advanced economies as they took on their more natural, more competitive roles in the international scene.

Notwithstanding the fact that conservative criticism regarding the economic effects of government growth in the United States is wrong, another troubling aspect of the criticism is the implicit notion that evaluations of government performance must rest exclusively or even heavily on its putative effects on the economy. It is not that economic effects are unimportant. Rather, among the economic effects of government actions, potential costs and benefits other than those associated with whether the United States is maintaining its competitive edge regarding some product or service must be considered. It is possible that some portion of economic difficulty in the United States is attributable to the substance and growth of government. However, there have been a number of important achievements of a "noneconomic" nature stemming from government involvement in previously private matters. It is worth altering the language of the discussion. It is important to remind ourselves that when we discuss what "the government" is doing, it is "us" we are talking about. Among democratic systems, in principle, the policies of government reflect the actions of citizens acting through the interests and organizations comprising modern, economically advanced systems.

Government policies are the mediated expressions of the great variety of social organizations comprising a respective society, even though policies might occasionally be unwise, unfair, or inefficient. But among the objectionable things that citizens do through their democratically organized institutions of governing, there are also great achievements. All of the following have produced great advances in social justice: the effort of citizens to improve the treatment of minorities; protection against abuse (including economic abuse) by private institutions; regulation for the purpose of protecting the environment or conserving scarce natural resources; and the taming of private power through our governing instruments. We are often depressed by the contemporary figures regarding crime and other indicators of social pathology. These can obscure the fact that, for the vast majority of citizens, the policies that their fellow citizens in past and current generations enacted through their democratic institutions have greatly enhanced the quality of life and the treatment they receive from one another. Fair competition among businesses, equitable conduct between employer and employee, civilized relations among races and ethnic groups, and greater regard for the stresses that are placed on the physical environment are still goals that require continued exertions and remain incomplete. Progress on these fronts has been substantial and brought about, in some important way, through the humane and creative intervention of citizens through democratic systems of governing.

Although the costs of social justice and greater equity ought to be considered, we should not automatically denigrate social progress as a result of faulty assessments of their impact on the cost of producing widgets. There might be grounds for criticizing the growth of the public sector. Yet, how much value is there in using the size of the public sector as an explanation for economic problems? The data indicate that the cost of these public sector programs appears to have limited worth as an explanation for the mediocre performance of the U.S. economy during much of the past twenty-five years.

CHAPTER 7

DOES AN ACTIVE GOVERNMENT NECESSARILY MEAN OPPRESSIVE GOVERNMENT?

There is a vast library that deals with the role of public institutions in expanding the liberty of racial, ethnic, and religious minorities, as well as women, the handicapped, and children. It is unnecessary to recite that material here, although it is extremely important to realize that for many the role of government in expanding freedom and protection against abuse and prejudice is crucial. The way in which the public, through the control of governing power, has sanctioned and protected the rights of individuals testifies to how democracy sometimes requires the public to use the tools of government to liberate individuals from the constraints of bigotry and unfairness. In reviewing the lament of conservatives about the size of government, it is easy to conclude that the average citizen today, in the context of a larger, more powerful regime, is more oppressed than his or her eighteenth- or nineteenth-century counterpart. But is it reasonable to suggest that the poor, children in the workplace, laborers, Catholics, Jews, African Americans, other previous victims of widespread discrimination, or women are less free today than their counterparts living in an allegedly freer, less regulated period? Although local, state, and federal governments have been used to limit the freedoms of people and to discriminate invidiously against individuals, the public has also used these institutions to expand freedoms and choice and to dismantle many of the social and institutional buttresses of bigotry. It is important to remember the critical role that governing institutions have played in the twentieth century to obliterate racial, religious, ethnic, and other social barriers in the workplace, housing, public transportation, public recreation, and education.

Many of the policies and powers that comprise larger government—the greater regulatory powers, the broader range of things in which government is involved, and the higher levels of cost associated with government activities—are the result of responses to abusive and dangerous behavior in the private sector. Insofar as the public uses governing tools to prevent the harms and costs of undesirable "private" behavior, the result increases happiness and well-being, rather than reduces it. For many individuals, the amount of freedom, liberty, and personal security they possess results from using public institutions to deal with private sector threats to personal liberty and well-being.

It is impossible here to catalog all of the ways in which individuals can be and are threatened by private sector conduct, whether these threats emerge from the acts of individual or corporate criminality or misbehavior. Most people agree that the public ought to deploy governing power to protect itself from what is seen as conventional criminal conduct, although one can disagree at the margin as to what constitutes criminality or how severe sanctions for particular crimes might be. For example, there are debates over whether substance abuse by certified addicts ought to be "decriminalized." Others claim that implementing three strikes laws should pertain only to violent crimes. Of course, there is the venerable argument over the virtue or vice of capital punishment and under what circumstances it should be applied. In addition to conventional criminal conduct, however, there is a wide range of behavior that can detract from the overall satisfaction of individuals—when a neighbor uses his property dangerously or in an uncivil fashion (e.g., has raucous late night parties or raises smelly, noisy livestock); when a factory dumps waste in a stream and destroys its use for swimming or fishing; when people must manage the risk of unregulated drug manufacture; when elected officials are bribed; when workers have no right to bargain collectively to secure benefits or improve working conditions; or when people and organizations can restrict access to jobs, housing, recreation, or public amenities on the basis of race, gender, ethnicity, religion, or lifestyle.

It is not an original insight to argue that personal happiness can be undermined by the actions of nongovernmental actors. What is often overlooked, however, is the degree to which the powers of governing need to be deployed to restrain private sector threats to well-being. Societal well-being stems from a balancing among various configurations of public sector involvement in the private sector (Dahl and Lindblom, 1953; Lindblom, 1977). Arthur Okun (1975) assessed a similar balancing puzzle in his analysis of the tension between maximizing economic efficiency and, hence, tolerating whatever inequality arises, or maximizing equality and suffering potential declines in productivity and, hence, producing a smaller pie to share. In this chapter, however, the focus is on a smaller number of issues to make the argument that public sector involvement is required in some cases to maximize societal happiness and satisfaction. It is conceded that the balance and mix between the public and private sectors is an ongoing analytical challenge. Additionally, this chapter will focus on a few features of everyday life, and make the argument that threats to personal well-being in a modern society have been ubiquitous.

Notwithstanding the effects on government size, many people seek direct benefits through government policies. Put differently, government intervention leaves them better off, either materially or in terms of rights and privileges that improve well-being indirectly. In the words of formal rational choice theorists, *rent-seeking* by individuals and groups is a rational and endemic activity. After all, the automobile industry believes it is beneficial to have the public's representatives raise tariff barriers against the cars manufactured in other countries. It is far less costly for people interested in preserving historic sites and structures to have the public, through governing powers, restrict development of these places than it is to purchase development rights from the owners of these properties. Home builders and homeowners benefit significantly from the lavishness of public subsidies for home-ownership that increase the supply of housing, reduce the cost of making deals for housing purchases, exempt homeowners from capital gains taxation on the sale of homes, and reduce the risk of financing housing construction and sales, thereby reducing the cost of purchasing housing. Lawyers and doctors and other professions and occupations often benefit in the form of higher salaries and wages from publicly sanctioned barriers to entry into these professions. Establishing governmentally sanctioned standards regarding termite inspections, liability law and permissible lawyers' fees, inoculation requirements for school children, quality standards for beer and wine, and a host of other regulations have the effect of restricting supply (and hence producing higher prices and wages) for various occupations and services.

Of course, there are nearly always claims concerning the nationwide or community-wide benefit that such policies are supposed to provide. Perhaps they really do provide such benefits; sometimes they really do not. That is not the point, though. Our concern is that the public sector grows, at least in part, because there are groups who can realize great benefits from some sort of government involvement (a subsidy or regulation), while the costs of these actions might be widely and indirectly shared throughout the society, despite their potentially large aggregate impact. There are fairly powerful incentives for individuals and groups to capture gains that provide narrowly concentrated benefits, while spreading the costs over a larger and, hence, politically less motivated public. In this sense, individuals and groups seeking to enhance private well-being use public powers to achieve these gains. It is a compelling process—a process that has accounted for much of the pressure for government growth (Wilson, 1980). Although it is an important matter whether in actuality government policies produce greater benefits than costs, that is not the focus here. The main point is that for many individuals and groups there are perceived gains in having government intervene in previously private matters. That is all that is important for them.

In addition to seeking benefits through government action, individuals also seek to gain by reducing or eliminating the perceived misconduct or undesirable behavior of some individual or group. These policies often tend to focus on particular misbehaving individuals and groups, so suffering has to be sufficiently widespread and spectacularly heinous enough to produce the sort of public outrage or continuing public "pain" (e.g., rising unemployment, threats to public health, violations of sensibilities) that officials can marshal for political credit (Baumgartner and Jones, 1993; Cobb and Elder, 1972; Kingdon, 1984). The idea that public sector growth results from a "political class" that sits around conjuring up new ways to expand their budgets and authority is not supported by the data. Histories of the rise of the welfare state throughout Europe or in the United States do not square with the popular explanation that emphasizes the role of crafty bureaucrats and social engineers producing new ways for government to grow. As demonstrated in earlier chapters, the main breakthroughs in government growth are generated by the needs of the military or threats of war or by the efforts to ameliorate the effects of economic downturns. Joined with the impetus of war and depression are rent-seeking, as described previously, and social movements and political reactions that arise as a result of objectionable private sector behavior. Although there has always been a tradition of worry among the general population and among social thinkers that active governments can be abusive, people have used the authority and tools of government to ameliorate and address very serious, pervasive private sector abuse and misconduct, whether by individuals, groups, private organizations, businesses, or sometimes by other levels or components of government.

The history of government growth shows, then, that the unhappiness, abuse, or, in terms of economics, loss of utility experienced by individuals, is produced by both public and private actors. Being hassled by Internal Revenue Agents (public sector) or denied promotions because an employer or supervisor dislikes one's political beliefs (private sector) are surely both sources of unhappiness. The ultimate distress and cost to society of people distributing a drug that produces genetic mutations or other serious health threats (private sector) is surely as deplorable as the possibly excessive regulation of some industry's workplace safety (public sector). Government snooping might be no more heinous than espionage or violations of personal privacy by businesses and "ordinary" citizens. People's overall sense of well-being, security, privacy, and liberty can be jeopardized by private sector behavior as well as by the behavior of government actors.

Over time, the public can forget that the government agencies and the laws that created them often resulted from some serious, specific private sector abuse or problems. When we attack these government agencies for one reason or another (and the attacks might be justifiable) we also run the risk of reviving or encouraging the private sector misbehavior that the public sought to obviate. Or we risk so weakening the underlying legislation, legitimacy, or morale of the agency that the public deprives itself of the capacity to achieve important values or to avoid serious harms. The recent assault on the IRS is a good example of this. Without discounting abuses by IRS agents or the need for reform to deal with such abuse, we should not forget that in 1998 it was estimated that American citizens were being shortchanged $195 billion a year by people not paying their taxes (*Los Angeles Times*, May 2, 1998, Part A). Although it is easy and popular to criticize an agency as disliked as the chief federal tax collector, unfair tax burdens, nonpayment of taxes, and tax cheating are a perpetual, serious problem. Reforming the IRS or disciplining misbehaving IRS employees will not, it is hoped, result in more nonpayment of taxes, greater levels of evasion and increased tax inequity, and, consequently, even deeper ultimate cynicism regarding the tax code.

The remedy for the mischief of governing in today's world is not the generalized weakening of governing institutions or the erection of even greater barriers to the use of resources for public purposes than the formidable ones that already exist. We do not face the same issues that were arrayed before the founders of the nation as they designed the nation's constitution. As has been pointed out by historians of the period, the overriding concern at the time of the founding was to ensure many of the reluctant copatriots that a "more perfect union" would not recreate the monarchic abuses of power that incited the rebellion. Clearly, the purposes of the constitution included as a paramount objective the disciplining and circumscribing of governing power. The terms of the debate among states and national representatives expressed the concerns of the just-concluded struggle against the autocratic claims of the British monarchy. The *application* of social contract theorizing found in the debates over seeking independence and rebelling against the crown and in the public colloquy over ratification of our current constitution emerged almost entirely because of efforts to void monarchic claims on the colonists. To a degree, even the veneration of property rights was directed explicitly against the claim by the British court that all property rights flowed as grants from the crown (Adams, 1980).

Unfortunately, the terms of the debate that prevailed during the founding continue to pervade all discussion of reform and policy today. It is as if our current concern ought still to be dominated by the possible ascendancy of some abusive regime. The language of the current debate continues to conjure up the specter of an all-powerful, abusive government that is incompetent, awkward, and inefficient as well. Even efforts to require motorcycle helmets or airbags or smoke-free workplaces produce hot debates and images of a Big Brother, totalitarian regime. It is as if language is devoid of terms to describe government actions as either wise or silly, wasteful or efficient, precipitous or prudent, and that the only characterization available for any new government activity is the specter of a ruthless dictatorship. The imposition of workplace safety regulations or rules governing the development of land with historical or preservationist value, for example, are significant, direct bricks down the totalitarian road—the domino theory of Big Government, in which *any* increment of government action leads to more government and, ultimately, to abusive, totalitarian government.

These views are inappropriate to discussing the balance between public and private sector power. Of course, there are proposals to have government do things that clearly raise civil liberties issues (e.g., establishing what sort of language creates an inhospitable workplace, regulating commercial advertising, requiring drug testing, or easing the standards required to justify search warrants). Other policy areas involve government actions that do not rise to that level. It is possible to talk about individualized abuses of government power, as when some agency or individual oversteps authority or abuses the populace. Citizens, businesses, neighborhoods, state and local governments, and a host of other social, political, ethnic, religious, and economic organizations, however, stand poised to resist any genuine, systemic threat to political liberty. The real issue today is not whether the nation is about to be taken over by some totalitarian regime. Instead, the key issue is whether the public is capable of designing effective, efficient governing bodies that can advance its interests in public and private sector arenas through the array of tools of governing that are available. The struggle is between those who seek to marshal, when appropriate, governing power on behalf of their interests against those who would weaken government in a manner that protects their franchise in government, while making it far more difficult for others to get a hearing and a reasonable chance of achieving a worthwhile response. In describing the methodical approach to insulating government from widespread political demands, Johnson and Broder (1997) clearly document the focused effort to "defund the government" (Johnson and Broder, 1997: 11). The following are all examples of how there has been a fairly open and coordinated effort to undermine the ability of the public to use public powers to achieve public benefits for nonelite segments of the country: institutionalizing tax cuts; reducing tax rates on a broad front; eliminating government agencies and departments; requiring extraordinary majorities to increase any tax; fixing budgets to a prescribed proportion of the economy; requiring government compensation for losses due to noncriminal regulatory activities (e.g., land use regulation); and requiring elaborate, expensive evaluations of government regulations before they can be implemented.

By making it more difficult for anyone to get support for public/government involvement in previously private matters, *ceteris paribus*, the price necessary to achieve that involvement is increased. This is easily inferred from the standard laws of supply and demand. If a good is curtailed in supply (e.g., government spending or the range of things that the government is permitted to regulate), its price will increase. Those with fewer resources, then, will be less competitive for the higher-priced access. The effect is then to bias the system so that it is less likely that groups with fewer political resources will be able to achieve publicly supported responses on their behalf. When there are fewer revenues in general, the competition for the use of those revenues becomes costlier and more intense. Competition, then, is likely to be dominated by those who can invest the political resources to direct these resources to themselves or to produce the elaborate rationales to qualify under the far narrower rules justifying intervention by government. As constraints on government spending have increased, budget items for the less affluent have fared less well than budget items for middle and upper income entitlements.

In considering the constrained budgets of localities, states, and federal governments, job training, housing assistance, parks and recreation, welfare, legal assistance for the poor, and public transportation are examples of programs for the less affluent that have not fared as well as have mortgage interest deductions, social security for the affluent retired, investment incentives, and deregulation of key businesses. Local jurisdictions often fear that being sensitive to the less well-off will make them worse off relative to their neighbors. As a result, localities are constrained to minimize commitments to the poor or the troubled within their boundaries (Peterson, 1981). Limiting the tools and resources that are available for the purposes of governing or limiting the range of topics over which governing power can be applied might (1) produce a variety of undesirable effects that impose significant costs and harms on society if these topics involve aspects of public health and welfare, and (2) increase the influence of powerful interests able to compete for the smaller amount of "involvement" by government.

When we limit the range of things over which government might act or constrain officials in the choice of tools the public might use to achieve public objectives, we also deprive human beings of the capacity to defend themselves against the ravages of private power. This seems to pose yet another of the problematic trade-offs of governing: While weakening government reduces the prospect of government mischief, it sometimes reduces, in the context of democratic politics, the chances of citizens employing government to their benefit, and it increases the chances of private sector abuse.

A substantial source of growth in government activity in democratic societies is driven, first of all, by citizens and other groups using government to improve their life-chances. As there have been more constraints on governmental ability to respond to citizens, it has been the most affluent and prosperous segments of society that have been most successful in the competition for government responses. Over the years, powerful interests who routinely have access to government forums and public officials have been joined by less blessed and less influential segments of society seeking to improve their well-being, including children, women, and various religious, racial, and ethnic minorities. Certainly for many previously disadvantaged groups and victims of unfairness, exploitation, or bigotry, an active government is not necessarily one that results in an overall decline in liberty. For many citizens, government intervention has been essential to ensure that freedom is available, whether it is freedom from the violence of private, free market competition or freedom from religious, racial, gender, or ethnic persecution.

The amount of well-being a person has, including the freedom available to individuals, is not a fixed quantity that automatically declines every time governing authority is increased or some policy enacted or some tax imposed. Is there evidence that *private* power can also be a source of abuse and threaten personal liberty, a problem that might require government intervention? Consider, for example, the early involvement by government in limiting private discretion with respect to economic issues. What sorts of abuses, misconduct, or suffering led to the demand for government intervention? Included in the list were such "private" issues as slavery, the fixing of prices and markets, abuse of children and women in the workplace, the inherent weakness of labor versus capital in bargaining position, and invidious discrimination in employment, housing, and education on the basis of race, religion, ethnicity, and gender.

And what of more contemporary instances of private abuse of power, including corruption of the political process, political intimidation of employees in the workplace, intrusions by private institutions into the personal lives of individuals through review of credit purchases or insistence on lie detector screening for jobs, and ruthless, often hazardous commercial activity as a consequence of profit maximization or competition? The list of actions that some have labeled "corporate violence" (Hills, 1987) for even the past few decades includes some horrific acts of irresponsibility, at best, and criminal venality, at worst. As Clinard and Yeager (1980) enumerate the listing of various types of illegal business/commercial practices, the following are included: false advertising; price fixing; marketing of untested, unsafe products; pollution of the environment; political bribery; foreign payoffs; manufacturing and distributing unsafe products; unsafe work conditions; tax evasion; and falsifying and hiding records. Unfortunately, the economic and competitive pressure of the market often makes such behavior inevitable and probably far more prevalent than reported.

Insofar as we are concerned about the abuse of power, we need to remember that the private sector, as well as the public sector, is a major source of abuse of power. Our sense of alarm is roused during spectacular cases of corporate misconduct, but there is a constant supply of repugnant behavior by some segment of the private sector at all times, beyond ordinary street crime. Why is it that we seem to underplay or tolerate white collar crime? To some extent, white collar crime is more difficult for the media to cover and depict in film and photo, although that is sometimes possible, as when oil-drenched birds make the evening news or when someone is interviewed from a hospital bed after ingesting an adulterated product.

Another reason for the lower white collar crime profile is that business often has ample resources to alter public perceptions of the conduct under scrutiny (e.g., tobacco). Often, accused businesses stipulate to crimes or misconduct in return for keeping the information regarding their culpability from the public. Furthermore, information regarding private sector misconduct is not, by right, accessible to the public, whereas public sector records are, in principle, generally accessible (Clinard and Yeager, 1980). If public institutions are stripped of the authority and tools necessary to achieve democratically prescribed objectives, there will be an increase in the chances of abuse by private power. Recalling the nature of these private abuses and misconduct and the fact that they continue in both traditional and new forms is important.

Human happiness results from the proper functioning and disciplining of both private and public sector institutions and actors. With the prevalence of complex and powerful private sector entities and with the proliferation of increasingly arcane technological and social interactions, the public's health and welfare might also require in some sense new or "larger" public sector responses by means of a greater number of and more highly trained personnel. A larger or more active government, in these circumstances, does not necessarily imply an oppressive government. In order to avoid the oppressions of private sector misconduct, both petty and significant, and to enhance individual happiness and well-being, an expansion of some aspect of governing authority or some extension of a government tool is sometimes required.

LABOR AND CONSUMERS

Prior to 1913, when the Department of Labor was established, the federal government did virtually nothing, other than gather some information, to manage labor conditions. Before 1933, moreover, virtually no regulatory activity was attempted by the national government in the field of labor. The 1890 Anti-Trust Act, although incited by the excesses of business and commercial monopolies and trusts, was first used more vigorously against the efforts of labor to strike or boycott. It was not until 1932, through the Norris-LaGuardia, Anti-Injunction Act of 1932, that labor was exempted from the Anti-Trust laws. This legislation was the first instance in which the public acknowledged through law that it was a matter of public policy to foster labor organization and collective bargaining (Metz, 1945: 7–9). Most of the "rights" taken for granted regarding workplace safety, protection of children, and the guarantees for labor to engage in such concerted action as organizing, maintaining membership discipline, protecting against employers who discriminate against union members, and negotiating with employees would evaporate quickly without the structure of laws, agencies, and court decisions that have nurtured them since the New Deal years. We have moved from a time when the well-being of the employee "was precariously dependent upon a fortuitous conjunction of the humanitarian impulses and economic interests of those in power" (Morris, 1946: 523). Histories of the labor movement in the late nineteenth and twentieth centuries reveal the conditions that inspired workers to press for their right to unionize and to overcome the many collective action problems associated with expressing worker influence. Despite the relatively low level of unionization in the United States, there is a continuing effort to weaken the capacity of workers and wage earners to organize and to compete politically. Recent efforts to introduce "paycheck protection" legislation, which would require unions to seek prior approval from individuals before each political involvement launched by their unions, is an example of the ongoing struggle to maintain the modest gains that workers have made.

Contemporary life has provided new, difficult-to-manage methods whereby businesses can abuse their employees. Consider the case of privacy: (1) the compilation of extensive dossiers on employees even when not justified by the nature of the work, including aspects of spouse, family, and personal habits (sexuality, drinking habits, hobbies, political beliefs and community activities, as well as club and religious affiliations); and (2) the imposition of requirements to take psychological tests and the use of polygraphs, with no control by employees of how the results of these tests are interpreted, used, shared, or stored (Smith et al., 1992).

The degree to which private sector employers monitor and intrude into the lives of their employees and of customers is not equaled by the public sector, except in the case of the nation's security, tax, and police agencies. These routine intrusions into the lives of employees include a whole array of monitoring activity and threats. There is, for example, *telephone monitoring*—with employers listening in on phone calls at work, whether private or business calls, obtaining or keeping records of employee calls, and recording phone calls. There is *computer monitoring*— using software to enable employers to see what is on the employee's screen or stored on their terminals and disks, monitoring idle time and key-strokes to assess the volume of employee activity. There are also *employment background checks*, which are presumably regulated, but where there is still very little oversight about what sorts of things employers will seek, retain, or share with others. While the degree of privacy provided or promised to employees can be negotiated and such subsequent agreements can be legally enforced in courts, they are very difficult for employees to negotiate individually. The highly technical and subtle ways in which these privacy violations occur often keep employees unaware of the monitoring until they are confronted by their employers, usually during a performance evaluation. Even if one assumes the very debatable position that employees have absolutely no expectation of privacy at their work-site and that employers have full rights to communications and exchanges of the products that are generated through employer-owned equipment, modern methods of surveillance and recording of behavior often outpace the employee's sense of how vulnerable he or she is to employer information gathering.

Of course, one might claim that the traditional forms of employee abuse, such as exploiting children, imposing excessive hours, and tolerating and obscuring workplace hazards are a thing of the past. Yet there are many examples of current abuse of employees regarding workplace safety. Loopholes in the law and unethical and illegal conduct are still legion. The passage of the Occupational Safety and Health Act (OSHA) of 1970 marks only slightly more than a quarter-century of national commitment to the safety and health of workers. OSHA was enacted in large part because of the ongoing problems of mine safety. In the years immediately after OSHA's implementation, the public became increasingly aware of the often severe health effects on employees of an array of chemical and pesticide hazards, asbestos, cotton dust, and radioactivity. It is not surprising that the American public was educated regarding such terms as black and brown lung disease and asbestosis only after OSHA was enacted. It is also clear that employers subjected employees to remediable health risks, even though they knew about the long-term health risks to employees who worked in the coal mines, asbestos factories, and textile mills. Because of the recordkeeping that OSHA has mandated, it is now known how persistent dangerous workplaces are. It is only since 1992 that the Bureau of Labor Statistics, U.S. Department of Labor, began to collect fatality census data on work injuries. For 1995 alone, the data indicate that 6,210 workers were killed at work and millions of others suffered nonfatal injuries at work. While many of these injuries are not due to unsafe working conditions or employer negligence, many others are.

Maintaining workplace health and safety is an ongoing struggle. Just as the vast majority of residents are law-abiding and not a threat to others, most businesses and entrepreneurs do not seek to do harm. Just as a fairly small set of scofflaws or predatory criminals or a couple of serial killers can detract greatly from the quality of life and a community's sense of security, so misconduct, irresponsibility, and the callous and criminal conduct of a fairly small number of businesses can undermine public well-being or public trust, as well as inducing ruthlessness in the larger commercial community. The wanton disregard that some employers have for their workers, their communities, and their customers are the stuff of numerous, apocryphal stories. It is like a stocked lake, where it is easy to dip one's fishing pole in and have a catch in no time at all. So it is in the area of business misconduct. For example, in examining the Consumer Product Safety Commission's January 1998 press releases, among the listing of recalls and violations for the month there is the tale of the owner of a distributor of alternative energy products who was sentenced to nearly two years in jail for improperly storing and shipping a highly corrosive, clear electrolyte solution. The result of this criminal neglect was that a fifteen-year-old boy mistook the solution for water, drank it, and died two weeks later from severe internal injuries. This sort of violation occurs with regularity, whether it involves the dangerous packaging and transport of products, the use of tainted food products, or the polluting and hazardous dumping of commercial by-products. It is not surprising that this "white collar" criminal act produced a fairly light sentence. It is surprising that anyone thinks such behaviors would not be far more widespread and more injurious without some form of public policing, whether through regulation or the mandating of liability (Rosoff, Pontell, and Tillman, 1998).

This inclination among businesses to push the envelope on safe and responsible conduct is evident when some businesses export their dirtier, less healthy, and more hazardous operations to places with fewer compunctions about the dangers posed to employees and surrounding communities. It is not that business owners and officers are necessarily malevolent and uncaring, although as in all human conduct there is some of that. The compulsions generated by the forces of the market and competition, so constructive in some ways, pressure businesses to minimize costs. Sometimes this leads to the premature introduction of products (sometimes encouraging the trading of public safety for competitive advantage), the use of least-cost labor (sometimes resulting in exploitation of child labor), the use of least-cost production (sometimes producing unsafe work places), and the effort to evade costs of production (sometimes inciting the dumping, including the illegal dumping, of waste). There is an elaborate body of formal theory to explain the conditions under which it is rational for individual businesses to engage in this sort of conduct, and why it is that some sort of public intervention is appropriate on economic grounds (even though the nature of the intervention might still be a matter of substantial disagreement and debate—e.g., disputes over regulatory versus more market-like mechanisms). As Croall (1992: 8) explains it, "White collar crime, therefore, appears to be an inevitable concomitant of business, trading and commerce."

So, even though there are widely understood and clearly articulated standards regarding fire resistant children's clothing, every year there continue to be nearly monthly recalls of garments that blatantly disregard the standard. Again, looking at just the 1998 press releases for the Consumer Product Safety Commission, in January the Commission reported the recall of an estimated 16,800 fleece garments, many of which were for children and infants. The garments failed to meet federal standards and were in danger of igniting readily. Lest one think that the federal standard is unreasonable, fabrics that fail to comply with the federal standard typically burn faster than newspaper. Repeated recent failures to comply with well-known standards regarding children's products like toys and children's furniture are bountiful on a monthly basis. It is reasonable to assume that without the moderate level of regulation and enforcement that exists, the misconduct and resulting dangers to children and adults would increase.

The Progressive Movement, New Deal, and modern consumer movements have provided tools to address, monitor, prosecute, and punish economic misdeeds and illegality. Yet, just as the criminal code has not ended street or violent crime, neither have the plethora of laws ended the propensity of the business community to produce ongoing misconduct, even criminal behavior. These undesirable, often criminal behaviors impose burdens on society that are, according to many respected observers of corporate misconduct, costlier, more hazardous, and often more heinous than the consequences of conventional street crime.

WHITE COLLAR CRIME

It is not easy to assess the financial impact of business misconduct, since it generally comes under the heading of "white collar crime." The range of behaviors included in the definition of white collar crime varies, and data gathering on such behavior is uneven and lacks uniformity. But it is unambiguous that by any definition of corporate, business, commercial, economic, or white collar crime, the dollars involved dwarf the costs associated with conventional crime. The cost of embezzlement, health care fraud, consumer and personal fraud, insurance fraud, workplace safety violations, consumer product violations, environmental damage, antitrust violations, and political corruption range into the hundreds of billions of dollar per year. Calavita, Poutell, and Tillman (1997) estimate that the Savings and Loan Bailout (involving criminal conduct or conduct that would have been illegal in an earlier, more closely regulated period) will cost $8–15 billion annually for twenty to thirty years. Clearly, there are great potential gains in reducing business and commercial misconduct.

One might claim that significant and gross misconduct by private firms is a thing of the past, that new understandings and expectations produce more benign conduct—that the modern corporation can generally be trusted to do the right thing. Or, in any case, that even if there are many cases of reprehensible commercial behavior, government intervention is worse than the disease. Yet an examination of the behavior of corporations in places less able to police the conduct of the corporations (in third world nations, for example) shows that the merchandising of harmful products and the tolerance of dangerous practices is ubiquitous. The following are examples of common practices of modern corporations: the tragedy of Bhopal, India, where thousands were killed or injured as a result of poor management and shoddy, criminally negligent maintenance of a chemical plant; the marketing of baby formula in spite of its deleterious consequences on infant mortality; the energetic marketing of cigarettes overseas; the contracting with prison labor in countries where labor is not free to organize; the exploiting of foreign child labor; the dumping of hazardous wastes in other countries; and the introduction in other countries of drugs and products that have been banned or limited in developed countries. Even in nations with a substantial regulatory apparatus (i.e., Western Europe or the United States) "white collar" and business crime continue as a substantial, fixed feature of modern business life. Policies that might obviate bad private behavior could, therefore, produce major benefits, if the costs of producing improvements are less than the cost of the harms avoided.

PRIVACY ISSUES

When critics of a larger public sector express their concerns, they often emphasize privacy issues. There are legitimate concerns about the many data demands that come from government agencies at all levels, such as departments of motor vehicles, health agencies, taxing bodies, security and police departments, social security, and other social welfare agencies. Efforts to consolidate data bases and the possibility of snooping due to horizontal and vertical integration of data bases, usually on the grounds of efficiency, do raise issues of possible threats to civil liberties. In some ways, however, the current threats to and actual violations of privacy that occur in the private sector are far more substantial. These include matters such as the following:

Employee Records   Employee records are sensitive and often subjective, with few safeguards against petty or malicious assessments by supervisors. Employees have little access to information, yet the improper use or careless maintenance of records by employers can have devastating effects on an individual's career.

Direct-Mail Lists   As direct mail marketing becomes increasingly important, the value of targeting becomes more apparent, hence the sophistication of detailing the lives of individuals and placing them in various categories of lists, by lifestyle, region, tastes, disposable income, religion, previous charitable giving patterns, partisanship, and voting rates. As we ponder the impact on privacy, we should also consider whether aspects of our lives should be deployed for profit this way without our permission. If my consumer purchases are valuable information, why should I not have a voice as to how that value should be managed?

Credit Card Data Use   Customers use credit cards, club cards, and other special devices that permit businesses to track purchases and accumulate elaborate and valuable data bases. Information is gathered at the time of applying for cards and supplemented with data retrieved by point-of-sale equipment. Fairly detailed profiles on background and customer purchases can be developed and used for marketing and for sale. Apart from the propriety of having customers monitored in this way, there is the additional issue of having customers providing a commercial benefit without their consent or knowledge and without being compensated. Customers are often induced into participating through ruses. For example, the increasing popularity of supermarket "club" cards is marketed in terms of presumed savings in groceries, when the additional purpose is to provide the commercial establishment with a means of tracking purchases by individuals and inducing people into using these cards. What would the public's reaction be if they were informed that the government was monitoring daily habits such as grocery purchases without the consent of individuals? The various methods by which commercial interests monitor consumers is proliferating with technological advances. For example, even "Caller ID" services are allegedly being used for purposes of collecting profiles on calling patterns.

Credit Information   Credit information is gathered on most adults in the nation. The firms gathering the information often make mistakes, and it is not a simple thing for individuals to ensure that they know what information about them has been gathered and whether it is accurate—and if it is inaccurate, there is no simple way of correcting errors.

Health Data   Health data on individuals are gathered and stored by a number of different health care and insurance firms. Individuals often do not know what is contained in these records, and hence they are disarmed in defending against inaccuracies. Individuals have precious little information on how these data bases are used for either marketing or other information. Clearly the health data for an individual are a vitally important and often intimately private thing, and how the data are used can affect individuals' lives in dramatic ways. As genetic markers for this or that disease or ailment become available for predictive use, how will the information be used? Who will control personal information? Will people be required to undergo DNA screening? And will that information be subject to commercial exploitation?

Private actors sometimes not only disregard, violate, and profit from ignoring the individual privacy of clients and employees, but they are also sometimes ruthless in spying on competitors and other businesses. Infiltrating particular businesses and trash trawling (rummaging through the trash); bugging, wiretapping, and drop-by spying by technicians, maintenance people, and sales personnel; hacking/cracking computer systems; mobile phone eavesdropping; and purchasing information from employees are all examples of "industrial espionage" and fairly regular behaviors in the business world today (Cornwall, 1987).

Added to these extensive threats to privacy generated by private sector behavior are an array of new forms of privacy threats in the on-line services world. Because so much personal information is being provided by users of these services—background information, credit information, and purchase patterns—public officials and the customers of such services are increasingly worried that violations of privacy will occur. Approximately 85 percent of web sites gather personal information from consumers and very few indicate how the information is used or how it is to be secured. Initial efforts to manage these problems have been launched by the private sector, although it is clear that this is being incited by the public's watch guards, the Federal Trade Commission (*Los Angeles Times*, June 20, 1998: D1).

The point is simple. Privacy, personal autonomy, and freedom from manipulation are values that can be violated by public institutions. These cherished values and freedoms are at least as vulnerable to the machinations of the private sector, however. With respect to the monetary costs of violations, white collar misconduct in the private sector is substantially more serious than street crime.

EXPENSIVE LESSONS, EXPENSIVE RERUNS

In a variety of situations, then, the public in a democracy will use the tools of governing in order to achieve perceived gains and reduce or eliminate the prospect of perceived harms. Some of these efforts fail or perhaps create costs that are greater than the gains. The road to hell, and maybe the road to policy failure, is littered with unwise or poorly crafted public programs. Sometimes the perpetrators of the harms or bad practices that inspired the initial government intervention come to dominate policy and either nullify its original intent or alter it to protect vested, rather than public, interests. There is a sizable literature on the problem of "agency capture" (Bernstein, 1955). Yes, there are risks and failures when government intervenes.

On the other hand, when considering what appears to be government failure, we do need to be sensitive to a number of issues. First, much of the criticism directed at particular programs or government size in general is self-interested, and is orchestrated by those who are the very individuals and organizations whose behavior produced the government intervention in the first place, or those who have much to gain materially by having government withdraw from the field. Calls for deregulation and privatization in finance and lending, in communication and electronics, in education, in pharmaceutical and drug development, in income security, in transportation, in workplace safety, and in prison management raise important issues and deserve serious review and discussion. We need to be wary, however, of the tactical nature of these calls for getting government off our back and of promises of efficiency, great savings, and more choice. Proponents of these proposals do not approach the issues objectively. Be wary, even if intrigued, of self-interested, ideologically motivated advocates bearing data. That applies also to what is said in this book.

There are often serious private sector failures that give rise both to government intervention and to the specific form that the intervention takes (e.g., direct regulation, incentives, mandated legal liability, and the like). It is not always easy for the public to feel the sense of crisis or to experience the feeling of outrage that some private sector actions have produced and that have resulted in a government response. Over time, the public becomes complacent. Over time, government regulators occasionally overstep their bounds. Sometimes there is a deplorable case of corruption among officials who are supposed to be protecting the public. There are cases of antiquated policies that no longer work or are far more expensive than best-practice methods require. There are investigations by congressional opponents. With access to public records, the media finds it relatively inexpensive to provide a steady stream of stories about the day's violation of public trust, government dishonesty, or official incompetence. So as we move on from the time when public anger and outrage about some private sector misconduct results in a policy intervention, as the fury dissipates, those who are the targets of government policy have an unwavering incentive to undermine the legitimacy of government intervention. Their philosophical or economic or constituent allies contribute to officials who are sympathetic to less government involvement. In the meantime, the public's motivation to strengthen and improve programs becomes less powerful than the motivation of those interested in getting government to disengage.

A classic example of this process is the evolution of regulation in the savings and loan industry. The entire financial industry collapsed during the Great Depression. In the aftermath of that collapse, and as a result of unethical, criminal, and foolhardy behavior within the financial industry, the government implemented a complex and arcane apparatus to regulate that industry. Safety and stability of the financial and savings and loan system were key objectives of regulatory policy after 1932, resulting in a fairly conservative system of investment and interest paid to depositors. There are many descriptions of the conditions that produced the devastation of the thrift industry in the late 1980s (Rosoff, Pontell, and Tillman, 1998: 202–20). The short version is that the savings and loan industry was constrained in its practices so that it was unable to match the go-go double-digit returns on investment that the period of double-digit inflation was producing in other investment venues. The industry used its genuine problem in competing in this environment to mobilize the deregulatory élan of the Reagan administration's early period. Massive deregulation resulted. The rest is history. Although there is a lot of hand-wringing about how much of this financial calamity was produced by significant criminal conduct or the sheer foolhardiness and risky behavior encouraged by deregulation, the bills for the debacle are very expensive and will continue for a long time. The total costs to be borne by the public vary between hundreds of billions of dollars to well over a trillion dollars. As we consider whether we wish to "privatize" pensions and retirement investments, we might wish to remember the recurrent nature of peculation among these private institutions entrusted with people's insurance funds and savings on which they are depending for their future income (Rosoff, Pontell, and Tillman, 1998: 194–219).

Of course, this is not to suggest that it was unwise to explore some form of change and deregulation in the thrift industry. Real problems of viable competition did exist. Withdrawals by depositors seeking profitable earnings were devastating the thrift industry, and some changes were required. However, the ideologically motivated "reforms" of the early and mid-1980s, which were implemented by those with a general antigovernment agenda, should have been examined more carefully. Confidence that wholesale deregulation would not replicate the misconduct of the earlier period was naive and misplaced. It is clear that when technology and economic forces justify deregulation, a more deliberative and measured approach, such as that evolving in the airlines and communications industry, can produce substantial public benefits in the form of lower costs and product innovation. Even in these areas, however, public safety issues and massive mergers are beginning to again stimulate debate over the appropriate public response and whether new forms of regulation might be required.

THE DISCOUNTED MARKETPLACE

Most resource conservation and environmental problems have a serious "obligation to future generations" component (Sikora and Barry, 1978). For example, insofar as fossil fuels are more or less plentiful, current generations of users benefit from the relatively low price, even if we ignore the variety of social costs that are not reflected in current prices, chief among these being air pollution. As the supplies inevitably dissipate, since fossil fuels are in fixed supply, the cost of developing and introducing substitutes into the market will increase. New costs will also be involved in producing these fuels and in training individuals in the skills that are required to service these different sorts of engines. These costs will be mostly borne by a later generation. How precipitously this happens and how much intergenerational inequity is induced depends on whether public institutions are used to infuse current prices with these future costs. If current prices reflect future costs of new energy sources, then current energy users will contribute to paying the cost of alternatives for the future. It depends in part on whether the claims of future generations have any bearing on the current policy agenda and whether norms of intergenerational equity motivate current generations to consider what, if any, obligations they have to themselves in their future (some of the current population might be around when the substitute fuel problem hits the fan) or to future generations. As a collective entity, a society might have an interest in producing greater incentives to increase energy efficiency sooner, encourage investment in alternative energy supplies now, and smooth out the cost of energy transformation. It is clear that only in public and collective forums will these issues be addressed. The greater the emphasis on purely private motives and exclusively "free market" arrangements, the less likely these issues will be addressed. If it can be shown that real gains in productivity and equity can be achieved with higher energy prices for current generations, only government institutions are likely to produce policies to achieve these gains.

The history of human beings is filled with examples of how we tend to discount the future. This tendency poses profound difficulties for those who argue that societal welfare is maximized by individuals doing their own thing. Since most people are likely to react far more strongly to short-term stimuli than to less certain, less discernible future stimuli, there are likely to be some serious behavioral anomalies. For example, is it reasonable to believe that a teenage woman beginning smoking, even if she is informed of the risks of smoking, can "rationally" weigh the risks and pleasures of smoking? Films and images of cancer victims and the ravages of the disease are shown and, as horrific as these might be, the aversive effects are often not enough to prevent a long-term smoking habit. The individual faces daily depictions of cigarette use in romantic or daring settings, not to mention the chemical dependency resulting from nicotine use. The risks and associated consequences are distant and uncertain. Perhaps the individual subsequently develops, decades later, a cigarette-induced cancer and has to endure the pain of the disease and the devastation of the treatment. It is often claimed that full disclosure of risks means that individuals who consume a good or use a service must value the good or service more highly than the costs of using it. Some also believe that full disclosure of risks places full responsibility for consequences on the person taking the risk. Others claim that to deny people through government regulation the use of a good or service when they have been fully informed of the risks smacks of paternalism, at best, and, at worst, marks a Big-Brotherish step toward the loss of personal freedom. Seatbelt and motorcycle helmet requirements are examples of areas in which this issue arises constantly. But turn back to the hypothetical longtime cigarette smoker, now a cancer patient who has endured the loss of her lung and massive chemotherapy and its usual side effects. Based on a commitment to minimizing the role of government and affection for the economic model of decision making, are we obliged to say, "Well, that woman surely must have gotten a kick out of smoking!" Shall we now adorn her with a medal commemorating her status as Heroine of Marginal Utility?

When a person goes to the supermarket and makes trade-offs between certain items, he or she can refer to long histories of comparing actual experiences in eating apples, oranges, pears, or daikon radishes. It is possible to recall the actual pleasure or dissatisfaction with the use of a particular product. On the other hand, merely disclosing the side effects of some product and claiming that this fully permits assessment of risks and benefits is often a dangerous thing to claim. Most people do not have the close up and personal experience or actual memory of lung and heart disease, breathing difficulties, disfigurement, or organ loss, much less the pain of surgery and chemotherapy, to weigh against the benefits of smoking. If, somehow, one could really experience the sound and actuality of a doctor saying, "I am sorry, but I have to tell you that you have lung cancer, and there is a very good chance that within two years you will be dead," and if one could also have, in advance, a brain record of the pain of surgery and treatment and loss of function during treatment, then it might be possible to claim that a person is making a true trade-off.

These are not fanciful issues. In the field of workplace safety, for example, many critics of public regulation argue that a sounder approach is to permit workers to trade off greater risk for higher wages. After all, who are we to prohibit unsafe practices? Why should the public deny workers the opportunity to have higher wages in return for being less risk averse? The only public responsibility is, according to some libertarian critics of government regulation, to make workers fully aware of the risks. We can suspend our concern momentarily regarding how full disclosure of risk will be required and how public agencies will inspire employers to provide the data and information necessary for full disclosure. After all, it is obvious that employers have every reason to conceal risks and hazards from employees. The challenge of eliciting full disclosure is very complex. The headaches of regulating workplace safety are not any more onerous than what might be necessary to require and ensure that employers fully inform all their respective employees of the entire range of serious hazards and risks. Determining what constitutes the threshold over which one moves from a trivial to a serious hazard and risk connotes a fairly big role for government.

Full disclosure of risks and hazards at the workplace would, according to many gung-ho antigovernment sorts, permit employers to compete for workers, with some investing in costlier yet safer workplace environments and others offering workers higher wages to absorb greater risk.

The market will then produce the optimal combinations of workplace risk and safety. Goods and services will be produced most efficiently and social utility maximized.

The problem is similar to the one previously described, in that those who choose higher workplace risks are merely trading a prospective risk for a nearer-term benefit (higher wages). The worker is not actually experiencing the pain of a bad fall or disabling injury or illness. He or she cannot know the actuality of years of rehabilitation or the psychic, physical, and economic costs of chronic disability that might result. The worker might be fully and completely informed of the risks and yet not really be able to fully internalize the experience of losing in the gamble for higher wages. The worker will discount the risk and underestimate the cost of being afflicted.

There is yet another problem in assuming that people will make "rational" trade-offs once they are fully informed of risks and hazards. It is one of equity, and it incorporates our understanding of the theory of marginal utility and diminishing returns. It is not unreasonable to assume that for the poor, the value of an additional dollar is greater than it is for the wealthy. Obviously an additional $1,000 in the pocket of a fairly poor individual will be more meaningful (provide more utility) than for a millionaire. As incomes grow, however, the utility or satisfaction gained from the additional (marginal) increment of income declines. For a poor individual the initial income base is used to consume the essentials of life, while the marginal gain of a few thousand dollars is much less for someone who lives in a comfortable home and is served by the full array of modern conveniences. It is not necessary to develop a formal proof that it is the less affluent who are most likely to absorb higher risks in return for higher incomes. Not only are the poor more likely to value the income gains for higher risk, but also they will have an even higher rate of risk-discounting than the person at the median income level. The poorer the person, the greater the prospect that he or she will accept lower compensation for each increased unit of risk. For some of us this might be a fairly uncomfortable equity puzzle.

The tendency of people to discount the risk of current behavior regarding future well-being is a very serious issue for those who insist on maximizing the "freedom" we have to make choices. Rational individuals would agree that any decision-making unit—an individual, household, business, city, or nation—ought to maximize well-being over the life of the decision-making unit. Well-run businesses must balance sales, product research and development, marketing, and investment in inventory, training of personnel, and purchasing that supports other enterprises (horizontal and vertical integration). The most successful businesses, the ones that remain and prosper over the long haul, understand that it is not possible to maximize profit at every point in time. The critical thing is to identify a reasonable planning horizon, say, the proverbial five-year plan, and produce the maximum return, among other possible five-year returns. It is possible that the business could produce spectacular profits in the first two years of that period, but that might happen at the expense of doing things that produce very poor performance for the remaining three years of the period, so that after the five years the total earned profit is ordinary or even unacceptable.

The average person in the United States can expect to live into his or her mid-seventies, and it is clear that the "rational" thing is to maximize the benefits a person will accumulate over the seventy-plus years of his or her life. A person can "choose" to live for today, burn the candle at both ends, live it up, spend-spend-spend, party hearty, and avoid personal development such as education and training. Such a person is not likely to prepare adequately for the time when he or she is not able to work, or for the time later in life when income needs increase and there is insufficient skill or knowledge to compete adequately, or for the time when he or she is less healthy and more dysfunctional with aging. Permitted full control over their income without the burden of "forced" savings or required participation in income security programs, whether Social Security or something else that is forced or required, vast numbers of people will simply under-invest in their future well-being. They will spend on things that bring them happiness in the present or near-term. After all, the week's savings alone will not produce long-term security. Hence, since any given week's savings only contributes in a minuscule way to future well-being, there is every incentive to use that income for something now. It is always possible to start next week, right? But tomorrow does come, and the result will surely be a large and possibly much less prosperous senior citizenry. The hold of the present is too great, and the future is often too anemic in its capacity to induce behavior in the present.

On a number of grounds, removing public control and government regulation, while permitting more individual choice for business, employees, consumers, and parents, might very well reproduce the host of problems that engendered the public clamor that produced the public involvement in the first place. It is not as if there is no evidence regarding these matters. During the Great Depression and prior to the enactment of Social Security, and with the utter collapse of the U.S. economy and private and local social welfare programs, it was clear that Americans were unprepared to deal with the ravages of the modern business cycle. Many older employees were unprepared for the forced retirement that resulted from losing jobs. Those with private pensions saw them obliterated because of the collapse of businesses, financial institutions, and lending institutions (Bernstein, 1985; Trotlander, 1975).

A growing public sector, then, is important to enhancing the freedom and well-being of many members of society. We are always faced with choices as to how much we are willing to give over as matters of private and individual choice. We are always confronted by the decision about how much we are willing to place in the market's basket. In a completely unregulated, mythically free, unfettered market, in the context of contemporary technology, is there any doubt that we would have a market for human organs or the genetic engineering of various human attributes? Of course, we would also have a rich and varied leisure drug-use industry, traditional prostitution for both gay and straight people, child pornography, exceptionally dangerous sports, indentured servitude, perhaps even murder-for-hire, people selling themselves for dangerous experiments, and other things that no doubt would be utterly repugnant. We do routinely make choices, then, to limit or encourage behaviors. We choose to limit the production of products that are dangerous; sometimes we insist that businesses treat employees in a certain way; other times we encourage human beings to do things that are deemed healthier or more conducive to future productivity. In principle, this is no different from prohibiting the salacious filming and photographing of children or limiting or encouraging any other human conduct.

The collection of different things the public chooses to do through governing methods might be too much, unwise, imprudent, inept, inefficient, and awkward. How it is decided when the burden of government policies is too great and which policies ought to be curtailed, improved, or terminated is the critical issue in democracies when it comes to questions of government size. Conservative critics of government size have increasingly sought to develop hard boundaries over which the public will be prevented from going, or to erect walls that the demands for government help will have an increasingly difficult time scaling (e.g., extraordinary majorities to raise taxes, formulas fixing spending levels, and granting property rights explicit, civil rights status). Or it is argued that the public ought to privatize certain services or remove government from the field altogether through program termination or deregulation. The price to be paid in accepting the antigovernment conservative agenda, however, will be to replicate forgotten abuses and to reduce democratic access for individuals, especially those who are less affluent or who are not represented by powerful organized interests. The price for this sort of government reform is perhaps too high. It is undeniable that suspicions and skepticism regarding the use of governing tools is healthy. There is no denying that public tools have been used to inflict some terrible and often unwise things. But then so have the tools and institutions of the private sector. In the zeal to dismantle government programs and to make it more difficult to use governing tools, it is possible to overlook the many ways in which ordinary citizens are vulnerable to the abuse of private power. It is easy to neglect the critical ways in which government has been employed to liberate individuals and to provide the means by which the average household can protect itself from the wildfires of private passion through the proper and prudent use of democratically guided political power.

CHAPTER 8

HITLER DIDN'T COME TO POWER VIA THE HEALTH DEPARTMENT

Many critics of government make no distinction among the elements of government growth or size. Government assistance for the poor; mandatory participation in Social Security; forced loyalty oaths; motorcycle helmet requirements; workplace safety regulations; limitations on political participation; greater police powers of search, seizure, and surveillance; stricter requirements for assembling for political purposes; regulation of media content; and prohibition of discrimination based on race, ethnicity, religion, gender, or sexual preference—all these sorts of things are lumped together as if each might undermine personal liberty or encourage government abuse. The things that government does, however, differ greatly in terms of resources involved, degree of influence with respect to choices, and the level of intrusion into people's lives. Simply examining the size of budgets, counting pages in the Federal Register, and listing the number of laws enacted, then adding these things up as if each item or dollar or action is equal to the other, does not allow for valid inferences about the size of government.

THE BIG BROTHER ROAD TO DICTATORSHIP

The number of different things provided through government institutions and the resources extracted to support public policies do measure some aspects of government size. Regarding government size, however, there are other important features that are not incorporated into the equation. When the role of government is evaluated in areas such as crime, poverty, education, economic performance, food production, workplace safety, or personal health, the policies can be judged as wise and prudent or unwise and foolhardy. It is perfectly possible to have inept policies that waste time, dissipate resources, and produce very little or no net benefit, even while they have nothing to do with whether or not a society is losing personal freedom and slipping closer to dictatorship. If government growth is viewed as a major threat to freedom as a general matter or matter of principle, then it is much easier to oppose not only a particular government action but also to argue for disengaging from some policy area altogether. If it is believed that there is a threat to basic liberty in assigning to the federal government the responsibility of promulgating energy efficiency standards, for example, then it would seem reasonable to argue for disengaging government from the arena of energy conservation. If, however, the need for or wisdom of government involvement in promoting energy efficiency standards is accepted, it is still possible to have reservations over some particular energy conservation policy without inferring that the public should get out of the business of using government to encourage energy efficiency.

There is, in short, a strategic purpose in characterizing government growth as a threat to liberty—it is not only to argue over any given policy, but to undermine the legitimacy of government being involved in any policy domain. These are important issues when considering if a government is getting "bigger" and more oppressive, or whether the size of the public sector in one nation is larger than that of another. It is possible to have a nation with a small social service sector—that is, one that provides no publicly supported income security, produces only limited public educational opportunities, and asserts no role in publicly regulated consumer or worker safety. The overall tax burden might be fairly small, and public regulation of economic activity might be nonexistent, perhaps limited to prohibiting prostitution and pornography. That same regime, however, might limit all political participation to members of a single "official" political party. The media might be required to have all news reports reviewed by government censors first. The rights of people to assemble or criticize the regime might be strictly limited, even prohibited. Labor unions might be outlawed, the police might have summary powers to search, seize, and detain people, and the rights of the accused might be nonexistent. In short, it is possible to have a nation with a small social welfare sector and little government economic regulation and low taxes, yet that nation could still have a very repressive government. A social welfare component, then, need not be a precursor to repression.

Imagine another nation with a large tax burden, substantial economic involvement by the public in such areas as plant closures, workers' rights, consumer protection, education, and income security. Political parties are plentiful, the media are free to criticize officials, politics, and policies, and officials are circumscribed in their ability to monitor or police citizens.

Strong norms of due process are supported to protect citizens from official abuse, and there exist opportunities for widespread political participation through political parties and other groups and organizations.

In this comparison, one nation has a small tax burden and negligible social service sector, but also has a politically intrusive regime, and another nation has a large tax burden and substantial social service sector, but has very limited capacity for the regime to limit political opposition. Which nation has a larger public sector? If only the level of taxes and spending and government regulation of the economy as "the public sector" are condidered, the inclination might be to think of nations with large social service sectors as having "larger" governments. Insofar as these governments are thought of as leading to repressive, even totalitarian regimes, the twentieth-century trend to think in terms of the quest for greater social equality and fairness as a road to dictatorship is reflected. This perspective is referred to as the Big Brother Road to Dictatorship. It is a perspective that arose in large part because of the linkage between the promise of social justice associated with the celebrants of the rise of Soviet and Chinese communism and the contrasting actuality of the brutality and imperial conduct in those regimes.

If the governments that repressed people in the twentieth century are examined for the ways in which they took, consolidated, and abused power, very little evidence for the the Big Brother Road is found. There is a sense in which this discussion seems to have tackled a straw man. But the straw man is adorned in very fancy clothing designed by very important and popular thinkers. Consider the comment by Machan (1995: 103), a leading conservative scholar, who refers to the nondemocratic governments of the Soviet Union and East Germany as "honest" socialist regimes:

> A somewhat different, less honest but no less insidious, type of system is one we can only call fascism, whereby government allows individuals to keep legal title to valued items, but regulates nearly all of what they would do with these. We are nearing such a system in the United States and other Western democracies. We might label these systems "democratic fascism." They are characterized by an overwhelming measure of government regulation of people's lives, especially their economic affairs.

It *is* common among conservative critics of public sector activism to characterize government growth in the arena of social welfare, environment, consumer and worker protection, and income security as steps toward the loss of liberty and even totalitarianism. Many critics of the emergence of the modern social welfare state, whether that of the Scandinavian and Benelux variety or of the more anemic versions of North America, have tried to convey the sense that the road to a totalitarian hell is paved with the good intentions of the social democratic program. As listed by King (1987: 45), there are a number of distinct claims that summarize the ways in which governments with large social welfare sectors presumably reduce liberty:

- By threatening property rights with higher taxes
- By promoting uniformity and standardization of services and under-mining diversity
- By advancing paternalism through fostering socially engineered choices
- By imposing restrictions through bureaucracies and courts, thereby lim-iting choice and strengthening government
- By encouraging dependency and reducing initiative among individuals to develop and pursue their own options
- By creating a larger government apparatus whose members form a pow-erful interest in creating even larger government involvement, thereby accentuating the previously mentioned trends

These elements in the case against activist governments can be found in a variety of contexts: the thought and writing of scholars, novelists, and commentators—Friedrich Hayek's popularizing of the Austrian-soon-to-be-Chicago School of economic doctrine with his 1944 essay *The Road to Serfdom* (Hayek, 1944) and his subsequent work (Hayek, 1976; 1979; 1991); Ayn Rand's novels (Uyl and Rasmussen, 1984); Milton Friedman's further work and the institutionalization of libertarian economic attacks on the welfare state in the Chicago School of economics (Friedman, 1962; Samuels, 1993); and the more raucous forums of talk shows and other places where such things as requiring safety-belt use, no-smoking areas in buildings, truth-in-advertising and labeling, or efforts to preserve endangered species are discussed as Big Brother steps to unresponsive governments and bu-reaucracies at best and totalitarian regimes at worst.

Obviously, an active government can waste the public's resources and produce inefficiencies (as can the private sector). There is no record, however, of any oppressive regime having taken power by advancing on the social welfare front. Lenin and Stalin (Carr, 1979), Mussolini (Finer, 1964), Mao Tse-Tung (Thaxton, 1997), Fidel Castro (Bunck, 1994), and Chile's Pinochet (Spooner, 1994) did not consolidate political power by gradually increasing social welfare programs, taxes, and regulation of the environment or work-place. Rather, these assaults on personal freedom and democratic gover-nance involved limitations on civil rights and political rights, the legitimization of oppression and discrimination against disfavored or un-popular groups, and the centralization and expansion of military and police forces. Hitler did not become the supreme ruler of the Nazi State by first taking over the health department.

Economic misery and a sense of exploitation and the privations of war, however, have unleashed the wildfires of resentment, revenge, and desperation. These sometimes elicit an embrace of dictators and produce a willingness to trade critical freedoms or sacrifice the rights of particular groups for bread and security. Rather than stoically waiting for good times to return or waiting, like grand heroes of libertarian doctrine, for the next economic equilibrium to develop, people do desperate things. Tragically, this includes succumbing to dictatorship. Subsequent to taking power, totalitarian and dictatorial regimes might assert rigorous controls over the economy and social welfare, but this happens as effect rather than as cause. With all due respect to Keynes's observation that in the long run we are all dead, one might add a corollary—sometimes if the long-run looks bleak enough, before they are "dead," people turn to the iron fist and throw away freedom for bread and peace.

There is not much evidence that people attach themselves to the yoke of dictatorship because of a taste for public policies to protect consumers and workers from abuse and danger. They might wind up wasting money or fail to achieve their social welfare objectives. If history is any guide, people are not likely to jettison democracy or freedoms because a ruling coalition of citizens chooses to support an active social and economic welfare sector. Surely if officials are able to search or arrest citizens without cause, or if political groups must be approved first by public agencies, or if political speech must first be reviewed by government agencies, there is greater risk to freedom and liberty than when officials are authorized to regulate workplace safety or the safety of drugs and other consumer items. Causally linking such policies as health programs, higher taxes, environmental regulation, and consumer protection with the prospect of dictatorship and the loss of an energetic democratic system is simply not supported in history. The Big Brother Road to Dictatorship perspective is a good premise for a novel or film, but it is inaccurate as a social and historical analysis. It is an argument that is more easily understood as a political and propaganda tactic.

THE ANTIGOVERNMENT SPIN

What we have is a massive muddling of how we talk about government size and government performance. Prevailing moods and themes and terms have made it very difficult to talk favorably about an activist role for government, something that has been observed by numerous individuals (Schwarz, 1988; Hirschman, 1991; Dionne, 1991). According to data provided by the Pew

Research Center, as of 1997, 64 percent of Americans think that government is inefficient and wasteful, 76 percent feel government officials "lose touch pretty quickly," 64 percent feel that government controls too much of daily life, and 57 percent think that the regulation of business does more harm than good. These results indicate slight declines in antigovernment sentiment in the past five years, at least as of 1997. Of course, these results precede the recent events surrounding the congressional investigation and impeachment proceedings of President Clinton in 1998. Even with modest improvements in outlooks about government, today's public agenda is not a particularly congenial setting for proposing great new initiatives. Although much was made of the strategic and tactical errors in the campaign by advocates of the Clinton health care reforms in the first years of his presidency, it was also fairly easy for opponents of the proposals to rely on public distrust in government and to deploy the usual array of Big Brother bogeymen and symbols to destroy prospects for any reform (Johnson and Broder, 1997).

Clearly, Americans' views regarding the size, burden, and impact of public policies have been driven more by antigovernment hyperbole than by any reasoned, factual discourse. Although it is not a justification to raise taxes, Americans are among the least-taxed people in the economically advanced societies of the world. American tax burdens, either as a percent of incomes or Gross Domestic Product, have not varied much since World War II (Wildavsky, 1998). Moreover, when comparing OECD nations in terms of their correlation between public sector size and various indicators of economic performance, it has been shown that there seems to be no consistent pattern at all. Sometimes nations with large public sectors seem to perform better than those with smaller ones; sometimes the reverse is true. More often, among the better performers there are both larger and smaller public sector nations. Despite the facts, Americans feel overly taxed and believe that government size has been a major cause of economic malaise, if not in the prosperous last few years of the twentieth century, then certainly during previous periods. Because of the preeminence of the usual Big Brother concerns and the belief in government failure, discussion about new government policies today is almost immediately diverted into a debate over whether or not there is already a too powerful, overly intrusive public sector. In many cases, the whole conversation is encapsulated and truncated by a simple query, brimming with a sense of foreboding, "Do you really want to have the government do that?" Much of our contemporary public dialogue is symbolized in this query.

In a related manner, opponents of an active government imply that taxes are lucre, extracted from a helpless and ill-served public, and that public revenues should be transferred back to individuals, since the money does not belong to "the government." The separation of the public and its government makes sense to people in a society with the perception of some fundamental, universally adversarial conflict between the public and its government. As Barber says of democracies, however:

> The money does not belong to the government, it belongs to us. But government belongs to us too. "It" does not steal from "us." We pool resources so we can act on behalf of the commonweal—the weal (well-being) common to us. If we do not like how our government spends what it collects on our common behalf, we should change the government, not deprive it of resources to do the job it does for us. Taxes are not tithes imposed by tyrants, they are self-imposed duties that permit our government to discharge our common purposes. (1996: 21)

Let us examine more closely the reference to "the government." It is as if the expression "the government" refers to some malevolent, alien beast that has landed in some remote part of the nation and is sending sinister agents out to exploit or enslave us. This image is used repeatedly in newspapers, magazines, and television and radio programs. Officials, public policies, and government institutions are talked about and described as disembodied, disconnected entities that have an adversarial relationship with the public. Whether it is the Internal Revenue Service (the least liked of all federal government agencies), the local school board, congress and other state and local legislatures, or officials of various government agencies, their actions are sometimes discussed as if they were outbreaks of a disease. In other words, "the government" is pathogenic, and every once in a while the public comes down with some variation of the government disease in the form of new taxes, regulation, and waste.

In a democracy, the relationship of the public to its officials, public policies, and the resources that are extracted to support officials and policies is quite different from what the antipublic sector spin would have us conclude. The relationship between the public and its government is different from the relationship between consumers and the private economy. The "responsiveness" to public demands operates in somewhat different fashion than markets responding to consumers; there are similarities, but important differences, too. How public sector performance ought to be evaluated as compared to private sector performance, or how the methods and objectives of the two modes of social organization might be mingled, is a complex matter, and is discussed later. For now, the important point is that critics of the public sector and those who benefit from a "smaller" public sector or who prefer to limit the public's ability to use public tools to further public goals have succeeded in creating a generalized sense of disquiet and even disdain whenever the term "the government" pops up in any conversation. The linguistic hegemony by antigovernment language poses an immediate barrier for almost anyone initiating a conversation or proposal to launch some "government" policy.

In theory and often in practice, shopkeepers and businesses are responsive to consumer tastes and preferences, and the goods and services they provide need to satisfy customers. Otherwise businesses risk the serious prospect of failure. Private markets are generally viewed as more responsive in a continuous, creative, and inevitable way than is public sector provision of goods and services. In private markets customers presumably can pick and choose bundles of goods and services so as to maximize their satisfaction, within the constraints of income and tastes and preferences. In private markets there is choice, and customers pay for things they want and they do not get things for which they do not pay. Of course, there is a host of literature about the circumstances (the market failure literature) that detracts from market performance, but in terms of the public discourse of everyday life, it is clear that people view private markets as superior in providing them with what they want and can afford, as well as permitting them to avoid paying for things that they do not want. More important, despite the fact that the public sector involves goods and services with different rationales and objectives than the private sector, the criteria employed in judging the private sector are too often the same (e.g., greater efficiency due to profit motive).

As a result, government delivery of goods and services is generally judged to be much less satisfactory. After all, these goods are too often produced in uniform bundles by monopolistic or quasi-monopolistic public providers. Voting, bargaining, lobbying by organized interests, and currying to public opinion are the mix of factors that go into the production side of government services. These services often include things that one or another person does not want. Altering any prevailing mix of government services requires investment of private resources that might otherwise be spent on the great variety of private sector goods and services. The cost of supporting unwanted services, paying for things that are not wanted, or taking time and resources away from private pursuits are seen as impositions and often convey a sense of being coerced or having one's personal resources expropriated for some other unwanted use (welfare, parks, schooling for other people's children, or economic development projects on the other end of town).

While conservatives might, under some specified circumstances, agree that some kind of government provision is required, they also argue that it should be done in a way that most closely resembles a private market, through the use of market-like mechanisms, rather than so-called command-and-control approaches such as regulations, fines, and punishments (Neiman, 1980). The language of private market provision emphasizes choice, preferences, voluntary exchange, and matching preferences/resources to goods and services. Government services, on the other hand, involve coercion; there is nearly always an inevitable mismatch between what is preferred and what is actually provided. There are greater transaction costs required by electioneering, organizing, bargaining, and negotiating in affecting choice change by changing officials, influencing fellow citizens, or combinations of both.

The more positive connotations of private market over public sector provision of goods and services camouflage a number of problems, however. If we consider the issue of whether private sector exchanges reflect the costs of other people's behavior, we realize that when we purchase a private good or service we often pay a lot for other people's conduct and preferences. Auto insurance premiums reflect the average cost of people in particular categories of location, age, and driving record. Although it might be ideal to have insurance premiums that are based solely on individual driving records, the fact is that insurance premiums must also reflect some estimate of the likelihood of future accidents and the costs of fraud, and that will always be calculated in terms of what others do as well. Similarly, the cost of borrowing money reflects the risks to similarly situated people as well as the effort on the part of firms to recoup losses incurred by loans to others. Competition might force firms to absorb the costs of some of these loans, but some degree of "socializing" or rolling in the costs of other people's behavior inevitably occurs. Finally, the cost of theft and fraud and risky behavior by customers and employees is sufficiently high that a whole range of goods and services is affected by them.

It is simply untrue to suggest that when we purchase private sector goods and services we do not pay for the choices made by others. The public could support government programs that would make it more likely that producers not pass on the costs of others when a transaction is made between a party and the supplier. For example, insurance companies might be given special tax benefits for penalizing those customers whose behavior produces higher pay-outs and, hence, higher premiums. As a result, customers with high-risk health profiles or high-risk genetic markers or other risk factors might be assessed even greater surcharges by health insurance programs. As a result, it might be possible to reward people with better health prospects. Bankruptcy laws might be made much harsher, so that people who are higher credit risks are driven out of the market for borrowed money or forced to pay much higher charges, hence driving down the cost of borrowed funds for those who are more prudent or creditworthy. Proposals to make individuals less likely to have to pay for the foolhardy and unhealthy conduct of others pose substantial increases in public sector involvement in previously private matters.

In a democracy, "the government" is merely another social organization, with one of its main purposes being the expression of the public's preferences, albeit organized around different principles than those that govern private market behavior. In democracies people seek to express certain objectives that are less likely to be expressed at all in the private sector or that would be provided by the private sector in some objectionable way. When "the government" does something to one of us, it is doing so because of policies and authority that the public has mandated through democratic procedures—such as voting and lawful delegations of authority to a responsible civil service—and through ongoing public participation in hearings and the activities of organized interests. In some sense, there is a prior understanding that membership in a civil society means that one cost to society's members will be supporting decisions that are made by others, even when one is not necessarily in favor of these decisions. The only way to avoid the burdens of tolerating majority rule would be to rely on something like the rule of unanimity for all public policy decisions. That would, of course, practically paralyze a society, making it virtually impossible to do anything of significance. In an important way, if one agrees in advance to being or remaining a member of organized society, one has implicitly accepted the rules of public sector engagement. If the rules include initiating public policies with the legitimacy of properly organized, democratic decisions to do so, then having to tolerate policies that one does not prefer is simply an overhead cost of being a member of a representative democracy.

Among some of the overhead costs of democracy are legislators and officials who behave in ways that are contrary to the preferences of some or many or most of their constituents part of the time. There are a host of classic puzzles that attend the establishment of representative institutions (Pitkin, 1967; Eksterowicz, Cline, and Hammond, 1995) For example, citizens want their representatives to do what is best for the constituency as a whole over the long haul. That invariably means that short-term interests and the interests of different segments of the community might be neglected or sacrificed. It might even be that some officials will not act on behalf of their constituents at all and will intentionally trade their constituents' best interests for private gain. These are not new puzzles. Just as private sector organizations might perform below optimal levels, so there might be public, government failure. Increasingly, scholars are aware of the conceptual linkages between market and nonmarket failure (Wolf, 1988). Insofar as admirers of the private market wish to improve public sector performance (achieving public sector objectives) by introducing the mechanisms of the private market, that is to be welcomed. One objective of public education, for example, is to increase social opportunity for as broad a segment of society as possible. If this goal is advanced by public deployment of market tools like school vouchers, then there is a strong case for doing just that. But if marshaling school choice approaches and vouchers are merely tactics to weaken and reduce the public sector and to have government disengage altogether from the equal opportunity objectives of public education, that raises serious questions about these proposals. Contemporary discussion portrays the tools of governing through traditional public sector systems as mutually exclusive with the mechanisms of market-like approaches. If the intent is to improve performance in achieving some public objective (e.g., cleaning air, maximizing opportunity for all school-age children, extending health care to the poor, or training individuals who lack marketable skills), then there is no *a priori* reason to dismiss the idea of publicly directed, yet market-like production and/or distribution of goods and services like recreation, education, housing, or counseling.

Hirschman (1991) discusses how conservative doctrine has always employed the consistent themes of "perversity, futility, and jeopardy" in criticizing and opposing the use of government to advance social justice or broaden democratic norms. Most of the arguments that have been deployed against a governmentally active public in recent decades have been easily discernible at least as early as the French Revolution. In the case of perversity, government programs and efforts to improve things are almost always alleged to produce unwanted and unanticipated results that are more important than the original intent. The futility argument claims that social interventions cannot change human nature and that maladies like poverty and prejudice will always be present. Finally, jeopardy arguments deal with the concern of conservatives that in seeking to improve social and political justice, other important values, such as liberty and private property, might be jeopardized. The themes of perversity, futility, and jeopardy can be seen in virtually every conservative campaign against such things as expanding voting rights, helping orphans, helping the industrial unemployed, reducing exploitation of child labor, managing environmental and natural resource problems, or increasing the minimum wage. Just about the only time we do not hear from conservatives about how public intervention is perverse, futile, or dangerous is when it involves such sure-fire winners as throwing tax benefits at the wealthy so that their decisions might trickle down to the less blessed, or making it easier to resist unions, or throwing ever greater numbers of drug addicts into prison, or treating ever younger children as adults in criminal cases, or having the government support religious schools with tax dollars.

This is not to say that those who advocate government activism are devoid of comparable rhetorical shibboleths and slogans. It is just that their rhetoric is not especially effective just now. It is not being suggested that a more desirable state of affairs is some sort of balance between the contending propaganda factories of the right and the left. Dionne (1991: 11) conveys more accurately the sense in which the rhetorical rocks and ideological hard places of contemporary public discourse need to be overcome:

> ... [L]iberalism and conservatism are framing political issues as a series of false choices. Wracked by contradiction and responsive mainly to the needs of their various constituencies, liberalism and conservatism *prevent* [author's emphasis] the nation from settling the questions that most

trouble it. On issue after issue, there is consensus on where the country should move or at least on what we should be arguing about; liberalism and conservatism make it impossible for that consensus to express itself.

In actuality, the public has much to be proud of in terms of what has been accomplished through its support of various public programs. Clearing the public perceptions of the antipublic sector dogma is necessary if the public is to fathom how it is that "constituencies who had gotten jobs, gone to college, bought houses, started businesses, secured health care, and retired in dignity because of government decided, of a sudden, that 'government was the problem' ..." (Dionne, 1991: 144). Certainly by the time of Ronald Reagan's 1980 presidential election victory the public's disdain for government and public officials had been nurtured by a variety of policy failures; the antigovernment themes were not composed in a vacuum. But as others have demonstrated (Goodsell, 1994; Kelman, 1987; Schwarz, 1988), the sense of failure can, indeed often does, obscure important successes. Getting Americans to forget their public sector achievements in education, income security, consumer protection, and environmental quality (Schwarz, 1988) has been a tremendous victory by those who would benefit from a dismal view of politics and an interpretation of failure, rather than important successes, in public policy.

Since World War II, the people of the United States have worked to improve the well-being of senior citizens and to broaden tremendously the educational opportunities of people. Through government, the public has improved the safety and performance of a wide range of goods and services, made workplaces less hazardous, enhanced environmental quality, and conserved important amenities, including rivers, lakes, beaches, forests, and other elements critical to the quality of life. Unfortunately, much that has not gone well has been blamed on some presumed, inherent tendency for the public sector to fail. An enormous amount of energy and sophisticated analyses have been directed at reconstructing the view of the past, so that the public sector achievements of American society have been obscured and diminished (e.g., Freeman, 1975; Freeman, 1981; Mitchell and Simmons, 1994). It is worth quoting at length the words of a leading defender of public activism:

> Dazed and dispirited, Americans entered the 1980s disturbed by the sensation that the prior twenty years had been largely misspent, that during all those years, bit by bit, we had traveled down the wrong road. The record of those years in the domestic spheres indicates otherwise. It reveals an era of constructive actions by both the government and the private economy to meet awesome challenges that our nation faced. For nearly a decade, a spell of antigovernment rhetoric has taken hold.

> Evolving from a myriad of misunderstandings of the past, the spell has beckoned us to reject the twenty years of the post-Eisenhower era and the accomplishments that we as a nation, through government, achieved in those years. Only if we recognize the negative spell that has been cast can we draw renewed confidence from the knowledge that in the past we accomplished much through governmental activism to improve Americans' lives. Only then can we realize our capacity as a nation to do so again in the future. (Schwarz, 1988: 186–87)

The purpose here is not to have people suspend their skepticism or even fear of government power, something that is not likely to happen anyway. Rather, it is to underscore the continuing need for a vigorous, democratically directed public sector and to explain the strategic purpose of antigovernment rhetoric. That purpose is to discourage people from using public sector tools, even when doing so would produce gains for the public, as it has before.

CONSIDER THIS PERVERSE ARGUMENT

The manner in which language is confounded in discussions about government size is never more evident than in discussions concerning the presumed relationship between coercion, personal liberty, and government size. Conservatives tend to argue, and the public has evidently accepted the argument, that government size and coercion are positively related: The more things the government does, the more coercive a government becomes. What if on some occasions traditional, coercive forms of government intervention tend toward smaller government?

Let us briefly review the way in which a conventional regulatory proposal arrives on the agenda of government (Cobb and Elder, 1972; Kingdon, 1984): A problem ascends to the social and political agenda; advocacy groups emerge; media involvement grows; resistance from the targets of public concern is mobilized; possible responses by elected officials are crafted; law is enacted; implementation is designed; and a variety of impacts result. The tools involved in regulation are most often some kind of coercion, with rules and standards enforced by fines or other sanctions, often even criminal sanctions. Most consumer safety, environmental protection, toxic waste and hazardous materials management, and water quality policies rely on these sorts of coercive, "command-and-control" approaches. Conservatively inclined theorists often worry about this form of government response, since it tends to displace markets and the role of prices and costs and profit-seeking with bureaucratically determined outcomes, and, presumably, it reduces personal liberty. The costs of complying with many regulatory policies tend to be diffuse and indirect, so that the benefits of regulation are hard to ascertain relative to costs. After all, the costs of complying with workplace safety or equal opportunity regulations are borne by the private sector and filter through the private sector's production, distribution, and exchange process, so that it is not readily apparent what the cost of regulation in any particular case is, much less what the cost of all regulation might be for the society as a whole. The public, moreover, by not directly bearing substantial regulatory costs, might possibly demand more regulation than would be the case if these costs were more apparent and directly felt in the way costs and benefits presumably are in conventional, private market exchange.

As Wilson (1980) has demonstrated, there are times when demands for regulation are unlikely to get transformed into public policy. When there are diffuse regulatory benefits for a large public and concentrated costs borne by some set of powerful interests, the result is usually a defeat for these policies. It is not easy for the general class of utility consumers to derive a few dollars in benefits per year due to a regulation over the opposition of a small, but powerful group of utilities that might bear the brunt of the cost of these benefits for consumers. The motivation of consumers to seek a few dollars in benefits will be much smaller than the motivation of the utilities that have to bear the large aggregate cost of these benefits. In the relatively rare situations in which policies are enacted and implemented over resistant targets, the targets are indefatigable in opposing, altering, terminating, and otherwise weakening the scope, substance, and effectiveness of policies that are seen as costly or harmful to them. Once the officials who carried the public's interest in the legislative domain turn to other matters or are displaced by officials with different views and priorities, once the media is no longer interested in dwelling on the reasons that produced public concern, and once the public becomes complacent about the fact of regulation, then the political advantage often shifts to the opponents of regulation.

Alternatively, what if we take to heart the conservatives' worries regarding conventional command-and-control regulation and use market-like incentives and subsidies? Recall that conservatives and other private market advocates might concede that some kinds of situations ("market failures") can require public intervention. The preference, however, is that if public intervention can be justified, then public responses should stay as close to market-like approaches as possible. Additionally, it is assumed that by increasing the return for complying with public objectives, there will be more efficient production of desired behavior. After all, people are more likely to do the things for which they are rewarded. On the other hand, people are likely to try to evade and, when possible, attack and destroy those policies that inflict costs on them. The recent impetus toward privatization of public services is premised in some significant ways on the allegedly greater efficiencies of market-like responses to such matters as primary and secondary school education, job training, managing public parks, prison administration, and the delivery of a host of other physical and social services. When public authorities are *not* using coercive methods to achieve public purposes, they are presumably not as "big" or "powerful" as they might otherwise be. After all, if the public supports the use of civil and criminal sanctions in some new area, has it not somehow increased the government's coercive potential? Isn't personal liberty less likely to be threatened or abused if officials rely on incentives and moral persuasion, rather than sanctions and coercion? Instead of coercing corporations to comply with clean air standards, give them tax breaks, direct grants, and honors for achieving these standards. Instead of using affirmative action standards and rules to coerce employers to comply with employment targets and goals, provide tax breaks for each percentage increase in the proportion of previously underrepresented groups in the employer's workforce, with special premiums for increases in hiring above the "glass ceiling" (i.e., hiring more minority group members and women and promoting them to higher executive positions). No doubt with "incentives" to comply, rather than threatened sanctions, businesses would rush to demonstrate the many things they have done to improve air quality or reduce water pollution. Employers might dash to discover the many different ethnic, racial, and cultural backgrounds of their employees to receive the rewards derived from enhancing their workforce diversity.

The ordinary *motivation* that individuals and organizations have in resisting government interventions is in fact diminished greatly in the face of rewards, incentives, and subsidies. In fact, while the size of government might involve less coercion, government growth might actually accelerate as a consequence of the greatly increased *range* of things that government will be doing as various actors seek to qualify for subsidies. While government might not be more coercive, it might be far more active. This distinction leads to an important proposition: The size of government is a function of how coercive the method associated with some action is plus the number of actions/things the government does (the range of government activity). This is expressed in the following equation:

$$GS = a + m_1A_1 + m_2A_2 + \dots m_nA_n$$

Where GS = total Government Size

a = the level of government in the absence of any formal activity

m_i = the level of coercion employed to implement some activity

A_i = the particular activity or action or thing implemented

Other things being equal, the higher the value of m_i (i.e., the more coercive the proposal), the less likely its corresponding A_i is to be enacted.

For example, a proposal to provide information to adults about the fat content in food is more likely to be enacted than a proposal to punish food processors for distributing food with fat content above a certain level. In addition, a proposal to join a prohibition of high fat content with policies to inflict costs on obese Americans obviously has even less chance of enactment. It is possible, then, to have two jurisdictions engaging in the same range of actions, yet differing in the size of their governments, due to the differences in the methods they use to implement the range of activity. In other words, if we reduce the use of coercive methods, we might actually increase the range of government activity, since the chance of enacting something is higher when the level of coercion is lower. Figure 8.1 suggests the nature of this inverse relationship, indicating that the more coercive a proposal is, the less likely it is to be enacted or to persist in the face of opposition by those against whom the coercion is directed. In democratic societies, if coercive proposals are formulated, they are less likely to be enacted and, hence, *the range* of different things being done will be smaller. In democratic societies relying on incentives and market-like inducements, the range of things done in the public sector will be greater.

It is hard to judge whether a smaller range of coercive activities is "more" government than a wider array of *less* coercive activity. There is not

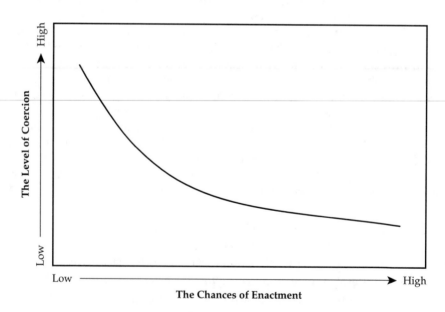

The Chances of Enactment

FIGURE 8.1   THE HIGHER THE LEVEL OF COERCION ASSOCIATED WITH A PUBLIC PROPOSAL, THE LESS LIKELY IT IS TO BE ENACTED

an adequate framework for developing weights and measures to come to some conclusion about these matters. Answering questions about which activities contribute the most to increasing the scale and/or burden of government is a very muddy issue. How do tax increases, fines, or threats of incarceration compare to substantive mandates (e.g., comparing an increase in sales taxes to government requirements that political demonstrations must receive prior, official approval)? Did Franco's Spain or Mussolini's Italy have a "smaller" government than contemporary Sweden because the former had a smaller social welfare component? Are citizens of the Netherlands more vulnerable to abuse than are citizens of the United States because the latter has a smaller social welfare component? Is every increment of government involvement equivalent to every other government action? Are restrictions or policies governing political participation of citizens and environmental or work-place safety standards or motorcycle helmet requirements and no-smoking areas equivalent in their relevance for personal liberty or government size?

Even public policies that do not involve coercion but that are administered through annual budgets, tend to come under intense political scrutiny and perhaps attack by their opponents. Most programs benefiting the poor require annual budget appropriations and government agencies to administer programs. Over the past twenty-five years, due to increasing pressures on budgets, many programs for the poor have been cut or otherwise grown much slower than inflation. Those who receive public benefits through the tax code, however, have fared much better, in the main. It is more difficult for the poor to receive their benefits as incentives and deductions from the tax code (these are called "tax expenditures"), since the poor do not usually file long-form tax returns. Benefits that are distributed through tax expenditures, however, tend to be less scrutinized since there is no automatic review of these expenditures in the same way that some program for the poor must experience through the usual budget process. So, while housing programs for the poor have been slashed substantially, just as one example, the tax expenditures for housing programs for the owner-occupied housing population has remained untouched. The estimated foregone revenue (tax expenditure) for just three categories of these items is enormous in the 1997 fiscal year. The estimated total of 1997 tax expenditures associated with interest on mortgage debt, state and local property taxes, deferral of capital gains on the sale of homes, and the one-time permanent exemption from capital gains is far greater than the total cost of all low-income housing programs.

Notwithstanding the current infatuation with the flat-tax rate, those who benefit from these tax benefits are not likely to accept quick reductions in them. The relative invisibility and complexity of tax provisions makes it unlikely that individual tax benefits will be assaulted by someone on mere principle. The apparently less coercive vehicle for providing benefits through the tax code receives relatively little scrutiny through fiscal review, and when it does, the review encounters intense opposition from beneficiaries of these benefits. Indeed, it is unclear whether the recipients of tax code largesse even see themselves as beneficiaries of government programs. Instead, they see any threats to the tax code as an assault on their disposable income.

So it is that the set of programs implemented through the relatively more visible arena of the conventional budget process comes to be fodder for the political process. Unlike the beneficiaries of tax code provisions, those who receive direct benefits through annually funded programs are seen as feeding at the public trough or as welfare dependents with no claim on public resources other than improving the utility of those whose taxes fund these programs. Naturally, recipients of tax benefits do not see themselves as being funded in part by those who do not qualify for the benefits and must make up the foregone revenue with higher taxes than would be the case if these tax benefits were eliminated.

During periods of constrained budgets, groups with fewer political resources are less able to defend the benefits they receive through budgeted programs, since these programs are regularly scrutinized through budget hearings. Government regulations are generally implemented by publicly funded commissions and agencies, and the budgets of these bodies can be assaulted by hostile interests and their representatives during every year the budgets of these entities are reviewed (usually on an annual basis). Put differently, during periods of budgetary stress, programs that are supported mainly through the conventional budget process are more likely to be cut than are programs supported as tax expenditures through the provisions of the tax code. As a corollary: Budgeted programs for the poor are more likely to be cut, *ceteris paribus*, than programs for the nonpoor, since the former tend to rely more on annually budgeted programs rather than through the tax code, which is less likely to receive ongoing, regularly scheduled oversight.

The equity issue is perhaps made more problematic since the tax code is less likely to be mined for budget savings, except intermittently as part of some overall tax reform effort, a relatively rare occurrence. It can be claimed that charitable contributions are encouraged through the tax code— true enough—and that these benefit the poor. However, the reality depends on how many of these contributions filter through to benefit lower income people. Remember that charitable contributions include a host of resources that do not always serve the poor directly, if they serve them at all (e.g., youth sports teams, university scholarships and capital campaigns, rescue and emergency organizations, hospitals and ballets, art museums, opera companies, theater groups, symphony orchestras).

Additionally, regulatory agencies or agencies that rely on coercion are often the subject of highly dramatized and publicized instances of abuse. In a sense, this is the obverse of highly dramatic events that causes public pressure to create some regulatory agency. Quite rightly, when officials of these agencies overstep their bounds or act like thugs, elected representatives and the media have a field day in investigating the conduct and scoring points for disciplining these misbehaving public employees. The result often is a loss of legitimacy for the agency and its purposes, as well as a tightening of its scope and its budget when it is reviewed during the budgetary process. During 1998, for example, tax opponents benefited from the possibly deserved public disclosure of misconduct by the nation's chief tax collector, the Internal Revenue Service. A parade of aggrieved and mistreated citizens recounted tales of abuse and misapplication of law and regulations, and the result was not only serious further reduction of IRS power, but also fairly major changes in the administration of the agency. There are many examples to indicate that when official mistreatment of citizens at the local, state, and federal levels occurs, it often results in the curtailment of agency power. Critics of government tend to exploit very quickly and publicize, as well they should, such misbehavior.

Noncoercive methods of achieving public objectives might actually produce more involvement by the public in previously private matters. While this involvement might appear to be less intrusive and imply "less government," incentives-based approaches might increase the range of things through which public influence is applied. It is possible that the increased range of public involvement, as noncoercive as it might seem, might still produce more government.

Examining the possible introduction of market incentives to the current prevailing public, private, and secondary schools—the so-called voucher approach to increasing school choice—it is possible to see some of these effects (Neiman and Stambough, 1998). The decline in academic performance of students in the public schools is often dramatized as one of the premier examples of government failure (Chubb and Moe, 1990). Ever since the early work of Milton Friedman (1955; 1962), conservative rational choice theorists and conservative economists have been formulating and advocating school choice and voucher proposals as alternatives, if not substitutes, for the current public school system. Advocates of school choice and vouchers argue that public schools are monopolistic and have no incentive to innovate and compete on the basis of the success they have in improving the educational performance of school children. Presumably, by introducing competition among schools and by permitting parents to choose the schools to which they send their children through the issuance of vouchers to parents to be redeemed at the school of their choice, a kind of educational market with all of its benefits will result. In implementing school choice, consider the issues (listed at the top of page 176) that arise (Neiman and Stambough, 1998).

- Assuming that parents will be able to choose schools that maximize the educational well-being and long-term interest of children, problems will result without standard consumer protection regulation of the education product of claims made by the schools, such as those regarding achievement or college placement.

- Will all schools, once they are accredited, be included in the program? Will there be no concern over schools that emphasize religious training, ethnic identification, or unusual life style questions (e.g., schools that are especially attentive to children who are gay)? Will all receive equal support or will some not?

- What about the value of the vouchers? They not only affect the cost of the programs, but also raise questions about equal opportunity. Should vouchers include travel costs? Perhaps sending a child to the school of choice requires one to send a student long distances at some considerable cost. What about tuition costs—what if one chooses a boarding school? What about including special assistance costs, such as training and preparing for the SAT exam? Should vouchers include the cost of extracurricular activities such as orchestra, drama, or sports? What standard of education should these vouchers minimally ensure? Will parents be allowed to supplement the vouchers at the schools; in other words can schools receive nonvoucher funds? Should the vouchers include costs for students with special needs due to some disability or for temporary disadvantages such as being a non-English speaker?

- If there are eligibility requirements for these vouchers, who will enforce them? Will there be price ceilings to receive the vouchers and how would these be enforced?

- What about competition among schools for vouchers and students? Might schools offer rebates for the best students in order to maximize the achievement profile of its students? How would this affect parents' choices? Would this be encouraged?

These sorts of post-implementation issues are budgetary and regulatory. While it is possible that school choice policies might provide more choice, it is also clear that a whole new area of budgetary and regulatory issues are likely to emerge, notwithstanding any claims made about the possible effects of greater school choice on children. It is likely that moving toward a more market-like setting for primary and secondary setting will open up substantial new arenas for public regulation. "Private" contractors delivering what were once "government" services will merely replace public employees (without the constraints imposed on public employees) as highly motivated lobbyists for public expenditure of "privatized" public services.

Imagine that the public could only use coercive methods of achieving public purposes. The demand for extending government to some new area would produce greater opposition than if that extension were implemented through noncoercive methods. It would be more difficult to garner support or maintain the zealousness of implementation over the long haul. Hence, *ceteris paribus*, requiring that any proposed activity of government must also employ coercion to accomplish its purpose means that a proposal is less likely to be enacted and less likely to overcome opposition from the coercion target as public attention diminishes. Assume, on the other hand, that the only way to accomplish proposed government activity is through incentives and subsidies. Clearly, less opposition is likely and more government will result, albeit with a soft touch and a carrot rather than a mailed fist and a stick.

Rational choice theories and empirical evidence are vague regarding what contributes more to government size—the method of doing something (coercion versus incentives) or extending government activity, however it is done, to some new area. Recall that rational choice theorists are concerned about two things: first, that government intervene in matters only when there is some solid extra-judgmental justification (e.g., public goods and market failure); second, when such justification exists government should replicate the workings of markets or market-like devices and rely on prices, rather than rule-enforcement and sanctions. The latter might produce more involvement by government, and hence conflicts with the prior, perhaps greater, concern that government scale be minimized. Surely a government that does an increasing range of things, even through the use of market-like incentives, can be intrusive, abusive, inequitable, and/or burdensome.

MEANING AND INTERPRETATION

One reason individuals feel that the range and cost of government is burdensome, even too large, derives from a sense of resentment about the justification for programs. Apart from the variety of highly technical criteria that are used in justifying a specific government program, the meaning people attach to programs can also be important. When individuals receive benefits that are paid by the general population, the meaning ascribed to the "redistribution" can be affected by the elements of context that are employed by the public. When someone is harmed and receives compensation, the public does not consider it welfare or "redistribution" in the charitable or social welfare sense of the term, but rather, thinks it is a matter of justice that a harmed party be compensated by those who inflicted the harm. In a related way, the public thinks that some people are deserving of help because the afflictions or disasters that befall them are not of their doing. The public is somewhat less sympathetic and less willing to help people whose choices and decisions knowingly invite disaster and difficulty. Obviously, the public might sympathize with the family of someone suffering permanent injury after going on a mountain climb or doing a bit of extreme skiing, but would probably feel little sense of obligation, charitable or otherwise, and might even resent a government program that would somehow compensate victims of injuries due to mountain climbing, extreme skiing, parachuting, and hang-gliding. Why? Because the public thinks that people who take on known, obvious risks in recreational activity should be a lower priority for help than others.

What of assistance to hurricane victims or to victims of wildfires in fire-prone areas? Is this sort of assistance considered to be redistribution? Might some members of the public object to helping people living in certifiably dangerous, vulnerable, hurricane-prone, and fire-hazardous areas? Did not these people "freely" choose to live in risky locales, thus inviting disaster? In many areas, the presence of large numbers of homes actually increases the likelihood of "natural" disaster. The equipment and facilities that are needed to manage fires when homes are built in fire-prone areas are expensive and impose high marginal costs on fire department budgets. These costs do not include the lucrative insurance subsidies that exist for middle-class and wealthy homeowners in flood and fire-prone areas. Yet, are the families of innocent bystander victims of gang violence more blameworthy than wealthy homeowners living in fire-prone areas? It does seem so, if actual policy indicates the revealed preferences of the public, since much more is provided in the way of assistance and subsidies to people living in flood-prone and fire-hazardous areas than to law-abiding victims of violent crime, especially those who are residents of crisis communities. It is not clear at all what principle explains the ready help given to victims of flood or other calamities, especially when the victims choose to live in areas with known hazards. Perhaps the barrio or ghetto family with a member or two gunned down in a drive-by shooting should have considered living in a gang-free area.

Of course, equal opportunity programs raise particular difficulties. Are these redistributive programs or are they compensatory efforts designed to redress prior injustices inflicted on particular groups? Individual viewpoints do depend on knowledge and acceptance of prior injustice, but also depend on views regarding the passing on of intergenerational burdens and obligations. When stockholders invest in a company, they assume, as well, liabilities that resulted *before* they invested. In other words, they assume fiscal responsibility, even though the stockholders might have had no role in the making of decisions that produced the liability. Tens of millions of Germans and Swiss citizens are taking on the cost of compensating victims of the Holocaust in World War II, even while contemporary

Germans and Swiss might have had no direct involvement in harming anyone during the Nazi era. A majority might not even have been alive then. Similarly, affirmative action programs might be seen as compensatory, rather than redistributive, and there might be a justification for having people bear the burden of affirmative action even if they did not discriminate against anyone.

The intent here is not to resolve the disputes over these sorts of issues; rather, the main point is that the meaning individuals attach to the exchange of resources, from taxpayers to one group or another, is affected by how individuals interpret the meaning of the exchange and how deserving they perceive the recipient to be. Our view of how imposing and burdensome government is depends partly on our sense of merit and justification for these kinds of actions or expenditures. Antigovernment critics have helped to undermine the sense of legitimacy for many of the groups or individuals for whom we once felt it useful or justified to provide public programs—many of the poor, immigrants, mentally ill, public school and college students, people living in crisis communities, and the unemployed.

There is a point at which the burden of "helping" or "compensating" various groups can become fundamentally too great, no matter how deserving some group is likely to be, and the result of trying to help might indeed be counterproductive (Okun, 1975). Despite the fact that Americans feel they are overtaxed, the United States is at the low end of the spectrum among advanced economies when it comes to the size of the public sector or the level of taxes. The sense of burden in the United States, then, is much less a function of some technical, objective level of spending and taxes. The general resentment reflects the success that antigovernment forces have achieved in labeling much of what the nation has done through the public sector as futile, perverse, and hazardous to other values, to paraphrase Hirschman (1991).

Americans have been convinced by the antigovernment campaign that a host of people who receive public support do not merit the help or that the help given them only compounds the problems these groups face. The politics of resentment, then, is coupled with the claim that a potentially abusive, even dictatorial government is being grafted onto the backs of the nation through the guise of a social welfare state. The success of conservatives comes from winning in the politics of meaning and fostering resentments about taxes, regulation, and welfare. There is nothing sinister about it, and there are a host of things that occurred in the world, the nation, and in the missteps of liberals that contributed greatly to the conservative ascendancy. Nor is it being suggested that the dominant liberal agenda or approach to social problems that existed prior to the conservative victories should necessarily be revived. The point is simply that how we view the array of government services, whether we consider them burdensome or justified, is partly a reflection of the meaning we attach to them. In the struggle for which set of understandings prevails among a ruling majority of Americans, the interpretations favoring the conservative agenda have prevailed, for now. Whether this is fair or not, whether conservatives are favored by institutional biases, whether they are blessed with far greater resources, or whether they are just better in this competition over political meaning is not relevant to the point being made. For now, they have won. Even in the context of a prosperous economy, there is a prevailing resentment among many Americans about the scope, burden, and purposes of contemporary politics.

Clearly, the process for making decisions about how to ease the sense of "burden" that public programs produce in a resentful public is not rigorous or formal. If it were, it would include a fair assessment of the panoply of regulations and expenditures and tax benefits that benefit those who are well-off. If the motivation were to generally eliminate programs that help the undeserving, it would include programs that underwrite home ownership and development in dangerous and environmentally sensitive areas. Such a general, fairer review would include some effort to recover the benefits from public regulation. For every landowner whose use of land is restricted, for example, there is another landowner whose land values increase because of that regulation. There are property owners whose land values skyrocket because of publicly financed water and road improvements, school construction, and the provision of public safety. There are middle-class homeowners whose neighborhoods are protected by government regulation against land uses that would conflict with residential-centered and family-centered lifestyles. There are middle-class and wealthy senior citizens who receive a host of government benefits. If it were true that a completely objective and rigorous review of the public sector is what conservatives are interested in, then all of these programs, as well as those for the poor and less advantaged, would be thrown into the hopper for a cost-benefit review.

Instead, the process of thinning the public sector is fraught with the capacity of various groups to maintain (or not maintain) the legitimacy of their claim on resources or the public's sense of merit for some group or interest. The programs that have tended to fare the worst in these budget cutting and program-thinning exercises are the programs for the poor, those on welfare, and those caught in crisis communities (e.g., disability insurance; Medicaid; Aid to Families with Dependent Children; housing assistance; federal aid to older, urban places; food stamp programs; more punishment for nonviolent criminals and drug addicts; and program cuts for immigrants, legal and illegal). As shown in the previous chapter, while we are busy increasing the severity of sentences and loading up the prisons with nonviolent criminals, we seem much less determined to do anything about white collar criminals whose misconduct is far costlier to society. We seem to choose imprisonment and skyrocketing prison system and court costs for those criminals whose misdeeds are far less expensive. With few exceptions, the politics of slashing budgets, reducing taxes, and reforming regulation avoids most policies that seem to benefit the affluent. Notwithstanding the occasional reference to corporate welfare, public discourse does not attach negative meanings to the lavish array of tax expenditures and direct payments and programs that benefit the politically influential.

CHAPTER 9

BEING DISMAL IN POLICY ANALYSIS OR LEARNING TO LOVE POLICYMAKING

Recent decades have seen the economic or rational choice approach to policy analysis become increasingly influential in the field of policy studies. Many works have chronicled the emergence of economics in policy analysis, and there is also a lively debate concerning the impact and implications of economic approaches for policy study. That debate is adequately summarized in a number of other places (Green and Shapiro, 1994; Coleman and Fararo, 1992; Johnson, 1991).

THE FLIGHT FROM POLITICS

The concern here is for another, perhaps more important, feature of the prevailing economic approach to policy analysis. Many applications of economics-based analysis are designed to displace the role of politics as a means of deciding when public policy interventions in previously private matters should occur, what sorts of public policy tools should be employed, when these interventions are justified, and how it is decided which policies to change or terminate. This mode of analysis is best understood as part of a centuries-long search for principles to determine when government intervention should happen and rules for designing institutions. A chief goal of this tradition is containing the growth and scale of government within limited bounds. The work of modern economics-oriented critics of politics and policy, such as Hayek, Friedman, Buchanan, Tullock, Nozick, and Rawls, is squarely within this tradition (Hampton, 1986).

Within democratic systems public policy emerges mainly from a complex mix of institutional design and such political processes as electioneering and voting, organizing and mobilizing groups, lobbying, assessing public opinion, and the interacting of views among the public, elected, and nonelected officials. The mix of traditional political forces is a matter of great suspicion among conservative thinkers, and has been since the founding of the nation and during the great public discourses expressed in the Federalist Papers and the ratification debates over the federal constitution. That is why economic approaches to politics and policy are more than just a technical issue regarding how best to deal with policy analysis. At its base, much of the work on rational or economic models of politics and policy is explicitly constitutional in nature. The word constitutional is quite intentional and refers to the work of Hayek, Friedman, Buchanan, Tullock, Nozick, and others. Their priority is to develop principles for limiting the boundaries of a political system in terms of what it does and how it does it. Their fundamental purpose is not to quibble about whether incentives or command-and-control approaches to policy ought to be used. Rather, it is to focus on what sets of principles will fix the scale of government so that it is contained within the bounds of what a reasonable person would refer to as "limited government." Not all economic or rational models of policy are conservative. Others have shown that such approaches are not necessarily compelled by logic to conservative conclusions (Elster, 1979; 1983; Levi, 1988; Samuels, 1993). However, most economic approaches to policy analysis and institutional design have been explicitly conservative in the sense of preferring that government be as limited as possible, and when government intervention is required, these approaches prefer that it be as market-like as possible.

Fretting about Democracy and Redistributive Demands

Rational choice approaches have popularized standards of performance such as returns on investment (cost/benefit analysis) and a host of other concepts critical to the variety of ways in which public interventions in society are justified and evaluated. The concepts of market failure, public goods, and externalities have been applied in a wide variety of contexts. Nevertheless, it is worth emphasizing the contributions of public/rational choice approaches:

1. Emphasizing the importance of opportunity costs in achieving public benefits and the principle that benefits must be considered relative to costs

2. Illustrating that there are a broad range of alternative ways of delivering public goods and services, other than hierarchical, government bureaucracies; for example, housing and education vouchers
   or the use of incentives and subsidies, rather than fines and sanctions

3. Emphasizing the importance of customer-oriented criteria for assessing satisfaction with government services

4. Demonstrating the fact that market-like incentives and price-like
   mechanisms are sometimes superior to rules and coercive sanctions
   in achieving public objectives

Despite these contributions, however, there is also a kind of imperialism in economic approaches to policy, in which the elegance and parsi-
mony of analysis overwhelms legitimate concern for the implications of
these various approaches. Kelman (1981) expressed this in his examination of the use of incentives to achieve public purposes in the areas of
health, safety, and environmental protection. The main concern here is the
commitment that many advocates of these theories have to a conservative
political agenda in the most fundamental sense. Some rational choice theorists begin with a deep repugnance for politics, even the politics of democracies, as a means of making choices. For them, rational choice models
provide an alternative to the processes of ordinary pluralistic decision
making.

At one level, economic or rational modes of analysis reflect nothing
more than an uncontroversial commitment to improving public policy
choices. After all, who is against knowing what works and what does not
work, or knowing which policy is less costly than another in achieving the
same results? Among rational model advocates, however, there is often
more than just a desire to improve technique in public sector activity. Advocates of privatization or the use of market-like mechanisms such as school
vouchers are not just interested in the narrow technical efficiency. There is
also a great fear of democratic political competition and great distrust of
governing institutions. This uneasiness has been manifested from the start
of the Republic by those concerned with majority tyranny or the evils of
faction (Berry, 1984). Specific concepts of public choice and rational model
approaches such as externalities, cost-benefit analysis, or privatization can
be seen as efforts to remove policy decisions from the turmoil of politics to
the domain of what is supposed to be more business-like and, therefore,
more rational, decision making.

In democracies, the way in which issues reach the public, policymaking agendas, how policies are formulated, and how they are assessed and
changed is often tumultuous (Baumgartner and Jones, 1993). Although life
in the state of nature might, according to Hobbes, be "nasty, brutish, and
short," the life of modern democratic politics is often unseemly, noisy, and
disorderly. No matter how the development of public policy is explained,

the policy process is, in actuality, complex and uncoordinated, and it lacks effective linkages between theories of how particular problems are caused and appropriate policy implementation methods for those problems (Rothstein, 1998: 57–70). Given the size and heterogeneity of the United States, its federal structure, the lack of consensus among experts, politicians and the public, and the legitimacy that is accorded to constituent interests, the American political process seems especially boisterous and inhospitable to the best-drawn blueprints of planners and policy analysts.

Social contract theorists and their classical liberal descendants were devoted to considering methods that would ensure that democratic politics did not produce a tyranny of the majority or excessive redistributive demands among the less affluent, propertyless classes. This was at one time a fairly explicit concern of American thinkers (Dietze, 1985). Separation of powers, bicameralism, indirect election of senators, and property qualifications to vote were often seen as methods to insulate policymaking from certain political forces that would detract from wise and just policy. The anxiety about egalitarian, direct democracy was explicit, and a preference for limiting the scale and scope of government, as well as avoiding redistributive public policy, was an important feature of the Lockean tradition so critical in the shaping of American institutions (Barber, 1984; Hartz, 1955). It was majoritarian democracy that worried conservatives.

The conservative nature of the uneasiness about the impact of democratic governance on government size and on the public is couched in terms of anxiety about redistributive policies or the role of public sector entities, most notably public bureaucracies themselves (Niskanen, 1971; Courant, Gramlich, and Rubinfeld, 1979). The fact that governments intervene far more extensively and vigorously on behalf of the affluent seems to be less an issue, although there are the occasional token expressions of worry about "welfare for the well-to-do" (Tullock, 1983).

Although anxiety about too much redistribution is often explicitly stated, these sentiments are regularly camouflaged in the language and rhetoric of cost-benefit analysis and economic efficiency and technical discussions about equilibria and marginal utility. The concern that conservative advocates of rational models have is really apprehension about too much access to politics by too many interests served by overly responsive officials, who, as a result, provide too much government. The fundamental problems for public choice theorists are, in short, too much access and too much responsiveness—too much democracy.

This chapter examines the use of economic or rational models of analysis in the area of urban government and housing policy. It also explores a number of ways in which economic approaches to policy analysis are used to guide public policies. Insofar as rational model advocates proclaim that they provide alternatives to the sound and fury of democratic politics, they are substantially wrong. The emphasis is on demonstrating the way in which the values of the advocates of these models affect what they do and a number of other issues that plague these sorts of approaches.

PUBLIC CHOICE AND METROPOLITAN ORGANIZATION

Although most people in the United States live in urbanized areas, none is governed by a single governmental entity. An examination of the great metropolitan centers of the United States—such as New York, Los Angeles, Chicago, Atlanta, Miami, New Orleans, Dallas, Houston, San Francisco, Portland, and Seattle—reveals that each of these areas comprises many units of government. Some of these areas still have a historically dominant area, such as Chicago's Loop or New York's Manhattan, but most urban areas are now multinucleated and governed by many different units of government. No single governmental entity is responsible for the range of local services and problems that are ordinarily associated with local governments. These local services and policies include street maintenance, traffic circulation, utility delivery, public transportation, education, public safety (police and fire protection), health and social services for the poor, solid waste management, air and water pollution regulation, and local planning and economic development. The chief feature of government organization in the metropolitan United States is fragmentation. A visit to the Los Angeles region results in a catalogue of hundreds of local governments, including cities, school districts, several counties, dozens of community college districts, library districts, several transportation entities, and so on. Even though a given metropolitan area constitutes an interrelated housing market, air and water basin, transport network, and ecological unity, there is little coordination among these many different local government bodies.

While consolidation of some government units might occur for a particular purpose, the key feature of America's metropolitan areas is the tremendous number and variety of local governments—cities, counties, and special purpose districts (e.g., school districts, soil conservation, water, and mosquito abatement districts). A citizen living in a large metropolitan region is likely to receive services from a city, a county, a school district, a community college district, and perhaps a water district. Moreover, he or she is likely to be subject to regulations by a number of different local or area governments and be taxed and governed by a number of different entities. For many years, government fragmentation has been criticized on the grounds that it obscures responsibility for services, and that it prevents public agencies from efficiencies that can be achieved by larger, regional units of government. Traditional reformers have claimed it would be less expensive, for example, to have one large metropolitan-wide police department with one communications hub than a multitude of local police departments within a single metropolitan region. Similar calls for consolidation on efficiency grounds have been voiced about transportation, planning, solid waste removal, library systems, and resource management generally.

Consolidation proposals have usually been rejected (Ross and Levine, 1996: 321–82). Suburban local governments resist consolidation with central cities. Indeed, newer suburbs tend to resist interaction with older suburban areas. In metropolitan areas, then, government consolidation occurs only for limited purposes (e.g., air and water quality management) and often even these consolidated entities leave out considerable portions of the region. For example, even though there is a transportation agency for all of Los Angeles county, there is no transportation agency for the entire Los Angeles region. The surrounding counties each have their own transportation agency, despite the obvious region-wide transportation challenges. Except for the state of California, there is no government entity with responsibility for the entire Los Angeles region. The same is true for Chicago, New York, Boston, Atlanta, or any other major metropolitan area. Critics of the current state of affairs in metropolitan governance tend to call for greater consolidation and regional governments with general powers of governing. In effect, they are calling for metropolitan-wide governments.

Despite these calls for metropolitan consolidation, there are defenders of the current decentralized, governmentally fragmented system. Among these defenders are some economic model advocates, often referred to as "public choice" analysts of metropolitan governance (Ross and Levine, 1996: 335; Lowery, 1998; Ostrom, 1974; Ostrom, Tiebout, and Warren, 1961; Ostrom, Bish, and Ostrom, 1988; Parks and Oakerson, 1989). These scholars, who mainly dissent from the calls for greater consolidation of urban government, have made a number of important contributions to the study of urban government and politics. Included are the following:

1. The existence of many different governments in a given metropolitan area cannot be assumed to be inefficient as many of the advocates of traditional reform and consolidation suggest.
2. There has been no evidence that the fragmentation of government in metropolitan areas has led to actual breakdowns in services.
3. Despite the desires and passion of consolidation advocates, a fairly broad coalition of central city and suburban residents, public officials, and private citizens arises to defeat consolidation proposals. Clearly many, if not most, metropolitan area residents are opposed to the consolidation of most functions into a single, regional, metropolitan government. Advocates of consolidation, then, seem elitist and too willing to impose their policies on an unwilling public.

4. Traditional reformers and consolidation advocates appear not to consider that many metropolitan residents place higher values on local control, access, and responsiveness.

5. Coordination does not require consolidation of governments. Voluntary agreements among clusters of local governments can produce coordination among those who value the results of such interaction, while permitting others who might value local autonomy more to operate individually. Approximations of regional cooperation around those issues where it is valued preserves freedom and local autonomy, yet produces wider cooperation without it being imposed.

6. Smaller local governments can contract with larger producers to receive services, thereby gaining production economies without sacrificing the intimacy of smaller local governments. For example, a small locality might contract with the county for policing, fire protection, and planning. Or it might even contract with a large, national firm to provide legal services, planning, or garbage collection.

7. Empirical work indicates that economies of scale in local government services do not simply occur in greater amounts with larger jurisdictions. At some point, larger jurisdictions produce a variety of diseconomies in labor costs and in the level of political conflict among different groups (transaction costs, Bish, 1971).

Insofar as public choice theorists have analyzed the arguments of traditional reformers and advocates of metropolitan consolidation, there is little to fault their work. Public choice theorists also claim that they are able to explain how the typical American metropolitan area is formed. The behavior of urban residents, according to public choice theorists, is couched in highly positive language. For them, the pattern of having metropolitan areas carved up into many different local governments is a reflection of a quasi-market-like expression of consumer choice. It is important to note how the creation and proliferation of suburban municipalities is characterized by references to motives like "the protection of property," "the maintenance of community norms," "the prevention of tyranny of the majority," "the defense of life styles," "the maximization of choice," "the assurance of citizen access," "the expression of consumer preference," and "emphasis on representativeness." Inferring these benign and commendable motives, goals, and consequences is not validated by empirical research, but appears to be embraced by rational choice theorists because of connotations that legitimize the pattern of metropolitan government fragmentation. However, one can explain the creation and spread of small, homogenous suburban communities in terms of less lofty motives. The impetus for suburbia also involves such impulses as expropriating tax base, excluding undesirable residents, minimizing public sector costs by shifting service demands to other jurisdictions, maintaining race and class exclusivity, and perpetuating unequal distributions of public service costs and resources.

Not surprisingly, small local governments are a "good" thing to public choice theorists, since they are more likely to be populated by individuals who share public policy preferences regarding such things as policing, parks and recreation, tax and spending levels, or local economic development. Small government, to public choice scholars of urban politics, is not simply a government that does as little as possible, but also one that contains a fairly limited population. The larger a local government is, the larger its area, and the greater the range of different groups, interests, lifestyles, ethnic and racial mixes, and social classes. Hence, in larger jurisdictions, like Chicago, Los Angeles, Portland, or Miami, the policies of the city government are more likely to be complex and more likely to make any given household or individual or group unhappy with some or many parts of the policy package. The smaller the government, the smaller the range of people and the narrower the range of tastes and preferences, and the more likely it is that policies of the smaller jurisdiction will approximate the tastes and preferences of its typical household. It strains the imagination to think of what the "typical" household represents in cities like New York, Atlanta, New Orleans, or Dallas, notwithstanding preconceived stereotypes about any of these places. For the public choice theorist, then, large cities pose coercion, loss of choice, and loss of freedom, since any individual, household, or group is likely to be paying for or tolerating a mix of public services and actions that are not what they want. By permitting metropolitan areas to exist as conglomerations of many different smaller local governments, each producing its own array of public services and tax and spending policies, individuals are provided choices. Hence, public choice theorists find that the current system reflects individuals "voting with their feet" and taking advantage of the freedom to choose. Therefore, any consolidation of metropolitan regions—so that services, taxes, and spending are decided in a single arena—would be a substantial loss of freedom. Worse yet, having a wide array of social classes, from the less well-off to the very affluent, living within the same locality creates a greater chance that policies that benefit the poor will be financed by the more affluent residents and businesses that are contained within the jurisdiction. And that would be, according to the public choice theorists, problematic. As one of the leading public choice thinkers has said:

> The demands of low income individuals for an increased share of resources without any sacrifice are regarded as non-economic or noneffective demands (like any "demand" of something for nothing) and does not increase economic efficiency in its broadest sense.... [Demands for income redistribution] are political externalities imposed through political processes on the individuals from whom resources are taken. (Bish, 1971: 141)

This is a fairly presumptuous statement. Not all income redistribution involves demands of something for nothing, although those who pay for it often feel that way. Of course, if people feel burdened by redistributive demands, and if these people have the political resources to successfully resist the demands, then the demands will fail to achieve policy status. The result might be very unfair and unjust, however, considering the immense subsidies directed at middle-class home ownership and the auto-based system of transportation. Tax benefits and government finance protection for housing loans are heaped on the owner-occupied housing market. The full cost of an auto-based transportation system, which serves primarily suburban commuters, contributes to excessive dependence on fossil fuels, makes air quality issues a public management nightmare, reduces agricultural productivity owing to the adverse impact of air pollution, vastly diminishes the amount of land in productive use (to make way for highways, streets, and parking lots), and otherwise produces a host of negative externalities that are not reflected in the cost of driving. The modest demands requiring affluent homeowners and auto commuters to consider some support for housing the less affluent or supporting a viable public transportation system (even at some ongoing subsidy level) are hardly redistributive. These demands might simply be requests for a modicum of compensation or equitable treatment for groups who have been treated unfairly and whose needs have not been generously tended to by public policy. Those who benefit from the current system of metropolitan governance will likely not see things this way; they are more likely to see such "demands" as a demand of "something for nothing." That would be the realistic conclusion. It has much less to do with efficiency, fairness, or justice.

It is very likely that there would be substantial race and class clustering in America's metropolitan areas as a "natural" reflection of the tastes, preferences, and income constraints of people. However, it is also true that the fragmentation of the typical American metropolitan area and its increasing amount of race and class segregation result from the way in which the better-off have advanced their well-being through the creation of great numbers of relatively homogenous, suburban municipalities. The process of massive sorting by race and class could not have happened on the scale that it has nor would this suburbanizing have occurred at artificially lower costs without very biased public policies and institutions. In addition to the subsidies and incentives for suburbanization of the middle class, there have also been contrived barriers, unintended or by design, that have impeded the participation of the less well-off, particularly minorities. Especially notable are exclusionary land use policies, policies favoring auto-based rather than mass transportation, and biased state and federal housing programs that favored stimulating single-family, detached home-ownership over the housing needs of the working poor and minorities (Neiman, 1975; Orfield, 1997).

The development of the American metropolis—with its high level of government fragmentation, race and class sorting behind increasing numbers of separate municipal boundaries—reflects the relative success and failures of different groups in designing institutions and policies to benefit themselves. What was once a pattern of intra-city segregation on a neighborhood basis has been grandly replicated on a municipality-by-municipality basis. The metropolis in America is not simply a reflection of individuals voting with their feet or expressing private preferences in a quasi-market of competing suburban localities. Urban development and the patterns of advantages and disadvantages and distributions of costs and benefits are reflections of the different capacities of different groups to influence institutions and policies. All of this might be inevitable; all of this might not be remediable; all of that, however, does not make it just or even efficient. The metropolitanization process raises important questions of fairness and justice, and they cannot be casually dismissed by adulating urban development as but one more arena of personal choice.

The way public choice theorists have wanted to anoint the status quo as benign and consistent with personal liberty is premature. A cheery conclusion about how nicely the current urban scene approximates the virtues of the private market is like legitimizing the effective demand of those whose income and resources have been attained through illegal or unsavory means. If the "good" communities and favored places are occupied mostly by the affluent, nonminority populations, at least partly because the result has been heavily subsidized or enabled by biased policies and rigged institutions, then how can it be assumed that the *status quo* is optimal or fair? The answer is that the question of optimality and fairness is problematic and very complex.

To the public choice theorists, urban areas pose a special difficulty when it comes to questions of limiting government. The higher densities and complex interactions among individuals, households, neighborhoods, businesses, and governments, and their use of resources and their behaviors are more likely to affect one another in both positive and negative fashion. In urban places, it is possible to assess the use of the concept of "externalities" that has been so critical in rational-model answers to the question, "When should government intervene in previously private matters?" Or, "When are externalities generated in parts of a metropolis requiring regional coordination?" Rather than having a large metropolitan-area government with a range of different responsibilities, public choice theorists prescribe different numbers of jurisdictions in order to manage different externalities. It is likely that some externalities will have different scales, and so there might be a variety of regional entities with specific responsibilities for different externalities with different boundaries. For example, there might be a regional entity to deal with air quality, another, less expansive entity to deal with the coastline (if there is one), yet another for groundwater management, several different community college entities, and another to deal with transportation. Each of these would be separate governing bodies, tailored with specific powers to deal with very specific issues. Unfortunately, in the world beyond the Emerald City of public choice, the concept of externality is not very useful for drawing boundaries.

Recall that an externality (often called a spillover effect) is a cost or benefit that is provided to people who are not part of the transaction that produces the externality. Spillover effects not only impart benefits and costs, but also can be concrete or symbolic. They can involve some measurable objective or physical change or they can be essentially psychological and subjective. Public choice theorists know these things, but seem not to internalize their implications. They seem to be in some sort of denial about the ramifications that result from the squishiness of the concept of externality. Unfortunately, there is little practical role for the concept of externality in providing some objective method for determining and justifying government intervention or increased government scale. It is the political process, instead, that determines what is regarded as an externality. Since the definition of externalities can encompass so much in urban places, where the interaction among people and jurisdictions clearly produces a host of externalities, almost everything becomes a source of external effects. Market failure in modern, urban settings is at least as frequent as optimal market exchanges. In urban settings, market failures in the form of spillover effects are intensified, indeed pervasive, not an occasional glitch in a smoothly functioning quasi-market.

We can approach a consensus that fouling air and water or polluting groundwater are externalities. But what of prostitution, adult book stores, liquor outlets, low-cost housing, apartment houses, music after midnight, teens hanging out at the local park on a summer night, an unusual design for a house, perhaps a unique ensemble of colors for a house's exterior—or what of conducting a business out of a residence? Anything that makes one person feel less satisfied can be an externality, all of which is multiplied in urban settings.

Consider the impact of local land use policies. Local governments regulate land use, and for most of the time since these policies were adopted in the late 1920s these policies have been used by communities to limit the supply of low cost and higher density housing in the newly suburbanizing fringe. This has produced a number of negative external effects: Lower- and moderate-income housing are more expensive than they might otherwise be; there is more race and class segregation than there otherwise would be. Local land use policies, then, can operate to restrict the supply of lower-income housing and higher density apartment dwellings, thereby making that sort of housing more expensive. After all, a restricted supply means higher prices, right? These local policies are combined with state and federal policies that provide enormously generous subsidies for the housing and auto-based transportation needs of the upwardly mobile middle-class, mostly white population, thereby combining to increase the supply of housing, making it less expensive than it would otherwise be.

Housing for the less affluent and higher density housing is more segregated, as are the people who tend to live in such housing. Externalities, deriving from a mix of both private and public sector forces, have created serious problems for the law-abiding poor, who are more concentrated in crisis communities, collapsing neighborhoods, and declining political jurisdictions than they would be under more equitable conditions. Consequently, the poor are more concentrated and more likely to be victims of violent crime and to suffer mental and physical problems that stem from crime-ridden and environmentally polluted neighborhoods. What sort of metropolitan government would be created to manage this set of externalities? What sort of powers would it have? Would it have the power to disperse low income housing into the suburbs? Would it have the capacity to assess communities with the most restrictive local land use policies to pay for the external effects these land use policies have on neighboring locales? The concept of externalities provides little in the way of some conceptual barrier to "more government." Someone sensitive to the externalities produced by the middle-class bias of public policy might readily understand that many redistributive demands are actually just compensation for previous injustice. It is just a thought, to be discussed at another time in a different forum.

Public choice approaches to metropolitan politics and organizations do function, then, as a justification for a governing system in urban places. Given the structure of most urban and metropolitan settings, there are no common arenas in which certain issues can be raised. The fact that the less affluent are concentrated in communities that are legally distinct government jurisdictions makes it very difficult to press redistributive demands that result from the spillover effects of other localities in the region. Since there is no shared political arena, issues of fairness and justice in areas such as housing and transportation or environmental quality cannot be addressed, short of appealing to state and federal governments. As Lowery (1998) observes, there is an appeal to thinking that the respective states and the federal government might produce a fairer system of metropolitan government. He goes on to say, "So too is the *Independence Day* notion that an invasion from outer space will erase ancient racial, ethnic, and class divisions as we discover shared interests in a common struggle to kill aliens. It remains unclear which will occur first" (Lowery, 1998: 8).

RATIONAL MODELS AS BLUEPRINTS
AND THE LACK OF RESOURCE FLUIDITY

Rational models of policy design have a blueprint view of problem solving (Faludi, 1973). The blueprint role for policy analysis suggests that it is possible to achieve a high degree of knowledge and certainty in policy-relevant knowledge. Rational models further assume that there are fairly clear ways to relate the elements of any policy program so that one can, as if guided by an architectural or engineering blueprint or a merchandising battle plan authored by corporate planners, bring about the desired results. All that is required is to follow the blueprint, or, in the case of rational models, follow the sequence of rational decision making (Dye, 1987). In these models, any given policy is a configuration of resources, including time, personnel, intelligence, data, skill, experience, or money. In rational models these are seen as inputs into the production of services and goods, which in the face of information or the results of evaluation can be reallocated. Just as a firm seeks to maximize return on investment and assesses its services and products in light of its bottom line, so a government should presumably deal with its products. The fact that governments most often do not accord with the blueprint qualities of rational decision making contributes to the scorn and derision that is felt about government policies and the apparent inability to make these policies in a way that approximates the presumably more efficient, private sector business.

There is, then, an assumption of fluidity in resources that even in the private sector is not always a good approximation of reality. Labor does not readily shift from one way of doing things to another, especially when extraordinary training investments are required. Industries do not merely respond to changing market forces; they sometimes seek to prevent them from changing in ways that detract from profit. When the risks of nuclear power, for example, made it difficult for utilities to raise money for investment, the nuclear power industry successfully sought liability limits against lawsuits. Similarly, when professions see lower-cost providers providing similar services, rather than lowering salaries in the face of competition or changing professions, they are likely to seek some barriers to their competitors' entry.

In rational or economic models, policy analysis in the public sector is supposed to work as prices or sales do in the private sector, signaling when to redirect resources from one activity to another. Just as in the private sector, however, there is no automatic reallocation of factors of production, even in the face of new market conditions. There is no necessary connection between the results of analysis and change in policy, at least not in an immediate way. Even if one assumes that the credibility and legitimacy of policy analysis is high, it is unlikely that application of rational models will produce new patterns of services immediately. Among businesses, when analysis of marketing results indicate that a service or item is losing money or that alternative methods would produce better results, it would be considered perverse if the firm or industry failed to change its policies or behavior. In reality that happens in the private sector more times than is readily admitted.

In the public sector, however, the results of policy analysis, no matter how rigorous and rational, cannot be thought about as if a consumer product were being marketed. In the public's efforts to reduce overall violence by reducing child abuse, the victims of which are a major source of social pathology, government policy must consider the rights of parents, weigh the societal commitment to the ideal of the nuclear family, maintain due process, and even manage issues over the meaning of child abuse. While the effects of a private sector campaign to sell a product are detectable in the short-term, changes in levels of child abuse and the hoped-for attendant effects are not observable for many years. Furthermore, the private sector can evaluate its conduct primarily in terms of its effects on the firm's rate of return, a fairly narrow, focused objective. That is very different from the multiple objectives involved in a single public policy. Evaluation of social programs requires time before the programs are suitable for analysis, and all the while a vested interest inevitably develops around the array of people, rules, resources, and interests associated with a particular program. Sometimes, when the data finally are available and indicate that the effects are not what was anticipated, or are even counter-productive, rearranging resources is not at all automatic. It is at this point that many critics of government policies emit their most sneering contempt, since, in their view, any private sector entity would suffer adverse market consequences if it persisted in producing unwanted services and goods or continued with costly practices when more efficient alternatives were available.

The analysis of public policies is often necessarily long-term, as beliefs that guide and influence public policy are either supported or gradually undermined, depending on whether analysis produces positive or negative results. The interval between the time the results of analysis first indicate program failure or waste and the time the results produce change, reform, or termination can be quite lengthy, since those who will be adversely affected by change will naturally resist the implications of the analysis. If policy analysis suggests the need for new arrays of actions, this might imply new configurations of resources, which, in turn, will involve new groups and interests who will benefit from the policy change. In a firm that decides it must place greater emphasis on research and development, the result might be that resources within the firm will be drawn from those departments that market the firm's products. The firm's research and development personnel may benefit at the expense of the sales force. In government, resources that are used to disrupt the production of illegal drugs and punish those who peddle them might be reallocated if the problem of drug abuse shifts from a criminal definition to a medical one. New configurations of resources in response to policy analysis imply benefits to different groups of people, from salespeople to research scientists, from police and district attorneys to doctors and social workers. Policy analysis as a catalyst for change must consider how to integrate the process of displacing one set of interests with another. When the results of policy analysis do not threaten the beneficiaries of the policy status quo or those who bear the costs of change, the issue is not that important. If it is otherwise, as it so often is, analysis must provide more than technical evaluations. Rational models of policy analysis clearly require a theory of interest and policy *displacement*. Resources are not fluid and are not easily transformed from one activity to another. Of course, some might contend that this difficulty is the very thing that is wrong with public policy and the public sector. On the other hand, change can and does occur; it is simply that change often occurs over a longer period (Brewer and deLeon, 1983; Kaufman, 1976).

Any model of policy evaluation or policy prescription must incorporate the issue of policy displacement if it is to be relevant. The inevitable and necessary role of democratic politics requires that the analyst overcome the tendency to view politics and political competition as evils that undermine rational, efficient policy prescription. Instead, policy analysis must begin with politics as one of the crucial components in which the practice of policy occurs and in which the results of analysis have to be shown.

Is there any hope, then, for policy analysis? Since most meaningful analyses of important issues often produce results that threaten important interests, how can analysis be useful? A meaningful, even impressive, role for policy analysis can be salvaged by accepting the following:

1. Public policies are nearly always designed in a way that, according to one or another criterion, are suboptimal; that is, public policies are multiple-objective phenomena that consolidate the interests and aspirations of contending, often conflicting, interests.
2. Public policies are, then, almost always seen by somebody as flawed.
3. Policy analysis, assuming that it is helpful in a given instance, is not a blueprint in the engineering or architectural sense. The lack of resource fluidity means that policy change comes from sustained, complex processes of social learning that occur over a period of time.

A necessarily brief foray into U.S. housing policy illustrates some of these points. It is possible to characterize housing policy as having either a supply-side or demand-side orientation. Supply-side housing policies focus on stimulating those who build and finance housing to build more or to provide more capital at more favorable terms for housing construction and purchases. The simplest, quintessential supply-side housing policy is when the public acts as landlord, owns public housing, and makes it available to those whose housing would otherwise be costlier or of much lower quality. Demand-side approaches are those that provide assistance directly to individuals and households to subsidize or underwrite their housing costs. Most housing experiments believe that demand-side approaches should be preeminent. Friedman and Weinberg, in their study of one of the most extensive and costly studies of any social program, concluded the following:

> Despite the huge volume of research under the Experimental Housing Allowance Program, its major implications for housing policy can be stated briefly ... we should replace all current programs involving the construction of new units or the rehabilitation of units selected by bureaucrats with some type of housing allowance program. (1983: 266)

By the early 1980s, then, an entirely new view of how to approach housing for the poor was established. Many scholars believed that the evidence for the efficacy of housing voucher programs had long been established, and that "politics" stood in the way of reform. For a variety of reasons, many of which are rooted in the processes of political competition, Americans have still made very little progress in implementing demand-side programs in housing (Heidenheimer, Heclo, and Adams, 1983).

The frustration reflects the lack of understanding of the historical context in which government housing programs developed in the United States. According to conventional wisdom, federal involvement in housing began in an *ad hoc* fashion during the New Deal. The supply-oriented policies reflected the dominant concern of the New Deal in putting people to work. Housing policy has been laboring ever since to overcome the vested interests and institutional commitments that the New Deal legacy created. In fact, this depiction is incorrect.

The Great Depression was, of course, one of the premier crises in American history. As such, it was managed in an atmosphere of crisis, often involving problems that were entirely unprecedented. However, the New Deal also provided opportunities for experts in particular fields and policy advocates with particular approaches to problems to advance their methods as public policy. By the time of the Great Depression there had developed a general understanding regarding the causes of housing problems and their solutions. Additionally, a set of housing activists from many fields had long been agitating for government activity in housing. Most of the lobbying was from a supply perspective, although at the time of the New Deal housing policies adopted in 1934 and 1937, the opponents of public housing proposed a number of model demand-side alternatives. The supply orientation launched during the Great Depression that prevailed until the 1970s had an established basis in research and analysis.

Essentially there were four components that produced the supply-oriented approach to housing launched in earnest by the federal government in the Housing Acts of 1934 and 1937. One was the Settlement House Movement and the rise of the social welfare movement during the late nineteenth and early twentieth centuries. Second was the emergence of public health as a field with the related specialties of epidemiology. Third was the rise of the city-planning (or town-planning) profession. Fourth was the concern in certain segments of the progressive business community about the relationship between adequate housing and social unrest.

The Settlement House Movement arose from the various charitable groups involved in the problems associated with rapid, industrial urbanization in the latter half of the nineteenth century. Of particular concern was the condition of children housed in urban slums and tenement districts. The immediate concern was to improve the shelter and, hence, the well-being of children. Most of the initial work on housing and other urban problems resulted from the anxiety over the well-being of children (Lawson, 1919; Clarke, 1920; Sykes, 1901).

In a related vein, the rapid growth of highly dense housing conditions of the growing cities of the late nineteenth and early twentieth centuries posed severe problems of health and sanitation. The technology to manage solid waste and the impact of high population densities on the communicability of disease led to increased worry about the design and distribution of housing as a means of improving health (Sykes, 1901; Robertson, 1920). Crowding, improper cooling and heating facilities, insufficient privacy, faulty ventilation, lack of light, and the absence of vegetation and open space were all linked to venereal disease, tuberculosis, rickets, and moral decay (with much concern about incest).

The juxtaposition of the Settlement House Movement with rapid industrialization and urbanization profoundly influenced how housing problems were evaluated. Along with other housing reformers, Settlement activists, many trained in the period's state of the art social science, exhibited a suspicion of the private market's ability to produce safe, sanitary, or adequate housing. The Settlement House Movement was a key force in the emergence of the city-planning profession in the United States; its strong, initial skepticism about the ability of the market to supply satisfactory housing situations for the poor and working classes became a persistent theme (Krueckeberg, 1983; Davis, 1967). Some of the research of the Settlement House Movement produced major inventories of housing conditions in places like New York, Chicago, Boston, Washington, D.C., San Francisco, and St. Louis. Even rural areas came under the view of the Settlement House Movement as major studies and commissions at the state and federal levels investigated housing conditions in farm labor camps and mining towns.

Zoning, building codes, and design standards were among the legacies of the Movement.

Finally, important elements of the business community became increasingly anxious about the supply and quality of housing and the capacity of the private finance markets to provide the capital for housing construction and purchases. As one researcher into the problem observed:

> Heretofore the demand for houses has been supplied by the speculative builder and the real estate operator. But at the present time he can no longer afford to build—in many cities he cannot get construction loans, and even if he does he cannot hope to sell in the open market at present prices and cannot be sure of any return on his money by renting, having in mind the possible trade depression during the reconstruction period which will come at the end of the war. (Allen, 1917: 6)

Businessmen were also concerned about the problem of "labor turnover," which referred to the great difficulty many employers had in getting and keeping workers. Part of that problem was due to inadequate housing in the face of labor shortages caused by wartime production during World War I (Gordon-Van Tine Co., 1918). There was also concern for the decline of home ownership and the increasing proportion of renters. As Miller (1920: 3) declared, "... a country of majority rule must be a country of majority home ownership." Or as an early housing lobbyist indicated, "The stability of American family life is threatened, as evidenced by the rapid growth of divorce and by the failure of the church in its spiritual hold on the people and by the reduction of home ownership" (Herman, 1929: 1). Yet others believed that the decline in home ownership and the quality of housing might further stimulate radicalism. "Bolshevism will make no headway if the city is everywhere peopled by a cooperative home-owning class ... it is doubtful whether anything will have a greater steadying effect upon the average man than for him to become the owner of his own home" (Roberts, 1922: 12–13). Or regarding the presumed lack of productivity among poorly housed workers: "The human tool is not unlike the machine tool in this respect, the better it is housed and cared for the greater will be its efficiency and its output" (Allen, 1917: 7).

For reasons of paternalism and self-interest, certain elements of the business community aligned themselves with the Progressive Movement and came to be involved in urging greater government incentives to the builders and suppliers of housing. The concern was to encourage home ownership and, if necessary, call for government to provide funds for the construction of improved housing for the worst-off. Many of the financial arrangements that characterized mortgage insurance and below-market interest subsidies, all designed to encourage housing and housing financial markets to provide more housing, were proposed at the turn of the century. Many of these proposals were widely discussed, for example, during the credit squeezes surrounding World War I.

The history of housing policy indicates that the experts and housing activists of the late nineteenth and early twentieth centuries took on a strong, prosupply orientation. There was considerable lack of confidence, if not disdain, for the private market's capacity to provide adequate housing, either in terms of quality or quantity. The problems of housing were not seen as linked to inadequate income (a demand orientation). Some of the worst housing problems emerged, after all, during World War I, when incomes grew rapidly. Perceived housing shortages during this period resulted in a frequently ignored, but exceptionally important event. In 1918, the federal government allocated $200,000,000 to build housing where the war effort needed it. The allotment was unprecedented and dissolved the ideological barriers at the federal government level, whose officials were strongly committed to free markets and had previously resisted efforts of this sort. The tight housing markets and labor shortages during World War I that existed in key ship-building and naval yard communities like Brooklyn, Philadelphia, Wilmington (Delaware), Baltimore, and Norfolk (Virginia), as well as the other exigencies of war, helped to fuel support for government efforts to stimulate housing supply and improve housing policy.

Other housing activists used the war emergency to press their housing agenda, which had existed before the strains posed by the war on housing finance and the cost of housing. Many entrepreneurs in the housing industry had long argued for federal underwriting of the risks of lending and borrowing for housing purchases; housing reformers who had long been appalled by the inadequacies of the tenements of the burgeoning, industrializing cities of the late nineteenth and early twentieth centuries were concerned about the design of safe and healthy housing; yet others saw federal involvement in housing as a means of blunting the rise of radical political movements. These individuals and groups, concerned with the problem of housing, pressed their views onto the local, state, and federal agenda. However, they were encapsulated in a world view that necessarily focused on government's need to regulate the building of homes, to manipulate the resources necessary for housing construction, and to have the public build housing directly if required.

Housing policy in the United States, then, began with a late nineteenth-century tradition of analysis. Housing policy represented the convergence of interests among a variety of different specialists, interests, and institutions. It was their efforts that enabled the first federal involvement in housing (after many local and state successes). It was analysis and politics and the exigencies of war that produced a federally sponsored, supply-oriented approach to housing. Any proposal at that time to directly supplement the incomes of individuals to support housing was viewed by federal legislators as too radical an intrusion into the private economy. (This is a terrific irony in light of today's tendency to see housing vouchers and direct grants to individuals as less intrusive and more market-like.) Early pre-Great Depression housing reflected the state of knowledge and social stresses of the time. All of the following understandably fostered a supply-side approach to housing: major levels of squalor; devastating epidemics of tuberculosis, pneumonia, and the flu; race and ethnic riots; rigidities in capital markets; war; unemployment; and housing shortages. The configuration of policy interests and resources produced a set of supply-side housing approaches, resulting in a sort of "iron triangle" (Peters, 1996: 28–30) of interests, understandings, and policies that functioned and resisted change until the 1970s. By that time there had been a considerable weakening of the triangle of interests (developers, financiers, big city mayors), understandings (the research and work of pre-Great Depression housing reformers), and policies (construction of public housing and underwriting riskier loans to lower-income families for housing purchases). The weakening stemmed from several sources, including the urban riots of the 1960s, with their clear implication that public housing had failed to produce acceptable housing, the increasingly anti-social welfare stance of victorious Republican presidential candidates (Nixon, Reagan, Bush), and fiscally prudent democratic presidents (Carter and Clinton).

Over time there has been a gradual dissolving of the structure of beliefs and of confidence in the "knowledge" that supported the older housing specialists' claims to housing policy wisdom. The emergence of rational models as a formal mode of analysis, no doubt, has contributed to the slow, disengagement from supply-side approaches to housing. Conversely, rational models have contributed to increasing support for a demand-side approach to housing assistance for the poor. The only thing missing is a political and financial commitment to support demand-side approaches that are equal in their commitment of resources to house the poor.

A REALISTIC ROLE FOR POLICY ANALYSIS

Using policy analysis is not a matter of finding a better architect and simply taking a new blueprint, tearing down an old structure, and building a new one. Policy structures cannot be reassembled like that. There is first a long period during which particular ways of doing things are displaced by new understandings, sometimes revealed by new analytical tools like rational models, and sometimes compelled by the concrete burdens and evidence of failure. The process of policy evolution is often tortuous, as new configurations of resources and administration imply new systems of status and prestige. Think, for example, of the tensions between those who see drug abuse as a crime control problem compared to those who view it as a medical one. Or what of the long-standing struggle between those who emphasize a rehabilitating approach to prison policy as compared to those who want to emphasize retribution and punishment. On the political side, the punishment approach is currently ascendant, and over time, there will be improved understanding of which crimes and criminals are more suitably managed by one or the other approaches. On the more technical side, it is interesting to observe the struggle between the technicians favoring manned space flight and those who claim that computer-directed, unmanned flight is more cost-effective and less hazardous.

These struggles are almost never simply between competing analytical structures, but are also struggles between who will have the esteem of doing things the "correct" way and all that implies. With all due respect to the creativity and energy of the private market, very few firms take on the problems of housing, educating, and medically caring for the poor, abating drug abuse, resolving ethnic and racial conflict, or confronting the challenges of crime. When the public addresses these issues, it should be with sensitivity to the severity of these problems and the tremendous difficulty of dealing with them in humane, democratic, and fair ways. If we think of such issues as comparable to the marketing of a commercial product, we are going to be frustrated and set for failure, since business-based models of policy analysis are often inappropriate. Hence, in many situations the disagreements in policy analysis and the glacial pace of change is normal. When the political will to invest more resources in housing the poor emerges once again, there will be a new array of understandings and "knowledge" about how best to deliver such services. Technical change is faster in the business world, to be sure, because what is done there involves simpler things and the decision-making structures are not democratic.

LIMITED GOVERNMENT AS A COMMON PROPERTY RESOURCE

It is possible to employ a fairly simple public choice model to make the point that it is an increasingly expansive view of democracy that worries public choice theorists. The key issue centers on the rules governing access to demand making and responsiveness to demands by institutions and officials. A special case of public goods termed a common property resource makes the argument (Hardin, 1968; Hardin and Baden, 1977; Haefele, 1974). A common property resource refers to any depletable asset or quality that is accessible to everyone and owned by no one; it is not governed, managed, or regulated by any individual or organization. Examples include the whales in the ocean, or the quality of air when it is not regulated or managed by anyone, but is available to all for waste dumping.

Since a common property resource—accessible to all and owned and managed by no one—is depletable, if it is used or exploited past a certain point it will deteriorate to unacceptable or unusable levels or disappear altogether. The users of a particular common property resource, say a fishery, might be aware of this possible outcome. Of course, all of the users have in their interest the continuing existence of the fishery, since it provides both income and food. All of the users of this "free," unregulated, and unmanaged fishery might fully comprehend that if they fish above certain levels, the fishery will decline and perhaps be depleted. However, if an individual decides to restrain himself, he has no guarantee, in this unmanaged, unregulated context, that others will restrain themselves. There is no assurance that the portion of fish that remains when an individual restrains himself will not simply be taken by others. Individual restraint, then, simply makes more fish available for other fishermen. It is obvious that the "rational" thing to do is to take as much fish as one can use. As all fishermen begin to do so, the fishery is stressed beyond its renewal levels and deteriorates inexorably. If the level of fishing becomes sufficiently high, the result might be the complete collapse of the fishery, something that has actually happened many times in many places.

The usual remedy for the common property resource problem is to develop a mechanism that reduces demands on the resource or asset. The process of developing these mechanisms is complex. It is possible to imagine, for example, that somehow the fishermen will come together and agree to draw lots and assign ownership of fishing rights to one of them. Disregarding the issue of enforcing the property right, the owner now has an incentive in maximizing the stream of income from the fishery, which also means that he will be motivated to extend the life of the fishery, as well as maximize the return from each fisherman. The owner will have an incentive to conserve the fishery, in order to maintain an ongoing stream of income.

It is also possible that the fishermen will estimate the amount of fishing that is consistent with the long-term survival of the fishery, assign a ration of fishing for each fisherman, and create an enforcement arm to police the ration. Perhaps it is discovered that if only a fraction of the fisherman catch fish, they can take as many fish as they want, and this fraction is then selected by lottery. A variety of ways to reduce access to the fishery and the amount of fish that can be taken or some combination of reducing access and fishing will be adopted to manage the common property resource problem.

It is also possible to think of "limited government" as a common property resource. Begin by defining limited government abstractly. Think of limited government as a range and mix of government activities. For now it is unimportant precisely what it is that makes up the mix. All that is required is to accept the simple idea that limited government exists somewhere between the conditions of no government (i.e., state of nature,

anarchy) and total government (i.e., Big Brother, dictatorship, or totalitarian regimes). Limited government is an interval on some continuum between no government and total government. It is possible to argue about
where the interval is on the continuum and how wide a band of government
activities should be included. That is not the issue here. It is enough to simply define limited government as an interval on the continuum between
the inelegantly named end-points of no government and total government.
It is possible, of course, that there is disagreement about the exact mix of
things that comprise limited government, even while there is agreement
on the desirability of avoiding total government. In this exercise, limited
government is preferred, in the sense of having a significant arena of life
that is secure from the reach of public authorities and public extractions.
Nevertheless, there is likely to be disagreement about what the mix is that
comprises limited government and what the point of no return is, the point
when government has been expanded so that it inexorably slides toward
total government and the dissolving of individual autonomy and personal liberty. Limited government is, in short, an unspecified mix of government actions, powers, and burdens, greater than no government and less
than total government.

Assume also that limited government, at a particular point in time,
is accessible to all. All groups and individuals in society are eligible and
able to participate in the process of making demands on officials who are
responsible for translating these demands into public policy. Officials are
assumed to be motivated to stay in office and hold on to their positions,
and to know that it is critical for them to be responsive to demands made
on them. Demands made on officials by individuals or groups are produced without knowledge of whether others will make demands or how
those demands will be received. Restraint in demand-making by one group
or set of individuals will have no influence on demand-making by other
groups and individuals. Under these circumstances, it is inevitable that
government activity will increase in its range of activities, even while there
might be widespread support for limited government. Government activities might advance well beyond the point preferred by many individuals and groups. If any individual or group restrains its own
demand-making, it will only provide opportunities for other groups to
press their demands. Hence, the rational thing for each individual and
group to do is to continue its own demand-making activity, thus ensuring
that the range of things that government does will be more than many individuals or groups might want.

In this sense, then, limited government has many of the attributes of
the general common property resource problem. The problem of dealing
with limited government can be managed by limiting access and reducing
responsiveness. Insofar as access to the tools of government and official responsiveness are important, if not sufficient, features of democracy, it is

possible to manage threats to limited government by reducing democratic rule. Access to government can be reduced by reestablishing property qualifications to vote or introducing strict literacy requirements to qualify as a registered voter. Voting can be limited to native-born, Christian, Jewish, or blue-eyed voters. These policies will have the effect of reducing access, although clearly such access reduction activity will be repugnant. Responsiveness or access can be reduced by insulating decision makers, reducing the number of elections, making it more difficult to create winning majorities, or reducing the range of policy demands that are considered legitimate. In some sense it is possible to reduce the pressure to stray from limited government by reducing officials' responsiveness in various ways, thereby reducing democratic governance. Democratization continues to affect the scale of governance. We might expect fewer pressures to do things through government bodies than might occur with less access to government or with public institutions that are made less responsive to public demands. The following are examples of methods that reduce access or responsiveness and that have been proposed in one form or another in recent years as a means of managing government growth and size: extraordinary voting requirements; making it more difficult for unions to function politically; increasing the barriers to citizenship; requiring compensation for property value losses due to public policy; elevating property rights to the status of First Amendment privileges; reducing the period of time when legislatures are in session; implementing strict balanced budget requirements; limiting overall spending and tax increases to some formula linked to population, GDP, or personal income; fixing the length of time that legislation is operative (sunset legislation); and privatizing current services and relying more on user fees and charges.

BEING RATIONAL IS A DIFFICULT AND SOMETIMES UNDESIRABLE THING TO TRY

Being rational is difficult for individuals and even more difficult for organizations composed of a multitude of diverse individuals with different utility profiles (Dunleavy, 1991; Green and Shapiro, 1994; Mansbridge, 1990; Neiman, 1975). Even in the most elementary sense, the extension of optimization through rational principles collapses of its own weight. For example, there are programs designed to reduce injuries to children due to unsafe toys and other products used by children. But why be concerned about the injury only to children? Well of course we are not concerned only with children's injuries. We also seek to reduce injury to workers and other adults in many different contexts. There are a host of different things done to improve the well-being of different groups. It is impossible to assess and prescribe the optimal array of societal resources and authority so that, given the information available and time permitted, such-and-such an alternative distribution of the current nearly $2 trillion federal budget will optimize social happiness and welfare. There is no rigorous, scientific, or rational way to make such a decision.

Consider a family that is involved in raising funds for research into Lou Gehrig's disease, which afflicts approximately 30,000 Americans a year. The family devotes enormous amounts of time to this illness because of the death of a parent who was afflicted with the disease. The disease is gruesome and inflicts considerable suffering on those afflicted. Yet it is a disease that is relatively rare, with little prospect of a cure in the near future. In a sense, society would be better served if the family devoted its energies to diseases with more victims and with some prospect of progress in treatment and cure. But sentiment and personal gratification have much more to do with the family's choice of how it expends its charitable impulse. From society's viewpoint, it would be more rational to invest the family's efforts in some other ailment, such as diabetes, AIDS, heart disease, breast cancer, or lung cancer, thus maximizing the "good" the family does. But people do not make decisions about where to spend their time, money, and energy on the basis of some methodical, rational calculus. Rather, they make decisions based on sentiment, personal involvement, friendship, memory, and loyalty. When people are willing to devote time, money, and energy to make themselves happy, they do not ask themselves which pattern of work, play, or charitable activity would maximize the bottom line for them in the long run.

Politics is the alternative to rational analysis in making the big choices. Rational models can be used to choose between alternative systems of city refuse collection (since there is agreement on the need to clear the garbage); rational models can be used to compare the relative net return of different ways to reduce drug use (since there is agreement on the desire to reduce drug use); and rational models can be used to determine which system best delivers a defined package of health care (assuming there is agreement on a desired health care component). However, the process of deciding whether to invest in cancer research, or agricultural research, or children's nutritional programs, or policies to reduce workplace injuries, or measures to minimize traffic accidents, or legislation to incarcerate more criminals, cannot be combined into some grand rational calculus to decide what levels of support each of these activities should receive.

There is also concern about the maintenance of democratic values. In a democracy there is the desire to maintain the capacity to participate in politics, to have officials who are wise and responsive, and to have a fairly broad band of society—comprising diverse, often disagreeing citizens—represented in policymaking. There are few policy areas in which there is a norm favoring less democracy (excepting perhaps monetary policy and decisions involving the prosecution of war). Foisting rational models on citizens and obliging them to abide by the analytical results produced from such analyses to the exclusion of democratic norms is an exceptionally, perhaps unacceptably, high price to pay for policy order or smaller government, such benefits being uncertain, if they exist at all.

CHAPTER 10

$\sim\!\!\ll\!\!\infty\!\!\gg\!\!\sim$

THE FREEDOM TO CHOOSE
DEMOCRATIC POLITICS

Has politics been such a terrible method for addressing the major issues of the time? A fair examination of the recent record suggests not. Several decades ago, Milton Friedman, one of the most distinguished antigovernment thinkers of the post-World War II era, declared his sadness at the onset of dictatorship in Chile, which he blamed on excessive commitment to social welfare (Friedman, 1976). He continued his lamentations stating the following:

> Lest you think that this tale of the history of Chile need not concern us, let me ask you to consider a case much closer. Cast your eyes across the Atlantic to the home of most of the ideas of freedom that we cherish—to the United Kingdom. Britain is a much richer country than Chile. It has a far stronger tradition of a belief in freedom and in democratic rights. Yet, the UK is going down the same path as Chile and, I fear, is headed for the same end. (1976: 9)

Friedman was wrong about Great Britain. Not long after he made the preceding comments, Margaret Thatcher and her Conservative Party launched a monumental assault on the British welfare state (Hoover and Plant, 1989). The result was a substantial decline in the British public sector—its rate of growth and its tax levels. Many national enterprises were privatized or sold to the private sector. With all due respect to Milton Friedman's accomplishments, his reputation as a political prognosticator is suspect.

Moreover, the recent collapse of communist dictatorships in Europe and in the former Soviet Union and the continuing pressure for popular participation in Latin America suggest that the presence of a sizable, tyrannical government might not prevent the onset of liberty and democracy. The worry today is whether the ravages and tumultuous movements of markets might not sour the taste for both capitalism and political freedom in a number of places. The notion that government growth is out of control and not capable of restraint without prescriptions suggested by conservative critics of government is not supported by the way in which the generally antigovernment mood has restrained government. Raising taxes, launching new regulatory initiatives, or producing new government programs is very difficult to advocate in the current political climate. Notwithstanding President Clinton's attempts to launch a variety of efforts to activate government programs—especially his effort to reform the delivery of health care and health insurance—he basically has adopted much of the GOP agenda for lower taxes, a balanced budget, and reducing the size of the federal labor force. Most notable has been the Clinton administration's embracing of a very conservative approach to welfare reform. As one observer states:

> Clinton also had promised welfare reform. He pledged to remove the impoverished from the rolls, offering a kind of "tough love" administered by the federal government. He would cut benefits after two or three years but ensure that welfare recipients received national health insurance and adequate child care. The proposal never left the drawing board. Instead, Clinton embraced the far more draconian GOP plan, eliminating the federal government's half-century commitment to the hard-core poor. (Schulman, 1998)

Notwithstanding the intense feelings that have emerged around President Clinton, he has presided over, facilitated, and celebrated the passing of Big Government and has helped to provide a relatively freer rein for the market in the nation and throughout the world.

Tax burdens in the United States have remained fairly constant, even declining somewhat. The overall proportion of the GDP represented by government spending and taxing is fairly constant over the past decade too. It is obvious that democratic politics has done a fairly reasonable job of addressing the issue of government size and burden. Supplanting the political process with rational choice algorithms for deciding when to initiate government action and using economic concepts to design these actions might reduce opportunities for democratic participation and merely create new forms of government intrusion in previously private matters.

Those who are skeptical and fearful about government are, as a matter of principle, likely to blame public policies and government for many harms and problems facing society. Government deficits, slowing economic growth, declining competitiveness, increasing crime, rising welfare dependency, declining personal freedom, deteriorating religious values, and the weakening of "family values" are considered by various antigovernment critics to be among the harms that have been produced by public policies. There is little in the preceding pages that will change the minds of these detractors. The most militant antigovernment critics, in any case, are mostly interested in magnifying and exploiting government failures. Anything that further undermines public confidence in the worth of public programs or that heightens a sense of incompetence, venality, or ill-will among government officials or that conjures up the specter of Big Brother is just fine with die-hard opponents of a vigorous public sector. Anything that disengages the public from its governing institutions, that prevents citizens from achieving important social gains through those institutions, and that insulates the well-off from the burden of supporting social justice and welfare is grist for their mill. Sardonicism, even prejudice, against public officials and public employees are part of the arsenal of rhetorical weapons used by the antigovernment coalition as it seeks to demolish the ideas and policies that have provided a modicum of social equity in the twentieth century. By imposing a general mood of despair and distrust about governing institutions, elected officials, and public employees, the antigovernment crowd hopes to sever the connection between the public and its representatives; they seek to shrink further the array of governing powers that have been used to achieve social objectives.

For the doctrinaire antigovernment troops, any instance of public policy failure is simply another opportunity to foment resistance to even the idea of using public policy. The greater the spectacle of disarray among government policies, the less attractive is public service and the more scorn there is for civil servants. If these kinds of sentiments also serve to reduce the chances to organize effective programs, much less get any support for their enactment, then so much the better. Demoralizing public employees by sneering at and debunking their abilities and work (unless they are police, prosecutors, prison guards, or members of the military) makes it more difficult to attract the best people into public service. Conservative government critics, therefore, further erode the inclination of the public to seek public solutions to a variety of problems. The perception of incompetence and ineffectiveness is clearly part of the mix of sentiments that has undermined, for example, public support to reform the medical insurance delivery system in the United States during the early Clinton administration (Johnson and Broder, 1997).

Rather than trying to convert the die-hard opponents of an activist government, my purpose here has been to provide an alternative to the automatic disdain and loathing that is commonplace when we think about issues associated with government size. The strategic weakening of governing authority advocated by antigovernment critics actually stems from a disguised fear and distrust of democratic politics. The fear of a vigorous democracy is a venerable feature of American political life. After all, as Barber (1984) argues, American democracy has always been a "thin democracy"—that is, a political system designed primarily to preserve the minimalist state and to insulate individuals from any demand that exceeds what is required to accomplish only very limited objectives. Fear of a "strong democracy" and its organized, informed, and effective popular majorities "is an integral disposition of American liberal democracy itself" (Barber, 1984: 17). The language and tactics of contemporary criticism of public policies and the scope of government is designed to underscore the lack of communal objectives and shared interests among Americans. Again, in the words of Barber (1984: 21), antigovernmental sentiments today function "by keeping men apart rather than by bringing them together. It is their mutual incompatibility that turns men into reluctant citizens and their aggressive solitude that makes them into wary neighbors." In his plea for a "strong democracy," Barber asserts, "In a public world reduced to the private marketplace, it is not only politics that vanishes but the very concept of a public and thus of public goods, public will, and public interest" (1998: 152). Many of the proposals to reform government, especially those posed by ideologically motivated antigovernment critics, *would reduce access* to governing institutions and leave large segments of the most vulnerable among us even more open to abuse by private sector forces. The effort to harden the political process and make government less capable of or less inclined to respond to political demands will not necessarily improve government performance, enhance personal liberty, or reduce government size. It will almost certainly worsen social inequity and further augment the already swelling personal fortunes of the most affluent.

SUMMARY

Although government in the United States has grown, measured in terms of tax burdens or as percentages of the Gross Domestic Product, the U.S. public sector, measured in fiscal terms, is relatively small when compared to the public sectors of other advanced societies. While it is probably true that the regulatory apparatus of the United States is extraordinarily adversarial and litigious, government size measured in terms of taxing and spending is relatively small in the United States when contrasted to most other advanced democracies. According to the standards of antigovernment critics, the public sector might nevertheless still be too large. In comparative terms, however, the U.S. public sector is fairly small.

The causes of government growth among democracies, including the United States, are varied. Among the most important are war and threats of war, economic downturns, democratization, and increased government responsiveness. Bureaucratic imperialism, by which public agencies generate an autonomous force for government growth, seems fairly insignificant as a cause of growing government size.

The fear that more egalitarian political systems and rampaging bureaucrats would savage the incomes and fortunes of the affluent citizens has not been realized. Income distributions in the United States have not changed much, and if they have in the past twenty years, it has been in the direction of worsening income inequality (Atkinson, 1995; Braun, 1991; Kraus, 1981; Maxwell, 1990; Ryu and Slottje, 1998; Weinberg, 1996). The public in the United States and throughout the advanced industrial world has also been fairly sensitive to the needs of market economies and balancing those needs against the claims of social justice. Advanced, industrial democracies have been solicitous of the competing needs of both social equality and economic efficiency (Okun, 1975). If anything, in the United States, wages and workers' benefits and the organization of business and tax burdens have, in recent years, clearly been subservient to the needs of the market economy. The privileged position of business, the global mobility of capital, and the inherent advantages in terms of political skill and resources that attend being among the middle and higher social classes provide an effective, ongoing check on rampant egalitarianism (Frey, 1971; Franklin, 1985; Piven and Cloward, 1988). Although the general public might tolerate and permit government size to reach slightly above the levels desired by some, it often resists government growth and size when these appear to undermine economic growth.

Even in countries with less extensive democratic traditions, working class and poorer citizens have tolerated heavy burdens of retrenchment, often to accommodate the needs of "sound" fiscal and economic policy as dictated by the International Monetary Fund.

There are also powerful arguments that the public sector is perhaps too small and overly sensitive to higher status groups because political participation tends to be heavily biased in favor of the most affluent and best organized. The "efficiency" gains, such as they are, to be had by making it more difficult to "grow the government" are not justified since societies do often act responsibly in balancing social and economic welfare. Barriers to public influence on public policy are not worth the loss in democratic access and might only serve to exacerbate social inequality. Arguments can be made that the lack of government access and the absence of more general political involvement have kept government size in the United States below "optimal" levels. Data indicate that the policies initiated during the 1980s, inspired largely by the antigovernment ideas of the Reagan administration, have not produced growth in jobs or income equal to that which occurred during the allegedly moribund 1970s (Schwarz, 1988: 147–85).

Government size can vary substantially and *independently* of economic performance. At some point, public sector burdens will detract from economic performance, although this point is likely to vary from one nation to another, and is certainly higher than where it currently is in the United States. The recent economic surge in the United States has occurred despite the slightly higher taxes and negligibly larger public sector that have been put in place under the Clinton administration.

Notwithstanding the possibilities of government failures and abuse, the public has deployed government policies to enhance the quality of its life and expand its freedoms. A public acting democratically through government can produce a larger public sector without producing an oppressive public sector. People are often severely mistreated and oppressed by the *private* sector. Sometimes private sector abuses can only be managed by the general public deploying government power through public policy. Recent reminders of this can be found in the monumentally expensive collapse of the savings and loan industry in the United States, in the commercial abuse of both adult and juvenile workers, and in the indifference to consumer safety and environmental quality. The public needs to be wary of the premise that a freer market will maximize general welfare. There is much to celebrate in terms of the public's achievements through the use of democratic governance, including a variety of environmental and conservationist achievements, including air and water quality improvements and wildlife and open space conservation. Greater equity in the treatment of citizens, a modicum of income security for citizens, dramatic reductions in senior citizen poverty, the extension of educational opportunity, and support of the greatest system of public higher education, by far, in the world are all very important attainments. They are the achievements of a democratically organized public, operating through its government institutions. A larger public sector in important ways merely reflects those achievements.

There are a variety of proposals to reduce the size of the public sector or make it more like the private sector (e.g., the privatization movement). These might, although it is by no means guaranteed, improve efficiency. Where gains are demonstrable, a strong case for adopting privatization can be made. It is not at all obvious, however, that the public sector would decline with privatization. There is reason to argue that "reforms" actually might produce a whole array of new, if less apparent, forms of government involvement in previously private matters and increase the scale of government. Applying private sector, business-based models to evaluate government performance can exaggerate the failures of public sector performance, since so much of what the public strives to accomplish through government would never be done by the private sector at all.

The Big Brother Road to Dictatorship suggested by many contemporary conservatives and popular critics of government is not supported by history. Some of the more intrusive government actions in nonmilitary contexts have been associated not with liberal, social welfare programs, but with conservative policy elements such as the drug war and the desire to police people's personal conduct. The specter of unrestrained redistributive demands among the less affluent or an out-of-control impetus for regulation and insatiable absorption of public revenues by a rapacious public bureaucracy turn out to be straw men. Insofar as the push for greater social welfare in the United States is a factor in explaining government growth, it is not among the poor that the big-ticket items are found. Rather, it is among the programs serving the more affluent segments of society that the most expensive components of domestic government programs—such as subsidies and incentives provided for business by every level of government, Social Security for affluent retirees, or the generous public support for owner-occupied housing finance, construction, and purchase—are located. In comparison to the extravagant support for middle-class home ownership, public policies designed to increase the supply of rental housing and housing for the less affluent, for example, are under-funded indeed.

ISSUES REGARDING FUTURE PUBLIC SECTOR INVOLVEMENT

Public sector growth has been described in terms of breakthrough and rationalizing politics (Brown, 1983). The former refers to the politics associated with true, qualitative increases in the public sector. Breakthrough politics involve situations in which the public considers and perhaps initiates involvement in previously private matters. Establishing public schooling where there is previously none, regulating business practices to protect consumers where heretofore there is only *caveat emptor* ("consumer, beware"), providing income security for the unemployed or for senior citizens where only private charity and family assistance prevail are examples of breakthrough issues. These issues tend to be accompanied at their inception by broadly ideological disputes about the wisdom or merit of government involvement. Political conflict about the appropriateness of public intervention tends to prevail during breakthrough politics.

Rationalizing politics, however, focuses on issues of improving or managing existing policies or substantive commitments. Experimenting with different service delivery systems, discussing funding levels, assessing effectiveness, making changes, and reforming are examples of rationalizing politics. Insofar as *terminating* a program results in a qualitative change in what the public is doing, it would, of course, conjure up the dynamics of breakthrough politics. For example, if the U.S. Congress were to consider terminating Social Security and declaring personal income security to be the sole responsibility of individuals, surely the general issues associated with the initiation of Social Security in 1935 would be revived. Brown (1983) argues that in contemporary U.S. politics most of the policy agenda will be preoccupied with rationalizing politics, and that there are fewer topics for which breakthrough issues are likely today. Perhaps—but it is possible to address a number of areas in which there are likely to be discussions and serious proposals regarding public intervention and government sector growth in the coming decades.

One of the areas in which the politics of breakthrough policies will occur is the domain of "industrial policy." During periods of substantial economic growth, a kind of "if-it-ain't-broke-don't-fix-it" perspective prevails. In the heady days of go-go growth of the late 1990s, talk about a role for government in promoting economic growth seemed beside the point or doomed to an ideological mismatch. Balancing government budgets and keeping taxes and government regulation to a minimum is all that is needed, many claimed. Yet during the onset of stagflation in the American economy in the late 1960s, and throughout the 1970s, and then again during the most recent economic downturn in the late 1980s and early 1990s, there was considerable interest in the notion of industrial policy (Johnson, 1984; Fallows, 1989; Reich, 1983; Reich, 1991).

Partly as a result of infatuation with Japanese successes and continued interest in more self-consciously planned policies in places like the Scandinavian nations, West Germany, and France, American scholars and some policy analysts have expressed interest in what is labeled industrial policy. The term *industrial policy* "is first of all an attitude, and only then a matter of technique. It involves the specific recognition that all government measures—taxes, licenses, prohibitions, regulations—have a significant impact on the well-being or ill health of whole sectors, industries, and enterprises in a market economy" (Johnson, 1984: 7). The prevailing mood and the strength of conservative criticism of any public intervention, however, makes it unlikely that any positive industrial policy activity will be a source of breakthroughs just now.

There is little doubt that the industrial policy debate will resurface if there is a sustained economic downturn again, as there surely must be. The nature of the debate regarding industrial policy will, of course, be hard to predict in terms of details. However, in the United States it is unlikely that proposals for industrial policy will seek to emulate countries in which industrial policy has figured more prominently—whether Japan or Western Europe. In the context of the United States, industrial policy will have less to do with targeting particular sectors and more to do with the general institutional, regulatory, fiscal, tax, infrastructure, and human resource context in which economic policy occurs. Unlike Japan, South Korea, France, or Germany, where governments have made very precise choices about targeting industries such as aerospace, computers, automobiles, or high resolution, flat-screen televisions, the United States has generally eschewed the practice of "choosing winners and losers" in the economy. When the debate over industrial policy occurs, it will, despite its generality, again incite a loud and intense ideological conflict.

Of course, despite the pretense of avoiding deliberate choices or acting as if there were no U.S. industrial policy, there is, *de facto*, such a policy in place. While free market advocates resist publicly directed industrial policy, they act as if there is not already a publicly directed flow of capital to a variety of different sectors of the economy, even to the extent of targeting a particular industry. The United States, for example, clearly has a policy of stimulating home construction and home ownership. There is in place today a hefty amount of public sector largesse for home construction and home ownership. An intricate array of public sector supports exists for the home mortgage market. Money for home ownership is given a great advantage over money borrowed for any other economic purpose. These advantages are exceptionally expensive and include tax expenditures (tax deductions) for homeowners—$90 billion *per year*, for the next five years, according to the Office of Management and Budget (1998). These tax subsidies to housing, moreover, do not include much of the cost of building and maintaining the physical infrastructure in the United States. Much of that physical infrastructure is dictated by the needs of the housing and land development business, including the construction of a vast system of roadways. A considerable portion of the nation's streets and highways, as well as the cost of constructing and maintaining them, is devoted mainly to serving suburban homeowners. There is also the required expansion of domestic utilities (water, power, and sewage treatment) and the variety of improvements (flood control) needed to serve an ever-expanding suburban terrain. Housing turnover, housing construction, and its collateral activities are a critical sector of the economy that has developed around a massive structure of public subsidies and incentives. Whether the United States will be able to afford this sort of lavish and high quality housing in the face of greater demands for capital will likely be a part of the future debate over industrial policy. But whether capital markets are best served by greasing the skids for money going into housing construction and finance or by other investment activities will be a matter of some debate. The mere question of whether money for the housing and land development sectors should compete equally with all other sectors is itself an important issue, much less whether there are other sectors that might be more beneficially stimulated than housing.

Not only has the United States had a policy that has massively favored owner-occupied housing construction and land development, there are a number of sectors that have historically been given focused and substantial assistance via public policy. For example, the elaborate system of land grant colleges and agricultural extension services has played an important role in the development of U.S. agriculture, both in the functioning of the agricultural market and in the developing of agricultural products and technology (Hudson, 1994; Hurt, 1994). Insofar as American agriculture is productive and competitive, and to the extent that American construction firms are among the world's biggest and most effective in providing very large supplies of housing, it is in part due to a kind of unintended industrial policy. Decades of investments by the public of very large amounts of capital in research and development for the military and for space programs has also had important spin-offs in such areas as aerospace, the development of the computer, and the emergence of the worldwide web and internet (Leslie, 1993).

Another policy domain that is a likely arena for breakthrough issues has to do with the impact of the globalization of markets on finance, labor, and environmental regulation. The global financial crisis that erupted into a worldwide scourge in the summer of 1998 and put Japan on the brink of deflationary depression has raised potentially significant issues regarding increased government involvement. Ironically, it is the least regulated sector of the insular financial sector of Japan and its untrammeled speculative forays throughout the world that has contributed to a kind of disenchantment with the push to establish "freer," virtually unregulated international flows of capital. Prior to the financial crisis of 1998, nations seeking to avoid being put at a competitive disadvantage had been falling all over one another in order to reduce regulatory barriers to investment. The lack of coordination and appropriate public or government regulation of these massive flows of capital will indeed pose regulatory policy challenges—not only in the United States, but also on the international scene—regarding such matters as investment and accounting standards (Kapstein, 1994, 1998).

Along with the deep, widespread economic misery that the fiscal collapse of 1998 has caused in Asia, Latin America, and parts of eastern Europe, there are a number of related issues that stem from concern for how the burdens of globalization are distributed. Throughout the world, capital and business activity has moved to its most rewarded location. In places like the United States, Canada, and Europe, labor has often been left behind. The fluidity of capital is high, while for labor it is necessarily low. Workers in the United States cannot simply pack their bags and join the labor force in the Philippines, Indonesia, Bangladesh, India, or Pakistan to take advantage of the capital inflow. American workers might be reasonably expected to invest in their education and retraining, and to absorb moving expenses within the United States to take advantage of changes in the American labor market. But unlike the waves of peasants and workers who have migrated from devastated nations to other places to make their homes, U.S. workers have no such experience. It would be a frightening thing to incite in any case. There is a major rigidity in labor that poses serious equity implications. While capital can be deployed quickly to take advantage of the most profitable prospects, labor is subjected to international forces with far fewer real options. Short of massive dislocations with horrid political and social implications, American workers are unlikely to take on the cost of moving out of the nation, in the unlikely event that they would find it "rational" to do so. It is likely, and rightly so, that workers and employees in the advanced industrial nations will seek to have their governments place some kind of burden or responsibility on businesses to share the benefits of the free flow of capital. The economic, social, and political consequences of increasing cross-national and domestic inequalities cannot be ignored without serious long-term peril to civic stability. The political unrest that has erupted in Asia, for example, stemming in some important way from the frustrated expectations of people who have tasted a bit of economic prosperity, is merely a hint of the political extremism that economic distress might bring. The globalism of capital and the transnational movement of people seeking a better life has inspired antiimmigrant and xenophobic movements in places like the United States, Australia, Sweden, and Germany. These and related issues having to do with reestablishing an effective educational system, managing the festering health care crisis, and dealing with the escalating surge of senior citizens and the problems of income security will provide additional arenas in which important issues of a breakthrough nature will be addressed.

Even though the generally antigovernment constraint on government growth will limit the size of public sector growth, the occasional ritual of breakthrough politics will continue to occur. In the absence of war and severe economic distress, however, public sector growth is likely to remain fairly limited when measured against the size of economies or as proportions of personal income.

SOME REMEDIES FOR SOME PROBLEMS

Concluding a book with a relatively short discussion of "remedies" makes one vulnerable to the charge of being long on criticism and short on remedies. There is truth to this charge. Among scholars, particularly among organized, professional political scientists, it is a debatable question as to what the appropriate role of scholars should be in the domain of "improving" or "informing" politics (Lowi, 1979; Meehan, 1967, 1990; Ranney, 1968; Riemer, 1962). In the impulse to be *scientific*, political scientists often insulate themselves in their subject matter and methods from systematic treatments of values and policy proposals on the ground that these sorts of issues are not amenable to scientific rigor. Despite the view that there are important civic dispositions in terms of tolerance, trust, respect, and public spiritedness that are necessary, even required, in democratic politics (Almond and Verba, 1965; Putnam, Leonardi, and Nanetti, 1993), organized political science has as yet not been able to define a large-scale, visible role in cultivating these values through its activities of teaching, advising, and researching. Yet, along with other disciplines, political science, insofar as it is itself the beneficiary of a flourishing democracy, should address more emphatically, more centrally, its role in cultivating such a democracy. The discipline should address questions of curriculum in schools at all levels as well as more disciplined reports, conferences, symposia, and media forums in which political scientists and other scholars engage the general question of how best to link individual citizens with the policy apparatus of the United States. The role of political parties, the impact of technology on the linkage between citizens and their governing institutions, the place of direct versus representative democracy, or the role of modern sampling and polling methods in both assessing sentiments and informing policymaking are examples of the issues for which political scientists as professionals might have valuable insights and proposals.

Improving the public's outlook and trust in public officials, elected and nonelected, is critical. It is not being proposed that such trust be a blind affection for or deference to authority. Rather, it is important that the public have real reasons to believe in the high quality of both the elected and nonelected public service. The issues confronted by citizens and the services they require—from the management of solid waste, to public safety, to regulation of complex commercial and scientific operations, to teaching at the K-12 and university levels, to managing the military, commercial, social, and ecological strains and challenges of a diverse and increasingly intertwined world—mean that legislators, public sector managers, and street-level public employees should strive for the highest standards of performance among themselves.

The objective here is not a loosening of institutional or political controls on the bureaucracy (Gruber, 1987), but rather an equal, even greater, emphasis on quality. Although higher incomes in a number of areas might remedy the problem of quality, that is not likely to happen in any sustained way without some greater confidence that the people who serve in the public sector, whether elected or not, provide quality service. However deserved it is, there is a prevailing view among people that those who work in the public sector are less competent in general, overpaid, and less responsive and less efficient than people in the private sector (Neiman and Riposa, 1986). Without public servants demanding from themselves highly publicized and rigorously enforced standards of professional conduct and training, public trust and support will, at best, remain fairly low, and perhaps will decline further. There are ample institutional and political controls on conventional bureaucracies (Goodsell, 1994), although there are continued disputes over such agencies as police and public safety organizations or the Internal Revenue Service. It is not necessary to control public bureaucracies and elected officials by making them objects of ridicule and scorn. Indeed, those kinds of sentiments are more likely to prevent the public from achieving important benefits, whether it is avoiding fiscal crisis due to banking practices or suffering the consequences of adulterated pharmaceuticals or a host of other private sector or natural difficulties (e.g., planning for and managing natural disasters).

Professional organizations or other entities that provide forums for public employees and elected officials to address these issues should be encouraged. Among teachers who wish to overcome a public perception that they lack qualifications and effectiveness, for example, there must be some greater emphasis on quality control and demonstrated competency. Teachers willing to achieve and document the attainment of the highest standards should organize around having reached these accomplishments and lobby to make these standards more general in their profession.

Recognizing that scrutiny of the public service is fairly inexpensive for the media and rife with opportunities for cheap-shot journalism, that is part of the heat of the public service kitchen. Even if misconduct and lack of quality is sometimes exaggerated, the best approach is not to whine or complain about media mistreatment. After all, what else is new? Public sector embarrassments must be acknowledged and addressed openly and remedied with as much dispatch as due process and professionalism permit. In the long run, a public that has trust and respect for the competence, honesty, and effective performance of its public servants is the best guarantor in a democracy of the *public servant's* material and professional well-being.

Among the most important needs is elevating the quality of political participation through the nurturing of public virtue, which requires tolerance and the capacity to feel personal satisfaction from advancing the public interest. Of course, choices must be made about the bounds of tolerance. An amendment to the constitution that would establish a national religion or one that would repeal the Bill of Rights would be unacceptable. Indeed, the entire issue of what tolerance demands and when tolerance must or should be supplanted by resistance is a fascinating issue.

There must be an expansion of political involvement in as wide a sphere of political life as possible. In a sense, this is advocating institutions and policies that enhance citizen involvement in processing political information, in participating in elections and campaigns, and in becoming more involved in affecting the formulation, enactment, and implementation of public policy. In order to accomplish this, there must be a concerted scholarship and widespread discussion of how larger proportions of the public can develop greater sophistication about their own interests, especially in light of mind-boggling and still growing levels of spending in political campaigns and lobbying. Equally important is the fostering of institutions, forums, and values that permit members of the public to advance public discourse with civility. These are some modest conditions for providing individuals with the opportunity to choose and celebrate a civil and gallant democratic politics.

References

Aaron, Henry J. 1973. *Why Is Welfare So Hard to Reform?* Washington, D.C.: The Brookings Institution.

Adams, Willi Paul. 1980. *The First American Constitutions Republican Ideology and the Making of State Constitutions in the Revolution Era.* Chapel Hill, NC: University of North Carolina Press.

Advisory Commission on Intergovernmental Relations. 1987. *Changing Public Attitudes on Governments and Taxes.* Washington, D.C.: Advisory Commission on Intergovernmental Relations.

Aharoni, Yair. 1977. *Markets, Planning and Development: The Private Sector and Public Sectors in Economic Development.* Cambridge, MA: Ballinger.

———. 1981. *The No Risk Society.* Chatham, NJ: Chatham House Publishers.

Ahrens, John. 1983. *Preparing for the Future: An Essay on the Rights of Future Generations.* Bowling Green, OH: Bowling Green State University, Social Philosophy and Policy Center.

Alexander, Herbert. 1976. *Financing Politics: Money Elections and Political Reform.* Washington, D.C.: Congressional Quarterly Press.

Allen, Leslie H. 1917. *Industrial Housing Problems.* Boston, MA: Aberthaw Construction Company.

Almond, Gabriel A., and Sidney Verba. 1965. *The Civic Culture.* Boston, MA: Little, Brown.

Alt, James, and K. Alec Chrystal. 1983. *Political Economics.* Berkeley, CA: University of California Press.

Amacher, Ryan C., Robert D. Tollison, and Thomas D. Willett. 1975. "A Budget Size in a Democracy: A Review of the Arguments." *Public Finance Quarterly* 3 (April): 99–121.

Amacher, Ryan C., Richard Higgins, William Shughart II, and Robert Tollison. 1985. "The Behavior of Regulatory Activity over the Business Cycle: An Empirical Test." *Economic Inquiry* 23 (January): 7–18.

American Assembly, The. 1954. *The Federal Government Service: Its Character, Prestige and Problems*. New York: Graduate School of Business, Columbia University.

Anderson, James E., ed. 1986. *The Rise of the Modern State*. Sussex, UK: Harvester Press.

Anderson, James E., and Jared E. Hazleton. 1986. *Managing Macroeconomic Policy: The Johnson Presidency*. Austin, TX: University of Texas Press.

Anderson, Terry L., and Peter J. Hill. 1980. *The Birth of a Transfer Society*. Stanford, CA: Hoover Institution Press, Stanford University.

Anton, Thomas J., Jerry P. Cawley, and Kevin Kramer. 1980. *Moving Money: An Empirical Analysis of Federal Expenditure Patterns*. Cambridge, MA: Oelgeschelager, Gunn & Ham.

Apgar, William C., and H. James Brown. 1987. *Microeconomics and Public Policy*. Glenview, IL: Scott, Foresman, and Company.

Arrow, Kenneth. 1951. *Social Choice and Individual Values*. New York: John Wiley and Sons.

Ashford, Douglas E. 1981. "The British and French Social Security Systems: Welfare State by Intent and by Default." Prepared for delivery at the 1981 annual meeting of the American Political Science Association, September 3–6.

Ashley, Anne. 1912. *The Social Policy of Bismarck: A Critical Study, with a Comparison of German and English Insurance Legislation*. London: Longmans.

Atkinson, Anthony Barnes. 1995. *Income Distribution in OECD Countries: Evidence from Luxembourg Income Study*. Paris, France: Organisation for Economic Cooperation and Development.

Auerbach, Joseph, and Samuel L. Hayes III. 1986. *Investment Banking and Diligence: What Price Deregulation?* Boston, MA: Harvard Business School Press.

Ball, Howard. 1984. *Controlling Regulatory Sprawl*. Westport, CT: Greenwood Press.

Baran, Paul. 1957. *The Political Economy of Growth*. New York: Monthly Review Press.

Barber, Benjamin. 1984. *Strong Democracy: Participatory Politics for a New Age*. Berkeley, CA: University of California Press.

———. 1996. "A Civics Lesson: Must We Remind You That Government Is Not the Enemy? We Must, Alas." *Nation* 263 (November 4): 20–21.

———. 1998. *A Passion for Democracy: American Essays*. Princeton, NJ: Princeton University Press.

Barber, William J. 1985. *From New Era to New Deal: Herbert Hoover, the Economists and American Economic Policy, 1921–1933*. New York: Cambridge University Press.

Bardach, Eugene, and Robert Kagan. 1981. *Going by the Book: Unreasonableness in Protective Regulation*. Philadelphia, PA: Temple University Press.

Bardach, Eugene, and Robert A. Kagan, eds. 1982. *Social Regulation: Strategies for Reform*. San Francisco, CA: Institute for Contemporary Studies.

Barrow, Clyde W. 1993. *Critical Theories of the State: Marxist, Neo-Marxist, Post-Marxist*. Madison, WI: University of Wisconsin Press.

Barry, Brian H. 1970. *Sociologists, Economists and Democracy*. London: Collier-Macmillan.

Baumer, Donald C., and Carl E. Van Horn. 1985. *The Politics of Unemployment*. Washington, D.C.: Congressional Quarterly.

Baumgartner, Frank, and Bryan D. Jones. 1993. *Agendas and Instability in American Politics*. Chicago, IL: University of Chicago Press.

Baumol, W. J. 1965. *Welfare Economics and the Theory of the State*. Cambridge, MA: Harvard University Press.

Baxter, William F. 1974. *People or Penguins: The Case for Optimal Pollution*. New York: Columbia University Press.

Bean, Charles R., Richard Layard, and Stephen Nickell III. 1986. *The Rise of Unemployment*. Oxford: Basil Blackwell, London School of Economics and Political Science.

Beck, James M. 1932. *Our Wonderland of Bureaucracy: A Study of the Growth of Bureaucracy in the Federal Government and the Growth and Its Destructive Effect upon the Constitution*. New York: The Macmillan Company.

Beck, Morris. 1976. "The Expanding Public Sector: Some Contrary Evidence." *National Tax Journal* 29 (March): 15–21.

———. 1979. "Public Sector Growth: A Real Perspective." *Public Finance* 34, no. 3: 313–56.

———. 1981. *Government Spending Trends and Issues*. New York: Praeger.

Becker, G. S. 1983. "A Theory of Competition among Pressure Groups for Political Influence." *Quarterly Journal of Economics* 98: 371–400.

Beer, Samuel H. 1977. "Political Overload and Freedom." *Polity* 10 (fall): 5–17.

Bennett, J. T., and M. H. Johnson. 1980. *The Political Economy of Federal Government Growth: 1959–1978*. College Station, TX: Center for Education and Research in Free Enterprise.

Bentley, Arthur F. 1967. *The Process of Government*. Cambridge, MA: Harvard University Press.

Bernstein, Irving. 1985. *A Caring Society: The New Deal, the Worker, and the Great Depression: A History of the American Worker, 1933–1941*. Boston, MA: Houghton Mifflin.

Bernstein, Marvin H. 1955. *Regulating Business by Independent Commission*. Westport, CT: Greenwood Press.

Berry, Jeffrey M. 1984. *The Interest Group Society*. Boston, MA: Little, Brown and Company.

Berry, William D., and David Lowery. 1984. "The Growing Cost of Government: A Test of Two Explanations." *The Social Science Quarterly* 65 (summer): 734–49.

———. 1984. "The Measurement of Government Size: Implications for the Study of Government Growth." *Journal of Politics* 46 (November): 1193–206.

———. 1987. *Understanding United States Government Growth: An Empirical Analysis of the Postwar Era*. New York: Praeger.

Best, Gary Dean. 1991. *Pride, Prejudice and Politics: Roosevelt versus Recovery, 1933–1938*. New York: Praeger.

Best, Michael, and William E. Connolly. 1982. *The Politicized Economy*. 2nd ed. Lexington, MA: D.C. Heath and Company.

Bhide, Amar. 1984. *Of Politics and Economic Reality: The Art of Winning Elections with Sound Economic Policies*. New York: Basic Books.

Birdsall, William C., and John L. Hawkins. 1975. "The Future of Social Security." *Annals of the American Academy of Political and Social Science* 479 (May): 82–100.

Bish, Robert. 1971. *The Public Economy of Metropolitan Areas*. Chicago, IL: Markham Publishing.

Block, Fred. 1977. "The Ruling Class Does Not Rule: Notes on the Marxist Theory of the State." *Socialist Revolution* 23 (May–June): 6–28.

Borchardt, Knut. 1991. *Perspectives on Modern German Economic History and Policy*. New York: Cambridge University Press.

Borcherding, T. E. 1977. "The Sources of Growth of Public Expenditures in the United States, 1902–1970." In *Budgets and Bureaucrats: The Sources of Government Growth*, ed. T. E. Borcherding. Durham, NC: Duke University Press.

Borjas, George J. 1984. "Electoral Cycles and the Earnings of Federal Bureaucrats." *Economic Inquiry* 22 (October): 447–59.

Bourgin, Frank. 1989. *The Great Challenge: The Myth of Laissez-Faire in the Early Republic*. New York: George Braziller.

Braeman, John. 1988. *Before the Civil Rights Revolution: The Old Court and Individual Rights*. New York: Greenwood Press.

Braithwaite, John. 1985. *To Punish or Persuade: Enforcement of Coal Mine Safety*. Albany, NY: State University of New York Press.

Braun, Dennis Duane. 1991. *The Rich Get Richer: The Rise of Income Inequality in the United States and the World*. Chicago, IL: Nelson-Hall Publishers.

Brennan, Geoffrey, and James Buchanan. 1977. "Towards a Tax Constitution for Leviathan." *Journal of Public Economics* (December): 255–73.

———. 1980. *The Power to Tax: Analytical Foundations of a Fiscal Constitution*. New York: Cambridge University Press.

Brenner, Philip, Robert Borosage, and Bethany Weidner, eds. 1974. *Exploring Contradictions: Political Economy in the Corporate State*. New York: David McKay Company, Inc.

Breton, Albert, and Ronald Wintrobe. 1975. "The Equilibrium Size of a Budget Maximizing Bureau: A Note on Niskanen's Theory of Bureaucracy." *Journal of Political Economy* 83 (February): 195–207.

Brewer, Garry D., and Peter deLeon. 1983. *The Foundations of Policy Analysis*. Homewood, IL: The Dorsey Press.

Brewster, Lawrence G. 1987. *The Public Agenda: Issues in American Politics*. New York: St. Martin's Press.

Brigham, John, and Don W. Brown, eds. 1980. *Policy Implementation: Penalties or Incentives?* Beverly Hills, CA: Sage Publications.

Brittain, Samuel. 1978. "Inflation and Democracy." In *The Political Economy of Inflation*, ed. Hirsch and Goldthorpe. Cambridge, MA: Harvard University Press.

Brooks, Thomas R. 1974. *Walls Come Tumbling Down: A History of the Civil Rights Movement, 1940–1970*. Englewood Cliffs, NJ: Prentice Hall.

Brown, Lawrence D. 1983. *New Policies, New Politics: Government's Response to Government's Growth*. Washington, D.C.: The Brookings Institution.

Bruchey, Stuart. 1988. *The Wealth of the Nation: An Economic History of the United States*. New York: Harper & Row.

Buchanan, James H. 1968. *The Demand and Supply of Public Goods*. Chicago, IL: Rand McNally and Company.

Buchanan, James H., and Gordon Tullock. 1962. *The Calculus of Consent*. Ann Arbor, MI: University of Michigan Press.

———. 1977. "The Expanding Public Sector: Wagner Squared." *Public Choice* 31 (fall): 147–50.

Buchanan, James M. 1967. *Public Finance in Democratic Process: Fiscal Institutions and Individual Choice*. Chapel Hill, NC: University of North Carolina Press.

Buchanan, James M., John Burton, and R. E. Wagner. 1978. *The Consequences of Mr. Keynes: An Analysis of the Misuse of Economic Theory for Political Profiteering, with Proposals for Constitutional Disciplines*. Sussex, UK: The Institute of Economic Affairs.

Bucholz, Rogene A. 1989. *Business, Environment and Public Policy.* 3rd ed. Englewood Cliffs, NJ: Prentice Hall.

Budge, Ian, and Richard I. Hofferbert. 1990. "Mandates and Policy Outputs: U.S. Party Platforms and Federal Expenditures." *American Political Science Review* 84 (March): 111–31.

Buechler, Steven M. 1990. *Women's Movements in the United States: Woman Suffrage, Equal Rights, and Beyond.* New Brunswick, NJ: Rutgers University Press.

Bumck, Julie Marie. 1994. *Fidel Castro and the Quest for a Revolutionary Culture in Cuba.* University Park, PA: Pennsylvania State University Press.

Bundett, Loomis A., and Allan J. Cigler. 1987. "Introduction to Interest Groups." Pp. 372–76 in *Congress and Public Policy: A Source Book of Documents and Readings.* 2nd ed. Edited by David C. Kozak and John D. Macartney. Chicago, IL: Dorsey Press.

Burnham, Walter Dean. 1987. "The Turnout Problem." Pp. 97–133 in *Elections American Style*, ed. A. J. Reichley. Washington, D.C.: The Brookings Institution.

Burton, John. 1985. *Why No Cuts? An Inquiry into the Fiscal Anarchy of Uncontrolled Government Expenditure.* London: Institute of Economic Affairs.

Calavita, Kitty, and Henry N. Pontell. 1990. "'Heads I Win, Tails You Lose': Deregulation, Crime and Crisis in the Savings and Loan Industry." *Crime and Delinquency* 36: 309–41.

Calavita, Kitty, Henry N. Pontell, and Robert H. Tillman. 1997. *Big Money Crime: Fraud and Politics in the Savings and Loan Crisis.* Berkeley, CA: University of California Press.

Calleo, David P. 1982. *The Imperious Economy.* Cambridge, MA: Harvard University Press.

Cameron, David R. 1978. "The Expansion of the Public Economy: A Comparative Analysis." *American Political Science Review* 72 (December): 1243–61.

———. 1982. "On the Limits of the Public Economy." *Annals of the American Academy of Political and Social Science* 459 (January): 46–62.

———. 1988. "Distributional Coalitions and Other Sources of Economic Stagnation: On Olson's Rise and Decline of Nations." *International Organization* 42: 561–603.

Campbell, Ballard C. 1995. *The Growth of American Government: Governance from the Cleveland Era to the Present.* Bloomington, IN: Indiana University Press.

Caporaso, James. 1982. "The State's Role in Third World Economic Growth." *Annals of the American Academy of Political and Social Science* 459 (January): 103–11.

Carr, Edward Hallett. 1979. *The Russian Revolution: From Lenin to Stalin.* New York: Free Press.

Carvounis, Chris C. 1987. *The United States Trade Deficit of the 1980s: Origins, Meanings, and Policy Responses.* New York: Quorum Books.

Catterall, J. S. 1992. "Theory and Practice of Family Choice in Education: Taking Stock— Review Essay." *Economics of Education Review* 11: 407–16.

Center for the Study of Public Choice. 1970. *Education Vouchers: A Report on Financing Elementary Education by Grants to Parents.* Cambridge, MA.

Champagne, Anthony, and Edward J. Harpham. 1984. *The Attack on the Welfare State.* Prospects Heights, IL: Waveland Press, Inc.

Chandler, Lester V. 1970. *America's Greatest Depression, 1929–1941.* New York: Harper & Row.

Chenery, Hollis, H. Ahiuwalia, C. L. E. Bell, J. H. Duloy, and J. Jolly. 1974. *Redistributions with Growth.* New York: Oxford University Press.

"Child Labor." 1905. *Annals of the American Academy of Political and Social Science* 25 (May).

"Child Labor." 1907. *Annals of the American Academy of Political and Social Science* 29 (January).

Choi, Kwang. 1983. *Theories of Comparative Economic Growth*. Ames, IA: Iowa State University Press.

Christainsen, Gregory B., and Robert H. Haveman. 1982. "Government Regulations and Their Impact on the Economy." *Annals of the American Academy of Political and Social Science* 459 (January): 112–22.

Chubb, J. E., and T. Moe. 1990. *Politics Markets and America's Schools*. Washington, D.C.: The Brookings Institution.

Clarke, Harold D., Marianne C. Stewart, and Gary Zuk, eds. 1989. *Economic Decline and Political Change*. Pittsburgh, PA: University of Pittsburgh Press.

Clarke, John J. 1920. *The Housing Problem: Its History, Growth, Legislation, and Procedure*. New York: Sir Isaac Pitman and Sons, Ltd.

Clinard, Marshall B., and Peter C. Yeager. 1980. *Corporate Crime*. New York: The Free Press.

Cobb, Roger W., and Charles D. Elder. 1972. *Participation in American Politics: The Dynamics of Agenda Building*. Boston, MA: Allyn and Bacon, Inc.

Cochran, Bert. 1984. *Welfare Capitalism—And After*. New York: Schocken Books.

Coleman, James S., and Thomas J. Fararo. 1992. *Rational Choice Theory: Advocacy and Critique*. Newbury Park, CA: Sage Publications.

Comanor, W. S. 1976. "The Median Voter Rule and the Theory of Political Choice." *Journal of Public Economics* 5 (August): 169–77.

Conklin, Paul. 1967. *The New Deal*. New York: Crowell.

Consumer Product Safety Commission, United States. "January, 1998 Press Releases."

Coons, J., and S. D. Sugarman. 1978. *Education by Choice*. Berkeley, CA: University of California Press.

Cornwall, Hugo. 1987. *Datatheft: Computer Fraud, Industrial Espionage and Information Crime*. London: Heinemann.

Cornwall, John. 1983. *The Conditions for Economic Recovery*. Oxford: Martin Robertson & Company, Ltd.

Corwin, Edward S., ed. 1964. *The Constitution of the United States of America: Analysis and Interpretation*. Washington D.C.: U.S. Government Printing Office.

Coughlin, Cletus. 1985. "Domestic Content Legislation: House Voting and the Economic Theory of Regulation." *Economic Inquiry* 23 (July): 437–48.

Courant, P. N., E. H. Gramlich, and D. L. Rubinfeld. 1979. "Public Employee Market Power and the Level of Government Spending." *American Economic Review* 69 (December): 806–17.

Croall, Hazel C. 1992. *White Collar Crime: Criminal Justice and Criminology*. Philadelphia, PA: Open University Press.

Cullis, John G., and Philip R. Jones. 1987. *Microeconomics and the Public Economy: A Defense of Leviathan*. New York: Basil Blackwell, Inc.

Cunningham, Hugh. 1987. "Child Labor in the Industrial Revolution." *The Historian* 14 (spring): 3–8.

Dahl, Robert A. 1982. *Dilemmas of Pluralist Democracy*. New Haven, CT: Yale University Press.

Dahl, Robert Alan, and Charles E. Lindblom. 1953. *Politics, Economics, and Welfare: Planning and Politico-Economic Systems Resolved into Basic Social Processes.* New York: Harper.

Dahrendorf, Ralf. 1959. *Class and Class Conflict in Industrial Society.* Stanford, CA: Stanford University Press.

Dalton, Russell J. 1988. *Citizen Politics in Western Democracies: Public Opinion and Political Parties in the United States, Great Britain, West Germany, and France.* Chatham, NJ: Chatham House.

Davies, G. D. 1970. "The Concentration Process and the Growing Importance of Non-Central Government." *Public Policy*: 649–57.

Davis, Allen F. 1967. *Spearheads for Reform: The Social Settlements and the Progressive Movement, 1890–1914.* New York: Oxford University Press.

Davis, Otto, M. A. H. Dempter, and Aaron Wildavsky. 1966. "A Theory of the Budgetary Process." *American Political Science Review* 60: 529–47.

DeGrasse, Robert W., Jr. 1983. *Military Expansion, Economic Decline: The Impact of Military Spending on U.S. Economic Performance.* Armonk, NY: M. E. Sharpe, Inc.

Denham, Andrew. 1996. *Think-Tanks of the New Right.* Brookfield, VT: Dartmouth.

Denison, E. F. 1979. *Accounting for Slower Economic Growth: The United States in the 1970s.* Washington D.C.: The Brookings Institution.

Denison, Edward F. 1983. *The Interruption of Productivity Growth in the United States.* Washington, D.C.: The Brookings Institution.

Denzau, A., R. J. Mackay, and C. L. Weaver. 1979. "Spending Limitations, Agenda Control and Voters' Expectations." *National Tax Journal* 32: 189–200.

Dionne, E. J. 1991. *Why Americans Hate Politics.* New York: Simon & Schuster.

Dietze, Gottfried. 1968. *America's Political Dilemma: From Limited to Unlimited Democracy.* Baltimore, MD: Johns Hopkins Press.

———. 1985. *Liberalism Proper and Proper Liberalism.* Baltimore, MD: Johns Hopkins University Press.

Dobelstein, Andrew W. 1980. *Politics, Economics and Public Welfare.* Englewood Cliffs, NJ: Prentice Hall, Inc.

Dogan, Mattei. 1995. "Erosion of Class Voting and of the Religious Vote in Western Europe." *International Social Science Journal* 47 (December): 525–39.

Downs, Anthony. 1957. *An Economic Theory of Democracy.* New York: Harper & Row.

———. 1960. "Why the Government Budget Is Too Small in a Democracy." *World Politics* 12 (July): 541–63.

Doyle, Brian John. 1995. *Disability, Discrimination, and Equal Opportunities: A Comparative Study of the Employment Rights of Disabled Persons.* New York: Mansell.

Drucker, Peter. 1969. "The Sickness of Government." *The Public Interest* (winter): 3–23.

Dryzek, John S. 1996. *Democracy in Capitalist Times: Ideals, Limits, and Struggles.* New York: Oxford University Press.

Dubin, Elliott. 1977. "The Expanding Public Sector: Some Contrary Evidence—a Comment." *National Tax Journal* 30 (March): 95.

Duncan, Greg J. 1984. *Years of Poverty, Years of Plenty: The Changing Economic Fortunes of American Workers and Families.* Ann Arbor, MI: Institute for Social Research, University of Michigan.

Dunleavy, Patrick. 1985. "Bureaucrats, Budgets and the Growth of the State: Reconstructing an Instrumental Model." *British Journal of Political Science* 15 (July): 299–328.

————. 1991. *Democracy, Bureaucracy, and Public Choice: Economic Explanations in Political Science.* London: Narvester Wheatsheaf.

Dye, Thomas R. 1976. *Policy Analysis: What Governments Do, Why They Do It, and What Difference It Makes.* Tuscaloosa, AL: University of Alabama Press.

————. 1987. *Understanding Public Policy.* Englewood Cliffs, NJ: Prentice Hall.

Easton, David. 1965a. *A Framework for Political Analysis.* Englewood Cliffs, NJ: Prentice Hall.

————. 1965b. *A Systems Analysis of Political Life.* New York: Wiley.

Edsall, Thomas Byrne. 1984. *The New Politics of Inequality.* New York: W. W. Norton & Company.

Edwards, Richard. 1993. *Rights at Work: Employment Relations in the Post-Union Era.* Washington, D.C.: The Brookings Institution.

Ehrenhalt, Alan. 1992. *The United States of Ambition: Politicians, Power, and the Pursuit of Office.* New York: Times Books.

Eichner, Alfred S. 1983. *Why Economics is Not Yet a Science.* New York: M. E. Sharpe, Inc.

Eksterowicz, Anthony J., Paul C. Cline, and Scott J. Hammond. 1995. *American Democracy: Representation, Participation, and the Future of the Republic.* Englewood Cliffs, NJ: Prentice Hall.

Elster, Jon. 1979. *Ulysses and the Sirens: Studies in Rationality and Irrationality.* Cambridge, MA: Cambridge University Press.

————. 1983. *Sour Grapes: Studies in the Subversion of Rationality.* Cambridge, MA: Cambridge University Press.

Epple, Dennis, and Allan Zelenitz. 1981. "The Implications of Competition among Jurisdictions: Does Tiebout Need Politics?" *Journal of Political Economy* 89 (December): 1197–217.

Ermann, H. David, and Richard J. Lundman. 1978. *Corporate and Governmental Deviance: Problems of Organizational Behavior in Contemporary Society.* New York: Oxford University Press.

Esping-Anderson, Gosta. 1985. *Politics Against Markets: The Social Democratic Road to Power.* Princeton, NJ: Princeton University Press.

Eulau, Heinz, and Michael S. Lewis-Beck, eds. 1985. *Economic Conditions and Electoral Outcomes: The United States and Western Europe.* New York: Agathon Press.

Fabricant, Solomon. 1952. *The Trend of Government Activity in the United States Since 1900.* New York: National Bureau of Economic Research, Inc.

Fairris, David. 1996. "Institutional Change in Shopfloor Governance and the Trajectory of Postwar Injury Rates in U.S. Manufacturing, 1948–1970." Unpublished paper, Department of Economics, University of California, Riverside, August.

Fallows, James. 1989. *More Like US: Making America Great Again.* Boston, MA: Houghton Mifflin.

Faludi, Andreas. 1973. *Planning Theory.* New York: Pergamon Press.

Farnam, Henry W. 1938. *Chapters in the History of Social Legislation in the United States to 1860.* Baltimore, MD: Waverly Press, Carnegie Institution of Washington.

Ferris, J. Stephen, and Edwin G. West. 1996. "Testing Theories of Real Government Size: U.S. Experience, 1959–89." *Southern Economic Journal* 62 (January): 537–54.

Finer, Herman. 1964. *Mussolini's Italy.* London: Frank Cass and Company, Ltd.

Fiorina, H. P., and R. G. Noll. 1978. "Voters, Bureaucrats, and Legislators: A Rational Choice Perspective on the Growth of Bureaucracy." *Journal of Public Economics* 9: 239–54.

Fisse, Brent, and John Braithwaite. 1993. *Corporations, Crime, and Accountability*. Cambridge, MA: Cambridge University Press.

Fladiman, Richard. 1987. *The Philosophy and Politics of Freedom*. Chicago, IL: University of Chicago Press.

Flanigan, William H., and Nancy H. Zingale. 1987. *Political Behavior of the American Electorate*. 6th ed. Boston, MA: Allyn and Bacon, Inc.

Flemming, J. S. 1978. "The Economic Explanation of Inflation." Pp. 13–36 in *The Political Economy of Inflation*, ed. Hirsch and Goldthorpe. Cambridge, MA: Harvard University Press.

Flora, Peter, and A. J. Heidenheimer, eds. 1981a. *The Development of Welfare States in Europe and America*. New Brunswick, NJ: Transaction Books, Inc.

———. 1981b. "The Historical Core and Changing Boundaries of the Welfare State." Pp. 17–34 in *The Developments of Welfare States in Europe and America*, ed. P. Flora and A. J. Heidenheimer. New Brunswick, NJ: Transaction Books, Inc.

Flora, Peter, and Jens Alber. 1981. "Modernization, Democratization, and the Development of Welfare States in Western Europe." Pp. 37–79 in *The Development of Welfare States in Europe and America*, ed. P. Flora and A. J. Heidenheimer. New Brunswick, NJ: Transaction Books, Inc.

Foltz, E. K. 1909. *The Federal Civil Service as a Career*. New York: Putnam.

Ford, Henry Jones. 1974 (1909). *The Cost of Our National Government*. New York: Arno Press.

Forte, Francesco, and Alan Peacock, eds. 1985. *Public Expenditure and Government Growth*. New York: Basil Blackwell, Inc.

Frankel, Marvin W. 1994. *Faith and Freedom: Religious Liberty in America*. New York: Hill & Wang.

Franklin, John Hope. 1978. *From Slavery to Freedom*. 5th ed. New York: Knopf.

Franklin, Mark N. 1985. *The Decline of Class Voting in Britain: Changes in the Basis of Electoral Choice, 1964–1983*. Oxford: Oxford University Press.

Fraser, Steve, and Gary Gerstle, eds. 1989. *The Rise and Fall of the New Deal Order, 1930–1980*. Princeton, NJ: Princeton University Press.

Frederickson, H. G. 1967. "Understanding Attitudes toward Public Employment." *Public Administration Review* 27 (December): 411–20.

Freeman, Roger A. 1975. *The Growth of American Government: A Morphology of the Welfare State*. Stanford, CA: Stanford University Press.

———. 1981. *A Preview and Summary of "The Wayward Welfare State."* Stanford, CA: Hoover Institution Press, Stanford University.

Frey, D. E. 1992. "Can Privatizing Education Really Improve Achievement? An Essay Review." *Economics of Education Review* 11: 427–38.

Frey, Bruno S. 1971. "Why Do High Income People Participate More in Politics?" *Public Choice* 11: 101–05.

Friedman, Jeffrey, ed. 1996. *The Rational Choice Controversy: Economic Models of Politics Reconsidered*. New Haven, CT: Yale University Press.

Fritschler, A. Lee, and Bernard Ross. 1980. *Business Regulation and Government Decision-Making*. Cambridge, MA: Winthrop Publishers.

———. 1978. *Modern Political Economy*. London: Macmillan.

Friedland, Roger. 1980. "Corporate Power and Urban Growth: The Care of Urban Renewal." *Politics and Society* 10, no. 2: 203–23.

Friedman, Joseph, and Daniel H. Weinberg, eds. 1983. *The Great Housing Experiment.* Beverly Hills, CA: Sage Publications.

Friedman, M. 1955. "The Role of Government in Education." In *Education and the Public Interest,* ed. R. A. Solo. New Brunswick, NJ: Rutgers University Press.

———. 1962. *Capitalism and Freedom.* Chicago, IL: University of Chicago Press.

———. 1976. "The Line We Dare Not Cross: The Fragility of Freedom at 60%." *Encounter* 47 (November): 8–14.

———. 1986. "Economists and Economic Policy." *Economic Inquiry* 24 (January): 1–10.

Friedrich, Carl J. 1974. *Limited Government: A Comparison.* Englewood Cliffs, NJ: Prentice Hall, Inc.

Frohock, Fred H., and David J. Sylvan. 1983. "Liberty, Economics, and Evidence." *Political Studies* 31: 541–55.

Furniss, Norman, and Timothy Tilton. 1977. *The Case for the Welfare State: From Social Security to Social Equality.* Bloomington, IN: Indiana University Press.

Fyfe, Alec. 1989. *Child Labour.* Cambridge: Polity Press.

Galbraith, John Kenneth. 1973. *Economics and the Public Purpose.* Boston, MA: Houghton Mifflin Company.

Galloway, David. 1976. *The Public Prodigals: The Growth of Government Spending and How to Control It.* London: Temple Smith.

Garson, David C. 1978. *Group Theories of Politics.* Beverly Hills, CA: Sage Publications.

Gati, S., and B. R. Kolluri. 1979. "Wagner's Law of Public Expenditures: Some Efficient Results for the United States." *Public Finance* 34: 225–33.

Gatti, James. 1981. *The Limits of Government Regulation.* New York: Academic Press.

George, Vic, and Paul Wilding. 1976. *Ideology and Social Welfare.* London: Routledge & Kegan Paul.

Gerston, Larry N., Cynthia Fraleigh, and Robert Schwab. 1988. *The Deregulated Society.* Pacific Grove, CA: Brooks/Cole Publishing Company.

Gibson, F. K., and G. A. James. 1967. "Student Attitudes toward Government Employees and Employment." *Public Administration Review* 27 (December): 429–35.

Gilbert, Michael. 1986. *Inflation and Social Conflict: A Sociology of Economic Life in Advanced Societies.* Brighton, Sussex: Wheatsheaf Books, Ltd.

Ginsburg, Benjamin, and Alan Stone, eds. 1986. *Do Elections Matter?* Armonk, NY: M. E. Sharpe, Inc.

Goldberg, Joseph P., Eileen Ahern, William Haber, and Rudolph A. Oswald, eds. 1976. *Federal Policies and Worker Status since the Thirties.* Madison, WI: Industrial Relations Research Association.

Goldsmith, M. M. 1984. "Liberty and Economics: A Reconsideration." *Political Studies* 32: 603–10.

Goldwin, Robert A., and William A. Schambra, eds. 1982. *How Capitalistic Is the Constitution?* Washington D.C.: American Enterprise Institute for Public Policy Research.

Goletze, Rolf. 1983. *Rescuing the American Dream: Public Policy and the Crisis in Housing.* New York: Holmes and Meier Publishers.

Gooby-Taylor, Peter. 1986. "Privatization, Power and the Welfare State." *Sociology* 20 (May): 228–46.

Goodsell, Charles T. 1994. *The Case for Bureaucracy: A Public Administration Polemic.* 3rd ed. Chatham, NJ: Chatham House Publishers.

Gordon-Van Tine Co. 1918. *Housing Labor: A Book Written by Businessmen for Businessmen and Dealing with Housing as a Means for Getting and Holding Labor to Meet Today's Need for Increased Production.* Davenport, IA: Gordon-Van Tine Co.

Gould, Frank. 1983. "The Growth of Public Expenditures: Theory and Evidence from Six Advanced Democracies." In *Why Governments Grow: Measuring Public Sector Size*, ed. C. L. Taylor. Beverly Hills, CA: Sage Publications.

Grafstein, Robert. 1990. "Missing the Archimedean Point: Liberalism's Institutional Presuppositions." *American Political Science Review* 84 (March): 177–93.

Gramlich, E. M., and D. L. Rubinfeld. 1982. "Voting on Public Spending: Differences between Public Employees, Transfer Recipients, and Private Workers." *Journal of Policy Analysis and Management* 1, no. 4: 516–33.

Grant, Wyn, and Shiv Nath. 1984. *The Politics of Economic Policymaking.* Oxford: Basil Blackwell, Inc.

Green, Donald P., and Ian Shapiro. 1994. *Pathologies of Rational Choice Theory: A Critique of Applications in Political Science.* New Haven, CT: Yale University Press.

Greenberg, Edward S. 1974. *Serving the Few: Corporate Capitalism and the Bias of Government Policy.* New York: Wiley.

———. 1979. *Understanding Modern Government: The Rise and Decline of the American Political Economy.* New York: Wiley.

———. 1985. *Capitalism and the American Political Ideal.* Armonk, NY: M. E. Sharpe.

Greene, K. 1973. "Attitudes toward Risk and the Relative Size of the Public Sector." *Public Finance Quarterly* 2: 205–18.

Gretton, J., and A. Harrison. 1982. *How Much are Public Servants Worth?* Oxford: Basil Blackwell, Inc.

Groth, Alexander J., and Larry L. Wade, eds. 1984. *Comparative Resource Allocation: Politics, Performance, and Policy Priorities.* Beverly Hills, CA: Sage Publications.

Gruber, Judith E. 1987. *Controlling Bureaucracies: Dilemmas in Democratic Governance.* Berkeley, CA: University of California Press.

Haefele, Edwin, ed. 1974. *The Governance of Common Property Resources.* Baltimore, MD: John Hopkins University Press.

Hall, Peter A. 1986. *Governing the Economy: The Politics of State Intervention in Britain and France.* New York: Oxford University Press.

Hampton, Jean. 1986. *Hobbes and the Social Contract Tradition.* London: Cambridge University Press.

Handlin, Oscar, and Mary Flug Handlin. 1969. *Commonwealth—A Study of the Role of Government in the American Economy: Massachusetts, 1774–1861.* Rev. ed. Cambridge, MA: The Belknap Press of Harvard University.

Hansen, Alvin. 1964. *Business Cycles and National Income.* New York: W. W. Norton Company.

Hardin, Garett. 1968. "The Tragedy of the Commons." *Science* 162: 1243–48.

Hardin, Garett, and John Baden, eds. 1977. *Managing the Commons.* San Francisco, CA: W. H. Freeman.

Hardin, Russell. 1982. *Collective Action.* Baltimore, MD: John Hopkins University Press.

Hartz, Louis. 1948. *Economic Policy and Democratic Thought: Pennsylvania, 1776–1860.* Cambridge, MA: Harvard University Press.

———.1955. *The Liberal Tradition in America.* New York: Harcourt Brace Jovanovich.

Harvey, David. 1982. *The Limits to Capital.* Oxford: Basil Blackwell, Inc.

Hayek, Friedrich. 1944. *The Road to Serfdom.* Chicago, IL: University of Chicago Press.

———. 1976. *The Mirage of Social Justice.* Chicago, IL: University of Chicago Press.

———. 1979. *Unemployment and Monetary Policy: Government as Generator of the Business Cycle.* San Francisco, CA: CATO Institute.

———. 1981. *The Political Order of a Free People.* Chicago, IL: University of Chicago Press.

———. 1991. *Economic Freedom.* Cambridge, MA: B. Blackwell.

Heady, Bruce. 1978. *Housing Policy in the Developed Economy: The United Kingdom, Sweden, and the United States.* London: Croom Helm.

Heidenheimer, Arnold J., Hugh Heclo, and Carolyn Teich Adams. 1983. *Comparative Public Policy: The Politics of Social Choice in Europe and America.* New York: St. Martin's Press.

Heilbroner, Robert L. 1970. *Between Capitalism and Socialism.* New York: Random House.

Hennock, E. P. 1987. *British Social Reform and German Precedents: The Case of Social Insurance, 1880–1914.* New York: Oxford University Press.

Herber, Bernard P. 1975. *Modern Public Finance: The Study of Public Sector Economies.* Homewood, IL: R. D. Irwin.

Herman, S. James. 1929. "Why 'Public Credits' Is the Logical and Practical Solution of the Housing Problem of the Low Income Group." Read before Conference of Town Planning. Institute of Canada. Winnepeg, Manitoba. June 17–19.

Herring, Pendleton. 1967 (1929). *Group Representation before Congress.* New York: Russell & Russell.

Hewitt, Christopher. 1977. "The Effect of Political Democracy and Social Democracy on Equality in Industrial Societies." *American Sociological Review* 42 (June): 450–64.

Hewitt, Daniel. 1985. "Demand for National Public Goods: Estimates from Surveys." *Economic Inquiry* 23 (July): 487–506.

Hibbs, Douglas A., Jr. 1977. "Political Parties and Macroeconomic Policy." *American Political Science Review* 71 (December): 1467–87.

———. 1987. *The American Political Economy: Macroeconomics and Electoral Politics in the United States.* Cambridge, MA: Harvard University Press.

Higgs, Robert. 1971. *The Transformation of the American Economy, 1865–1914: An Essay in Interpretation.* New York: John Wiley and Sons, Inc.

———. 1983. "Where Figures Fail: Measuring the Growth of Big Government." *Freeman* 33: 151–56.

———. 1985. "Crisis, Bigger Government, and Ideological Change: Two Hypotheses on the Ratchet Phenomenon." *Explorations in Economic History* 22 (January): 1–28.

———. 1987. *Crisis and Leviathan: Critical Episodes in the Growth of American Government.* New York: Oxford University Press.

Highton, Benjamin. 1997. "Easy Registration and Voter Turnout." *Journal of Politics* 59 (May): 565–75.

Hills, Stuart L., ed. 1987. *Corporate Violence: Injury and Death for Profit.* Totowa, NJ: Rowman & Littlefield, Publishers.

Hines, Thomas. 1998. "The Eve of Destruction: Los Angeles and the Apocalyptic Temptation." *Los Angeles Times, Book Review,* August 16: 3–4.

Hirsch, Fred, and John G. Goldthorpe. 1978. *The Political Economy of Inflation.* Cambridge, MA: Harvard University Press.

Hirschman, Albert O. 1991. *The Rhetoric of Reaction: Perversity, Futility, Jeopardy.* Cambridge, MA: Belknap Press of Harvard University Press.

———. 1992. *Rival Views of Market Society and other Recent Essays*. New York: Viking.

Hoberg, George, Jr. 1986. "Technology, Political Structure, and Social Regulation." *Comparative Politics* 18 (April): 357–76.

Hochstedler, Ellen, ed. 1984. *Corporations as Criminals*. Beverly Hills, CA: Sage Publications, Inc.

Hodge, R. W., et al. 1964. "Occupational Prestige in the United States, 1925–1963." *American Journal of Sociology* 70 (November): 286–302.

Hofstadter, Richard. 1948. *The American Political Tradition and the Men Who Made It*. New York: A. A. Knopf.

Holcombe, Randall, G. 1983. *Public Finance and the Political Process*. Carbondale, IL: Southern Illinois University.

Holmwood, John. 1996. *Founding Sociology?: Talcott Parsons and the Idea of General Theory*. New York: Longman.

Hooks, Gregory. 1984. "The Policy Response to Factory Closings: A Comparison of the United States, Sweden and France." *Annals of the American Academy of Political and Social Science* 475 (spring): 110–24.

Hoover, Kenneth, and Raymond Plant. 1989. *Conservative Capitalism in Britain and the United States: A Critical Appraisal*. London and New York: Routledge.

Horowitz, Horton J. 1977. *The Transformation of American Law, 1790–1860*. Cambridge, MA: Harvard University Press.

Huang, Wei-Chiao, and Gary McDonnell. 1997. "Growth of Government Expenditure: The Case of the USA." *Social Science Journal* 34 (July): 311–23.

Hudson, John C. 1994. *Making the Corn Belt: A Geographical History of Middle-Western Agriculture*. Bloomington, IN: Indiana University Press.

Hughes, J. R. T. 1977. *The Governmental Habit: Economic Controls from Colonial Times to the Present*. New York: Basic Books.

———. 1991. *The Governmental Habit Redux: Economic Controls from Colonial Times to the Present*. Princeton, NJ: Princeton University Press.

Hughes, Thomas P. 1989. *American Genesis: A Century of Invention and Technological Enthusiasm, 1870–1970*. New York: Viking.

Hula, R. 1986. "Introduction: Market Based Public Policy." *Policy Studies Review* 5: 583–87.

Hurt, R. Douglas. 1994. *American Agriculture: A Brief History*. Ames, IA: Iowa State University Press.

Husted, Thomas A., and Lawrence W. Kenny. 1997. "The Effect of the Expansion of the Voting Franchise on the Size of Government." *Journal of Political Economy* 105 (February): 54–83.

Huxley, Aldous. 1955. *Brave New World*. New York: Bantam Books.

Janowitz, Morris, and Deil Wright. 1956. "The Prestige of Public Employment: 1929 & 1954." *Public Administration Review* 16 (winter): 15–21.

Johnson, Chalmers, ed. 1984. *The Industrial Policy Debate*. San Francisco, CA: Institute for Contemporary Studies.

Johnson, David B. 1991. *Public Choice: An Introduction to the New Political Economy*. Mountainview, CA: Bristlecone Books.

Johnson, Haynes, and David S. Broder. 1997. *The System: The American Way of Politics at the Breaking Point*. Boston, MA: Little, Brown, and Company.

Kapstein, Ethan B. 1994. *Governing the Global Economy: International Finance and the State*. Cambridge, MA: Harvard University Press.

———. 1998. "Back to Basics." *Los Angeles Times*, September 6, Section M.

Katzenstein, P., ed. 1978. *Between Power and Plenty*. Madison, WI: University of Wisconsin Press.

Kau, James B., and Paul H. Rubin. 1981. "The Size of Government." *Public Choice* 37, no. 2: 261–74.

Kaufman, Herbert. 1976. *Are Government Organizations Immortal?* Washington, D.C.: The Brookings Institution.

Keech, William R., and Carl P. Simon. 1983. "Inflation, Unemployment, and Electoral Terms: When Can Reform of Political Institutions Improve Macroeconomic Policy?" Pp. 77–107 in *The Political Process and Economic Change*, ed. K. R. Monroe. New York: Agathon Press, Inc.

Keith, Nathaniel S. 1973. *Politics and the Housing Crisis Since 1930*. New York: Universe Books.

Keller, Horton. 1963. *The New Deal: What Was It?* New York: Holt, Rinehart and Winston.

———. 1977. *Affairs of State*. Cambridge, MA: Harvard University Press.

Kelly, Allen C. 1976. "Demographic Change and the Size of the Public Sector." *Southern Economic Journal* 43: 1056–66.

Kelman, Steven. 1981. *What Price Incentives? Economists and the Environment*. Boston, MA: Auburn House.

———. 1987. *Making Public Policy: A Hopeful View of American Government*. New York: Basic Books.

Keman, Hans. 1982. "Securing the Safety of the Nation-State." Pp. 189 ff in *The Impact of Parties*, ed. F. G. Castles. London: Sage Publications.

Kemp, Kathleen A. 1987. "Growth in the Regulatory State: Social Regulation, Prosperity, and State Fragmentation." Paper presented at the 1987 annual meeting of the American Political Science Association, September 3–6, Chicago, Illinois.

Kendrick, H. Slade. 1955. *A Century and a Half of Federal Expenditures*. New York: National Bureau of Economic Research, Inc.

Kendrick, John W., ed. 1984. *International Comparisons of Productivity and Causes of the Slowdown*. Cambridge, MA: Ballinger Publishing Company.

Key, V. O. 1964. *Politics, Parties and Pressure Groups*. New York: Thomas Y. Crowell Company.

Kilpatrick, Franklin P., Milton C. Cummings, Jr., and H. Kent Jennings. 1964. *The Image of the Federal Service*. Washington, D.C.: The Brookings Institution.

Kinder, Donald R., and Walter R. Mebane, Jr. 1983. "Politics and Economics in Everyday Life." Pp. 141–80 in *The Political Process and Economic Change*, ed. K. R. Monroe. New York: Agathon Press, Inc.

King, Desmond S. 1987. *The New Right: Politics, Markets, and Citizenship*. Chicago, IL: The Dorsey Press.

King, Wiliford Isbell. 1915. *The Wealth and Income of the United States*. New York: The Macmillan Company.

Kingdon, John W. 1984. *Agendas, Alternatives, and Public Policies*. Boston, MA: Little, Brown.

Kluegel, James R., and Eliot R. Smith. 1986. *Beliefs about Inequality: Americans' Views of What Is and What Ought to Be*. New York: Aldine de Gruyer.

Kramer, Ronald C. 1983. "A Prolegomenon to the Study of Corporate Violence." *Humanity and Society* 7 (May).

Kraus, Franz. 1981. "The Historical Development of Income Inequality in Western Europe and the United States." Pp. 187–236 in *The Development of Welfare States in Europe and America*, ed. P. Flora and A. J. Heidenheimer. New Brunswick, NJ: Transaction Books, Inc.

Kriegel, Blandine. 1995. *The State and the Rule of Law*. Princeton, NJ: Princeton University Press.

Krueckeberg, Donald A., ed. 1983. *Introduction to Planning History in the United States*. New Brunswick, NJ: Center for Urban Policy Research, Rutgers University.

Ladd, Everett C., and Karlyn H. Bowman. 1998. *Attitudes Toward Economic Inequality*. Washington, D.C.: American Enterprise Institute Press.

Lambro, Donald. 1984. *Washington—City of Scandals: Investigating Congress and Other Big Spenders*. Boston, MA: Little, Brown and Company.

Lane, Roger. 1979. *Violent Death in the City: Suicide, Accident, and Murder in Nineteenth-Century Philadelphia*. Cambridge, MA: Harvard University Press.

Lansburgh, Richard H., ed. 1926. "Industrial Safety." *Annals of the American Academy of Political and Social Science* 123 (January): 1–224.

Larkey, Patrick, Chandler Stolp, and Mark Winer. 1981. "Theorizing about the Growth of Government." *Journal of Public Policy* 1 (May): 157–220.

Lars, Osberg. 1984. *Economic Inequality in the United States*. Armonk, NY: M. E. Sharpe, Inc.

Lawless, Edward William. 1977. *Technology and Social Shock*. New Brunswick, NJ: Rutgers University Press.

Lawson, Dick. 1919. *Defective Housing and the Growth of Children*. London: George Allen and Unwin, Ltd.

Lee, W. R., ed. 1991. *German Industry and German Industrialization: Essays on German Economic and Business History in the Nineteenth and Twentieth Centuries*. London: Routledge.

Leff, Mark H. 1984. *The Limits of Symbolic Reform: The New Deal and Taxation, 1933–1939*. Cambridge, MA: Cambridge University Press.

Leighley, J. E., and Jonathan Nagler. 1992. "Socioeconomic Class Bias in Turnout, 1964–1988: The Voters Remain the Same." *American Political Science Review* 86: 725–26.

LeLoup, Lance T. 1986. *Budgetary Politics*. 3rd ed. Brunswick, OH: King's Court Communication, Inc.

Lens, Sidney. 1973. *The Labor Wars: From the Molly Maguires to the Sitdowns*. New York: Doubleday & Company, Inc.

Leslie, Stuart W. 1993. *The Cold War and American Science: The Military-Industrial-Academic Complex at MIT and Stanford*. New York: Columbia University Press.

Leuchtenburg, William E. 1963. *Franklin D. Roosevelt and the New Deal, 1932–1940*. New York: Harper & Row.

———. 1964. "The New Deal and the Analogue of War." In *Change and Continuity in Twentieth Century America*, ed. J. Braemon, R. H. Bremner, and E. Walters. Columbus, OH: Ohio State University Press.

Levi, Margaret. 1988. *Of Rule and Revenue*. Berkeley, CA: University of California Press.

Levin, H. M. 1991. "The Economics of Educational Choice." *Economics of Education Review* 10: 137–49.

Lewis-Beck, Michael S. 1988. *Economics and Elections: The Major Western Democracies*. Ann Arbor, MI: The University of Michigan Press.

Lewis-Beck, Michael S., and Tom W. Rice. 1985. "Government Growth in the United States." *Journal of Politics* 47 (February): 2–30.

Lieberson, Stanley. 1971. "An Empirical Study of Military Industrial Linkages." *American Journal of Sociology* 76: 562–84.

Lilley, William, and James Miller. 1977. "The New Social Regulation." *Public Interest* 47 (spring): 49–62.

Lindbeck, Assar. 1985. "Redistribution Policy and the Expansion of the Public Sector." *Journal of Public Economics* 28: 309–28.

Lindberg, Leon N., and Charles S. Haier, eds. 1985. *The Politics of Inflation and Economic Stagnation: Theoretical Approaches and International Case Studies.* Washington, D.C.: The Brookings Institution.

Lindblom, Charles Edward. 1977. *Politics and Markets: The World's Political Economic Systems.* New York: Basic Books.

Llewellyn, Chris. 1987. *Fragments from the Fire: The Triangle Shirtwaist Company Fire of March 25, 1911: Poems.* New York: Viking.

Long, Edward V. 1966. *The Intruders: The Invasion of Privacy by Government and Industry.* New York: Frederick A. Praeger, Publishers.

Lovrich, Nicholas, and Max Neiman. 1984. *Public Choice Theory in Public Administration: An Annotated Bibliography.* New York: Garland Publishing, Inc.

Lowery, David. 1998. "Sorting in the Fragmented Metropolis: Updating the Social Stratification-Government Inequality Debate." Paper delivered at the annual meeting of the American Political Science Association, Boston, MA, September 4–7.

Lowery, D., and L. Sigelman. 1982. "Party Identification and Public Spending Priorities in the American Electorate." *Political Studies* 30 (June): 221–35.

Lowi, Theodore J. 1979. *The End of Liberalism: The Second Republic of the United States.* 2d ed. New York: Norton.

Lustig, R. Jeffrey. 1982. *Corporate Liberalism: The Origins of Modern Political Theory, 1890–1920.* Berkeley, CA: University of California Press.

Lybeck, Johan A. 1986. *The Growth of Government in Developed Economies.* Brookfield, VT: Gower Publishing Company.

Machan, Tibor. 1995. *Private Rights and Public Illusions.* New Brunswick, NJ: Transaction Books, Inc.

Maddison, Angus. 1984. "Comparative Analysis of the Productivity Situation in the Advanced Capitalist Countries." Pp. 59–92 in *International Comparisons of Productivity and Causes of the Slowdown,* ed. John W. Kendrick. Cambridge, MA: Ballinger Publishing Company.

Maier, Charles S., ed. 1987. *Changing Boundaries of the Political: Essays on the Evolving Balance between the State and Society. Public and Private in Europe.* New York: Cambridge University Press.

Maier, Charles S. 1987. "The Politics of Inflation in the Twentieth Century." Pp. 37–72 in *The Political Economy of Inflation,* ed. F. Hirsch and J. G. Goldthorpe. Totowa, NJ: Rowman and Littlefield, Publishers.

Maital, Shiomo. 1982. *Minds, Markets, and Money: Psychological Foundations of Economic Behavior.* New York: Basic Books, Inc.

Mansbridge, Jane J., ed. 1990. *Beyond Self Interest.* Chicago, IL: University of Chicago Press.

Manza, Jeff, Michael Hout, and Clem Brooks. 1995. "Class Voting in Capitalist

Democracies since World War II: Dealignment, Realignment, or Trendless Fluctuation." *Annual Review of Sociology* 21 (Annual): 137–63.

Margonis, F., and L. Parker. 1995. "Choice, Privatization, and Unspoken Strategies of Containment." *Education Policy* 9: 375–403.

Markham, Edwin, Benjamin Lindsey, and George Creel. 1914. *Children in Bondage: A Complete and Careful Presentation of the Anxious Problem of Child Labor—Its Causes, Its Crime, and Its Cure.* New York: Hearst's International Library Company.

Marshall, T. H. 1964. *Class, Citizenship and Social Development.* New York: Doubleday.

Martin, Andrew. 1973. *The Politics of Economic Policy in the United States: A Tentative View from a Comparative Perspective.* Beverly Hills, CA: Sage Professional Paper, Comparative Politics Series, Sage Publications.

Maxwell, Nan L. 1990. *Income Inequality in the United States, 1947–1985.* New York: Greenwood Press.

McCormick, B. J. 1988. *The World Economy: Patterns of Growth and Change.* Totowa, NJ: Barnes & Noble Books.

McCurry, Dan C., ed. 1975. *Children in the Fields.* New York: Arno Press

McGuire, Martin. 1974. "Group Segregation and Optimal Jurisdictions." *Journal of Political Economy* 82 (January/February): 112–32.

McLean, Lain. 1982. *Dealing in Votes: Interactions between Politicians and Voters in Britain and the U.S.A.* Oxford: Martin Robertson.

———. 1987. *Public Choice: An Introduction.* New York, Oxford: Basil Blackwell, Inc.

Medley, Richard, ed. 1982. *The Politics of Inflation: A Comparative Analysis.* New York: Pergamon Press.

Meehan, Eugene. 1967. *Contemporary Political Thought: A Critical Study.* Homewood, IL: Dorsey Press.

———. 1990. *Ethics for Policymaking: A Methodological Analysis.* New York: Greenwood Press.

Meltzer, Alan H., and Scott F. Richard. 1978. "Why Government Grows (and Grows) in a Democracy." *Public Interest* 52 (summer): 111–18.

———. 1981. "A Rational Theory of the Size of Government." *Journal of Political Economy* 89 (October): 914–27.

———. 1983. "Test of a Rational Theory of the Size of Government." *Public Good*: 403–18.

Mendeloff, John M. 1979. *Regulating Safety: An Economic and Political Analysis of Occupational Safety and Health Policy.* Cambridge, MA: MIT Press.

Metz, Harold. 1945. *Labor Policy of the Federal Government.* Washington, D.C.: The Brookings Institution.

Milibrand, Ralph. 1969. *The State in Capitalist Society.* New York: Basic Books.

Mintz, Morton. 1985. *At Any Cost: Corporate Greed, Women and the Daikon Shield.* New York: Pantheon Books, Inc.

Mitchell, Broadus. 1971. *Depression Decade.* New York: Holt, Rinehart, and Winston.

Mitchell, William C., and Randy T. Simmons. 1994. *Beyond Politics: Markets, Welfare, and the Failure of Bureaucracy.* Boulder, CO: Westview Press.

Mokhiber, Russell. 1988. *Corporate Crime and Violence: Big Business Power and the Abuse of the Public Trust.* San Francisco, CA: Sierra Club Books.

Monks, Robert A., and Nell Minow. 1991. *Power and Accountability.* New York: Harper Collins.

Monroe, Kristen R., ed. 1983. *The Political Process and Economic Change*. New York: Agathon Press, Inc.

———. 1991. *The Economic Approach to Politics: A Critical Reassessment of the Theory of Rational Action*. New York: Harper Collins Publishers, Inc.

Monroe, Kristen R., and Maurice D. Levi. 1983. "Economic Expectations, Economic Uncertainty, and Presidential Popularity." Pp. 214–31 in *Political Process and Economic Change*, ed. K. R. Monroe. New York: Agathon Press, Inc.

Moon, Bruce E., and William J. Dixon. 1985. "Politics, the State, and Basic Human Needs: A Cross-National Study." *American Journal of Political Science* 29 (November): 661–94.

Moore, D., and S. Davenport. 1990. "School Choice: The New, Improved Sorting Machine." In *Choice in Education*, ed. W. Boyd and H. Walberg. Berkeley, CA: McCuthan.

Moran, Michael. 1986. "Theories of Regulation and Changes in Regulation: The Case of Financial Markets." *Political Studies* 34 (June): 185–201.

Morris, David. 1979. *Measuring the Condition of the World's Poor: The Physical Quality of Life Index*. New York: Pergamon.

Morris, Richard B. 1946. *Government and Labor in Early America*. New York: Columbia University Press.

Mueller, Dennis C., and Peter Murrell. 1985. "Interest Groups and the Political Economy of Government Size." Pp. 13–36 in *Public Expenditures and Government Growth*, ed. F. Forte and A. Peacock. Oxford: Basil Blackwell, Inc.

———. 1985. "Interest Groups and the Size of Government." *Public Choice* 48: 125–45.

Munns, Joyce Matthews. 1975. "The Environment, Politics, and Policy Literature: A Critique and Reformulation." *Western Political Quarterly* 28 (December): 646–67.

Murray, Charles. 1984. *Losing Ground: American Social Policy, 1950–1980*. New York: Basic Books.

Murrell, Peter. 1985. "The Size of Public Employment: An Empirical Study." *Journal of Comparative Economics* 9: 424–37.

Musgrave, Richard A. 1959. *The Theory of Public Finance*. New York: McGraw-Hill.

———. 1981. "Leviathan Cometh—Or Does He?" Pp. 77–120 in *Tax and Expenditure Limitations*, ed. H. Ladd and T. N. Tideman. Washington, D.C.: The Urban Institute.

Musgrave, Richard, and A. Peacock, eds. 1958. *Classics in the Theory of Public Finance*. London: Macmillan.

Nagler, Jonathan. 1991. "The Effect of Registration Laws and Education on U.S. Voter Turnout." *American Political Science Review* 85: 1393–405.

Neenan, William B. 1972. *Political Economy of Urban Areas*. Chicago, IL: Markham Publishing.

Neiman, Max. 1975. *Metropology: Toward a More Constructive Research Agenda*. Beverly Hills, CA: Sage Publications.

———. 1980. "The Virtues of Heavy-Handedness in Government." *Law and Policy Quarterly* 2 (January): 11–34.

Neiman, Max, and Catherine Lovell. 1981. "Mandating as a Policy Issue: The Definitional Problem." *Policy Studies Journal* 9 (spring): 667–81.

———. 1982. "Federal and State Mandating: A First Look at the Mandate Terrain." *Administration and Society* (November): 343–72.

Neiman, Max, and Gerald Riposa. 1986. "Tax Rebels and Tax Rebellion." *Western Political Quarterly* 39 (September): 435–45.

Neiman, Max, and Stephen J. Stambough. 1998. "Rational Choice Theory and the Evaluation of Public Policy." *Policy Studies Journal* 26: 449–65.

Nell, Edward. 1988. *Prosperity and Public Spending: Transformational Growth and the Role of Government.* Boston, MA: Unwin-Hyman.

Niskanen, William A. 1971. *Bureaucracy and Representative Government.* Chicago, IL: Aldene, Atherton.

———. 1973a. *Bureaucracy—Servant or Master? Lessons from America.* London: Institute of Economic Affairs.

———. 1973b. *Structural Reform of the Federal Budget Process.* Washington, D.C.: American Enterprise Institute for Public Policy Research.

Nitti, F. S. 1920. "Principles of Public Finance." Pp. 33–47 in *Selected Readings in Public Finance.* 2nd ed. Edited by C. J. Bullock. Cambridge, MA: Ginn and Company.

Nordaus, William D. 1975. "The Political Business Cycle." *Review of Economic Studies* 42: 160–90.

Nordlinger, Eric A. 1981. *On the Autonomy of the Democratic State.* Cambridge, MA: Harvard University Press.

Norgaard, Richard B. 1992. *Sustainability and the Economics of Assuring Assets for Future Generations.* Washington, D.C.: Policy Research Dissemination Center, World Bank.

Norpoth, Helmut, Michael S. Lewis-Beck, and Jean-Dominique Lafay. 1991. *Economics and Politics: The Calculus of Support.* Ann Arbor, MI: University of Michigan Press.

North, Douglass C. 1981. *Structure and Change in Economic History.* New York: W. W. Norton & Company.

Nutter, G. Warren. 1978. *Government Growth in the West.* Washington, D.C.: American Enterprise Institute.

Oates, Wallace E. 1985. "Searching for Leviathan: An Empirical Study." *American Economic Review* 75 (summer): 748–57.

O'Conner, James R. 1973. *The Fiscal Crisis of the State.* New York: St. Martin's Press.

Odell, John S. 1982. *U.S. International Monetary Policy: Markets, Power, and Ideas as Sources of Change.* Princeton, NJ: Princeton University Press.

Office of Management and Budget, Executive Office of the President. 1998. *Government-Wide Performance Plan: Budget of the United States Government, Fiscal Year, 1999.* Washington, D.C.: United States Government Printing Office.

Okun, Arthur M. 1975. *Equality and Efficiency: The Big Tradeoff.* Washington, D.C.: The Brookings Institution.

Olson, James Stuart. 1988. *Saving Capitalism: The Reconstruction Finance Corporation and the New Deal, 1933–1940.* Princeton, NJ: Princeton University Press.

Olson, Mancur. 1965. *The Logic of Collective Action.* New York: Schocken.

———. 1982. *The Rise and Decline of Nations: Economic Growth, Stagflation and Social Rigidities.* New Haven, CT: Yale University Press.

———. 1983. "A Less Ideological Way of Deciding How Much Should Be Given to the Poor." *Daedalus* (fall): 217–36.

Orfield, Myron. 1997. *Metropolitan Politics: A Regional Agenda for Community and Stability.* Washington, D.C.: The Brookings Institution.

Organisation for Economic Cooperation and Development (OECD). 1997. *National Accounts.* Vol. I and II. Paris: OECD Publications.

Ornstein, Norman, and Shirley Elder. 1978. *Interest Groups, Lobbying and Policy Making.* Washington, D.C.: Congressional Quarterly Press.

Orwell, George. 1977. *Nineteen Eighty-Four: A Novel.* New York: Harcourt, Brace and World.

Osberg, Lars. 1984. *Economic Inequality in the United States.* Armonk, NY: M. E. Sharpe.

Oshima, H. T. 1957. "The Share of Government in Gross National Product for Various Countries." *American Economic Review* 47: 381–90.

Ostrom, Vincent. 1974. *The Intellectual Crisis in American Public Administration.* Tuscaloosa, AL: University of Alabama Press.

Ostrom, Vincent, Charles M. Tiebout, and Robert Warren. 1961. "Organizing Government in Metropolitan Areas: A Theoretical Inquiry." *American Political Science Review* 55 (December): 838–42.

Ostrom, Vincent, Robert Bish, and Elinor Ostrom. 1988. *Local Government in the United States.* San Francisco, CA: ICS Press.

O'Toole. George. 1978. *The Private Sector: Private Spies, Rent-a-Cops, and the Political-Industrial Complex.* New York: W. W. Norton and Company.

Pacelle, Richard L. 1987. "The Supreme Court and the Growth of Civil Liberties: The Process and Dynamics of Agenda Change." Paper presented at the American Political Science Association Meetings, Chicago, IL, September 3–6.

Page, Benjamin I. 1983. *Who Gets What from Government.* Berkeley, CA: University of California Press.

Parenti, Michael. 1995. *Democracy for the Few.* 6th ed. New York: St. Martin's Press.

Parks, Roger B., and Ronald J. Oakerson. 1989. "Metropolitan Organization and Governance: A Local Public Economy Approach." *Urban Affairs Quarterly* 25 (September): 18–30.

Peacock, Alan T. 1979. *The Economic Analysis of Government and Related Theories.* New York: St. Martin's Press.

Peacock, Alan T., and Jack Wiseman. 1961. *The Growth of Public Expenditures in the United Kingdom.* Princeton, NJ: Princeton University Press.

Pechman, Joseph A. 1983. *Federal Tax Policy.* 4th ed. Washington, D.C.: The Brookings Institution.

Pechman, Joseph A., and Mark J. Mazur. 1985. *The Rich, the Poor, and the Taxes They Pay: An Update.* Washington, D.C.: The Brookings Institution.

Peirce, William Spangar. 1981. *Bureaucratic Failure and Public Expenditure.* New York: Academic Press.

Peltzman, S. 1980. "The Growth of Government." *Journal of Law and Economics* 23 (October): 209–87.

Pen, Jan. 1987. "Expanding Budgets in a Stagnating Economy: The Experiences of the 1970s." Pp. 323–61 in *Changing Boundaries of the Political*, ed. C. S. Maier. New York: Cambridge University Press.

Peretz, Paul. 1983. *The Political Economy of Inflation in the U.S.* Chicago, IL: University of Chicago Press.

———. 1996. *The Politics of American Economic Policy Making.* 2nd ed. New York: M. E. Sharpe.

Perritt, Henry H. 1995. *Civil Rights in the Workplace.* 2nd ed. New York: Wiley Law Publications.

Peters, B. Guy. 1996. *American Public Policy: Promise and Performance.* 4th ed. Chatham, NJ: Chatham House Publishers, Inc.

Peterson, Paul E. 1981. *City Limits*. Chicago, IL: University of Chicago Press.

Peterson, Wallace C. 1994. *Silent Depression: The Fate of the American Dream*. New York: W. W. Norton.

Pigou, A. C. 1946. *The Economics of Welfare*. 4th ed. New York: Macmillan.

Pitkin, Hanna. 1967. *The Concept of Representation*. Berkeley, CA: University of California Press.

Piven, Frances Fox, and Robert A. Cloward. 1988. *Why Americans Don't Vote*. New York: Pantheon.

Plattner, Marc F. 1982. "American Democracy and the Acquisitive Spirit." Pp. 1–21 in *How Capitalistic Is the Constitution?* Edited by R. A. Goldwin and William A. Schambra. Washington, D.C.: American Enterprise Institute for Public Policy Research.

Pole, J. R. 1993. *The Pursuit of Equality in American History*. Berkeley, CA: University of California Press.

Poulantzas, Nicos. 1973a. *Political Power and Social Classes*. London: New Left Books.

———. 1973b. "The Problem of the Capitalist State." In *Ideology in the Social Sciences*, ed. R. Blackburn. New York: Vintage Books, Random House.

Poveda, Tony G. 1994. *Rethinking White-Coller Crime*. Westport, CT: Praeger.

Price, Barry, and Roslyn Simowitz. 1986. "In Defense of Government Regulation." *Journal of Economic Issues* 20 (March): 165–77.

Proxmire, William. 1980. *The Fleecing of America*. Boston, MA: Houghton Mifflin Company.

Pryor, F. L. 1968. *Public Expenditures in Communist and Capitalist Nations*. London: George Allen and Unwin, Ltd.

Przeworski, Adam. 1991. *Democracy and the Market*. Cambridge, MA: Cambridge University Press.

Putnam, Robert D., with Robert Leonardi and Raffaella Y. Nanetti. 1993. *Making Democracy Work: Civic Traditions in Modern Italy*. Princeton, NJ: Princeton University Press.

Radosh, Ronald. 1972. "The Myth of the New Deal." In *A New History of Leviathan: Essays on the Rise of the Corporate State*, ed. R. Radosh and N. Rothbard. New York: Dutton.

Rae, Douglas, Douglas Yates, Jennifer Hochschild, Joseph Morone, and Carol Fessler. 1981. *Equalities*. Cambridge, MA: Harvard University Press.

Ram, Rati. 1986. "Causality between Income and Government Expenditure: A Broad International Perspective." *Public Finance* 41, no. 3: 393–414.

———. 1986. "Government Size and Economic Growth: A New Framework and Some Evidence from Cross-Section and Time-Series Data." *American Economic Review* 76 (March): 191–203.

Ranney, Austin, ed. 1968. *Political Science and Public Policy*. Chicago, IL: Markham Publishing Co.

Ratner, Sidney, James Soltow, and Richard Sylla. 1979. *The Evolution of the American Economy: Growth, Welfare, and Decision Making*. New York: Basic Books, Inc.

Rauch, Jonathan. 1996. "The End of Government." *National Journal* 28 (September 7): 1881–932.

Reich, Robert B. 1983. *The Next American Frontier: A Provocative Program for Economic Renewal*. New York: Penguin Books.

———. 1991. *The Work of Nations: Preparing Ourselves for 21st-Century Capitalism*. New York: A. A. Knopf.

Rhoads, Steven E. 1984. *The Economist's View of the World*. Cambridge, MA: Cambridge University Press.

Ricci, David. 1984. *The Tragedy of Political Science: Politics, Scholarship, and Democracy*. New Haven, CT: Yale University Press.

Rice, Tom W. 1986. "The Determinants of Western European Government Growth, 1950–1980." *Comparative Political Studies* 19 (July): 233–57.

Riemer, Neal. 1962. *The Revival of Democratic Theory*. New York: Appleton-Century-Crofts.

Riker, William H. 1962. *The Theory of Political Coalitions*. New Haven, CT: Yale University Press.

Rizzo, Ilde. 1985. "Regional Disparities and Decentralization as Determinants of Public-Sector Expenditure Growth in Italy (1960–1981)." Pp. 65–82 in *Public Expenditure and Government Growth*, ed. F. Forte and A. Peacock. Oxford: Basil Blackwell, Inc.

Roberts, Isaac. 1922. *Rent Reduction and Home Ownership through Cooperation*. New York: White Oak Publishing Co.

Robertson, John. 1920. *Housing and the Public Health*. New York: Funk and Wagnalls Co.

Robinson, Ann, and Cedric Sandford. 1983. *Tax Policy-Making in the United Kingdom: A Study of Rationality, Ideology and Politics*. London: Heinemann Educational Books.

Roediger, David R. 1989. *Our Own Time: A History of American Labor and the Working Day*. New York: Greenwood Press.

Romer, Thomas, and Howard Rosenthal. 1978. "Political Resource Allocation, Controlled Agendas, and the Status Quo." *Public Choice* 33: 27–43.

———. 1979. "The Elusive Median Voter." *Journal of Public Economics* 12: 143–70.

Rose, Richard. *The Influence of Laws Upon the Growth of Government*.

———. 1981. "What, if Anything, Is Wrong with Big Government?" *Journal of Public Policy* 1 (February): 5–36.

———. 1984. *Understanding Big Government*. London and Beverly Hills, CA: Sage Publications.

———. 1985. "The Program Approach to the Growth of Government." *British Journal of Political Science* 15 (January): 1–28.

Rosenfeld, Raymond. 1984. "An Expansion and Application of Kaufman's Model of Red Tape: The Care of Community Development Block Grants." *Western Political Quarterly* 37 (December): 603–20.

Rosoff, Stephen M., Henry N. Pontell, and Robert Tillman. 1998. *Profit without Honor: White Collar Crime and the Looting of America*. Upper Saddle River, NJ: Prentice Hall.

Ross, Bernard H., and Myron W. Levine. 1996. *Urban Politics: Power in Metropolitan America*. Itasca, IL: Peacock Publishers, Inc.

Rothstein, Bo. 1998. *Just Institutions Matter: The Moral and Political Logic of the Universal Welfare State*. Cambridge, MA: Cambridge University Press.

Ryu, Hang K., and Daniel J. Slottje. 1998. *Measuring Trends in U.S. Income Inequality: Theory and Applications*. New York: Springer.

Samuels, Warren J., ed. 1993. *The Chicago School of Political Economy*. New Brunswick, NJ: Transaction Books, Inc.

Samuelson, Paul Anthony. 1955. *Foundations of Economic Analysis*. Cambridge, MA: Harvard University Press.

Sassen, Saskia. 1996. *Losing Control?: Sovereignty in an Age of Globalization*. New York: Columbia University Press.

Savage, James D. 1988. *Balanced Budgets and American Politics*. Ithaca, NY: Cornell University Press.

Schattschneider, E. E. 1960. *The Semisovereign People*. New York: Holt, Rinehart and Winston.

Schlegel, Kip, and David Weisburd, eds. 1992. *White-Collar Crime Reconsidered*. Boston, MA: Northeastern University Press.

Schlozman, Kay Lehman, and John T. Tierney. 1986. *Organized Interests and American Democracy*. New York: Harper & Row, Publishers.

Schmidt, Manfred. 1983. "The Growth of the Tax State: The Industrial Democracies, 1950–1978." Pp. 261–85 in *Why Governments Grow: Measuring Public Sector Size*, ed. C. L. Taylor. Beverly Hills, CA: Sage Publications.

Schott, Kerry. 1984. *Policy, Power, and Order: The Persistence of Economic Problems in Capitalist States*. New Haven, CT: Yale University Press.

Schulman, Bruce J. 1998. "Clinton's Reaganite Legacy." *Los Angeles Times*, September 12, Metropolitan Section, p. 2.

Schultze, Charles L. 1977. *The Public Use of Private Interest*. Washington, D.C.: The Brookings Institution.

Schumpeter, Joseph A. 1950. *Capitalism, Socialism, and Democracy*. New York: Harper & Row.

Schwarz, John E. 1988. *America's Hidden Success: A Reassessment of Public Policy from Kennedy to Reagan*. Rev. ed. New York: W. W. Norton and Company.

Shariff, Zahid. 1978. "How Big Is Big Government?" *Social Policy* 8 (March/April): 22–27.

Shefrin, B. M. 1980. *The Future of U.S. Politics in an Age of Economic Limits*. Boulder, CO: Westview Press.

Shergold, Peter R. 1982. *Working-Class Life: "The American Standard" in Comparative Perspective, 1899–1913*. Pittsburgh, PA: University of Pittsburgh.

Siegan, Bernard H. 1980. *Economic Liberties and the Constitution*. Chicago, IL: University of Chicago Press.

Sikora, R. I., and Brian Barry, eds. 1978. *Obligations to Future Generations*. Philadelphia, PA: Temple University Press.

Skocpol, Theda. 1980. "Political Response to Capitalist Crisis: NeoMarxist Theories of the State and the Case of the New Deal." *Politics and Society* 10, no. 2: 155–201.

Skocpol, Theda, and Kenneth Feingold. 1982. "State Capacity and Economic Intervention in the Early New Deal." *Political Science Quarterly* 97: 255–78.

Skowronek, Stephen. 1982. *Building a New American State: The Expansions of Administrative Capacities, 1877–1920*. Cambridge, MA: Cambridge University Press.

Smith, M. J., P. Carayon, K. J. Sanders, S. Y. Lim, and D. LeGrande. 1992. "Employee Stress and Health Complaints in Jobs with and without Electronic Performance Monitoring." *Applied Ergonomics* 23: 17–28.

Smith, K. B., and K. J. Meier. 1995. "Public Choice in Education: Markets and the Demand for Quality Education." *Political Research Quarterly* 48: 461–78.

Sorkin, Alan. 1988. *Monetary and Fiscal Policy and Business Cycles in the Modern Era*. Lexington, MA: Lexington Books.

Spooner, Mary Helen. 1994. *Soldiers in a Narrow Land: The Pinochet Regime in Chile*. Berkeley, CA: University of California Press.

Stein, Arthur A. 1980. *The Nation at War.* Baltimore, MD and London: The Johns Hopkins University Press.

Stein, Herbert. 1984. *Presidential Economics: The Making of Economic Policy from Roosevelt to Reagan and Beyond.* New York: Simon & Schuster.

Stigler, George J. 1975. *The Citizen and the State: Essays on Regulation.* Chicago, IL: University of Chicago Press.

Stone, Alan. 1982. *Regulation and Its Alternatives.* Washington, D.C.: Congressional Quarterly Press.

Striner, Herbert E. 1984. *Regaining the Lead: Policies for Economic Growth.* New York: Praeger Publishers.

Sutherland, Edwin H. 1949. *White Collar Crime.* New York: Holt.

Sykes, John F. 1901. *Public Health and Housing: The Influence of the Dwelling upon Health in Relation to the Changing Style of Habitation.* London: P. S. King and Son.

Szirmai, Adam. 1988. *Inequality Observed: A Study of Attitudes Towards Income Inequality.* Brookfield, VT: Gower Publishing Company.

Tarschys, Daniel. 1975. "The Growth of Public Expenditures: Nine Modes of Explanation." *Scandinavian Political Studies Yearbook* 10: 9–31.

Tax Foundation, The. 1944. *Facts and Figures on Government Finance, 1944.* New York: The Tax Foundation.

Tax Foundation, Inc. 1962. *Growth of Federal Domestic Spending Programs, 1947–1963.* New York: Tax Foundation, Inc.

Taylor, Charles Lewis, ed. 1983. *Why Governments Grow: Measuring Public Sector Size.* Beverly Hills, CA: Sage Publications.

Taylor, Ronald B. 1973. *Sweatshops in the Sun: Child Labor on the Farm.* Boston, MA: Beacon Press.

Thaxton, Ralph. 1997. *Salt of the Earth: The Political Origins of Peasant Protest and Communist Revolution in China.* Berkeley, CA: University of California Press.

Thielbar, G., and S. D. Feldman. 1969. "Occupational Stereotypes and Prestige." *Social Forces* 48 (September): 64–72.

Thomas, John C. 1980. "The Growth of American Public Expenditures: Recent Trends and Their Implications." *Public Administration Review* 40 (March/April): 160–65.

Tiebout, Charles M. 1956. "A Pure Theory of Local Expenditures." *Journal of Political Economy* 64: 416–24.

Tobin, Gary, ed. 1987. *Divided Neighborhoods: Changing Patterns of Racial Separation.* Newbury Park, CA: Sage Publications.

Tocqueville, Alexis de. 1966. *Democracy in America.* New York: Harper & Row.

Toscano, Guy, and Janice Windau. 1996. "National Census of Fatal Occupational Injuries, 1995." Bureau of Labor Statistics, Department of Labor, United States. *Compensation and Working Conditions.* Washington, D.C.: U.S. Government Printing Office, September.

Truman, David B. 1971. *The Governmental Process.* 2nd ed. New York: Alfred A. Knopf.

Tufte, Edward R. 1978. *Political Control of the Economy.* Princeton, NJ: Princeton University Press.

Tullock, Gordon. 1976. *The Vote Motive: An Essay in the Economics of Politics, with Applications to the British Economy.* Churchill Industrial Estate, Lancing, Sussex: The Institute of Economic Affairs.

———. 1983. *Welfare for the Well-to-Do.* Dallas, TX: The Fisher Institute.

Turner, Jonathan H., and Alexandra Maryanski. 1979. *Functionalism*. Menlo Park, CA: Benjamin/Cummings Pub. Co.

Twiss, Benjamin R. 1942. *Lawyers and the Constitution: How Laissez Faire Came to the Supreme Court*. New York: Russell and Russell, Inc.

United Nations. 1997. *National Accounts Statistics: Analysis of Main Aggregates*. New York: United Nations.

United States Bureau of the Census. 1975. *Historical Statistics of the United States, Colonial Times to 1970*. Bicentennial edition. Parts I and II. Washington, D.C.: U.S. Government Printing Office.

United States. 1985. *American Exports: Why Have They Lagged?* A Study Prepared for the Use of the Subcommittee on Trade, Productivity, and Economic Growth of the Joint Economic Committee Congress of the United States, May 14, 1985. Washington, D.C.: U.S. Government Printing Office.

———. 1985. *Report of the President's Commission on Industrial Competitiveness*. Hearing before the Subcommittee on Economic Stabilization of the Committee on Banking, Finance and Urban Affairs, House of Representatives, 99th Congress, March 5, 1985. Washington, D.C.: U.S. Government Printing Office [Gov Pub Y4 .B22/1: 99–97).

———. 1986. *Trends in Family Income: 1970–1986*. Congressional Budget Office, Congress of the United States. Washington, D.C.: U.S. Government Printing Office, February.

———. 1987. *To Enhance the Competitiveness of American Industry, and for Other Purposes*. Hearing before the Subcommittee on Economic Stabilization of the Committee on Banking, Finance and Urban Affairs House of Representatives, 100th Congress, March 10, 1987. Washington, D.C., U.S. Government Printing Office.

———. 1987. *The Threat of Inflation*. Hearings before the Subcommittee on Domestic Monetary Policy of the Committee on Banking, Finance and Urban Affairs, House of Representatives, 100th Congress, June 4, 10, 11, and 17, 1987. Washington, D.C.: U.S. Government Printing Office [Gov Pub (100) Y4 .B22/1: 100–114].

———. 1994. *The Fair Housing Amendments Act of 1988—The Enforcement Report: A Report of the United States Commission on Civil Rights*. Washington, D.C.: The United States Commission on Civil Rights.

Usher, Dan. 1981. *The Economic Prerequisite to Democracy*. New York: Columbia University Press.

Uyl, Douglas J., and Douglas B. Rasmussen., eds. 1984. *The Philosophic Thought of Ayn Rand*. Urbana, IL: University of Illinois Press.

Valdes, Juan Gabriel. 1995. *Pinochet's Economists: The Chicago School in Chile*. New York: Cambridge University Press.

Vanneman, R., and F. C. Pampel. 1977. "American Perception of Class and Status." *American Sociological Review* 42 (June): 422–37.

Vartebedian, Ralph. 1998. "Unpaid Tax Total Put at $195 Billion a Year by IRS." *Los Angeles Times*, May 2, part A.

Verba, Sidney, and Gary R. Orren. 1985. *Equality in America: The View from the Top*. Cambridge, MA: Harvard University Press.

Vig, Norman J., and Steven E. Schier, ed. 1985. *Political Economy in Western Democracies*. New York: Holmes and Meier.

Viscusi, W. Kip. 1979. *Employment Hazards: An Investigation of Market Performance*. Cambridge, MA: Harvard University Press.

Vogel, David. 1986. *National Styles of Regulation: Environmental Policy in Great Britain and the United States*. Ithaca, NY: Cornell University Press.

Wade, Robert. 1990. *Governing the Market: Economic Theory and the Role of Government in East Asian Industrialization*. Princeton, NJ: Princeton University Press.

Wallerstein, Immanuel. 1984. *The Politics of the World Economy: The States, the Movements, and the Civilizations*. New York: Cambridge University Press.

Ward, Michael Don. 1978. *The Political Economy of Distribution: Equality versus Inequality*. New York: Elsevier North Holland.

Weatherford, H. Stephen. 1983. "Parties and Classes in the Political Response to Economic Conditions." Pp. 181–213 in *Political Process and Economic Change*, ed. K. R. Monroe. New York: Agathon Press, Inc.

Weaver, P. H. 1978. "Regulation, Social Policy, and Class Conflict." *Public Interest*: 45–63.

Weicher, John C. 1980. *Housing: Federal Policies and Programs*. Washington, D.C.: American Enterprise Institute for Public Policy Research.

Weidenbaum, Murray L. 1977. *Business, Government, and the Public*. Englewood Cliffs, NJ: Prentice Hall.

Weinberg, Daniel H. 1996. *A Brief Look at Postwar U.S. Income Inequality*. Washington, D.C.: Bureau of the Census, Economics and Statistics Administration, U.S. Department of Commerce.

Weingast, Barry R. 1984. "The Congressional-Bureaucratic System: A Principal Agent Perspective (with applications to the SEC)." *Public Choice* 44: 147–91.

Weisbrot, Robert. 1990. *Freedom Bound: A History of America's Civil Rights Movement*. New York: Norton.

Wertheimer, Barbara Mayer. 1977. *We Were There: The Story of Working Women in America*. New York: Pantheon Books.

West, Darrell M. 1987. *Congress and Economic Policymaking*. Pittsburgh, PA: University of Pittsburgh Press.

West, E. G. 1991. "Public Schools and Excess Burden." *Economics of Education Review* 10: 159–70.

White, Gerald. 1982. *The United States and the Problem of Recovery after 1893*. Tuscaloosa, AL: University of Alabama Press.

White, Lawrence. 1983. *Human Debris: The Injured Worker in America*. New York: Seaview/Putnam.

White, Leonard D. 1929. *The Prestige Value of Public Employment in Chicago*. Chicago, IL: University of Chicago Press.

Whiteley, Paul. 1986. *Political Control of the Macroeconomy: The Political Economy of Public Policy Making*. London: Sage Publications.

Wildavsky, Aaron. 1980. *How to Limit Government Spending*. Berkeley, CA: University of California.

Wildavsky, Ben. 1998. "A Taxing Question." *National Journal* 30 (February, 18): 440–44.

Wilensky, Harold. 1975. *The Welfare State and Equality*. Berkeley, CA: University of California Press.

———. 1981. "Leftism, Catholicism, and Democratic Corporatism: The Role of Political Parties in Recent Welfare State Development." Pp. 345–82 in *The Development of Welfare States in Europe and America*, ed. P. Flora and A. J. Heidenheimer. New Brunswick, NJ: Transaction Books, Inc.

Williamson, Clinton. 1960. *American Suffrage from Property to Democracy, 1760–1860.* Princeton, NJ: Princeton University Press.

Williamson, Jeffrey G., and Peter H. Lindert. 1980. *American Inequality: A Macroeconomic History.* New York: Academic Press.

Williamson, Oliver. 1985. *The Economic Institutions of Capitalism.* New York: The Free Press.

Wilson, Graham K. 1985. *The Politics of Safety and Health.* New York: Oxford University Press.

Wilson, James Q. 1973. *Political Organizations.* New York: Basic Books.

———. 1980. *The Politics of Regulation.* New York: Basic Books.

Wilson, John Oliver. 1985. *The Power Economy: Building an Economy That Works.* Boston, MA: Little, Brown and Company.

Wirth, Louis. 1938. "Urbanism as a Way of Life." *American Journal of Sociology* 44 (July): 1–24.

Wolf, Charles. 1988. *Markets or Governments: Choosing between Imperfect Alternatives.* Cambridge, MA: MIT Press.

Wolff, Edward N. 1996. *Top Heavy: The Increasing Inequality of Wealth in America and What Can Be Done about It.* New York, NY: The New Press.

Wolff, Nancy Lee. 1987. *Income Redistribution and the Social Security Program.* Ann Arbor, MI: University Microfilms.

Yergin, Daniel, and Joseph Stanislaw. 1998. *The Commanding Heights: The Battle between Government and the Marketplace That Is Remaking the Modern World.* New York: Simon & Schuster.

Zald, Mayer N. 1985. "Political Change, Citizenship Rights, and the Welfare State." *Annals of the American Academy of Political and Social Science* 479 (May): 48–66.

Zysman, John. 1983. *Governments, Markets, and Growth: Financial Systems and the Politics of Industrial Change.* Ithaca, NY: Cornell University Press.

INDEX

Absolute fiscal growth, 17–21

Activism, government
Big Brother Road to Dictatorship critique of, 157–61
opponents of, 161–69

Activism, institutional, 95

Adair v. United States, 61

Adams, Carolyn Teich, 197

Adams, Willi Paul, 136

Adkins v. Children's Hospital, 61

Adversarial conflict between the public and its government, perception of, 163–64

Agencies. *See* Public agencies

"Agency capture," problem of, 148

"Agency domination," 110, 112

Age of population, as stimulant of government growth, 45

Agricultural Adjustment Act, 66

Agricultural extension services, 217

Aharoni, Yair, 45, 95–96

Ahrens, John, 75

Airlines, deregulation of, 150

Alber, Jens, 89

Aldrich, Nelson, 16–17

Allen, Leslie H., 199, 200

Allgeyer v. Louisiana, 61

Almond, Gabriel A., 219

Alt, James, 114

Amacher, Ryan C., 46

Antigovernment sentiment, 2–4, 161–69
concerns over, 3–4
conservative arguments against activism, 167
government growth as threat to liberty, 10–11, 158, 160
on government size and coercion, 169–77
harms produced by public policies, 209–10
promoting perception of public incompetence and ineffectiveness, 210
sense of unremitting failure, 4
strategic purpose of, 169

Antiquated policies, 148

Anti-Trust Act (1890), 141

Apgar, William C., 71, 74, 77

Ashley, Anne, 49

Atkinson, Anthony Barnes, 212

Attitudes, as macro-deterministic variable, 46–47

Auto-based transportation system, subsidies of, 190

Baden, John, 203

Ball, Howard, 78

Banking, regulation of, 37

Barber, Benjamin, 163, 185, 211

Barber, William J., 93

Bardach, Eugene, 41

Barrow, Clyde W., 44, 65

Barry, Brian, 75, 103, 109, 150

Baumgartner, Frank, 135, 185

Baumol, W. J., 68

Bean, Charles R., 116

Benefits, government
administered as direct payments, 106, 134, 174
remoteness of, 85
as tax expenditures, 103–6, 173–74, 216

Bennett, J. T., 78

Bernstein, Irving, 155

Bernstein, Marvin H., 35, 36, 148

Berry, Jeffrey M., 184

Berry, William D., 88, 110

Best, Michael, 103

Bhopal, India, tragedy of, 145

Big Brother Road to Dictatorship, 157–61, 214

Big Government, domino theory of, 137

Bish, Robert, 188, 190

Bismarck, Otto von, 48, 49

Black political participation, 55

Block, Fred, 65

Blueprint role for policy analysis, 194–202

Borchardt, Knut, 48

Borcherding, T. E., 78

Borrowing, rate of, 13–14

Bourgin, Frank, 35, 97

Bowman, Karlyn H., 109

Braeman, John, 58

Braun, Dennis Duane, 107, 212

Breakthrough politics, 53–54, 214

future issues for, 215–18

Brennan, Geoffrey, 8, 16

Breton, Albert, 111

Brewer, Garry D., 196

Brigham, John, 69

Broder, David S., 137, 162, 210

Brooks, Clem, 90, 99, 101

Brooks, Thomas R., 47

Brown, Don W., 69

Brown, H. James, 71, 74, 77

Brown, Lawrence D., 53, 214, 215

Bruchey, Stuart, 16

Buchanan, James H., 8, 16, 68, 69, 182

Bucholz, Rogene A., 35, 36, 39, 40

Budget(s). *See also* Deficits, budget

contrast between public sector and family or business, 13–14

federal, 29, 30

ignorance regarding benefits/costs and size of, 84–86

public policies administered through annual, 173–74

self-interest of bureaucracy to maximize, 81–82

Budget maximizing approach of agency bureaucrats, 111–12

Budget surpluses, 5, 17, 18

Bumck, Julie Marie, 160

Burden of government

complexity of assessing, 26

perceived burden of deficit, 86

regulation, 41–42

subjective component to perceptions of, 15

taxes, perception of burden of, 85–86, 162, 179

Bureau behavior, formal model of, 81

Bureaucracy, need for emphasis on quality in, 219–20

Bureaucracy and Representative Government (Niskanen), 81

Bureaucratic determinism model, 6, 80–82

critiques of, 110–13

Bureau of Labor Statistics, 143

Burnham, Walter Dean, 101

Burton, John, 58, 78

Business. *See also* Private sector

government's promotional role in, 50

housing programs and, 199–200

illegal business/commercial practices, 139–40

Business-based models of policy analysis, 202

Calavita, Kitty, 145

Cameron, David R., 89, 118, 123, 124

Campbell, Ballard C., 47

Capital

globalism of, 217, 218

mobility of, 111

world demands for, 125

Capital formation

national saving relative to GDP and, 127, 128

size of public sector and growth in (1960–95), 118, 119

Capitalism, Marxist explanations of government growth under, 62–65

Carayon, P., 142

Carr, Edward Hallett, 160

Carter, Jimmy, 94

Castro, Fidel, 160

Charitable contributions, 174–75

Chicago School of economics, 160

Children, Settlement House Movement and well-being of, 198

Chrystal, K. Alec, 114

Chubb, J. E., 175

City planning profession, emergence of, 199

Civil Rights Acts of 1964 and 1968, 55

Civil War

budget deficits incurred during, 27, 91

federal expenditures in, 20

federal regulation during and after, 36

fiscal growth after, 17, 92

Clarke, John J., 198

Class friction

class clustering in metropolitan regions and, 191–92

in Germany, 49

regulation to reduce, 38

Classical liberalism, 45–46

view of government in, 48

Class struggle perspective, 64–65

Class voting, decline of, 99–100

Clinard, Marshall B., 139, 140

Cline, Paul C., 166

Clinton, William J., 2

conservative approach to welfare reform under, 209

on big government, 1

fiscal growth under, 34

impeachment trial of, 3, 4, 162

proposed balanced budget (1998), 3

sexual misconduct and investigation of, 3

Clinton-Gingrich-Lott budget of 1998, 95

Cloward, Robert A., 101, 102, 212

Cobb, Roger W., 135, 169

Coercion, government size and, 169–77

inverse relationship of, 171–73, 175, 177

market-like incentives vs., 170–72, 175–77

Coercion-voluntarism distinction, 6

Coleman, James S., 68, 182

Common property resource, 203–6

remedy for, 203–4

Communications industry, deregulation of, 150

Communist dictatorships in Europe, collapse of, 208

Competition, regulation of, 37

Computer monitoring, 142

Confidence in business institutions, regulation to promote, 38

Congress, deregulation by, 110

Conklin, Paul, 47, 93

Connolly, William E., 103

Conservative doctrine arguments against government activism, 167

Conservatives. *See also* Antigovernment sentiment

emergence of political strength of (1970s), 115–16

fear of majoritarian democracy, 185

Consolidation, metropolitan, 187

resistance to, 187–91

Conspiracy, assault on governing as, 2–3
Constraints on government responses to citizens, results of, 138–39
Consumer Product Safety Commission, 38, 143
recalls by, 144
Consumer protection, 98–99
Consumer sovereignty, 71, 78
Consumption taxes, 127
Contract with America, 4
Coordination among local governments in metropolitan regions, 188
Cornwall, Hugo, 147
Corporate income taxes, 24–26
Corporate violence, 139–40. *See also* White collar crime
Corruption, 148
Cost of Our National Government: A Study in Political Pathology, The (Ford), 16–17
Costs and benefits of the future, 75–76
Courant, P. N., 111, 185
Court system, government growth and, 58–61
Credit card data use, use/abuse of, 146
Credit information, use/abuse of, 146–47
Criminal conduct
criminalizing of drug use, 77
governing power deployed against, 133
white collar crime, 140, 143–45, 180–81
Croall, Hazel C., 144
Cultural achievement, governing institutions used for, 6–7
Culture, political, 46–47
Cynicism, climate of, 5

Dahl, Robert Alan, 133
Dahrendorf, Ralf, 44
Dalton, Russell, J., 99, 115
Davis, Allen F., 199
Debt, interest payments on national debt, 30–31. *See also* Deficits, budget
Declining public sector prediction, anomalous case of, 83–86
Deductions, tax. *See* Tax expenditures

Defense as percent of federal budget (1950–1996), 30, 31
Deficits, budget, 26–31
economic performance indicators and, 124
federal (1909), 16
historical pattern of, 26–30
perceived burden of, 86
as percent of total federal budget and GNP, 29
table of (1792–1997), 18
deLeon, Peter, 196
Demand and supply, laws of, 138
Demand for security, impact of, 95–96
"Demand side" explanations of government growth, 56
Demand-side housing policy, 197, 202
Democracy
causes of government growth in, 211–12
fear of, 3, 184, 185, 210–11
"government" as social organization in, 166
maintenance of values of, 207
majoritarian, 54–61
overhead costs in, 166
public-government relationship in, 163–64
reducing access to limited government in, 205–6
repugnance of rational choice theorists for politics of, 184–85
role of political science in cultivating, 219
social achievements of, 130–31
sources of public policy in, 183
strong, 211
thin, 211
Democratization
government growth and, 95–96, 114
income distribution and, 106–7
Demographic changes, government growth and, 44–47
Denison, Edward F., 126
Density, population, 45
Department of Labor, U.S., 140, 143
Depressions, displacement effect hypothesis and, 52

Deregulation, 41
in airline and communication industry, 150
by Congress, 110
tactical nature of calls for, 148–49
in thrift industry, 149–50
Developed nations, government growth in, 89–90
Dictatorship
Big Brother Road to, 157–61, 214
reasons for succumbing to, 161
Dietze, Gottfried, 57, 185
Diminishing returns, 153
Dionne, E. J., 161, 167–68
Direct benefits, 106
through government policies, 134
vulnerability of, compared to tax expenditure benefits, 174
Direct-mail lists, use/abuse of, 146
Disclosure of future risks, discounting of, 151–54
Discounted marketplace, 150–56
Diseconomies, 76
Displacement effect hypothesis, 51–54, 90–95
Dixon, William J., 56
Dogan, Mattei, 90, 99
Domino theory of Big Government, 137
Downs, Anthony, 83–86, 103
Doyle, Brian John, 47
Drug use, costs of criminalization vs. decriminalization of, 77
Due process, substantive, 59–61
Dunleavy, Patrick, 111, 112, 206
Dye, Thomas R., 46, 194

Easton, David, 44, 45
Economic base, government size and growth and, 45–46
Economic choice approaches to policy. *See* Public choice explanations of government size and growth
Economic choice models of interest group behavior, 83
Economic decline
federal deficits associated with, 27–28

Economic decline (*cont.*)
  government growth and, 88, 89, 92–93, 95
  prior to Great Depression, 92
  in U.S., catching-up of rest of world and, 129
Economic development
  tailoring theories to, 89
  Wagner's Law of Increasing State Activity and, 47–51
Economic distress
  blaming government for, 116
  conservative vs. liberal response to, 62
  displacement effect hypothesis and, 52
  malaise of 1890s, government growth and, 92
  rise of conservative political strength resulting from, 115–16
  tendency for less affluent not to place demands on affluent during, 108–9
Economic performance, government size/growth and, 6, 115–31, 213
  capital formation, 118, 119
  fiscal growth and, 33–35
  government size and productivity, 125–29
  national wealth and income, 118–22
  regulation and, 41
  unemployment and inflation, 122–25
Economic performance indicators, 124
Economic progress, government growth during, 93–94, 114
Economic Recovery Act of 1981, 107
Economic regulation, 36, 39–40
Economies of scale
  metropolitan consolidation and, 188
  service responsibilities pushed to federal level for, 53
Economy, fiscal growth relative to total, 21–26
Edsall, Thomas Byrne, 103, 107
Education
  market incentives introduced in, 175–77
  public vs. private, 77

Eksterowicz, Anthony J., 166
Elder, Charles D., 135, 169
Electoral process, government size and, 54–58
Eligibility requirements, changes in population meeting, 45
Elster, Jon, 183
Employee abuse, 142–44
  workplace safety, 142–44, 152–53
Employee records, use/abuse of, 146
Employment, public, 110
  employees, 113, 219–20
Employment background checks, 142
Environmental protection, explaining increased government involvement in, 7–8
Environmental Protection Agency, 38
Equal distribution of knowledge and ignorance, 75
Equal Employment Opportunity Commission, 38
Equal opportunity programs, redistributive vs. compensatory, 178–79
Equity, government involvement on grounds of, 77–78
Esping-Anderson, Gosta, 99, 115
Ethnic background of population, 45
Eulau, Heinz, 90, 116
Evaluation of social programs, 195–96
Expectations, public
  displacement effect hypothesis and, 51–52
  as macro-deterministic variable, 46–47
Externalities, 73–74, 97–98, 114, 189, 192–94
  defined, 192
  local land use policies, 193–94
  in metropolitan regions, 192–94
  negative, 73, 74, 98
  positive, 73

Fallows, James, 215
Faludi, Andreas, 194
Fararo, Thomas J., 68, 182
Farnam, Henry W., 35
Fascism, 159
Fatality census data on work injuries, 143

Fear of democracy, 3, 184, 185, 210–11
Federal agencies. *See* Regulatory agencies
Federal budget. *See* Budget(s); Fiscal growth
Federal Deposit Insurance Corporation, 66
Federal Energy Regulatory Commission, 38
Federalist Papers, The, 57–58, 183
Federal Reserve Act, 66
Federal Reserve System, 37
Federal Trade Commission, 110, 147
Feingold, Kenneth, 62, 65
Ferris, J. Stephen, 110
Fifteenth Amendment, 55, 57
Fifth Amendment, 59
Financial crisis of 1998, 89, 217
Finer, Herman, 160
Fire department, development of professional, government-employed, 98
Fiscal decentralization, utility-maximizing behavior of individuals and, 8–9
Fiscal growth, 16–35
  absolute, 17–21
  comparative size of U.S. spending and taxing, 31–35
  federal vs. local or regional, 52–53
  government deficits, 26–31
  historical perspective on, 16–17
  political and ideological antagonism to, example of, 90
  relative, 21–26
Fiscal illusion analysis, 82
Fiscal review of budget vs. tax expenditures, 174
Fishery, as common property resource, 203–4
Flanigan, William H., 55
Flight from politics, 182–83
Flora, Peter, 89, 93, 100
Fluidity of resources, lack of, 195–96, 197
Food and Drug Administration, 37
Ford, Henry Jones, 16–17
Founders, influence of issues of concern to, 136–37
Fourteenth Amendment, 55, 60
Fragmentation of metropolitan government, 186–91

Fraleigh, Cynthia, 35, 41
Franco, Francisco, 173
Franklin, John Hope, 55
Franklin, Mark N., 212
Fraser, Steve, 93
Freedom, growing public
    sector to enhance, 155.
    See also Liberty
Freeman, Roger A., 78, 168
Free market assumptions, 72
Free-rider problem, 75, 97,
    150
Frey, Bruno S., 68, 99, 212
Friedman, Jeffrey, 68
Friedman, Joseph, 197
Friedman, M., 76, 160, 175,
    182, 208
Fritschler, A. Lee, 36
Functionalist Marxists, 63–64
Futility argument against gov-
    ernment activism, 167
Future, discounting the, 150
Future generations, obliga-
    tion to, 150–51
Future public sector involve-
    ment, issues regarding,
    214–18

Galloway, David, 78
Gatti, James, 38
GDP. *See* Gross Domestic
    Product
GDP/Man-Hour indicator,
    125
Gender, electoral participa-
    tion and, 55
George, Vic, 93
Germany, Wagner's Law
    shaped by history of,
    48–50
Gerstle, Gary, 93
Gerston, Larry N., 35, 41
Globalization
    distribution of burdens of,
        217–18
    limitation of government
        growth and, 111
    of markets, impact of, 217
GNP. *See* Gross National
    Product
Goldwater, Barry, 93–94
Goods and services
    public goods, 50, 51, 69,
        74–75
    supplied by government,
        26
Goodsell, Charles T., 168, 219
Gould, Frank, 46, 89–90
Governing
    recent assault on, 2–3
    trade-offs of, 138–39
    use of term, 2

Government, use of term, 2
Government failure, 166
    antigovernment view of,
        209–10
    bureaucratic determinism
        and, 80–82
    declining public sector
        prediction, anomalous
        case of, 83–86
    economic choice models of
        interest group behavior
        and, 83
    fiscal illusion analysis and,
        82
    government growth as, 70,
        78–86
    median-voter redistribu-
        tion, 79–80
    in public education,
        voucher approach to re-
        duce, 175–77
Government growth
    approaches to explanation
        of, 7–9. *See also* Macro-
        deterministic explana-
        tions of government
        growth; Public choice
        explanations of govern-
        ment size and growth
    causes of, among democ-
        racies, 211–12
    economic decline and, 88,
        89, 92–93, 95
    fiscal growth. *See* Fiscal
        growth
    as government failure, 70,
        78–86
    median-voter model of.
        See Median-voter model
    need for context in assess-
        ing, 13–16
    private benefits and pres-
        sures for, 134–35
    regulation, growth of,
        35–42
    step-like increases in, 90–91
    as threat to liberty, strate-
        gic purpose in character-
        izing, 158
Government size. *See also*
    Economic performance,
        government
    size/growth and; Public
    choice explanations of
    government size and
    growth
    coercion and, 170–77
    distinction among ele-
        ments of, 157–58
    economic base and, 45–46
    electoral process and,
        54–58

growth in GDP and,
    118–20
inflation and, 123–25
interest rates and, 124, 125
productivity and, 125–29
technology and, 45–46
unemployment and,
    122–23
U.S. compared to other ad-
    vanced democracies, 211
Government successes, 6–7,
    168–69, 213
Gramlich, E. H., 111, 185
Gramm-Rudman legislation,
    5
Great Britain, social welfare
    in, 208
Great Depression, 66, 198
    fiscal policy making in, 108
    government growth to
        counter, 38, 89, 92–93,
        154–55
Great Society, 4, 93, 94
Green, Donald P., 68, 182, 206
Greenberg, Edward S., 63, 65,
    66, 67
Gross Domestic Product
    capital formation as per-
        centage of, among
        OECD nations, 119
    government size and
        growth in (1960–95),
        118–20
    per person employed, per-
        cent change in real, 121
    total government expendi-
        tures as percent of, 32,
        116–17
Gross National Product
    deficit as percent of, 29
    federal budget as percent
        of, 30
    fiscal data as percentage
        of, 21–24
    interest paid on national
        debt as percentage of, 30
*Growth of Public Expenditure
    in the United Kingdom,
    The* (Peacock and Wise-
    man), 51–54
Gruber, Judith E., 219

Haefele, Edwin, 203
Hamilton, Alexander, 48
Hammond, Scott J., 166
Hampton, Jean, 182–83
Hansen, Alvin, 92
Hardin, Garett, 203
Hardin, Russell, 50, 51
Hartz, Louis, 46, 48, 59, 185
Harvey, David, 44
Hayek, Friedrich, 160, 182

Health data, use/abuse of, 147
Heclo, Hugh, 197
Heidenheimer, Arnold J., 89, 93, 100, 197
Hennock, E. P., 49
Herber, Bernard P., 48, 50, 51
Herman, S. James, 200
Heterogeneity of population, 45
Heterogeneous republic, purpose of large, 58
Hewitt, Christopher, 56
Hibbs, Douglas A., Jr., 93, 95, 114
Higgins, Richard, 46
Higgs, Robert, 68, 100–101, 114
Highton, Benjamin, 101
Hills, Stuart L., 139
Hirschman, Albert O., 161, 167, 179
Hitler, Adolf, 5, 11, 161
Hobbes, Thomas, 185
Hoberg, George, Jr., 35
Holmwood, John, 44
Home construction and ownership
    decline in early twentieth century, 199–200
    encouragement of, 199–200, 216
    middle-class, subsidies for, 104–6, 173, 180, 190, 214, 216
Hooks, Gregory, 93
Hoover, Kenneth, 94, 208
Housing Acts (1934 and 1937), 198
Housing policy, U.S., 197–202
    demand-side, 197, 202
    historical context of, 198–201
    implemented through budget appropriations vs. tax expenditures, 173
    local land use policies and, 193–94
    supply-side, 197, 198–202
    support for government efforts to stimulate supply, 200–201
    tenement housing and, 97
Housing voucher programs, 197
Hout, Michael, 90, 99, 101
Huang, Wei-Chiao, 110
Hudson, John C., 217
Hughes, J. R. T., 78, 97

Human resources, as percent of federal budget (1950–1996), 30, 31
Hurt, R. Douglas, 217

Ideology, as constraint on median voter redistribution, 108–9
Ignorance, rational political, 84–85
Imperialism of public choice approach, 184–85
Income
    as constraint in market system, 71
    discounting risk of current behavior on future well-being and, 153
    growth of social welfare in 1960s, 93, 95
    mean tax expenditure by, 104
    of median voter vs. average earner, gap between, 79
    national, government growth/size and, 118–22
    ratio of mean to median, 100, 101
    as stimulant/constraint of government growth, 45, 121–22
Income distribution
    median-voter model and, 106–7
    in United States, 100, 106–7, 212
Income inequalities
    acceptance of relatively high degree of, 109
    in 1990s, 107
Income maintenance, direct payments for, 106
Income taxes, proportion of total federal revenue derived from, 24–26. See also Taxes
    corporate income taxes, 24–26
    individual income taxes, 24–25
Income transfer system, 96
Industrialization
    government involvement and, 49–50, 51
    market failure generated by, 97
Industrial policy, 215–17
Industrial Revolution, 45–46
Inflation, 116, 123–25
Information, unequal, 72, 75–76

Infrastructure, physical, 216
Inspection effect, 94
Institutions
    activism of, government growth and, 95
    as macro-deterministic variables, 46
    pattern of government growth and, 54–61
Instrumentalist Marxist theory, 63
Interest group behavior, economic choice models of, 83
Interest group egotism, 7
Interest payments on national debt, 30–31
Interest rates
    global influences on, 125
    government size/growth and, 124, 125
Intergenerational inequity, 150–51
Internal Revenue Code, 104
Internal Revenue Service, 136, 175
International Monetary Fund, 212
Interstate Commerce Commission, 37

Japan
    financial crisis of 1998 and, 217
    productivity growth rates in post-1973 period, 126
Jefferson, Thomas, 48
Jeopardy arguments against government activism, 167
Johnson, David B., 68, 182, 183
Johnson, Haynes, 137, 162, 210
Johnson, Lyndon B., 4, 93
Johnson, M. H., 78
Jones, Bryan D., 135, 185
Justification for programs, resentment about, 177–81

Kagan, Robert A., 41
Kapstein, Ethan B., 217
Kaufman, Herbert, 112–13, 196
Keller, Horton, 27, 92, 93
Kelman, Steven, 168, 184
Kemp, Kathleen A., 35
Kendrick, H. Slade, 94–95
Kennedy, John F., 4, 93
Key, V. O., 46
Keynes, John Maynard, 161

King, Desmond S., 115, 116, 160
King, Wiliford Isbell, 16
Kingdon, John W., 135, 169
Kluegel, James R., 108, 109
Korean War, federal deficits during, 28
Kruas, Franz, 212
Krueckeberg, Donald A., 199

Labor, equity implications of rigidity in, 217–18
Labor conditions, regulation of, 140–44
Labor movement, 141
"Labor turnover," problem of, 199
Labor unions, 99
Ladd, Everett C., 109
Lafay, Jean-Dominique, 116
Laissez faire economics, 61
Land grant colleges, 217
Land use policies, 76, 193–94
Language of private vs. public sector provision of goods and services, 164–65
Larkey, Patrick, 79, 82, 101
Law of Increasing State Activity, Wagner's, 47–51, 87, 88–90, 113–14
Lawson, Dick, 198
Layard, Richard, 116
Lee, W. R., 48
Leff, Mark H., 108
Legislative oversight of bureaucracy, 81–82
LeGrande, D., 142
Lenin, V., 160
Leonardi, Robert, 219
Leslie, Stuart W., 217
Less developed countries, government growth in, 89
Leuchtenburg, William E., 47, 93
Levi, Margaret, 47, 183
Levine, Myron W., 187
Lewis-Beck, Michael S., 90, 114, 116
Liberalism, classical, 45–46, 48
Liberty
government growth as threat to, 10–11, 158
government size and coercion and, 169–77
private sector power and, 11
reduction by large social welfare sectors, claims of, 160

Lieberson, Stanley, 83
Lilley, William, 35
Lim, S. Y., 142
Limited government
access to, 204–5
as common property resource, 203–6
defined, 204
Lindbeck, Assar, 100
Lindblom, Charles E., 133
Lindert, Peter H., 106
Literacy tests, 55
Llewellyn, Chris, 98
Local governments
public choice view of, 189–90
services and policies of, 186
Local land use policies, impact of, 193–94
Lochner v. New York, 61
Los Angeles region, fragmentation of, 187
Lovell, Catherine, 37, 164
Lovrich, Nicholas, 10
Lowery, David, 88, 110, 187, 194
Lowi, Theodore J., 218
Lybeck, Johan A., 68, 100

McDonnell, Gary, 110
Machan, Tibor, 59, 78, 159
McLean, Lain, 68–69
Macro changes
challenges and demands for government created by, 43–44
effect on individual, 43
Macro-deterministic explanations of government growth, 43–67
displacement effect hypothesis, 51–54, 90–95
majoritarian democracy, 54–61
Marxist explanations, 62–67
social and demographic changes, 44–47
Wagner's Law, 47–51, 87, 113–14
Maddison, Angus, 126, 127
Madison, James, 57
Maier, Charles S., 47, 90
Majoritarian democracy, 54–61
fear of tyranny in, 184, 185
Mansbridge, Jane J., 206
Manza, Jeff, 90, 99, 101
Mao Tse-Tung, 160
Marginal utility, theory of, 153

Market economy
conditions defining market efficiency, 72
globalization of markets, impact of, 217
idealized private market model, 71
public sensitivity to needs of, 212
Market failure, 96–99
as episodic, belief in, 6
equal distribution, unequal information, 75–76
externalities and, 73–74, 97–98, 114, 189, 192–94
free-rider problems and, 75, 97, 150
government growth to remedy, 70, 71–78
losses before government intervention in, 98
market-like approaches to public intervention in, 170–72, 175–77
in metropolitan regions, 192–94
monopoly as, 73, 98
as pervasive, 7
public goods, 50, 51, 69, 74–75
transaction costs, 72, 76–78
Marketplace, discounted, 150–56
Marxist analysis, 46
explanations of government growth, 62–67
view of government, 48
Maryanski, Alexandra, 44
Maxwell, Nan L., 107, 212
Mazur, Mark J., 107
Meat Inspection Act, 66
Median-voter model, 56, 99–110
conclusions regarding, 109–10
income distribution and, 106–7
median-voter redistribution, 79–80, 108–9
stringent conditions required by, 101
tax expenditures and, 103–6
in U.S. context, 100–109
weak empirical support for, 100–101
Medicare, 53
Meehan, Eugene, 44, 218
Meltzer, Alan H., 56, 68, 79, 80, 99, 100

Metropolitan organization
  fragmentation in, 186–91
  metropolitanization
    process, 191
  public choice and, 186–94
  resistance to consolidation
    of, 187–91
  segregation by race and
    class, 191–92
  variety of local govern-
    ments within, 187
Metz, Harold, 141
Middle class, tax expenditures for, 103–6
Middle-class home owner-
  ship, subsidy directed
  at, 104–6, 173, 180, 190,
  214, 216
Military-Industrial Complex,
  83
Military spending, Wagner's
  Law on, 49
Miller, James, 35, 199
Misconduct, government ac-
  tion sought to reduce,
  135
Missouri Compromise, 59–60
Mitchell, William C., 78, 168
Mobility of capital, limitation
  of government growth
  and, 111
Moe, T., 175
Monitoring activity and
  threats by employers,
  142
Monopoly, 73, 98
  Slaughterhouse Cases and,
    60–61
Monroe, Kristen R., 68
Moon, Bruce E., 56
Morris, Richard B., 141
Mortgage interest deduction,
  104–6, 216
Motivation to resist govern-
  ment interventions, re-
  ducing, 171
Motorcycle helmet require-
  ments, 151
Mueller, Dennis C., 109
Multicausality, 9
Munn v. Illinois, 61
Murrell, Peter, 109, 110
Musgrave, Richard A., 16, 78
Mussolini, B., 160, 173

Nanetti, Raffaella Y., 219
National Industrial Recovery
  Act, 66
National Labor Relations
  Board, 38, 141
National Recovery Adminis-
  tration, 67

National Transportation
  Safety Board, 38
National wealth and income,
  government growth/size
  and, 118–22
Nazi State, 161
Negative externalities, 73, 74,
  98
Neiman, Max, 10, 12, 37,
  164, 175, 176, 191, 206,
  219
Nell, Edward, 124
Netherlands
  income distribution in,
    109–10
  preference for equality in,
    108
New Deal
  federal expenditures in, 20
  housing policies, 198
  inspection effect during
    late, 94
  labor legislation in, 141
  Marxist view of, 64, 66–67
  regulatory growth with,
    37–38
  as response to Great De-
    pression, 47
  U.S. Supreme Court on, 61
New Frontier, 4, 93
Nickell, Stephen, III, 116
Nineteenth Amendment, 55
Niskanen, William A., 68, 81,
  110, 185
Nixon, Richard M., 4
Nonexcludability of public
  good, 74–75
Nonrivalry in consumption
  of public good, 74–75
Nordlinger, Eric A., 65
Norgaard, Richard B., 75
Norpoth, Helmut, 116
Norris-LaGuardia, Anti-
  Injunction Act of 1932,
  141
North, Douglass C., 78
Norway
  income distribution in,
    109–10
  preference for equality in,
    108
Nozick, 182
Nuclear Regulatory Com-
  mission, 38

Oakerson, Ronald J., 188
Oates, Wallace E., 9
Obligation to future genera-
  tional, 150–51
Occupational Safety and
  Health Act (OSHA) of
  1970, 142–43

Occupational Safety and
  Health Administration,
  38
Okun, Arthur M., 133, 179,
  212
Olson, James Stuart, 93
Olson, Mancur, 68, 83, 99
On-line services, privacy
  threats in, 147
Oppression. *See also* Coer-
  cion, government size
  and
  government size and, 213
  methods of, 160–61
Optimal point of redistribu-
  tion, 109
Orfield, Myron, 191
Organisation for Economic
  Cooperation and Devel-
  opment (OECD), 31
OECD nations, 33, 34, 119,
  120, 121
Orren, Gary R., 106
Osberg, Lars, 107, 110
Ostrom, Elinor, 188
Ostrom, Vincent, 187, 188
Over-supply of goods or ser-
  vices, problem of, 74

Pacelle, Richard L., 58
Page, Benjamin I., 96
Panic of 1893, 65
Parenti, Michael, 44
Parks, Roger B., 188
Parliament, government
  growth and, 58–59
Partial ignorance, 84
Patent rights, 76
Peacock, Alan T., 51–54,
  90–95
Pechman, Joseph A., 107
Peltzman, S., 109
Personal liberty. *See* Liberty
Perversity argument against
  government activism,
  167
Peters, B. Guy, 201
Peterson, Paul E., 138
Peterson, Wallace C., 107
Pew Research Center,
  161–62
Physical resources, as per-
  cent of federal budget
  (1950–1996), 30, 31
Pigou, A. C., 78
Pinochet, A., 160
Pitkin, Hanna, 166
Piven, Frances Fox, 101, 102,
  212
Plant, Raymond, 94, 208
Plateau, public sector, 51, 52
Plattner, Marc F., 58

Policy analysis
  blueprint role for, 194–202
  business-based models of, 202
  comparison to private sector marketing, 195–96
  economic approach to, 182–83, 184
  as long-term, 196
  policy displacement and, 196–97
  realistic role for, 202–3
  resource fluidity and, lack of, 195–96, 197
  of U.S. housing policy, 197–202
Policy displacement, 196–97
Policy evolution, process of, 202–3
Political culture, as macro-deterministic variable, 46–47
Political economy origin of public choice, 68–70
Political functionalist Marxists, 63–64
Political ignorance, rational, 84–85
Political participation
  black, 55
  democratization of, as force for government growth, 54–58
  need for expansion of, 220–21
Political parties, working-class, 99–100
Political Redistribution Hypothesis. *See* Median-voter model
Political science, role in cultivating democracy, 219
Politics
  breakthrough, 53–54, 214, 215–18
  flight from, 182–83
  rationalizing, 53–54, 214–15
  of resentment, 177–81
Poll taxes, 55, 56
Pontell, Henry N., 143, 145, 149
Poor, the
  curtailing of government responsiveness to, 4–5
  vulnerability of programs for, 180, 181
Population, social and demographic changes in, 44–47
Positive externalities, 73
Postindustrial stage, government growth in, 51

Power, private abuse of, 139–47
Preindustrial agricultural era, 50–51
Preponderant ignorance, 84
Privacy
  government agencies and, 145–46
  private sector threats to and violations of, 142, 146–47
Private abuse of power, 11, 139–47
  access to information about, 140
  examples of, 139–40
  origins of government agencies and laws in, 136
  personal liberty and, 11, 133–34, 135
  regulation of labor conditions due to, 140–44
  white collar crime, 140, 143–45, 180–81
Private benefits, publicly produced, 83
Private market, public sector performance improved by mechanisms of, 166–67. *See also* Market failure
Private sector
  balance between public and, 137–39
  public's view of superiority of, 6, 164–65
Privatization movement, 12, 148–49, 213
Productivity
  government size and, 125–29
  regulation and, 126–27
Progressive Era, 200
  Marxist views of, 64, 66
Progressive taxes, 80
Promotional role of government, 50
Property ownership, electoral participation and, 55, 56, 57. *See also* Home construction and ownership
Property resource, common, 203–6
Property rights, 57–61
  concern for hazards to, 57–58
  court limitation on regulation of, 59–61
Property taxes, state/local personal, 104–6

Przeworski, Adam, 99
Psychic costs and benefits of public policy, 69–70
Public agencies. *See also* Bureaucratic determinism model
  abuse by, curtailment of power and, 175
  congressional control of, 110
  costs of, 39
  creation in 1960s of new, 38–40
  hazards to life of, 113
  persistence of, 111–12
Public choice explanations of government size and growth, 68–86, 96–113, 177
  anxiety about too much redistribution, 185–86
  bureaucratic determinism model, 6, 80–82, 110–13
  contributions of, 184
  flight from politics and, 182–83
  government failure and, 70, 78–86
  imperialism of, 184–85
  interest group behavior, models of, 83
  limited government as purpose of, 183
  market failure, 70, 71–78, 96–99
  median-voter model, 56, 99–110
  metropolitan organization and, 186–94
  political economy origin of, 68–70
Public distrust of government, 162
Public employees
  motivations of, 113
  perceptions of, 219–20
Public employment, 110
Public goods, 50, 51, 69, 74–75
Public health, emergence of, 98, 198–99
Publicly produced private benefits, 83
Public policies
  achievements or successes, 6–7, 168–69, 213
  as mediated expressions of society, 130
  psychic costs and benefits of, 69–70
  social progress through, 130–31

Public policies (*cont.*)
  sources of, in democracy, 183
Public sector growth. *See Fiscal growth; Government growth*
Pure Food and Drug Act, 66
Putnam, Robert D., 219

Quantitative vs. qualitative change in public sector, 14–15

Race
  electoral participation and, 55
  segregation in metropolitan regions by, 191–92
Rand, Ayn, 160
Ranney, Austin, 218
Rasmussen, Douglas B., 160
Rational analysis
  limits of usefulness of, 206–7
  politics as alternative to, 207
Rational choice approach. *See* Public choice explanations of government size and growth
Rationalizing politics, 53–54, 214–15
Rational models of policy design, blueprint view of problem solving in, 194–202
Rational political ignorance, 84–85
Rawls, 182
Reagan, Ronald, administration, 94, 168, 212
  cutbacks since election of, 107
  deficits under, 29, 34
  deregulation of S & L industry under, 149
  fiscal growth under, 21
  legacy of, 4
Real estate tax deduction, 104–6
Recessions, government growth to counter, 89
Redistribution
  conservative anxiety about too much, 185–86
  "demands" for, 190–91
  in fragmented metropolitan region, difficulties of, 194
  meaning ascribed to, 177–81
  median-voter, 79–80, 108–9

net redistributive impact, 103–6
  optimal point of, 109
  propensity to resist vs. propensity to seek, 102–3
Regulation, government, 140–44, 169–73
  burden of, 41–42
  of business, government growth since 1930s and, 92–93, 95
  command-and-control approaches, 169–70
  cost of, 82, 170
  definition of, 35
  denying goods and services through, 151–52
  economic, 36, 39–40
  economic performance and, 41
  fairer assessment of benefits covered by, 180
  growth of, 35–42
  historical perspective on, 35–36
  implementation in U.S. vs. Europe, 127
  as important public policy issue, 35
  of labor, 140–44
  periods of regulatory growth, 37–42
  permanent full-time regulatory agency positions, 40
  presumption against, as matter of principle, 41
  productivity and, 126–27
  of property rights, court limitations on, 59–61
  in savings and loan industry, 149
  social, 36–37, 38, 40
  tools involved in, 169
  of workplace safety, 152–53
Regulatory agencies. *See* Public agencies
Regulatory martyrs, class of, 148
Reich, Robert B., 129, 215
Relative fiscal growth, 21–26
Rent-seeking, 134, 150
Research and development, government-sponsored, 50
  spinoffs from, 217
Resentment, politics of, 177–81
Resistance to government imposition

lack of growth in median family income and, 121–22
  in post-Nixon era, 94–95
Resources
  common property resource, 203–6
  lack of fluidity of, 195–96, 197
  misallocation of, 75, 76
Retirement, saving for, 75–76
Richard, Scott F., 56, 68, 79, 80, 99, 100
Riemer, Neal, 218
Right, assault on governing from the, 2–4. *See also* Antigovernment sentiment
Rights
  of citizenship, 46
  patent, 76
  property, 57–61
  vested, 59
  voting, 55–58
Riposa, Gerald, 219
Risks of current behavior on future well-being, discounting, 151–54
  income and, 153
Road to Serfdom, The (Hayek), 160
Roberts, Isaac, 200
Robertson, John, 199
Romer, Thomas, 101
Rose, Richard, 88
Rosenthal, Howard, 101
Rosoff, Stephen M., 143, 149
Ross, Bernard H., 36, 187
Rothstein, Bo, 93, 185
Rubinfeld, D. L., 111, 185
Ryu, Hang K., 107, 212

Samuels, Warren J., 160, 183
Samuelson, Paul Anthony, 50
Sanders, K. J., 142
Sassen, Saskia, 111
Savage, James D., 26
Saving relative to GDP, national, 127, 128
Savings and loan crisis, 39, 41, 145
Savings and loan industry, regulation in, 149
Schmidt, Manfred, 88
School choice, voucher approach to increasing, 175–77
Schott, Kerry, 47
Schulman, Bruce J., 209
Schwab, Robert, 35, 41
Schwarz, John E., 161, 168–69, 212

Scientific achievement, governing institutions used for, 6–7
Scott v. Sandford, 60
Seatbelt requirements, 151
Security, demand for, 95–96
Segregation, local land use policies and, 193–94
Settlement House Movement, 198, 199
Sherman Antitrust Act of 1890, 37, 66
Shughart, William, II, 46
Sigelman, L., 194
Sikora, R. I., 75, 150
Simmons, Randy T., 78, 168
Simple democratic hypothesis, 56
Skocpol, Theda, 47, 62, 64–65
Slottje, Daniel J., 107, 212
Smith, Eliot R., 108, 109
Smith, M. J., 142
Smoking, disclosure of risks of, 151–52
Social activism of 1960s and 1970s, regulation associated with, 38–40
Social changes, government growth and, 44–47
Social contract tradition, 182–83, 185
Social justice, government used for, 6–7
Social progress, achievements of, 130–31
Social regulation, 36–37, 38, 40
Social Security Act, 67
as breakthrough politics, 53
Social welfare
direct payments for, 106, 134, 174
major beneficiaries of, 96
for poor vs. affluent, 214
Social welfare state
critics of emergence of, 159–61
meaning ascribed to redistribution in, 177–81
Soviet Union, collapse of, 208
Spanish-American War (1898), 20, 91
Spending priorities, shifts in, 5
Spillover effect. *See* Externalities
Spooner, Mary Helen, 160
Stagflation, 115, 215
Stalin, Josef, 5, 160
Stambough, Stephen J., 175, 176

State/local government spending as percent of GNP, 21–24
State/local personal property taxes, 104–6
State management perspective, 64–65
Stein, Arthur A., 91
Stolp, Chandler, 79, 82, 101
Stone, Alan, 35
Strong democracy, 211
Subsidies
auto-based transportation system, 190
housing, 104–6, 173, 180, 190, 214, 216
Substantive due process, 59–61
Suburbanization, 189, 191
barriers impeding participation by race and class, 191–92
infrastructure required by, 216
local land use policies and, 193–94
Suburban local government, resistance of metropolitan consolidation by, 187
Successes, government, 6–7, 168–69, 213
Supply and demand, laws of, 138
Supply-side housing policy, 197, 198–202
disengagement from, 201–2
Surpluses, budget, 5, 17, 18
Sweden
income distribution in, 109–10
preference for equality in, 108
Sykes, John F., 198, 199
Szirmai, Adam, 108

Tarschys, Daniel, 48, 56
Tax code, charitable contributions and, 174–75
Tax cuts, 84
Taxes
consumption, 127
fiscal illusion of, 82
income, federal revenue derived from, 24–26
as percentage of GDP, 32, 33, 34
perception in U.S. of burden of, 85–86, 162, 179
poll, 55, 56
progressive, 80
U.S. compared to OECD nations, 162

Tax expenditures
benefits provided as, 103–6, 173–74
for mortgages, cost of, 104–6, 216
shares of, relative to share of tax liability, 104–5
Taxing and spending. *See* Fiscal growth
Tax tolerance, 51, 52, 114
Technologies
government size and growth and, 45–46
regulation to promote new, 38
Telephone monitoring, 142
Tenement housing, 97
Thatcher, Margaret, 208
Thaxton, Ralph, 160
Thin democracy, 211
Thirteenth Amendment, 60
Thrift industry. *See* Savings and loan industry, regulation in
Tiebout, Charles M., 8, 187
Tillman, Robert H., 143, 145, 149
Tocqueville, Alexis de, 46
Tolerance
bounds of, 220
tax, 51, 52, 114
Tollison, Robert, 46
Totalitarian government, images of, 137
Total war, 91
Trade-offs, 151–53
of governing, 138–39
Transaction costs, 72, 76–78
Transfer payments, 82, 107. *See also* Benefits, government
Transportation
auto-based, subsidies for, 190
government's promotional role in, 50
regulation of, 37
Triangle Shirtwaist fire in New York City, 98
Trotlander, 155
Tufte, Edward R., 114
Tullock, Gordon, 68, 80–81, 96, 99, 100, 182, 185
Turner, Jonathan H., 44
Twiss, Benjamin R., 90

Under-supply in goods or services, problem of, 73
Unemployment, 116, 122–23, 124
Unequal information, 72, 75–76

United States
  government growth/size,
    31–35, 97, 116–17
  losses before government
    intervention in, 98
  rate of capital formation
    for, 118, 119
U.S. Supreme Court
  interpretation of due
    process, 61
  on Missouri Compromise,
    59–60
  Slaughterhouse Cases, 60–61
Urban areas. *See* Metropoli-
    tan organization
Urbanization
  industrial, social frictions
    intensified by, 49–50
  public health and, 198–99
Uyl, Douglas J., 160

Values, as macro-determinis-
    tic variable, 47
Verba, Sidney, 106, 219
Vested rights, 59
Vietnam War, 4, 28
Vogel, David, 127
Voluntarism, coercion vs., 6
Voter knowledge of impact
    of political agendas, 102
Voting rate differences
    among income and class
    groups, 101–3. *See also*
    Median-voter model
Voting rights, government
    growth and, 55–58

Voucher approach
  to housing, 197
  to school choice, 175–77

Wages, annual rate of growth
    of real manufacturing,
    121
Wagner, Adolph, 47–51, 52
Wagner Labor Relations Act
    (1935), 67, 141
Wagner's Hypothesis/Law,
    47–51, 87, 113–14
  problems with, 88–90
Wallerstein, Immanuel, 67
War
  government growth and,
    91–92, 95, 114
  as source of displacement,
    51–52
  total, 91
War of 1812, budget deficits
    incurred during, 91
Warren, Robert, 187
Watergate scandal, 4
Wealth. *See* Income
Weatherford, H. Stephen, 99
Weaver, P. H., 37
Weidenbaum, Murray L., 126
Weinberg, Daniel H., 107,
    197, 212
Weingast, Barry R., 110
West, Edwin G., 110
White collar crime, 143–45
  cost of, 145, 180–81
  lower profile of, 140
Wildavsky, Ben, 24, 162

Wilding, Paul, 93
Wilensky, Harold, 100
Williamson, Clinton, 55, 59
Williamson, Jeffrey G., 106
Willingness to pay, 71
Wilson, James Q., 35, 103,
    135, 170
Winer, Mark, 79, 82, 101
Wintrobe, Ronald, 111
Wirth, Louis, 44–45, 97
Wiseman, Jack, 51–54, 90–95
Wolf, Charles, 70, 166
Working-class political par-
    ties, 99–100
Workplace safety, 142–44,
    152–53
World War I
  federal deficit during, 27, 28
  federal expenditures in, 20
  housing shortages during,
    200
  labor shortages during,
    199
World War II
  federal deficits during, 28
  federal expenditures in, 20
  income taxes as proportion
    of federal revenue dur-
    ing, 25
Wynehamer v. People, 59

Yeager, Peter C., 139, 140

Zero ignorance, 84, 85
Zingale, Nancy H., 55
Zysman, John, 46